The Aftermath of the Arab Uprisings

Unlike other books on the Arab uprisings of 2010–2011 which focus on why they occurred, this book looks instead towards the future of three countries—Syria, Libya, and Yemen—where the violence and instability initiated by the uprisings persist. It additionally examines the case of Iraq which continues to suffer from a precarious political situation introduced by the US-led invasion of 2003. The book investigates what should be done to achieve inclusive political and economic development and eventually a lasting peace. It describes the particular circumstances in each of the four countries, and analyses the common challenges facing them such as the need to achieve economic diversification, control inflation, raise employment levels, husband fiscal expenditures, control corruption, and implement transparent policies. It argues that in the four countries any lasting settlement must involve an explicitly stated new social contract that lays the foundation for inclusive socio-economic development and a genuinely democratic environment. In addition, a massive transformation is required of the institutional fabric of society, that is, the set of key institutions that helped create the conditions for conflict. Moreover, the book argues that any successful transition hinges on anticipating the potential for political and economic development that an eventual peace agreement will open. This can only be done by envisioning and planning the reforms that ought to be implemented, and building up political support for the transition phase.

Samir Makdisi is a Professor Emeritus of Economics at the American University of Beirut, Lebanon.

Raimundo Soto is a Professor of Economics at the Pontificia Universidad Católica de Chile, Santiago, Chile.

Routledge Political Economy of the Middle East and North Africa
Series editor: Hassan Hakimian, Professor of Economics and Director,
Middle Eastern Studies Department, College of Humanities and Social
Sciences (CHSS), Hamad Bin Khalifa University (HBKU), Qatar

Editorial board:
David Cobham, Professor of Economics, Heriot-Watt University
Numan Kanafani, Associate Professor, Emeritus, Department of Food and
Resource Economics, University of Copenhagen
Jeffrey B. Nugent, Professor of Economics, USC
Jennifer Olmsted, Professor of Economics, Drew University
Subidey Togan, Professor of Economics and Director of the Center for
International Economics, Bilkent University
Wassim Shahin, Professor of Economics and Dean, Adnan Kassar School of
Business, Lebanese American University (LAU)

11 Economic and Trade Policies in the Arab world: Employment, Poverty
Reduction and integration
Edited by Mahmoud A.T. Elkhafif, Sahar Taghdisi-Rad and
Mutasim Elagraa

12 Iran and the Global Economy
Petro populism, Islam and economic sanctions
Edited by Parvin Alizadeh and Hassan Hakimian

13 State-Business Alliances and Economic Development
Turkey, Mexico and North Africa
Işık Özel

14 Social Policy in Iran: Main Components and Institutions
Edited by Pooya Alaedini

15 Tunisia's Economic Development
Why Better than Most of the Middle East but Not East Asia
Mustapha K. Nabli and Jeffrey B. Nugent

16 The Aftermath of the Arab Uprisings
Towards Reconstruction, Democracy and Peace
Edited by Samir Makdisi and Raimundo Soto

The Aftermath of the Arab Uprisings
Towards Reconstruction, Democracy, and Peace

Edited by
Samir Makdisi and
Raimundo Soto

LONDON AND NEW YORK

First published 2023
by Routledge
4 Park Square, Milton Park, Abingdon, Oxon OX14 4RN

and by Routledge
605 Third Avenue, New York, NY 10158

Routledge is an imprint of the Taylor & Francis Group, an informa business

© 2023 selection and editorial matter, Economic Research Forum;
individual chapters, the contributors

The right of Economic Research Forum to be identified as the
authors of the editorial material, and of the authors for their
individual chapters, has been asserted in accordance with sections
77 and 78 of the Copyright, Designs and Patents Act 1988.

All rights reserved. No part of this book may be reprinted or
reproduced or utilised in any form or by any electronic, mechanical,
or other means, now known or hereafter invented, including
photocopying and recording, or in any information storage or
retrieval system, without permission in writing from the publishers.

Trademark notice: Product or corporate names may be trademarks
or registered trademarks, and are used only for identification and
explanation without intent to infringe.

British Library Cataloguing-in-Publication Data
A catalogue record for this book is available from the British Library

Library of Congress Cataloging-in-Publication Data
Names: Makdisi, Samir A., 1932- editor. | Soto, Raimundo, editor.
Title: The aftermath of the Arab uprisings / edited by Samir Makdisi
and Raimundo Soto.
Description: First Edition. | New York : Routledge, 2023. |
Series: Routledge Political Economy of the MENA |
Includes bibliographical references and index. | Identifiers:
LCCN 2022046057 (print) | LCCN 2022046058 (ebook) |
ISBN 9781032383026 (Hardback) | ISBN 9781032383033 (Paperback) |
ISBN 9781003344414 (eBook)
Subjects: LCSH: Arab Spring, 2010—Influence. | Democratization—
Arab countries. | Economic development—Arab countries. | Peace-
building—Arab countries. | Protest movements—Arab countries.
Classification: LCC JQ1850.A91 A358 2023 (print) | LCC JQ1850.A91
(ebook) | DDC 909/.097492708312—dc23/eng/20230105
LC record available at https://lccn.loc.gov/2022046057
LC ebook record available at https://lccn.loc.gov/2022046058

ISBN: 978-1-032-38302-6 (hbk)
ISBN: 978-1-032-38303-3 (pbk)
ISBN: 978-1-003-34441-4 (ebk)

DOI: 10.4324/9781003344414

Typeset in Times New Roman
by codeMantra

To all those who have endeavoured, in writing or in action, to open the doors of Arab countries to growth, justice, and freedom

Contents

List of Figures	ix
List of Tables	xi
Acknowledgements	xiii
List of Contributors	xv
Preface	xix

Part I
Post-Conflict Development and Democratic Governance   1

**Introduction: On the Causes of Conflict and the Premises for
Reconstruction**   3
SAMIR MAKDISI AND RAIMUNDO SOTO

1   Economic Agenda for Post-Conflict Reconstruction   23
SAMIR MAKDISI AND RAIMUNDO SOTO

2   Grievances and Civil Wars: The State of the Literature   54
CRISTINA BODEA AND CHRISTIAN HOULE

3   Power-Sharing and Peace-Building   67
NICHOLAS SAMBANIS

Part II
Country Studies   95

4   Causes, Consequences, and Future Directions of the Syrian Conflict   97
NADER KABBANI AND ALMA BOUSTATI

5   Conflict, Institutions, and the Iraqi Economy, 2003–2020   121
BASSAM YOUSIF, RABEH MORRAR, AND OMAR EL-JOUMAYLE

viii *Contents*

6 Conflict, Peace-Building, and Post-Conflict Reconstruction in Yemen 151

MAHMOUD AL IRIANI, HIBA HASSAN, AND IRENE MARTINEZ

7 Investigating the Libyan Conflict and Peace-Building Process: Causes and Prospects 185

AMAL HAMADA, MELIKE SÖKMEN, AND CHAHIR ZAKI

Concluding Remarks 219

SAMIR MAKDISI AND RAIMUNDO SOTO

Bibliography 223
Index 253

Figures

1	Real GDP per worker and total factor productivity (normalized 2010=100)	6
1.1	Human development index	29
A3.1	Global patterns of onset and prevalence of civil war by 5-year period; 1945–2012	90
A3.2	Strength of national vs ethnic identification by power status	91
4.1	Overview of the Syrian context: timeline	99
4.2	Main macroeconomic indicators	100
4.3	Entry points for post-conflict engagement	113
5.1	Total factor productivity and real GDP	129
5.2	Wages and salaries as a proportion of public expenditure	130
5.3	Violence and growth in fixed capital formation	131
5.4	Gross capital formation as proportion of GDP	132
5.5	Value added by economic sector	133
5.6	Oil and key macroeconomic variables	134
5.7	Fiscal balance, 2004–2020	134
5.8	Real GDP, unemployment, and consumer prices	135
5.9	Military and health expenditures	136
5.10	Growth in government revenues and jobs growth	137
5.11	Governance indicators, 2002–2017	139
5.12	Employment by economic sector and employer	141
6.1	Pre-conflict development profile of Yemen (2010)	157
6.2	Pre-conflict contributions of economic sectors to Yemen's GDP (%)	157
6.3	Actual real GDP and per capita GDP in Yemen, 1990–2018 (USD)	174
6.4	Actual and counterfactual GDP in Yemen, 1990–2018	177
7.1	Gaddafi's conceptualization of popular conferences and people's committees	189
7.2	Indicator of ethnic fractionalization	191
7.3	Labour Force by job status, 2010	193
7.4	Fuel exports (% of merchandise exports)	194
7.5	Oil rents per capita (current USD), average 2000–2017	195

x *List of Figures*

7.6	GDP/capita of oil exporters in the MENA region, (USD)	195
7.7	Unemployment rates (%), 2000–2020	196
7.8	Youth unemployment rates (%), 2000–2019	197
7.9	Female unemployment rates (%), 2000–2019	197
7.10	Fragile state index	198
7.11	GDP growth in Libya (%), 2000–2020	203
7.12	GDP per capita in PPP, constant USD of 2011, 2000–2019	203
7.13	Number of physicians and beds per 1000 people, 2014	205
7.14	GDP composition by expenditure (%)	210
7.15	Growth rates in input factors per five-year periods in Libya (1970–2014)	211
7.16	Correlation between oil rents and GDP	212
7.17	GDP growth volatility	213
7.18	Labour productivity	213

Tables

1	Average Growth in Real GDP per Capita by Region (%)	5
2	Rates of Unemployment	8
1.1	Main Macroeconomic Indicators (%)	28
1.2	Rates of Unemployment and Youth Employment	31
1.3	Recent Macroeconomic Indicators, 2016/2017 Averages	36
1.4	Central Bank Independence and Transparency Indices	37
1.5	Structure of Government Expenditures (%)	38
1.6	Doing Business Indicators	46
A3.1	Replication of Graham et al. (2017)	87
A3.2	Multinomial Logit Regressions of Conflict on Lost Autonomy and Exclusion	88
A3.3	Reproducing Results from Bormann, Toukan, and Sambanis (2019) on the Effect of Territorial Autonomy on Post-conflict risk of War Recurrence	89
5.1	Transparency International's Corruption Perceptions Index	138
5.2	Illiteracy in Iraq, (%)	140
5.3	Basic Income: Three Scenarios (USD)	145
6.1	Selected Economic and Social Indicators in Pre-conflict Yemen and MENA (2010)	156
7.1	Financial Aggregates in Libya	193

Acknowledgements

This book is the outcome of a research project on national peace-building and development in the post-conflict phase with a focus on selected Arab countries—Iraq, Libya, Syria, and Yemen—sponsored by the Economic Research Forum for the Arab Countries, Iran, and Turkey (ERF) with the financial support of the Ford Foundation.

The editors are very grateful for the unflinching support of ERF management during the course of this project, from its initiation a few years back to its completion. In particular, we wish to acknowledge our debt to Ibrahim Elbadawi, the managing director who, before taking leave from the ERF to assume a ministerial position in Sudan in 2019, was closely involved in co-managing and steering the project. We would also like to extend our gratitude to Sherine Ghoneim who, as acting ERF Managing Director, provided all the administrative support we needed and to Faiza Jaafar who patiently handled all administrative aspects pertaining to the team of researchers who accepted our invitation to collaborate on this project.

We owe gratitude to Noha El Mikawy, Ford Foundation's representative for the Middle East and North Africa at the start of this project, for her ever-helpful comments and insights at various stages of the project's progress. And to our colleagues in the research team for their absolute cooperation in helping us fulfil the project's objectives, especially given that at times we might have been too demanding of them. We also extend thanks to our editor Isabel Miller for her excellent work.

Two workshops were held to discuss the drafts of the papers for the project: the first as part of a wider conference on Conflicts, Governance, and Post-Conflict Economic Agenda in War Afflicted Arab Countries held in Casablanca on 25 October 2018, and the second, Conflict, National Peace Building, and Post-Conflict Economic Agenda, held in Cairo on 19 September 2019, which was a more restricted event specifically devoted to the papers prepared by the project's team of researchers. Highly beneficial comments were received from participants at the two events; regretfully limitations of space do not permit us to acknowledge each individual by name.

Samir Makdisi would like to acknowledge the support of the Institute of Financial Economics at the American University of Beirut that provided xiv *Acknowledgements*

not only a congenial environment for work but over the years 2018–2020 the most able research assistance of Razan Amine and Rasha Fattouh. He owes his wife Jean a profound debt of gratitude for her support and penetrating comments on issues taken up in this volume that he brought to her attention.

Raimundo Soto would like to thank his wife Camila for her love and unfailing support.

Contributors

Cristina Bodea is an Associate Professor of Political Science at Michigan State University. She has a PhD degree in Political Science from the University of Rochester (2006) and was a Postdoctoral Fellow at Princeton University. She has also worked for the European Central Bank in Frankfurt, Germany, and the World Bank. Her interests include reputation building in exchange rate policy, central bank independence and government spending, the fiscal policy of developing countries, as well as civil war, coups, and low-intensity violence as alternative manifestations of domestic conflict. She is an Editor for the *British Journal of Political Science*. Her work has been published in the *Journal of Politics,* the *British Journal of Political Science, International Organization,* the *European Journal of Political Economy, Public Choice*, and *Economics and Politics*.

Alma Boustati is an Independent Researcher. She received her PhD in Economics from SOAS, University of London, in May 2020 and has collaborated with the Economic Research Forum on several research projects. Her research interests include the economics of gender, development, and labour markets with a focus on the Middle East.

Amal Hamada is an Assistant Professor of Political Science and Gender Studies at the Faculty of Economics and Political Science, Cairo University, Egypt. Her research interests include gender issues in the Middle East with a special focus on women's daily strategies for their lives and on conflict-related issues. She directs the women's studies unit and is the Academic Coordinator of the Professional Master's in Gender and Development, Cairo University.

Hiba Hassan is an Associate Professor at Blanquerna University. She is a Researcher and Political Expert with over twelve years of experience in political analysis and research on Yemeni and Gulf affairs in particular and on the Middle East in general. She holds a Master's in International Security from the Institut Barcelona D'Estudis Internacionals and is currently completing her PhD in Political Science at the University of Barcelona. She has written many research papers and analytical reports on security and the political environment in Yemen and the Gulf.

xvi *List of Contributors*

Christian Houle is an Associate Professor of Political Science at Michigan State University. He obtained his PhD from the Department of Political Science at the University of Rochester in 2011. Before joining Michigan State University, he was an Assistant Professor in the Department of Political Science at Trinity College, Dublin, between 2010 and 2013. His research interests fall within the field of the comparative politics. He is particularly interested in issues related to democracy and regime change, political instability, and inequality and redistribution. His work has been published in several journals, including *World Politics*, the *Journal of Politics, International Organization, Comparative Political Studies*, the *Journal of Conflict Resolution*, and the *Journal of Peace Research.*

Mahmoud Al-Iriani is a Senior Economic Advisor at the Kuwait Fund for Arab Economic Development (KFAED) and a Non-resident Research Fellow at the Economic Research Forum (ERF). Before joining KFAED, he was an Economic Advisor at the Economic Policy Research Center of Dubai Economic Council, and Professor of Economics at the United Arab Emirates University (UAEU) and Sana'a University. Apart from lecturing obligations, he carried out policy research and the economic evaluation of KFAED development projects in Africa, Asia, and Eastern Europe. He has published in regional and international journals.

Omar El-Joumayle is an Independent Scholar. He obtained his PhD in Economics and Management from the University of Pavia (2017). He holds a Bachelor and an MSc Degree in Economics from the University of Baghdad. He also has a post-graduate degree in Management of Development from the University of Turin (2006). He was an Associate at the Centre for Arabic and Middle Eastern Studies, American University of Beirut (2014). Some of his work has appeared in peer-reviewed journals. His current work focuses on the political economy of the oil industry and the economic consequences of armed conflicts in the Middle East region.

Nader Kabbani is the Director of Research at the Brookings Doha Center (BDC) and a Senior Fellow with the Brookings Global Economy and Development Program. Prior to joining BDC, Kabbani served as Director of Policy and Research at the Silatech Foundation and Founding Director of the Syrian Development Research Centre at the Syria Trust for Development. He has held academic positions with the American University of Beirut and served on the research staff of the US Department of Agriculture and the California State Senate. He has a PhD in Economics from Johns Hopkins University, 2001.

Samir Makdisi is Professor Emeritus of Economics and Founding Director of the Institute of Financial Economics at the American University of Beirut (AUB). He is a former Minister of Economy, Republic of Lebanon (1992), Deputy President of AUB (1992–1998), Chair of the Board of Trustees, Economic Research Forum (1993–2001), and an elected member of the Board, 2012–2022. Recipient of several honours including the AUB medal (1998), he is widely published in academic journals and has written books in the areas of financial policies, civil conflict, and democratic transitions, among others, with special reference to the Arab World. He is Co-editor (with Ibrahim Elbadawi) of *Democratic Transitions in the Arab World*. He received his PhD in Economics from Columbia University, New York.

Irene Martinez is an Associate Professor of Economics at Blanquerna University (Barcelona) and a Researcher at the Institute for Statecraft (London). She holds an MSc in Development Economics from the School of Oriental and African Studies, University of London, and has wide experience as a Consultant in multilateral financing projects in the MENA region and strategic development in Europe and Asia.

Rabeh Morrar is a Senior Researcher at the Centre of International Development at Northumbria University, UK. Previously he was an Assistant Professor in Economics and Head of the Economics Department from 2011 to 2016 at An-Najah National University, Palestine. He received his PhD in Innovation Economy from Lille 1 University for Science and Technology, Lille, France in 2011. His current research interests include Knowledge Economy, Innovation Economy, and International Development, and is a Fellow of the Economic Research Forum (ERF), Arab Council for the Social Sciences (ACSS), Turkish Economic Research Forum, American Economic Association (AEA), and Middle East Economic Association (MEEA).

Nicholas Sambanis is Presidential Distinguished Professor of Political Science, University of Pennsylvania. He writes on inter-group conflict, ranging from everyday forms of discrimination to violent protests and civil wars. With Michael Doyle, he published *Making War and Building Peace* (2006), the first quantitative analysis of the effectiveness of United Nations' peacekeeping operations after civil war. He co-authored *Breaking the Conflict Trap: Civil War and Development Policy* (2003) and designed and implemented the first multi-country mixed-method research project exploring the causes of civil war in a two-volume book, *Understanding Civil War: Evidence and Analysis* (2005).

Melike Sökmen is a Researcher, who has been involved in Horizon 2020 projects at the Barcelona Centre for International Affairs (CIDOB), focusing on issues such as diaspora studies, migration, Turkish foreign policy, and EU-Mediterranean relations. She has a BA in History from Koç University, Istanbul, and an MA in International Security from IBEI, Barcelona.

Raimundo Soto is Associate Professor of Economics and researcher at the Center for Asian Studies, Pontificia Universidad Católica de Chile. He received his PhD in Economics from Georgetown University and has published extensively on long-run growth, the resource curse, institutions and conflicts, and fiscal and monetary affairs. He has been a Visiting Scholar at institutions in the United States, Asia, and Latin America and at international organizations such as the World Bank, IMF, the Federal Reserve Bank of Minneapolis, and the Economic Research Forum. He was the Director of International Development at the Dubai Economic Council between 2010 and 2012. He is the Managing Editor of the *Middle East Development Journal*.

Bassam Yousif is a Professor of Economics at Indiana State University. He received his PhD in Economics from the University of California, Riverside. He has written extensively on the economic development and political economy of the Middle East, concentrating on Iraq. His book, *Human Development in Iraq, 1950–1990,* was published by Routledge in 2012. His research on the role of institutions in development has been published in *Contemporary Arab Affairs* (2016) and the *Journal of Institutional Economics* (2019).

Chahir Zaki is an Associate Professor of Economics at the Faculty of Economics and Political Science, Cairo University. He conducts research into trade policy and macroeconomics. He is also the Director of the French section of the faculty, a part-time Senior Economist at the Economic Research Forum (Cairo, Egypt), and a Consultant for several international organizations. He has published numerous studies in refereed journals on international trade, trade policy, trade in services, applied economics, and macroeconomic modelling.

Preface

Since achieving independence after World War II, and despite their steady development, the majority of Arab countries have generally failed to break out of the grip of their autocratic regimes[1] This failure stands in contrast with an emerging trend in other regions of the world, whereby a positive correlation between democracy and development has been widely documented (e.g., Alesina and Perotti, 1996; Acemoglu et al., 2014). While this evidence is uncontested, its interpretation is controversial. Inferring causality from correlation is notoriously difficult, but mutual causation between democracy and development is likely to be present. One strand of the literature takes an 'optimistic view' of the correlation whereby sustained economic development empowers the citizens and provides a counterweight to the power of elites and governments, thus creating space for a society that would promote civil and political freedoms and, in turn, democracy can increase economic growth due to its positive effect on political stability and democratic institutions (Alesina and Perotti, 1996; Acemoglu and Robinson, 2006 2006). The 'pessimistic view' would rationalize the correlation as an indication of reverse causality whereby bad economic performance would push or catalyse the end of autocratic regimes whereas good economic performance would facilitate transferring resources to buyout the opposition (e.g., O'Donnell, 1973; Remmer, 1993; Ruiz Pozuelo et al., 2016).

Notwithstanding the evidence for other regions of the world, it remains that democracy has been largely absent from Arab countries and that it does not appear to be correlated with economic development. Several explanations have been posited to explain this failure to democratize. Of note is the role of oil resources and the prevalence of conflicts in the region, along with their consequent disruptive foreign interventions.[2] But also religious, cultural, societal, and historical explanations have been advanced for the lack of inclusive political participation in most, if not all, of the Arab countries.[3]

These explanations, nevertheless, tend to conceal the fact that there is a significant popular appetite for political inclusion and a growing demand for participation in the region, especially by women and the youth. The uprisings that the five Arab countries (Egypt, Libya, Syria, Tunisia, and Yemen) experienced in 2011 vividly reflected the extent of the deep popular discontent and the clamour for change. Furthermore, they were a stark reminder that, sooner or later, a fundamental transformation in the socio-economic and political order of the Arab countries would be in the offing.

What course such a transformation would take and what type of new social contract would emerge remain uncertain being largely dependent on how the elites of these countries respond to the popular clamour for change. Of the above five countries, Tunisia is the only one that has been, since the uprising, undergoing a process towards political inclusion via fair and free democratic elections. However, as its political crisis of 2021 has shown,[4] the path has certainly not been easy for the Tunisians. Some observers note that the same factors that allowed its transition—including a willingness to compromise, a weak security sector, and a powerful civil society—may have, in their own ways, inhibited the consolidation of Tunisia's democracy by not allowing substantive action on political and economic reforms (Grawal, 2021). It remains to be seen whether the post-2021 phase will yet witness an overdue solid consolidation of its democratic experiment. Egypt, on the other hand, has all but returned to autocracy, largely resulting from the inability of key political actors to resolve their ideological and strategic differences and provide the country with a viable transition agenda and importantly the latent opposition of the military to having their privileges dismantled (see Quandt, 2020).

This volume focuses on the dramatic cases of those Arab countries that fell into civil wars in the aftermath of the 2011 uprisings. Libya, Syria, and Yemen show that the unwillingness and/or inability to respond to a popular clamour for change can quickly lead to violent conflict with devastating social, institutional, and economic consequences. They also attest to the pervasive effects that external actors can have on aggravating conflicts and inhibiting fundamental transformations that would support political inclusion and broad-based economic development. Our research also considers Iraq, a country less affected by the Arab uprisings, but that has equally struggled to reduce its level of sectarian conflict and political instability without, however, any notable success. Its experience demonstrates that *even if modernizing reforms are adopted*, non-inclusive top-down transformations may fail to ensure longer-term national peace and stability.

The ample spectrum of political and economic reforms needed for reconstruction in conflict-afflicted economies calls for the design of a comprehensive agenda whereby neither political nor economic elements become limitations to its success. Such an agenda ought to be based on a solid and sound diagnosis of the existing conditions and a thorough assessment of the institutions and policies that led to the fracturing of the social contract, so that the proposed set of reforms responds adequately to the needs of the country and articulates properly both the economic and political dimensions of the transformation.

Experience shows that the future course of countries experiencing civil conflict will largely be defined not only by the nature of the peace settlement but also by the extent to which such settlement is capable of enticing a common vision of a possible future, by the capacity of authorities to neutralize those opposing the peace agreement, and by their response to unforeseen contingencies and external pressures.

Whatever form these settlements take, a major premise of this volume is that in today's world *any transformation leading to lasting national peace in any of the Arab countries will be conditional on laying the foundations for an inclusive form of socio-economic development in the context of a genuinely democratic environment.* The latter can be characterized by two elements: one is that it is a system of governance in which the rulers are held accountable for their actions (Schmitter and Karl, 1991) and the other is that a society can choose to replace those rulers through open, free, and fair elections (Huntington, 1991). Irrespective of the form it adopts, a democratic system, as we define it, implies a political system characterized by equality before the law, basic human rights, guarantees of minority rights, accountability, transparency, and fair competition between political parties.

A second premise of the volume is that *whatever form the new social contract takes in each Arab country, it would require a massive transformation of the institutional fabric of society—that is, the set of key institutions—that had helped to create the conditions which made a conflict inevitable.* Such transformation is not limited to reforming institutions in the political arena, but it must also deal with far-reaching economic reforms that would ensure that the benefits of the peace agreement are passed on to the population. We should keep in mind what experience has shown namely that, parliamentary elections, even if free, are not necessarily sufficient to ensure accountability in governance. Any institutional reform should allow for its regular implementation.[5]

Such a fundamental transformation is inevitable for success. Failing to materialize would signal a return to pre-conflict forms of governance with their latent instability that, we submit, sooner or later would lead to a renewed upheaval. But should it take roots in the countries emerging from conflict, it is expected to help diminish resistance to the democratization of the region as a whole which, except for a few countries, remains characterized by varying shades of autocracy.[6] The speed of this transition (its timing and regularity), its nature (the extent and depth of reforms), and the path it takes (peaceful or not, constitutional or not) could very well differ from one Arab country to another, most likely as a result of their initial political and economic conditions as well as of the nature of any agreed settlement of the prevailing conflicts. And while the scope of socio-economic reforms is vast, given the Arab region's generally entrenched autocracy, those in the political arena assume special significance.

A major aim of this volume is, therefore, to study the conditions for a sustained political and economic transformation in countries emerging from civil conflicts, with a focus on the above four Arab countries whose conflicts are yet to be resolved and for which a fully fledged post-conflict recovery strategy is yet to be designed and implemented. Its research is intended to contribute to improving the design of political and economic reform agendas that would eventually support the reconstruction of conflict-afflicted Arab economies, provide for democratic change, and, hopefully, achieve national peace.

The volume is divided into two main parts preceded by a detailed introduction. The first part (Chapters 1 to 3) takes up the root causes of civil conflicts as background for an argued post-conflict political model and overall socio-economic agenda for the four Arab countries. On the causes of conflicts, the effects of horizontal inequality and its conditionality on oil resources and government spending and their interaction turn out to be crucial for our understanding of the Arab uprisings and the subsequent civil wars. This is followed by an analytic review of the empirical evidence on the relationship between power-sharing institutions and post-conflict trajectories in countries that have experienced civil war. It affirms that 'constraining' power-sharing has a positive effect on the probability of democratic survival, and that in post-war settings the only type of power-sharing that produces positive outcomes on democratic stability is 'inclusive' power-sharing. In turn, the accompanying reconstruction policies should aim at changing altogether the pre-conflict institutional fabric of the country, with the aim of achieving wider economic inclusion and lesser inequality; more generally socio-economic reforms and policies ought to be in line with the establishment of an implicit or explicit new form of the social contract that incorporates the principles of democracy.

The second part of the volume (Chapters 4–7) is devoted to detailed case studies of the four countries in conflict (Iraq, Libya, Syria, and Yemen) whose civil wars have wrought a large magnitude of human havoc and material destruction, albeit to varying levels from one country to another, and invited a multitude of direct outside military involvements most notably in the case of Syria where armed intervention by fundamentalist groups succeeded for a while in establishing their own state in the north-eastern part of the country. Accounting for the analyses of Part I, the case studies explore the causes of the respective conflicts, trace subsequent politico-economic developments, identify major national questions and issues faced in the post-conflict phase, and identify the major areas of reform that need to be implemented to achieve the objectives of equitable economic reconstruction and national peace. Looking beyond the eventual settlement of any ongoing conflict, the case studies assert that if these objectives are to be sustained, a new social contract would have to be put in place; one that would reflect socio-economic inclusivity, institutional reform, and democratic political governance that ensure equitable power sharing and accountability

The Introduction (Makdisi and Soto) to this volume presents an overview of the underlying factors for the discontent which led to conflict; the premises of reconstruction in the post-conflict phase; and the prospects for a regional democratic breakthrough. Noteworthy is that the four countries under study made good economic progress prior to the uprisings and managed to improve levels of human development by reducing extreme poverty and boosting shared prosperity. Nonetheless, other major economic factors continued to fuel social and political discontent, principally high rates of unemployment and a high level of inequality in expenditure, income, or wealth, in addition to institutional and social factors such as cronyism, corruption, and the abuse of power by public servants. The long-term durability of any post-conflict transition is founded, according to the authors, on the fulfilment of three vital premises: gearing reconstruction towards changing, improving, or in an extreme case, eliminating altogether the pre-war institutional fabric of the country; focusing economic rebuilding on achieving wider economic inclusion and reducing inequality as well as generating greater employment opportunities; and establishing a new form of social contract, implicit or explicit, that would enshrine the attributes of democratic government. Of course, as long as the multi-dimensional military conflicts in Syria, Yemen, and Libya continue to rage, the prospects for any democratic transition are limited. But once the conflicts are settled, the path to change will lie open. Among the factors pushing in the direction of democratic change are a growing middle class, a growing incompatibility between exclusive political institutions and the greater openness of economic institutions, and an expanding popular demand for freedom, equal political rights, and social justice.

Chapter 1 (Makdisi and Soto) focuses on the design and implementation of economic reforms, which are an integral part of the process of peace and reconstruction. The challenge facing any economic reform is immense. On the one hand, economic policies should aim at minimizing the risk of conflict recurrence, restoring confidence in economic institutions, generating employment and fostering investment, and enhancing the ability of the state to provide security for communities and households, to enforce the rule of law and deliver essential services. On the other hand, since the pre-conflict economic structure did very little to avert conflict and became highly distorted as a result of the war, reconstruction policies should be primarily geared towards changing, improving, or, even in an extreme case, eliminating altogether the pre-conflict institutional fabric of the country, i.e., the set of economic institutions—and their embedded structure of incentives—that helped to create the conditions for failure.

Chapter 2 (Bodea and Houle) reviews the long-standing debate on the origins of political conflict—social grievances versus economic calculations and greed—with a focus on political exclusion and economic inequality. They argue that while the 'greed approach' focuses on the factors that motivate individuals to initiate conflict, the grievance hypothesis focuses on those that create the opportunity for conflict to erupt. Both issues and their interaction are crucial for our understanding of the Arab uprisings and the subsequent civil wars. Furthermore, they posit that these two approaches may not be independent. Greed-based factors, such as oil rents, can aggravate grievances caused by political or economic inequality. By themselves, grievances may not be sufficient for conflict. A group with incentives to rebel may refrain from initiating a civil war if it does not have the opportunity to do so. In particular, Bodea and Houle find that the effects of horizontal inequality (which is associated with the grievances-based approach) on the civil war in the Arab world have been conditional on oil resources (which is associated with the greed-based approach).

The chapter provides empirical support to the notion that dwindling oil proceeds may have been at the root of the collapse of the social contract in Libya, Iraq, and Yemen. The empirical evidence indicates that horizontal inequality only increases the likelihood of civil war in oil-rich countries: countries that spend oil revenues on repression and/or cooptation are less vulnerable to civil war. Furthermore, the effect of horizontal inequality is conditional on a country's level of government spending: as government spending increases, its effect weakens. Conversely, a sudden drop in oil prices and/or exports might force the government to cut subsidies and transfers to certain groups in the population, thus igniting discontent and conflict. Such a decline in oil prices might also lead to an increasing inability on the part of the government to effectively repress discontent.

Chapter 3 (Sambanis) reviews key questions and the empirical evidence about the relationship between power-sharing institutions and post-conflict trajectories in countries that have experienced civil war. Different measures and concepts of power-sharing are discussed, and a broad set of empirical results is reviewed and replicated. The author refers to three types of power-sharing. The first is 'inclusive' which mandates the participation of several parties of groups in particular offices or in the decision-making processes; the second is 'dispersive', dividing authority between individuals in a well-defined pattern (e.g., territorial decentralization); and the third is 'constraining', limiting the power of any individual and thus protecting ordinary citizens and vulnerable groups against encroachment and abuse. He emphasizes the point that a key distinction that can be drawn is between 'inclusive' and 'dispersive' power-sharing. The conditions favourable to different types of power-sharing are considered, as are the consequences of power-sharing as regards the risk of war recurring and democratic stability. Differences between constraining and dispersive power-sharing are discussed and the pacifying effects of dispersive power-sharing are analysed, providing new insights regarding the implications of external intervention in respect of the post-war stability of power-sharing institutions.

Reviewing the literature, the author finds that only 'constraining' power-sharing has a positive effect on democratic survival and that in post-war settings the only type of power-sharing that produces positive outcomes for democratic stability is 'inclusive' power-sharing. This implies that agreements on regional autonomy, which are frequently negotiated as solutions to ethnic or separatist civil wars, have no positive effect on this outcome. This review shows, however, that it is possible to find substantial support for the claim that regional autonomy (i.e., 'dispersive' power-sharing) reduces the risk of a return to conflict. Further, it shows that patterns of external intervention in the civil war will also shape the stability of power-sharing arrangements post-war. Replicating and extending a published study by Cederman et al. (2015) who use data from the Ethnic Power Relations database to study the consequences of 'downgrading' the political inclusion of ethnic groups, this chapter indicates that the effects of autonomy agreements are conditional on patterns of external intervention. Pro-rebel intervention provides groups with an 'outside option' that makes the government hostage to external interference. The more extensive the inclusion of former rebels in the power balance among intervening powers, the more it weakens the parties' commitment to power-sharing.

Turning to the country studies, the Syrian case study (Nader and Boustati, Chapter 4) discusses in detail the various causes of the country's conflict and identifies specific pathways to the country's recovery in the absence of a yet comprehensive political settlement. The analysis points to the continuing 'authoritarian bargain' and its consequent lack of power-sharing that has characterized the country's political regime since the 1950s, a regime that has also discriminated politically against its Kurdish population. The civil wars over the years that followed the 2011 uprising have led to devastating economic, social, and political costs, borne mostly by a few cities and towns. But until a final inclusive political settlement is reached, the implementation of a comprehensive plan for economic and social recovery does not seem feasible. Rather reconstruction efforts would necessarily have to be less ambitious focusing on identifying feasible entry points for recovery. Among others that the study identifies, this includes revitalizing the agricultural sector and supporting high-value-added export-oriented manufacturing and high-tech services. For the longer term, however, achieving lasting national peace and sustained economic recovery would call for a new social contract that embodies genuine and inclusive political governance.

The Iraqi case study (Yousif, Morrar, and El-Joumayle, Chapter 5) demonstrates how, following the overthrow of its autocratic regime in 2003, the absence of properly functionating national institutions in multiethnic countries such as Iraq perils attempts to transit from an autocracy to democracy-hence the relevance of its experience to the countries of the 2011 uprisings that are yet to settle their conflicts and aspire to traverse the road to a democratic order. The De-Ba'athification of the country following the Allied invasion of 2003, which dismantled Saddam's authoritarian regime, initially led to the creation of a Governing Council drawn from among the returning exiles and based on a system of ethno-sectarian apportionments between Sunnis, Shi'is, Kurds, and other groups. Sectarian political groupings, however, came to dominate specific government ministries, allocating jobs and other patronage to their supporters, while the long-standing question of Kurdish self-rule has still to be finally resolved. Dismantled institutions have remained unrepaired, while new institutions that the US created, with the help of the new Iraqi elites, have often proved fragile. In consequence, despite the country's massive oil wealth, economic rebuilding since 2003 has been slow, inequitable and inefficient, largely due to the decline of those institutions that are central to economic policy formation and implementation. Thus, the primary challenge that Iraq has been facing since 2003 is institutional reform that addresses existing ethno/sectarian divisions, permits the implementation of equitable national economic policies, and promotes the establishment of democratic governance.

The Yemen case study (Al Iriani, Hassan, and Martinez, Chapter 6) stresses the point that the equal power-sharing arrangement following the country's unification in 1990 proved unsuccessful; the country experienced years of instability, which together with existing tribal structures contributed to lack of a strong central authority. Government control outside the major cities was minimal, leading several marginalized local groups to begin speaking up against the political elite in Sana'a. As of mid-2020, the conflict seems to have reached a deadlock with neither side being able to achieve total victory and apparently no imminent prospect for a peaceful solution. The study proposes a return to the power-sharing formula adopted by the National Dialogue Conference of 2013 but not implemented when the state was dismantled in September 2014. The formula adopted postulated political (non-sectarian) power-sharing arrangements that guaranteed the inclusion of all segments of the society. This type of governance should in turn encourage the implementation of growth-enhancing and equitable socio-economic policies.

The Libya case study (Hamada, Sokmen, and Zaki, Chapter 7) points out that since the uprising of 2011 and the overthrow of the Qathafi regime the country has been suffering from a cycle of social, political, security, and economic crises, as well as tribalism, ethnic divisions, and foreign interventions, all of which have reinforced one another. They have greatly weakened state institutions and the economy, the country's oil wealth notwithstanding, and in consequence facilitated fragmentation, disunity, and dysfunction, creating a fertile ground for the growth of violence and a war-driven economy. It would be greatly desirable were a post-conflict transition model of reconstruction to embody an inclusive settlement with balanced power-sharing (e.g., the Skhirat Agreement of 2015). But this may not be feasible in the immediate future. Rather, coping with prevailing economic and political challenges might require a transitional government that brings together the warring parties. The main function of this government would be to facilitate a dialogue on establishing stability as a first step, to be followed by agreement on the form of governance to be adopted nationally through a constitutional referendum. Support from the international community for reconciliation would greatly facilitate such a process.

Notes

1 Lebanon with its consociational democracy established at independence in 1943 is one notable exception though its political system has not since evolved to becoming a fully fledged democracy.
2 See for example Ross (2012) and Elbadawi and Makdisi (2011 and 2017).
3 For a review see Huntington (1991) and Hinnebusch (2006).
4 Parliament was suspended by the President on July 25, 2021, on the promise of reforms, with consequent political turmoil. As of end 2021, the crisis had yet to be settled.
5 While there has been an increase in violent conflicts in a global context, at the same time, the number of societies that have adopted more inclusive forms of political, economic, and cultural governance has grown rapidly over the last 30 years. The 2018 World Bank study *Pathways for Peace, Inclusive Approaches to Preventing Violent Conflict* argues that success in preventing violent conflicts would call, among other things, for inclusive decision-making, as well as long-term policies to address economic, social, and political issues.
6 According to the Economist Index of Democracy for 2020, the vast majority of Arab countries remain classified as authoritarian; a few, namely, Lebanon and Morocco as hybrid regimes; and only one, Tunisia, as a flawed democracy. A flawed democracy is characterized by free and fair elections and basic civil liberties, but suffer from problems in governance, an underdeveloped political culture, and low levels of political participation. A hybrid regime is characterized by substantial election irregularities, government pressure on opposition parties, serious weaknesses in political culture, functioning of government and political participation, and widespread corruption.

Part I
Post-Conflict Development and Democratic Governance

Introduction

On the Causes of Conflict and the Premises for Reconstruction

Samir Makdisi and Raimundo Soto

The Arab uprisings of 2011 that initially erupted in Tunisia on 17 December 2010, spread rapidly and strongly to four other countries, Egypt, Libya, Syria, and Yemen. They led to the immediate toppling of the regimes in all of them, followed by civil wars in the last three that, as of the beginning of 2022, are yet to be resolved. In addition, sustained street demonstrations also took place in Algeria, Iran, Iraq, Jordan, Kuwait, Morocco, Oman, and Sudan. Minor protests occurred in Djibouti, Mauritania, the Palestinian National Authority, and Saudi Arabia. Tunisia managed to introduce democratic governance though not free from serious domestic strains, while subsequent political changes in Egypt led in 2014 to the emergence of a ruling regime that essentially reflects a return to the pre-2011 military-influenced mode of government. Thus, taken together the uprisings have not resulted in any significant move towards a genuinely Arab regional democratic order. The old social contract has not been replaced with a new one.

The intensity of the demonstrations and the speed at which the Arab uprisings spread from one country to the next are striking and attest to the existence of profound and enduring factors underlying the expression of discontent and the subsequent outbreak of armed conflict. Hence, any meaningful reconstruction plan must be based on a valid diagnosis of these factors. A quote from George Santayana expresses it eloquently: 'those who cannot remember their past are doomed to repeat it' (*The Life of Reason: The Phases of Human Progress*, 1905, vol. I, p. 284). Correctly recognizing the deep roots of these conflicts constitutes the first major prerequisite for identifying the counterbalancing/remedial measures that need to be implemented as an integral part of the reconstruction effort and the establishment of national peace associated, we submit, with democratic governance. In what follows we take up these issues under three headings: factors of discontent, premises of reconstruction, and prospects for a regional democratic breakthrough. They constitute an introductory background to the thematic papers and case studies taken up in this book.

1 Factors of Discontent

Cross-country research on the economic causes of civil conflicts has largely focused on the 'greed vs. grievance' issue: greed determinants would include mainly economic factors, such as poverty or appropriable natural resources, while grievance determinants include political exclusion, social polarization, or ethnic fractionalization. Bodea and Elbadawi (2008b) provide cross-country empirical evidence that once political violence is correctly modelled as a complex process with multiple manifestations (one of which is civil war), both grievance and economic factors are all relevant for explaining the risk of violent conflicts.

More recently, scholars have been tackling the important issue of the differences between the determinants of two types of civil resistance: violent and non-violent conflict. These are often considered to be very different phenomena, despite the accounts demonstrating close links between the two experiences. As noted by Witte et al. (2020), the relationship between grievances and uprisings is expected to be stronger in the case of peaceful uprisings than in violent revolts, largely because participation in peaceful uprisings is associated with a lower risk of violent government retaliation—and lower expected costs—than when engaging in violent rebellion, and also because it does not require the legitimization of the use of violence, nor the resources for purchasing weaponry. Possibly, the Arab uprisings are a singularity in the sense that, although peaceful at inception, they met with significant repression and, not surprisingly, turned violent very quickly.

Focusing on factors of discontent underlying the conflicts in the Arab region, we may group them into economic, political, and social categories. We refer to them in general terms leaving their deeper individual country analysis to the case studies of section II.

1.1 Economic Factors

There is an ongoing debate among scholars and politicians regarding the importance of economic factors in sparking the recent conflicts in the MENA region vis-à-vis other sociological, historical, and political determinants (see, for instance, Campante and Chor, 2012; Malik and Awadallah, 2013). Arguably, all of them are important but might have affected the events in each country in idiosyncratic ways. The country studies in this volume shed light on their relative importance and the ways in which they are connected and influence each other. This, in turn, forms the basis for the reconstruction agendas that would function as markers for the post-conflict transition period.

From a broad perspective, economic factors may not seem to be at the root of the conflicts in Arab countries. Prior to the uprisings, the region had been making steady progress towards eliminating extreme poverty, boosting prosperity, increasing school enrolment, and reducing hunger, and infant and maternal mortality (World Bank, 2017a). The Arab countries had embarked on significant programmes of structural reform and had made progress in creating environments more conducive to private sector development and shifting their economic systems to include more private sector-market-driven approaches. It has been pointed out that in the 1990s MENA economies lagged behind the rest of the world in terms of economic reform and when reforms were implemented, they had a limited impact in terms of economic growth and job creation (Nabli and Véganzonès-Varoudakis, 2004). On the other hand, reforms implemented in the twenty-first century have been more comprehensive, thus allowing for a reduction in the oversized and coercive style of state apparatus that was set up throughout the MENA region in the 1950s, and for increasing the role of the private sector. However, the limited liberalizing reforms undertaken lacked a clear strategic focus and have strengthened cronyism by generalizing politically oriented cooption and patronage, thereby establishing economies that are strongly averse to innovative behaviour (Malik and Awadallah, 2013; Diwan et al., 2015).

Nonetheless, the Arab region's economic growth in the pre-2010 period although moderate was generally in line with growth trends in other regions of the world. For the ten years preceding the uprisings, its average rate of growth exceeded the world average as well as the averages of most other regions of the world (see Table 1).

Furthermore, as shown in Figure 1, real GDP per working-age individual in the countries that experienced uprisings had increased in the two decades before 2010. Growth was, nevertheless, slow and unsteady in the two oil-abundant countries—Iraq and Libya—where the increase of GDP per working-age individual was below 1 per cent per year on average between 1990 and 2010. In the other two countries, economic growth was steady yet rather modest—around 2 per cent per year on average. In any case, these growth rates indicate that all these countries were unable to catch up significantly with those of more advanced economies.

Table 1 Average Growth in Real GDP per Capita by Region (%)

	World	Arab World	Middle East & North Africa*	Euro Area	OECD Members	High Income	Middle Income	Low Income
2000–10	1.7	2.2	2.5	1.3	1.1	1.2	4.8	1.9
2010–17	1.6	1.1	0.6	1.2	1.2	1.2	3.7	2
2000–18	1.7	1.7	1.8	1.3	1	1.3	4.2	2.2

Source: World Economic Indicators 2020, The World Bank.

Note: *excludes MENA high-income economies.

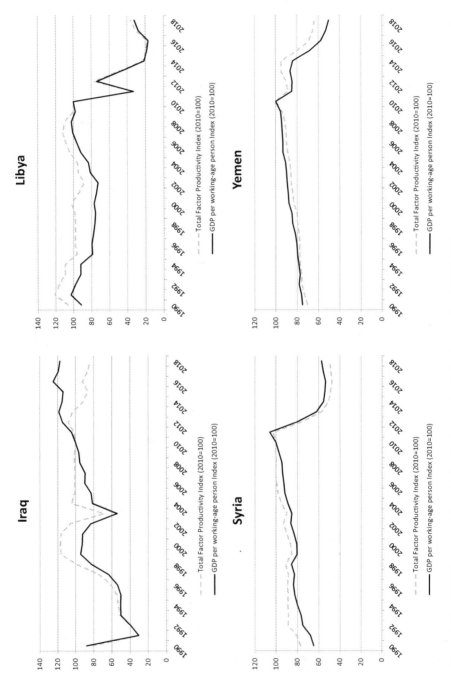

Figure 1 Real GDP per worker and total factor productivity (normalized 2010=100)
Source: Own elaboration

Introduction 7

More indicative of the impact of economic development on the livelihood of the population is the evolution of total factor productivity, TFP.[1] While employment is usually directly related to economic activity and GDP growth, the evolution of wages and workers' incomes is more tightly related to TFP gains. Higher productivity allows for sustainably higher wages. It can be seen in Figure 1 that TFP continued to be stagnant in the economy of every one of these countries, with the exception of Yemen, in the decade before the Arab uprising of 2011. In Yemen, TFP growth was, nevertheless, low (around 1.5 per cent). In Iraq, the combination of stagnating TFP and rising GDP per working-age person indicates that growth is largely driven by accumulating capital—and to a lesser extent employing more workers—and not by becoming more efficient at producing goods and services.

In the absence of labour market indicators—wages and unemployment rates—in these countries, TFP indices allow us to indirectly grasp the situation of the average worker. TFP stagnation suggests that social discontent may have arisen as a result of increasing dissatisfaction with the opportunities that sustained but slow growth had to offer the population.

Figure 1 also shows the extent of the damage brought on by the conflicts. It can be seen that GDP per working-age person and TFP collapsed after the Arab uprisings in Libya, Syria, and Yemen. In the latter two countries, cumulative decline in GDP per working-age individual is around 40 per cent. In Libya, the decline is significantly greater.

These countries had also made progress towards eliminating extreme poverty and boosting shared prosperity: although about half of the poor in these countries had moved out of poverty by the end of the 2000s, tough chronic poverty remained high; upward mobility was stronger in Syria and Tunisia, whilst downward mobility was pronounced in Yemen and Egypt (see Dang and Ianchovichina, 2018).

GDP growth is, obviously, not an all-encompassing measure of economic development or welfare that, on its own, determines the stability or instability of a given country or region. And other economic factors could have played a role in fuelling the social and political discontent that eventually led to the uprisings (Tucker, 2012; Ianchovichina et al., 2015). Two classic candidates would be: the high rates of unemployment and the high degree of inequality in expenditure, income, or wealth of the MENA region. In what follows we review the evidence.

1.1.1 Unemployment

Studies of unemployment in the countries where the uprisings broke out indicate that high unemployment, in particular youth unemployment, was one of the factors contributing to the uprisings (Elbadawi and Makdisi, 2016). Table 2 reveals that in the pre-uprising period, youth unemployment in Egypt, Syria, and Tunisia was significantly higher than elsewhere in the world with averages ranging from 19 to 30 per cent for the period 2000–2009.

Table 2 Rates of Unemployment

	General Unemployment. Ages 15 and Older		Youth Unemployment: Ages 15 to 24	
	Average 2000–2009	Average 2010–2018	Average 2000–2009	Average 2010–2018
Arab Countries	9.18	10.04	22.35	26.38
• Algeria	18.72	10.69	35.73	26.32
• Egypt	9.77	12.03	27.76	32.09
• Morocco	10.93	9.22	17.52	20.18
• Syria	9.18	8.52	19.17	20.07
• Tunisia	13.83	15.73	30.24	35.35
Sub-Saharan Africa	7.66	5.93	13.02	11.52
Latin America	8.33	6.98	16.44	15.22
Southern Asia	4.75	5.09	10.64	18.27
East Asia	4.29	4.04	9.52	10.01

Source: Own elaboration based on ILO database, ILO (2021).

High unemployment weakened the ability of the regimes to trade public goods and other economic benefits in exchange for the withholding of political rights and participation (the authoritarian bargain).

Indeed, as the table reveals, yet higher unemployment rates have continued to prevail in the post-uprising phase even in countries where political settlements have been reached, such as Egypt and Tunisia. The presence of high unemployment poses major challenges for political stability in all these countries, but in particular in Tunisia which has embarked, and in those other countries that might embark, on the road to democratic governance. Whereas, in what might be termed non-democracies high unemployment might play a role in bringing about regime change, for newly established democracies the concern would be its possible ability to undermine their democratic path.

1.1.2 Inequality

There is no consensus on the degree of inequality in the Arab region relative to what prevails in other regions of the world. Recent studies (UN ESCWA, 2019) point out that both income and wealth inequality in the Arab region are the highest worldwide.[2] Similarly, Alvaredo et al. (2017) argue that household survey data greatly underestimate inequality in the region and extend the types of data used in estimating income concentration in the Middle East to include national accounts, income tax data, and wealth data. Their estimates for the period 1990–2016 indicate that the Middle East is one of the most financially unequal regions in the world, due not only to an enormous inequality between countries (particularly between oil-rich and population-rich countries) but to a considerable economic inequality within countries.

The most affluent in the population (with the top 10 per cent of income levels) had appropriated around 60–66 per cent of the total income, while the share of the bottom 50 per cent of society varied between 8 per cent and 10 per cent of the total income. Thus, the degree of inequality in the Middle East is significantly higher than the highest levels in Latin America (Brazil, 55 per cent) or Asia (India, 54 per cent).

In contrast to this, the World Bank estimates indicate that the degree of income inequality in Arab countries is not much greater than in the rest of the world (World Bank, 2019d). Data provided by WIR (2018) shows that the income of the top 10 per cent of the population in the Middle East declined steadily between 1990 and 2010, whereas in all other regions in the world it either stagnated or increased sharply. Other studies similarly reveal that, prior to the Arab uprisings, inequality did not increase in Middle East countries (see Bibi and Nabli, 2010; Joffé, 2011). Looking at expenditure inequality in the Arab countries during the 2000s, Devarajan and Ianchovichina (2018) conclude it was low or moderate and, in many cases, declining. Examining the cases of Syria, Yemen, and Iraq, the UNU-WIDER database reveals that income inequality, measured by the Gini coefficient, declined slightly in these countries in the 2000s.

Certain researchers have assigned a key role to actual inequality in the igniting of the uprisings of 2011 (Klassen, 2018). However, there is increasing consensus that the actual high levels of income, or even wealth, inequality in the MENA region might not have been a significant underlying factor in these uprisings and the degree of political violence that followed (Joffé, 2011; World Bank, 2017a). Rather, what did play a crucial role in the social—and thereby, political—discontent were the prevailing perceptions of inequality and injustice that did not improve despite two decades of sustained growth before the outbreak of the Arab Spring. Devarajan and Ianchovichina (2018) find that measures of subjective well-being in Arab countries were relatively low and falling sharply, especially for the middle class, and in the countries where the uprisings eventually broke out. There was a growing and broadly shared dissatisfaction with the quality of life; the middle class, in particular, felt frustrated by deteriorating standards of living, lack of job opportunities in the formal sector, the poor quality of public services, and the absence of government accountability.[3] According to Verme (2014), significant differences between perceived and actual income distribution emerged in Egypt between 2000 and 2008. In 2000, people viewed themselves as more affluent than they actually were, but by 2008 it was the reverse, despite income data showing that in fact Egyptians had become more affluent. Arampatzi et al. (2018) found that over time, perceptions about corruption became increasingly more important in people's assessments of their satisfaction with their lives, particularly in the countries where the uprisings were most intense.

The above review leads to the conclusion that perceived, more than actual, income and wealth inequality in the Arab region was one of the triggers contributing to the uprisings. It gains added potency as a trigger when set alongside ethnic or sectarian inequality.

1.2 Political and Institutional Factors

A high level of income inequality and a lack of inclusion are usually the result of an economic ordering where rent-extraction dominates rent-creation: institutions are built so that a privileged few can capture the benefits of natural resources, economic growth, and overall development that would otherwise accrue to the population as a whole. The Arab countries are no exception. Usually, there is a high correlation between economic inequality and political inequality because when politicians are overly responsive to small affluent groups, policies inevitably are directed towards promoting their interests (Rosset et al., 2013). Conversely, citizens who are not part of the affluent group may become less engaged with politics. As noted by Przeworski (2015), citizens are not politically equal in economically unequal societies. When the political influence of certain individuals increases with their income and decisions are made by coalitions with greater political influence, the extent of income redistribution through taxes and transfers is always less than what is desired by the citizens (Karabarbounis, 2011). The end result is that representative institutions do not mitigate economic inequality, in the way that they would in more egalitarian systems.

The increasing unhappiness voiced during the Arab uprisings was associated with dissatisfaction with the quality of public services, the shortage of formal-sector jobs, and corruption, as well aspirations for a politically freer society. These sources of dissatisfaction suggest that the old social contract, where governments provided jobs, free health services and education, and subsidized food and fuel, in return for the rest of the population stifling its voice, could no longer be sustained (Devarajan and Ianchovichina, 2018). The Arab uprisings and their aftermath indicate that a new social contract was called for, one where the government promotes a regulatory environment that encourages the creation of private-sector jobs and accountability in service delivery, and where citizens are active and freer participants in the economy and society.

Growing dissatisfaction with the quality of life and income inequality is not the monopoly of Arab economies; most emerging economies in Africa or Latin America share similar if not deeper problems. What distinguishes our group of Arab economies from other countries in the Middle East or other regions of the world is recourse to untamed violence on the part of the authorities and other political actors.[4] The issue of violence in the Arab World and its determinants is a long-standing debate among scholars and experts. On one hand, there is the issue of political repression. The disproportionate response of governments to popular dissent, with the widespread use of repression, is characteristic of societies where political participation is limited, reluctantly tolerated by the authorities, and/or reserved only for the elite. As discussed in Lawrence (2016), however, identifying the impact of repression on protest presents a thorny problem because both the policing of protest and protest itself are endogenous processes and it can be difficult to assess whether police action is a cause or consequence of protests. On the other hand, there is the use of collective violence as a political tool for achieving particular objectives. As noted by Tilly (2003) there is little consensus on the appearance of violence (why does violence comes in waves?), its spread once ignited (why do peaceful people shift rapidly into violence and then may shift back to relatively peaceful interactions?), and the intensity of violent acts (why do different political regimes experience different levels and forms of collective violence?).

The onset of large-scale civil violence which can escalate to civil war is, nevertheless, prima-facie evidence of the breaking of the social contract between the people and the government. Rougier (2014) reviews the political literature on the Arab uprisings and argues that they may well have been motivated by a common feature, that is, the lack of structural change experienced by most economies in the region during the second half of the twentieth century. To explain why economic transformation slowed down after the 1960s, a variety of cultural, geographical, political, and institutional causes have been put forward. Even though these analyses all indicate crucial obstacles to long-term growth and structural transformation, none of them really explain why, after fifty years of calm, most of the MENA politico-economic equilibria were, ultimately, so abruptly rejected. The MENA structural change deficit can therefore be considered as a symptom of the persistent lack of reform to the social contract. Rougier concludes that as a consequence of the growing gap between the socioeconomic expectations and the real opportunities available to the population, and in the absence of any willingness to significantly reform on the part of entrenched elites, relative frustration increased until people were driven to protest and, eventually, to commit to violence.

1.3 Social Factors

Social inequality—in the form of fractionalization and polarization—has also the potential to spark conflicts, both in the region and elsewhere. There is a rich literature that attempts to link different forms of social inequality (polarization, fractionalization, or Lorenz-domination) in different characteristics (ethnicity, language, or religion) to various specifications of conflict (onset, incidence, or intensity).[5] The evidence, however, remains inconclusive. Most of the literature fails to find any significant evidence of ethnic fractionalization as a determinant of conflict (e.g., Fearon and Laitin, 2003; Hegre and Sambanis, 2006), and could not identify a link between fractionalization and conflict. The study by Montalvo and Reynal-Querol (2005), on the other hand, revealed a significant relationship between ethnic polarization and the incidence of conflict.

It is useful to distinguish between inter-group and intra-group inequality. Religious intergroup inequality—particularly, the Sunni-Shi'a schism—has always been at the front of popular explanations for conflict in Arab countries. Ethnic or sectarian inter-group inequality, however, may have also played an important role in the increased incidence of conflict in the MENA region. Most civil conflicts are rooted in ethnic, sectarian, or other identity groups (Doyle and Sambanis, 2000; Fearon and Laitin, 2003), making it important to consider arguments about how economic inequality measured with respect to groups affects their propensity to participate in civil war. Huber and Mayoral (2019) distinguish between group-based economic inequality and the onset of civil conflict, on one hand, and group-based inequality and the intensity of civil conflict, on the other. In their empirical analysis, they find that there is a robust association between intragroup inequality and conflict intensity, but a much weaker link with conflict onset.

They also find essentially no evidence to show that horizontal economic inequality is related to conflict onset and find that previous claims are not robust. Esteban and Ray (2008, 2011) argue that it is not clear why the relative wealth of a group should be systematically related to its propensity to start a war and offer an alternative rationale based on polarization and ethnicity. They take the position that 'prize-grabbing' on a large scale—often economic but possibly political, cultural, or religious in nature—is frequently at the heart of the ethnic conflict, both for the elites as well as for the masses. The 'prize' comes in the form of government 'budgets' or 'policies' that produce various public goods. Such budgets or policies may be used to benefit one class over another (e.g., public versus private health, primary versus higher education), and they may have distinct ethnic implications (e.g., funding for religions, the proclamation of 'secular' or 'majoritarian' identities). To gain control of these budgets, class-based or ethnic alliances must be formed. In this context, they show that ethnic, as opposed to class, conflict may be focal, and precisely so in the presence of economic inequality. The reason lies in the fact that a class division creates groups that display strong internal economic homogeneity and a sense of common purpose, while ethnic alliances display high levels of internal group economic inequality and open the door for redistribution conflicts.

Intergenerational inequality is another potential source of conflict, particularly when societies are polarized along ethnic or sectarian lines. Both the fact of a large proportion of young adults in the population and a rapid increase in the working-age population tends to exacerbate unemployment, prolongs dependency on parents, diminishes the individual's self-esteem, and fuels frustrations, indicating the low cost to these young adults of engaging in a violent political uprising. Paasonen and Urdal (2016) blame what they term the large 'youth bulges' in Middle Eastern economies—and the repressive response of governments—for the armed conflicts that broke out in the early 2010s. As mentioned above, before the Arab uprisings double-digit unemployment was the norm in the four countries of interest, with youth unemployment generally above 25 per cent. It was in this context that, after the onset of the uprisings, many countries in the region seemed primed to fall into disarray. Countries become even more prone to conflict when economic conditions decline and, notably for the young, opportunities in the labour market dwindle (Urdal, 2006), or when there are abundant rents from natural resources, and the expected benefits of rebellion seem much higher than those of not rebelling (Karakaya, 2016).

Bodea and Houle (this volume) revisit the research, linking together grievances and civil war in various political regimes, institutions, and intergroup relations, as well as society-wide and group-level inequality. In contrast to the argument in the early literature that grievance is too ubiquitous to be analytically useful, they argue that measuring grievances and injustices caused by political exclusion and economic inequities at the ethnic-group level explains the onset of civil war. Their key observation is that the use of economy-wide measures of grievances fails to account for the intergroup rivalries that might lead to violent conflict. Their empirical work on the youth—which more clearly delineates the boundaries between ethnicity and inclusion in political power as well as the fact that economic inequality is overlaid with social factors—supports their argument.

While ethnicity is not a dominant issue in Arab countries, in our view it is reasonable to conclude that the high levels of exclusion from political power and economic inequality in the region must have played a significant role in the uprisings of the 2010s (Elbadawi and Makdisi, 2017). Bodea and Houle also point to another dominant factor in the MENA region that bears responsibility for fuelling the conflicts: natural resources. Grievances not only increase the likelihood of conflicts and violence but also interact with the abundance of natural resources which may serve as a catalyst for political polarization and conflict. This is certainly an issue in Arab countries where oil has become a key determinant of political and economic power (e.g., Iraq, Libya, Algeria, and, to some extent, Yemen). But it also permeates other Arab economies in various forms. Oil price volatility affects foreign currency flows to non-oil Arab countries in the form of workers' remittances and direct foreign investment. Geopolitics and foreign intervention in the MENA region have also been largely driven by oil wealth. We, therefore, argue that both economic considerations as well as grievances are at the root of the conflicts we review in this volume.

2 The Premises of Reconstruction

The above analysis of the causes of civil conflict points to a major conclusion, namely that they are the inevitable result of long-standing and deep-rooted institutional failures. Hence, in contrast to development in relatively normal times which takes place in a given political and economic structure, post-conflict reconstruction will involve a drastic transformation of pre-war economic, social, and security sectors (Tzifakis and Tsardanidis, 2006).

At the political and social levels, the main goal of post-conflict reconstruction will be to induce a major shift in the developmental ideology and operations of the political system. It encompasses state building (the creation of the institutions of the state) as well as nation building, that is, the forging of a sense of common nationhood, intended to overcome ethnic, sectarian, or communal differences, and which would counter alternative sources of identity and loyalty, and mobilize the population behind a parallel state-building project.

At the economic level, the reconstruction agenda is necessarily more broadly defined than post-war stabilization to include not only the rehabilitation or creation of basic services and infrastructure destroyed during the war, but also the modernization or creation of the basic macro and microeconomic institutional and policy framework that is necessary for creating a viable and healthy economy. Successful macroeconomic policies are the backbone of successful reconstruction: maintaining relative price stability sustains growth, permitting the provision of much-needed resources to the government so that reconstruction initiatives can be properly financed. Furthermore, sustained and vigorous growth will also result in employment and higher levels of real wages that in turn will sustain the return of ex-combatants to productive occupations.

With the above in mind, we posit that the long-term durability of any post-conflict transition is founded on the fulfilment of three vital premises, discussed in further detail in chapter one.

The first is that *post conflict reconstruction should be primarily geared towards changing, improving or in an extreme case, eliminating altogether the pre-war institutional fabric of the country, i.e., the set of key institutions that helped to create the conditions that made conflict inevitable.*

As amply demonstrated by the Arab uprisings, and those elsewhere, nation-states fail when their governments lose legitimacy (Rotberg, 2003). Failed states have flawed institutions. Democratic debate is noticeably absent. If legislatures exist at all, they are rubber-stamping machines. Only the institution of the Executive functions. The Judiciary is derivative of the Executive rather than being independent of it, and the people know that they cannot rely on the court system for significant redress or remedy, especially against the state. The bureaucracy exists mainly to carry out the orders of the Executive and to oppress the people. The armed forces of failed states are often highly politicized. Hence, eliminating altogether the pre-conflict institutional fabric of the country, i.e., the set of key institutions that helped to create the conditions for failure is an essential post-conflict endeavour.

The literature on post-conflict economic recovery shares the assumption that failed nation-states fail in their own unique way and that, accordingly, each reconstruction effort is unique (Tzifakis, 2013). Every situation differs in terms of initial conditions (including the causes of the outbreak of conflict and the level of development of the economy); the scope of destruction; the nature of its resolution (the total (or otherwise) cessation of hostilities in the territory); and the extent of international support for the settlement, both in political and economic terms.

Consequently, one would be tempted to conclude that reconstruction plans ought to be tailor-made to the particular needs of each country. Undoubtedly, idiosyncratic political, economic, and sociological elements will largely shape the national post-conflict reconstruction work in any given country. Nevertheless, any plan for reconstruction will have to deal with a number of socio-economic challenges common to all post-conflict situations. These would include the repatriating of human and financial resources, dealing with the donor community, reversing the deterioration of human development and security conditions, overcoming the destruction of infrastructure, facing the increase in the number of people needing social assistance; coping with large fiscal deficits caused by high levels of military expenditure (usually at the expense of social services); curtailing the rise of inflation; managing the increase in debts that were not serviced during wartime; or normalizing external trade disrupted by the hostilities.

The second premise is that *reconstruction work ought to focus on achieving wider economic inclusion and less inequality as well as generating increasing employment opportunities if it is to gain legitimacy and be sustainable.* Coping with unemployment is essential for their future democratic development: importantly, non-democratic parties could exploit actual and potential popular resentment associated with high levels of unemployment in order to change the democratic political process underway.

Undoubtedly, sustained economic growth and stability are mutually reinforcing. Growth is important for achieving stability and that, in turn, stimulates investment and growth. Therefore, the prospects for stable growth are vital for reconstruction work in that such prospects will further spur the private sector to provide opportunities for investment, greater employment, and higher wages, and thus provide the government with a sustainable, steady flow of resources to support reconstruction and improve living standards.

The experiences in the Arab countries and elsewhere indicates that the benefits of growth should materialize not only in increasing levels of employment and/or worker remuneration but also in better access and quality of public goods and services. Consequently, the prospects for improving welfare conditions (i.e., economic growth benefiting the entire society and not only those in positions of power) are also vital for reconstruction.

The third premise is that if *the Arab countries are to embark on a genuinely inclusive process of reconstruction that would cement the transition to peaceful and sustainable national development, the proposed economic reforms* *and policies ought to be in line with the establishment of a new form of social contract, implicit or explicit, that would reflect the attributes of democratic governance.* Of the five Arab countries where uprisings broke out, so far only Tunisia appears to be moving in this direction though it is yet to establish solid economic foundations necessary for sustaining democracy.

In this regard, economic policies deemed to be optimal from a technical viewpoint ought to be weighed against their ability to support the proposed social contract. Otherwise, they will prove unviable and politically damaging in the long run. As discussed by del Castillo (2008), war-affected countries may initially be forced to adopt sub-optimal economic policies (e.g., maintain certain non-profitable production units) in consideration of political and security requirements (e.g., the preservation of jobs). But the long-term objective would nonetheless remain the reconciliation of efficient economic policies with a democratic transition.

3 National Peace: Prospects for a Regional Democratic Breakthrough

Except in the case of Tunisia, the uprisings have not, so far, led to a democratic breakthrough in the region.[6] Instead, the civil conflicts that have broken out in their wake are yet to be settled. This phenomenon is probably strongly linked to the fact that the major factors that account for the persistence of the Arab democracy deficit in the pre-2010/2011 period (i.e., oil, state incapacities, conflicts, and their accompanying foreign interventions) continued to prevail after 2010–2011 (Elbadawi and Makdisi, 2017). Indeed, the level and intensity of conflicts in the region, fed by growing sectarian divisiveness including the intensification of identity politics and the rise of fundamentalist groups, have since further increased. The region continues to be one of the most conflictual in the world having in the period 2011–2017, the greatest number of the world's war-related deaths (UNDP, 2018). At the same time, oil resources have continued to exert a negative influence on the political scene in the region, though perhaps to a lesser degree than before.

The eventual various outcomes of the brutal civil conflicts in Syria, Yemen, and Libya will determine the nature of the political regimes that will follow, and to what extent, if any, these future regimes will come to reflect the attributes of democratic governance rather than those of new autocratic orders. The delay, so far, of a substantive move to democracy in Egypt is associated with the continuing political dominance of the military elite and maybe, to a lesser extent, continued political divisions there, not to mention the influence of the persisting, indeed expanding conflicts in the region with all their corrosive effects on the transition process.

These foregoing remarks raise the question of whether, after the 2011 uprisings, a successful region-wide transition to democratic governance remains more an aspiration than a concrete reality. What about prospects in the longer run? Presumably, as long as the multi-dimensional military conflicts in Syria, Yemen, and Libya continue to rage, the prospects for any democratic transition in the region are still remote. As remarked these conflicts are manifestations of a counter-revolution (partly linked to foreign interventions) intended to stifle transitions towards democratic forms of governance. But ultimately, they will be resolved, opening the door, however narrowly, to the emergence of accountable democratic political institutions.

Pushing in the direction of democratic change in the post-conflict phase are growing socio-economic and political processes that will further weaken the prevailing authoritarian regimes, their counter-revolutions or 'authoritarian upgrading' in the wake of the 2011 uprisings notwithstanding.[7] These processes include: the building modernizing influences (e.g., a growing middle class,[8] improving levels of education, and growing female participation in the economic and political domains) which the civil conflicts have slowed down or disrupted; an increasing incompatibility between exclusive political institutions and the increasing openness of economic institutions; an expanding popular demand for freedom, equal political rights, and social justice, reinforced by decreasing fundamentalist influence (Makdisi, 2021).

Furthermore, the corrosive political effects of relatively abundant oil resources will, with the passage of time, be countered by the influences forcing change, such as mounting socio-economic inequities that breed growing popular dissatisfaction, the weakening of the rentier effect due in part to changing internal economic conditions and a growing democratic neighbourhood as more and more countries tend to move to partial if not full democracies under the influence of the factors pushing for change. Moreover, to the extent that the global oil market tends to lean towards a potential long-term deceleration of prices and resulting in low 'equilibrium' prices will further threaten the sustainability of the authoritarian bargain, even in the richly endowed societies of the Gulf (Elbadawi and Makisi, 2021).

Were the process of democratization to unfold on a solid basis in those countries that have experienced uprisings (in 2011 as well as more recently), it would tend to gain an added momentum that would positively affect other countries in the region which are yet to democratize. The reason is that undemocratic societies that are located in democratic neighbourhoods are more susceptible to democratic transition. In turn, this would also diminish the potential threat of reversal (see Poast and Urpelainen, 2015). In the case of the Arab region, not only would the factors pushing for conflict recede but the significance of resource rents as a constraint to democratic transition would diminish, even for societies endowed with great resources.

3.1 The Challenges Ahead

The design and implementation of economic reforms are an integral part of the process of peace and reconstruction. The challenge for economic reformers is arguably daunting. On one hand, they must succeed in instilling in a country previously unobserved levels of self-control and political generosity, intergroup confidence, and economy-wide governance. Reforms should aim at minimizing the risk of conflict recurrence, restoring confidence in economic institutions, generating employment and fostering investment, and enhancing the ability of the state to provide security for communities and households, to enforce the rule of law, and to deliver essential services. On the other hand, and concurrently with jump-starting the economy, deep structural reforms should be promptly implemented with a view to changing, improving or, even in an extreme case, eliminating altogether the pre-conflict institutional fabric of the country, that is, the set of economic institutions—and their embedded structure of incentives—that helped to create the conditions for failure.

Sustainable reconstruction requires the implementation of a balanced macroeconomic policy, one that would help overcome social discontent and so the risk of renewed hostilities. A poor macroeconomic approach might constitute a serious limitation for any hoped-for reconstruction. Another immediate and crucial concern is the resumption of economic growth and, in particular, increasing levels of employment. The political support for reconstruction work depends primarily on the population perceiving an improvement in their standard of living. Therefore, the creation of employment opportunities—particularly for the youth—ought to be at the centre of the reconstruction agenda. In most emerging economies, economic recovery from a crisis has been accompanied by the substantial creation of employment (see Stein, 2016 for the African case and Chaturvedi and Saha, 2019 for the South Asian case). This may not necessarily be the case for the MENA region mainly due to the poor performance of the labour market. It would require a paradigm shift to correct this, in which governments abandon the use of public employment as a key mechanism for generating political allegiance and instead allow a well-managed private sector to become the main source of the earned income of the family unit. Reforms to the labour market should be considered a crucial component of the reconstruction agenda.

Accordingly, this agenda must be geared towards a vigorous resumption of economic activity. Four areas of macroeconomic management are deemed crucial for the success of the reconstruction process: inflation control, fiscal policies, exchange rate policy, and physical infrastructure. First, macroeconomic policies ought to set up the institutions necessary for the establishment of a modern monetary policy framework, in which inflation control is the sole task of an independent monetary authority, accountable only to the population via a formal political procedure (e.g., periodic and scheduled reports to a congress or parliament as well as publicly available minutes of the meetings of the Central Bank on monetary policy). Second, there should be a restructuring of government finances away from military ends and towards welfare-improving programmes and the provision of public services. Reforms that guarantee fiscal stability and responsibility must also be implemented. Building or re-establishing fiscal institutions should be aimed at strengthening fiscal solvency and sustainability (i.e., attaining sustainable levels of government deficit and debt), contributing to macroeconomic (or cyclical) stabilization (i.e., reducing fiscal policy pro-cyclicality or raising policy counter-cyclicality), and making fiscal policy design and execution resilient against government corruption and private-sector lobbing. Third, exchange rate management and the choice of the exchange regime is an essential consideration in the design of the reconstruction agenda. Exchange rate regimes influence inflation, economic growth, investment, and productivity. Furthermore, the successful provision of a stable currency lends credibility to the reconstruction process and a single, national currency can be a unifying symbol, contributing to a sense of national identity. Fourth, given a shortage of domestic resources, reconstruction of physical and institutional infrastructure would have to rely mainly on foreign resources. One important source is a foreign direct investment (FDI). Attracting FDI requires the appropriate institutional setup that provides investors with an environment in which they can conduct their business profitably and without incurring unnecessary risk.

Macroeconomic structural reforms by themselves are insufficient to generate sustained welfare gains for the population beyond the initial impact of the peace dividend. Reconstruction of institutions at the microeconomic level is vital for sustainable development and, more importantly, for the appropriation of the benefits of such development by the population. In turn, these reforms can increase the legitimacy of the reconstruction process. In Chapter 1, we identify a number of key issues that need addressing in the economic agenda. Briefly, these issues are organized along three guiding principles. First, the need to ensure the enforcement of property rights—and sometimes restore and expand them—so that the levels of economic confidence improve and the returns on an enterprise are accrued to their legitimate owners. Second, a proper distinction between those sectors best served by private sector initiatives and those where markets fail due to 'imperfections' such as natural monopoly power, informational asymmetries, and external factors. The latter would call for public sector intervention. Third, the design of a proper regulatory setup for each type of market. Competition in free markets will not provide advances in development and welfare unless adequate regulation and supervision are in place. Similarly, where the market fails, interventions must be designed so that efficiency is preserved, and benefits accrue to the population and not to interest groups or those bureaucrats in charge of running state-controlled businesses.

We thus submit an economic agenda for reconstruction that goes far beyond selecting policies to deal with the immediate post-conflict needs; it has to prepare the economy—and ultimately the society—to design and build the institutions needed for sustained development. If such reforms are able to align with the expectations of the population regarding the economic role of government in a post-conflict transition and can convince the elites to direct state resources towards building up the State's capacity for providing services and towards fulfilling those expectations, then there is a good chance that the construction of a new social contract will meet with success. This will occur through the establishment of an agreement between state and society on their mutual roles and responsibilities. Their successful implementation would positively align the expectations of the population as to the role of the government in the post-conflict transition and how it could contribute to the building of a new social contract between the state and society that redefines their mutual roles and responsibilities.

3.2 The Impact of the Covid-19 Pandemic

If the prospects for peace and development in conflict-afflicted Arab countries looked remote in the 2010s, matters have unfortunately taken a turn for the worse with the sudden and devastating effects of the Coronavirus pandemic. Beyond health issues, which by themselves constitute a severe blow to the fragile political and institutional fabric of Arab countries, the economic downturn unleashed by the plague is, perhaps, the worst global shock in almost a century. No country has escaped its effects. Already fragile contexts are at risk of becoming even more so. Conflicts are typically exacerbated by natural disasters and the situation of marginalized populations could rapidly worsen, in particular migrant and displaced communities, already living in poor sanitary conditions and with limited access to public services. While the rapid development of vaccines initially raised hopes of prompt alleviation, as of early 2022 the disease is far from being controlled and successive waves of new Covid-19 strains have reintroduced health concerns as well as fears of economic distress.

Pandemics, nevertheless, are both a major challenge to fragile economies in a myriad of areas (economic activity, government finances, health, education, etc.) and yet can also provide the opportunity for much-needed economic, political, and institutional reforms.

In the economic realm, the adverse effects have taken the form of a downturn in activity, an increase in unemployment and informal activity, and in levels of poverty. Most of these effects are associated with the containment and confinement measures taken by the authorities to control the spread of the disease. While these measures proved effective (see Blanco et al., 2020 for an assessment), the downturn has been very pronounced and contrary to initial expectations, bound to last for some time. International trade and particularly tourism have been severely damaged, but matters could have been much worse if not for the vigorous expansionary fiscal policies enacted by most governments in the world. Combatting health problems, enacting emergency transfers and a reduction in tax revenue have placed a significant strain on fiscal resources forcing the authorities to increase the national debt and/or curtail public investment. The latter will have a deleterious effect on economic growth in the medium to long term. An additional challenge to the economies of Arab countries includes the almost certain fact that the economic slowdown in the advanced economies is likely to cause a decrease in Official Development Assistance, a much-needed source of financing for post-conflict reconstruction.

On the political side, one possible outcome of a pandemic is political chaos and an increase in violence and destruction. The political opportunity theory (Tarrow, 1994) would suggest that armed groups could perceive the crisis as a chance to expand the areas under their control or to eliminate adversaries. Empirical evidence collected by Sedik and Xu (2020) suggests political unrest tends to peak two years after a typical epidemic starts and tends to be quite persistent. On the other hand, economic crises tend to bring to light the best in human nature. Government responses to the spread of the virus have led to the greater centralization of political decision-making. Emergency measures have been implemented in most of the countries suffering from the pandemic, increasing the reach of the oversight functions of the executive. Some observers have been warning about a possible surge in autocratic rule or the possible abuse of power, in particular in countries where oversight and accountability functions are insufficiently resilient. Maintaining the Rule of Law, Human Rights and compliance with basic liberties could prove to be a challenge in the coming years.

There is empirical evidence which suggests that some natural disasters—droughts or floods, for example—can operate as potential democratizing devices (Brückner and Ciccone, 2011; Aidt and Leon, 2016). Nevertheless, the support for the authorities during the pandemic does not necessarily continue in ex-post politics: most of the research on the political effects of natural disasters (Healy and Malhotra, 2009) and economic shocks (Margalit, 2019) demonstrates that those in power are often punished by events that produce a negative welfare shock on the population, even when they are beyond anyone's control.

In fact, evidence is already surfacing on the political impact of the pandemic. Amat et al. (2020) survey the population of Spain, one of the worst-affected countries in Europe, and finds a widespread demand for effective leadership, a willingness to surrender individual freedoms, and a marked increase in support for technocratic governance. In this shift, the authors fear that Covid-19 could provide an opportunity for those in power to centralize and further accumulate power, and increase surveillance and their control of society. Bol et al. (2021) take advantage of a unique representative web-based survey that was fielded in March and April 2020 in Western Europe to compare the political allegiances of those who took the survey immediately before and immediately after the implementation of the lockdowns in their respective countries. They have found that initially at any rate the lockdowns increased support for the party of the Prime Minister/President and the intention to vote for it, an increased trust in government, and satisfaction with democracy. Furthermore, generally speaking, while rallying individuals around current leaders and institutions, the lockdowns have had no effect on traditional left-right attitudes.

Gingerich and Vogler (2020) argue that the exceedingly high cost in terms of human lives of the deadliest pandemic of the last millennium (the Black Death, 1347–1351) weakened repressive regimes (notably serfdom in Western Europe) and, ultimately, led to the development of proto-democratic institutions and the associated political cultures that shaped the modalities of political engagement for generations. They find that areas in Germany hit hardest by the Black Death were more likely to adopt inclusive political institutions and equitable land-ownership patterns, and exhibited electoral behaviour indicating independence from the influence of the landed elite during the transition to mass politics.

Notes

1 Total factor productivity or multi-factor productivity is usually measured as the ratio of aggregate output (e.g., GDP) to aggregate inputs. Under some simplifications regarding production technology, growth in TFP becomes the portion of growth in output not explained by growth in traditionally measured inputs of labour and capital used in production. We use a Solow growth model to compute TFP.
2 It is argued that the Gini coefficients of income that show for 2019 comparatively low to moderate levels for most of the Arab countries are not an accurate measure of inequality in the Arab world (WIR, 2018). A more realistic assessment is given by the World Inequality Database estimates. For 2016 it reveals that the regional income inequality average is the highest of all regions. Similarly, the Arab regional Gini coefficient of wealth, estimated for 2016 at 83.9, is higher than the average for other regions. The UN ESCWA study (UN ESCWA, 2020) estimates that in 2019 the Arab region population held USD 5.79 trillions worth of wealth of which the top 10 per cent accounted for USD 4.39 trillion, or 75.8 per cent, of the total. Their average wealth was USD 182,939 compared to an average of USD 975 for the bottom 46 per cent of the population.
3 One study (UN ESCWA, 2014) points out that prior to the 1990s the authoritarian Arab regimes managed to gain the loyalty of the middle classes by providing them with economic privileges including well-paid jobs. Subsequently, however, declining economic opportunities along with flourishing patronage networks that favoured some groups over others and continued political repression, led the middle classes to join the 2011 uprisings (see also Cammett and Diwan, 2013).
4 In comparison, Latin American countries successfully transitioned from dictatorship to democracy without political unrest while having similar levels of inequality of conflict affected MENA countries, for example, Argentina and Uruguay, or much higher levels, such as Brazil or Chile where Gini coefficients are in the range of 0.50.
5 See, for example, Collier and Hoeffler (2004), Fearon and Laitin (2003), Montalvo and Reynal-Querol (2005), and Østby (2008a).
6 For an analysis of the Tunisian case see Boughzala and Ben Romdhane (2017) and El Ouardani and Makdisi (2018).
7 The concept of 'authoritarian upgrading' refers to economic and political changes introduced by the authoritarian regimes with the objective of placating their population and preserving their rule (see Aarts et al., 2012).
8 In particular, the Syrian civil war has led to a greatly depleted middle class in the country but once peace is restored it will grow again.

1 Economic Agenda for Post-Conflict Reconstruction

Samir Makdisi and Raimundo Soto

1 Introduction

By any standard, the challenges faced by post-conflict countries are daunting. In addition to recovering from the destruction of physical, human, and social capital, societies must cope with severely weakened state capacity, distorted economic incentives, widespread poverty, population displacement, and massive unemployment.

These conditions place war-torn countries at a continuing risk of relapsing into violent conflict. As discussed by Sambanis (in this volume), civil conflicts are notoriously persistent: the same reasons that ignited the conflict, make it difficult to reach a mutually enforceable settlement that might avoid the high cost of violence in settling disputes over resources or power. Power-sharing institutions, he argues, increase the political inclusion and the accommodation of minority groups and former rebels after a civil war, thereby reducing those grievances that might fuel violent conflict.

Beyond politics, institutions also matter for the maintenance of peace after conflicts (Fearon, 2011). Besley and Persson (2011) and Elbadawi and Soto (2014), among others, provide theories and empirical evidence showing that political violence is the result of a game where both the incumbent government and an opposition group may make an investment in political violence and where the ruling group at each period controls the government budget, which can be expended either on public goods or redistributed between the two groups. The main determinants of conflict include the level of resource rents, aid or other forms of income to the state, the level of wages and of the provision of public-goods. Importantly, however, the theory predicts these determinants will have an influence on violence only if the political institutions are non-consensual.

Resource and power control are key determinants of conflict, but grievances can also play a role. Bodea and Houle (this volume) review the long-lasting debate over the role of grievances, inequality, and natural resource rents in fuelling civil conflict and violence. They investigate the ways in which horizontal wealth inequality interacts with oil resources to increase or mitigate the risk of conflict: the inequalities of wealth between groups

DOI: 10.4324/9781003344414-3

generate an emotional reaction both as regards to one's perceived lack of resources as compared to that of other groups, or against a requirement to redistribute to poorer, less deserving groups. Oil revenue can be insidious in this context, compounding such emotional reactions.

While political, institutional, and sociological considerations play a crucial role in post-conflict reconstruction, an equally vital determinant of success is the quality of the economic policies implemented once peace has been restored. This chapter focuses on the design and implementation of economic reforms, which are an integral part of the process of peace and reconstruction. The challenge in implementing successful economic reforms is immense. On one hand, economic policy priorities for countries in post-conflict recovery should take into account the need to minimize the risk of conflict recurrence and to restore confidence in social, political, and economic institutions. In particular, it is important to enhance the ability of the state to provide security for households and communities, by enforcing the rule of law and delivering essential services. Economic recovery priorities must focus on employment, encourage productive investment, mitigate business risks, and reduce group inequalities. On the other hand, in order to avoid a relapse into conflict and give the peace process some hope of being sustainable, structural economic reforms cannot be postponed. It is most likely that the pre-conflict economic structure did very little to avoid the conflict, and the current economic structure may also be highly distorted as a result of the war. Reconstruction policies should, therefore, be primarily geared towards changing, improving or, even in an extreme case, eliminating altogether the pre-conflict institutional fabric of the country. That is, the set of economic institutions and their embedded structure of incentives that helped to create the conditions for failure. Reconstruction has to be a nation-building exercise as well as a peace-building endeavour.

Undoubtedly, idiosyncratic political, economic, and sociological elements largely shape national post-conflict reconstruction endeavours. Nevertheless, reconstruction must deal with common challenges, such as establishing genuinely inclusive and democratic governance; repatriating human and financial resources; dealing with the donor community; reversing the deterioration of human development and security conditions; overcoming the destruction of infrastructure; confronting the problem of an increase in the number of people needing social assistance; coping with large fiscal deficits caused by high levels of military expenditure (usually at the expense of social expenditure); curtailing the rise of inflation; managing the increase in the debt that was not serviced during wartime; or normalizing external trade disrupted by hostilities.

We submit that the reforms to be considered in the post-conflict economic agenda should be based on the three premises which we discussed in the introduction. First, in order to gain legitimacy and be sustainable, reconstruction policies should focus on attaining wider economic inclusion and reducing inequality, in addition to substantially reducing unemployment.

Second, reconstruction policies should be primarily geared towards changing, improving or, even in an extreme case, eliminating altogether the pre-conflict institutional fabric of the country. Third, proposed economic reforms and policies ought to be in line with the establishment of a new form of social contract, whether implicit or explicit.

OECD (2008) defines a social contract as a process for bargaining, articulating, and mediating society's expectations of the state. A social contract emerges from the interaction of five elements: (a) the expectations that a given society has of the state; (b) the state's capacity to provide services, including security, and to secure revenue to provide these services; and (c) an elite willing to direct the resources of the state and capacity to fulfil social expectations. It is crucially mediated by (d) the existence of political processes through which the bargain between state and society is institutionalized. Finally, (e) legitimacy plays a complex additional role in shaping expectations and facilitating the political process. Legitimacy is also produced and replenished—or, conversely, eroded—by the interaction between the other four factors. Structural reforms post-conflict ought to provide a new framework where such interaction is fruitful, by inducing an agreement between the state and society on their mutual roles and responsibilities.

As can be seen, our analysis points to the need to implement far-reaching, structural reforms. We are aware of the criticism that reconstruction often fails as a result of authorities aiming at transferring Western state institutions to post-conflict economies with a disregard for local interests. Englebert and Tull (2008) identify this as one of the main reasons why some countries—particularly in Africa—have obstinately resisted attempts at transformation. The limited success of market reforms and the promotion of democracy indicates that the grand vision of state building, with its one-size-fits-all approach, is likely to meet with resistance. To some extent, this is due to the absence of cooperation between supporters of reform (especially, donors) and national leaders, itself the result of conflicting views on both the causes of state failure and the goals of reconstruction. Political elites may seek to maximize the benefits accruing to them from existing institutions as well as from ongoing political instability.

We split post-conflict reforms into two main areas. The first pertains to macroeconomic stabilization and structural reforms, which would provide an appropriate framework for the resumption of growth and employment, for the control of economy-wide imbalances (such as inflation, fiscal deficits, and in the balance of payments), and for dealing with the financing of those essential public services that have an immediate impact on the welfare of the population. The second covers a number of crucial microeconomic reforms in areas concerning property rights, the regulation of markets left to the operation of the private sector (including privatization), and the management of markets where a market fails as a result of natural monopoly power, informational asymmetries, merit and demerit goods, missing undiversifiable risks of the markets, and externalities. These microeconomic reforms can have a significant impact on the welfare of the population in the short term as well as build defences against corruption and abuse in the medium run.

At the analytic and empirical levels, the literature on reconstruction agendas is vast. Our main goal is not to survey but to identify those insights, practices, and lessons learned, that best serve the purposes of illuminating the reconstruction challenges in conflict-affected MENA countries. The rest of the chapter is organized into four sections. Section 1 takes up reconstruction challenges. In our view reconstruction has to be a nation-building exercise as well as a peace-building one. Crucially, reforms should steer the economy and society away from the resumption of violence by changing the structure of those political and economic institutions that helped to create the conditions for failure. This is a very difficult challenge and needs support both at the macro- and microeconomic levels. In Section 2, we focus on the most important macroeconomic reforms that we submit should be implemented to deal with the pressing and crucial concern of the resumption of economic growth and, in particular, the creation of employment. These include monetary, fiscal, and exchange rate reforms, as well as policies dealing with the reconstruction of infrastructure, the role of direct foreign investment, foreign aid, and commodity price shocks. Section 3 is based on the notion that the reconstruction of institutions at the microeconomic level is vital for sustainable development and, more importantly, for the appropriation by the population of the benefits of peace and augmenting the legitimacy of the reconstruction. Microeconomic reforms are identified using three guiding principles. First, the need to restore property rights, so that security levels improve, and the returns on the effort accrue to their legitimate owners. Second, the identification of sectors where private initiative is best allocated by market forces from areas where markets fail as a result of natural monopoly power, informational asymmetries, and externalities. Third, the proper regulatory setup for each type of market. Competition in a free market would not fulfil its promise of gains in development and welfare unless adequate regulation and supervision are in place. Likewise, where the market fails, intervention must be designed so that efficiency is preserved, and benefits accrue to the population and not to interest groups or bureaucrats. Section 4 presents the main conclusions.

2 Reconstruction Challenges

We start from the premise that reconstruction policies should be primarily geared towards changing, improving or, even in an extreme case, eliminating altogether the pre-conflict institutional fabric of the country that helped to create the conditions for failure. As noted by Devarajan and Mottaghi (2017), reconstruction should be designed to steer the dynamics of conflict towards peace by changing the calculus of the belligerents.

Economic reforms must therefore be designed and implemented to change the incentives for the different agents in society at all levels; microeconomic, macroeconomic, and institutional. If, as documented in Bodea and Houle (this volume) and Campante and Chor (2012), inequality in incomes and opportunities is one of the main sources of civil conflicts in the Middle East, then the challenge for the authorities is to devise economic reforms that allow for an appropriate partake of the benefits of peace and sustained growth.

A number of researchers, for example, Malik and Awadallah (2013) and Salih (2013), have pointed out that the roots of the region's long-term economic and political failure are a statist model of intervention that is financed through external windfalls and rests on inefficiency and corruption. This would call for reforms that are designed to alter incentives such that a vibrant private sector emerges in areas where the government has been blatantly unsuccessful.

Political reforms also face daunting challenges. Political exclusion and repression have been repeatedly blamed for the violence of the Arab uprising of 2011 (Wimmer et al., 2009; Joffé, 2011). Devarajan and Ianchovichina (2018) claim that the underlying source of the conflict is in the fraying of a social contract where the government provided formal-sector jobs, education, and health care, and subsidized fuel and energy, in return for a limitation on political freedom. This social contract was becoming economically unsustainable, and the implicit promises of the government were being eroded or no longer fulfilled, leading to widespread dissatisfaction and a willingness to protest. They argue that a new social contract is, therefore, required; one that promotes private-sector jobs, accountability in service delivery, and active citizen participation in the economy and society. In particular, as pointed out in the Introduction and discussed by Elbadawi and Makdisi (2016), Arab countries recovering from conflict should strive to establish democratic governance if they are to embark on a genuinely inclusive reconstruction, so cementing their transition to peaceful and sustainable national development.

It may be tempting to conclude that the reconstruction agenda ought to be tailor-made to the particular circumstances and needs of each country (e.g., UNDP, 2008; Tzifakis, 2013). Certainly, idiosyncratic political, economic, and sociological elements largely shape the agenda of national post-conflict reconstruction. However, and as mentioned above, reconstruction must deal with challenges common to all post-conflict situations, including establishing a political system that allows for inclusive and democratic governance; reversing the deterioration in security conditions and confronting the increase in the numbers of people needing social assistance; repatriating human and financial resources; coping with large fiscal imbalances while at the same time overcoming the destruction of infrastructure; curtailing inflation and managing government debt; and normalizing external trade disrupted by the hostilities.

This commonality makes cross-country analysis and country case-studies complementary approaches and important sources for the purposes of understanding the challenges of reconstruction in conflict-affected Middle East economies which, as discussed in the introductory chapter, can be grouped into economic, political, and social categories.

2.1 Economic Challenges

Deceptively, economic factors appear not to have been at the root of recent conflicts in the Middle East. The region had made steady progress towards eliminating extreme poverty, furthering prosperity, increasing school enrolment, and reducing hunger, and child and maternal mortality (Ianchovichina et al., 2015). About half of those in poverty in the region in the 2000s had moved out of poverty by the end of the decade. Nevertheless, chronic poverty remained high. Upward mobility was strong in Syria and Tunisia, but downward mobility was pronounced in Yemen and Egypt (Dang and Ianchovichina, 2018).

Reforms were at least partially underway and economic growth was moderate and generally in line with growth trends in other regions of the world (see Panel A in Table 1.1). Nabli et al. (2008) evaluate the reforms prior to the uprisings and conclude that all these countries had embarked on significant structural reform and had made progress in creating environments more conducive to private sector development by allowing their economic systems to be more market-driven. However, they conclude that while the reforms of the last twenty-five years helped MENA countries to open up space for the private sector, the response to the reforms was weak and performance lagged significantly behind the rest of the world.

Table 1.1 Main Macroeconomic Indicators (%)

	World	Arab countries	Iraq	Libya	Syria	Yemen
Panel A: Period 1990–2009						
Annual GDP Growth	3.1	4.9	3.1	2.4	4.9	4.6
Per Capita GDP growth	2.1	1.9	0.2	0.6	2.1	1.1
Investment Ratio (% GDP)	23.8	20.6	8.6	25.7	22.1	18.4
Employment Growth	1.3	4.3	3.0	3.2	2.5	3.5
TFP Growth	0.2	0.2	1.6	0.1	1.4	−0.6
Panel B: Period 2010–2018						
Annual GDP Growth	3.4	2.3	5.7	3.7	−7.3	3.4
Per Capita GDP growth	2.1	−0.4	2.5	2.6	−6.1	2.1
Investment Ratio (% GDP)	23.5	23.5	21.8	42.0	27.0	23.5
Employment Growth	1.2	3.1	3.6	1.6	−1.7	1.2
TFP Growth	0.1	−2.1	2.3	4.2	−7.9	0.1

Source: Own elaboration based on World Development Indicators 2019, The World Bank, and Total Economy database, The Conference Board.
Note: Arab countries include Algeria, Egypt, Morocco, Sudan, Tunisia, Bahrain, Iran, Iraq, Israel, Jordan, Kuwait, Oman, Qatar, Saudi Arabia, Syria, United Arab Emirates, and Yemen.

Economic growth in the Arab economies outpaced the expansion of the world economy by a significant margin in the period 1990–2010 but slowed down noticeably thereafter (as shown in Panel B of Table 1.1). The experience of the four case studies in this volume is notoriously heterogeneous. Economic growth in Syria and Yemen was as strong as in other Arab countries and amply surpassed growth in the world economy as a whole. Iraq managed to recover from the 1980s conflict with Iran, and only Libya lagged significantly behind other Arab countries and the world economy. Per capita GDP—a limited yet informative indicator of welfare—grew steadily in Syria and Yemen in the two decades before 2010 but clearly stagnated in Libya and Iraq.

Per-capita income is, obviously, not an all-encompassing measure of economic development or welfare. Jones and Klenow (2016) identify leisure, mortality, morbidity, crime, and the natural environment, as some of the major factors affecting living standards in a country that are incorporated imperfectly, if at all, in GDP. Nevertheless, evidence from the Human Development Index elaborated by the UNDP (2019a)—a composite index measuring achievements in a long and healthy life, knowledge, and a decent standard of living—indicates that all the conflict-afflicted Arab nations had improved significantly in these terms during the two decades before 2011 (see Figure 1.1).

At the same time, as pointed out by studies on the Arab uprisings, other economic factors played a role in fuelling social and political discontent (e.g., Tucker, 2012; Ianchovichina et al., 2015). Two classic candidates are:

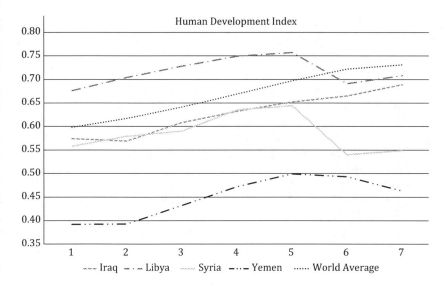

Figure 1.1 Human development index
Source: UNDP (2019).

the high levels of inequality in expenditure, income or wealth in the MENA region, and the high rates of unemployment. In what follows we review the evidence.

2.1.1 Inequality

The available data provide contrasting views on the role of inequality in conflicts in the Middle East. Certain studies indicate that the degree of income inequality in the Arab countries is not much different than in the rest of the world. In particular, the UNU-WIDER database reveals that the Gini coefficient of income in Syria in 2004 was 0.358—indicating a relatively equal distribution similar to that of the United Kingdom—and that it had improved to 0.32 by 2007. A similar trend is observed in Yemen (dropping from 0.395 in 1992 to 0.377 in 2005) and in Iraq (reducing from 0.351 in 2003 to 0.301 in 2007). Data provided by WIR (2018) show that the share in the income of the top 10 per cent of the population in the Middle East declined steadily between 1990 and 2010, whereas in all other regions in the world it either stagnated or increased sharply. Devarajan and Ianchovichina (2018) point out that during the 2000s, expenditure inequality in Arab countries was low or moderate and, in many cases, declining.

On the other hand, the demands for greater social justice associated with the Arab uprisings have led researchers to re-examine inequality in the region. Alvaredo et al. (2017) argued that previous results, based only on household survey data, greatly underestimated levels of inequality and they offered new estimates indicating instead that the Middle East is one of the most unequal regions in the world. The most affluent of the population (top 10 per cent of incomes) have appropriated around 60 per cent to 66 per cent of the total income, as compared to 37 per cent in Western Europe, 47 per cent in the USA and 55 per cent in Brazil. The share of the bottom 50 per cent varied between 8 per cent and 10 per cent of the total income. Hlasny and Al Azzawi (2019) find that there are significant differences in wealth at the household level across the urban-rural and educated-uneducated divides in three MENA countries (Egypt, Jordan, and Tunisia).

Whatever the prevailing inequality levels, there is increasing consensus that actual degrees of income or even wealth inequality in MENA might not have been a significant determinant in the uprisings (Joffé, 2011; Devarajan and Mottaghi, 2017); it remains a fact, however, that the two decades of sustained growth before the outbreak of the Arab Spring did little to improve perceptions of inequality and injustice. Indeed, it is perceptions that seem to have played a crucial role in social, and thereby political, discontent. Devarajan and Ianchovichina (2018) find that subjective measures of well-being were relatively low and falling sharply, especially for the middle class, in those countries where the uprisings were most intense. There was a growing and broadly shared dissatisfaction with the quality of life; the middle class, in particular, became frustrated by a lack of employment opportunities in the formal sector, the poor quality of public services, and the absence of government accountability. Arampatzi et al. (2018) documented the low and declining levels of subjective well-being in the run-up to the Arab Spring and found that perceptions of corruption became more important to people's sense of satisfaction with life, particularly in the countries which experienced the most intense uprisings. According to Verme (2014), significant differences between objective data and perception data and between perceived and actual income distribution emerged in Egypt between 2000 and 2008. While in 2000, people viewed themselves as more affluent than they actually were, by 2008 it was the reverse, despite data demonstrating that they had become more affluent.

2.1.2 Unemployment

Labour markets in Arab countries share certain common characteristics, including an oversized public sector, high youth unemployment, weak private sectors, rapidly growing but highly distorted educational attainment, and low or stagnant numbers for the female labour force. Several studies (e.g., Malik and Awadallah, 2013; Assad, 2014) identify these features as resulting from the Arab regimes using labour markets as a tool in political appeasement in the context of 'authoritarian bargain' social contracts.

Studies in conflict-affected Arab countries indicate that high unemployment, in particular youth unemployment, was one of the factors contributing to the uprisings (Elbadawi and Makdisi, 2016). The ILO estimates presented in Table 1.2 confirm that not only total unemployment has been much higher in MENA countries than the global average, but also that youth unemployment is significantly higher than elsewhere in the world. Unemployment problems are compounded by the fact that there are considerably greater numbers of those 15 and 24 years old in the population (the so-called 'youth bulge') of most MENA countries than elsewhere. Consequently, youth

Table 1.2 Rates of Unemployment and Youth Employment

	Total Unemployment: Ages 15 and older		Youth Unemployment: Ages 15–24		Employment to Population Ages: 15–24	
	Average 2000–2009	Average 2010–2018	Average 2000–2009	Average 2010–2018	Average 2000–2009	Average 2010–2018
World	4.1	4.4	13.0	13.5	43.6	38.8
MENA	7.1	7.6	21.1	26.7	25.0	22.4
Iraq	5.7	7.4	17.2	20.7	27.6	28.8
Libya	15.1	15.9	47.5	50.2	18.6	18.9
Syria	5.9	5.4	19.3	20.8	28.4	18.4
Yemen	8.6	20.3	9.3	24.1	23.5	19.8

Source: Own elaboration based on ILO database, ILO (2021).

employment is notoriously lower in MENA countries: on average, before 2011, only one out of five youngsters was employed. Youth employability deteriorated in the following decade, particularly in war-ravaged Syria and Yemen. Indeed, high unemployment rates have continued to prevail even in countries where political settlements have been reached, such as Egypt and Tunisia.

The poor performance of the Arab labour market is to a great extent due to an oversized public sector, with employment in government bureaucracy and the security forces constituting a large portion of the total employment, but also accounting for a dominant share of formal sector employment (Assaad, 2014). Malik and Awadallah (2013) point out that an oversized public sector has produced a formal, anaemic, and small private sector relying mostly on government welfare and rent-seeking for its survival. The distorting role of the public sector also affects the quality of human capital. Pissarides and Véganzonès-Varoudakis (2006) argue that the MENA countries have failed to deploy human capital efficiently despite high levels of education in the population because in most of the Arab countries the education system has been geared to the needs of the public sector, so the skills acquired are not necessarily used for growth-enhancing activities. Moreover, excessive regulation of the private sector further removes any incentive for employers to recruit and train good workers. Consequently, labour market reforms should be considered a crucial component of the reconstruction agenda.

High unemployment weakened the ability of these regimes to trade public goods and other economic benefits for a loss of political rights and participation (the authoritarian bargain). Unemployment poses major challenges to stability, in particular in countries that embarked on the road to democratic governance (e.g., Tunisia). Coping with unemployment is essential for their future democratic development: importantly, non-democratic parties could exploit any actual or potential popular resentment associated with high unemployment to alter the course of the democratic political process underway.

Undoubtedly, sustained economic growth and stability are mutually reinforcing. Growth is important for achieving stability that, in turn, stimulates investment and growth (Servén, 1999). Therefore, the prospects for stable growth are vital for the reconstruction efforts in that such prospects could further spur the private sector to provide opportunities for investment, higher employment, and wages. As a consequence, this could provide the government with a sustainable, steady flow of resources to support reconstruction and improve living standards. Experience in Arab countries and elsewhere indicates that the benefits of growth should materialize not only in rising employment and wages, but also in better access and quality of public goods and services. Consequently, the prospects for improving welfare conditions (i.e., economic growth benefiting the entire society and not only those in positions of power) are also vital for the reconstruction effort. This leads to our second premise, namely that, if they are to gain legitimacy and be sustainable, reconstruction policies should focus on achieving broader economic inclusion and lessening inequality, in addition to achieving substantial reductions in unemployment.

2.2 Political Challenges

High levels of income and wealth inequality and a lack of inclusion are usually the results of an economic ordering where rent-extraction dominates rent-creation: institutions are built so that a privileged few can capture the benefits of natural resources, economic growth, and overall development that would otherwise accrue to the entire population (Acemoglu and Robinson, 2012). The Arab countries are no exception. Usually, economic inequality and political inequality go hand in hand: when politicians are overly responsive to a small affluent group, policies are inevitably directed towards promoting their interests, further enhancing their political influence (Houle, 2018b). Citizens are not politically equal in economically unequal societies, as noted by Przeworski (2015). When the political influence of individuals increases concomitant to income and decisions are made by elite coalitions exerting greater political influence, redistribution of income through taxes and transfers is always at a lower rate than that desired by the citizens. The end result is that representative institutions do not mitigate economic inequality, as they would in more egalitarian systems.

The unhappiness voiced during the Arab uprisings was associated with dissatisfaction with the quality of public services, the shortage of formal-sector jobs, and corruption. These sources of dissatisfaction suggest that the old social contract, in which the governments in Arab countries provided jobs, free education, and health, and subsidized food and fuel, in return for the population stifling its voice, could no longer be sustained (Amin et al., 2012; Diwan et al., 2015). The uprisings and their aftermath manifest that a new social contract was called for, one where the government promotes an environment that encourages the creation of private-sector jobs and the accountability of services, and where citizens are active participants in the economy and society. The decline in public investment has not been replaced by even an equivalent growth in private investment (see Achcar, 2017).

Growing dissatisfaction with the quality of life and income inequality is not the monopoly of Middle East economies; most countries in Africa or Latin America share similar if not deeper problems. What distinguishes our group of Arab economies from other countries in the Middle East or in other regions of the world is the recourse to untrammelled violence on the part of both the authorities and the people.[1] The disproportionate response of governments to popular dissent, with the widespread use of repression, is characteristic of societies where political participation is limited, reluctantly tolerated by authorities, and/or reserved only for the elites (Besley and Persson, 2011). The onset of massive uprisings and large-scale civil wars is prima facie evidence of the breaking of the social contract between the people and the government.

This leads us to our third premise, namely, that *proposed economic reforms and policies ought to be in line with the establishment of an implicit or explicit new form of social contract*. Governments face two main challenges in trying to revive their countries' social contracts, as discussed by Derviş and Conroy (2019). They must ensure a strong and efficient safety net by adapting social and labour-market policies to the new world of work. And they must take concrete steps towards providing global public goods by securing domestic support for international cooperation.

In this regard, in post-conflict situations economic policies deemed to be optimal from a technical viewpoint ought to be weighed against their support for the proposed social contract. Otherwise, they will prove unviable and politically damaging in the long run. In this regard, the consolidation of peace should take precedence over the stimulation of development. As discussed by del Castillo (2008), war-affected countries may initially be forced to adopt sub-optimal economic policies (e.g., maintain certain non-profitable production units) due to political and security considerations (e.g., preservation of jobs). The subsequent move towards better sustainable policies is a crucial challenge of post-conflict reconstruction.

2.3 Social Challenges

Inequality of various kinds between ethnic or sectarian groups, however, may have also played an important role in the increased incidence of conflict in the MENA region (Hinnebusch, 2016). Rørbæk (2019) presents descriptive statistics showing that the Middle East is the only region in the world where religious (including sectarian) affiliation is the predominant identity marker and, furthermore, that on average Arabs are twice as likely as people in other developing regions to belong to identity groups excluded from legitimate political representation. In his view, the comparatively high level of identity-based political inequality in the region provides a better explanation for the intensity of the conflict than does the predominance of divisions based on religious identity.

Where societies are polarized along ethnic or sectarian lines, the combination of unemployed young men and natural resources also increases the risk of conflict (Karakaya, 2016). As discussed, prior to the Arab uprisings, double-digit unemployment was the norm in the four countries of interest and youth unemployment was above 25 per cent. It was in this context that after the onset of the uprisings, these countries in the region seemed primed to fall into disarray. Ethnic and sectarian inequality reinforced the destructive power of income and wealth inequality. Paassonen and Urdal (2016) blame the large proportion of the youth in Middle Eastern economies—and the repressive response of the government—for the eruption of the armed conflicts, with those participating in protests being the youngest and the best educated. Limited economic and political opportunities for the youth in the region remain a major concern.

3 Macroeconomic Policies for Balanced Growth and Employment

The sustainable reconstruction of conflict-ravaged countries requires the implementing of profound structural reform, as mentioned. But these costly efforts, in turn, necessitate a balanced macroeconomic stance to promote economic welfare, manage social discontent, and avoid renewed hostilities. A poor macroeconomic stance would, otherwise, constitute an important limitation to reconstruction. In what follows we review the main issues that, we submit, need addressing in post-conflict countries in MENA.

An immediate and crucial economic as well as political concern is the resumption of economic growth that, as in most emerging economies, is usually accompanied by substantial employment creation, a major objective of any reconstruction programme. Khan (2007) estimates the income elasticity of the demand for labour in developing economies to be around 0.7. Martins (2013) estimates similar values for African economies but also that elasticities have declined since the early 1990s, particularly if a country has invested in capital-intensive industries. Evidence indicates that, before and after the uprisings of 2001, GDP growth was on average around the same rate as that of total employment in both Arab countries and conflict economies and that it largely reflected the growth in the number of public employees. The implicit arch-elasticity of around one suggests that even if the post-conflict reforms are successful and growth resumes and is sustained, it will be nevertheless unlikely to significantly reduce the chronically high level of unemployment. Therefore, unless reforms open up a space for a vigorous private sector where it becomes the major source of employment creation, reconstruction will be jeopardized. If the public sector remains the main employer, employment creation will be anaemic, both because of the severe constraints on resources of the state in the post-conflict period and because government agencies are already heavily overstaffed.

In addition to the resumption of economic activity and the creation of employment opportunities the reconstruction agenda must be geared towards four areas of macroeconomic management: inflation control, exchange rate policy, fiscal policies, and physical infrastructure and FDI. As shown in Table 1.3, the four post-conflict economies suffer from internal and external imbalances. Inflation is high in three of them (and most likely it is underestimated due to price controls), fiscal imbalances are substantial in all conflict economies, public debt is high and unlikely to be serviced in the non-oil economies, and current account balances are sizable.

3.1 Inflation Control

Immediate priority should be given to reforms aiming at the reduction of inflation, re-monetization, and the design of a proper monetary policy (Lewarne and Snelbecker, 2004). In war-torn economies, the demand for

Table 1.3 Recent Macroeconomic Indicators, 2016/2017 Averages

Country	Annual Inflation	Government Deficit	Government Debt	Current Account Balance
	%	% of GDP	% of GDP	% of GDP
Iraq	0.2	14.0	66.7	−8.7
Libya	24.4	22.0	286.0	−22.4
Syria	45.0	18.0	150.0	−15.0
Yemen	20.0	13.5	85.4	−5.1

Sources: Annual inflation and GDP growth: IMF World Economic Outlook; Government deficit and debt, and current account balance: World Bank.

money is likely to be reduced both directly, as a result of the fall in income, and indirectly, as a result of activity and asset substitution. This exacerbates the seigniorage-inflation trade-off facing the government (Adam et al., 2008). In the medium term, however, macroeconomic policies ought to give priority to reforms aimed at setting up the new institutions needed for a modern monetary policy framework.

3.1.1 Monetary Policy Reforms

Reforms of monetary policy frameworks in the world were in response to the patent inability of central banks to control inflation during the 1970s and 1980s. High inflation resulted from the self-interest of decision-makers who, subject to political pressures, made it difficult for the Central Banks to credibly commit to long-term price stability (Kydland and Prescott, 1977; Barro and Gordon, 1983). To overcome this problem of time inconsistency, monetary policy, we submit, needs to be delegated to an institution that is sufficiently independent of political influence. Following the example of the Fed and Bundesbank, many countries have since the 1980s established independent and accountable central banks. In most cases, the conduct of monetary policy has been made more systematic by the use of policy rules, in particular by the explicit announcement of inflation targets. Evidence indicates that central bank independence (CBI) leads to lower inflation levels and to price stability which, in turn, are conducive to economic growth and high levels of employment, contributing positively to the welfare of citizens (Mishkin and Schmidt-Hebbel, 2007). CBI and transparency in the conflict-affected Arab economies rank comparatively low in contrast to the rest of the world, the only exception being Iraq which undertook significant reforms in 2004 (see Table 1.4). There is, therefore, considerable space for improvement in this area and post-conflict economies should seize the opportunity to instil discipline in their monetary policies with the objective of achieving long-term price stability.[2]

Table 1.4 Central Bank Independence and Transparency Indices

Country	Central Bank de jure Independence Index, 2012 (range 0=no independence to 1=fully independent)	Central Bank Transparency Index, 2010 (range 0=no transparency to 15=fully transparent)
Iraq	0.703	2.5
Libya	0.322	1.0
Syria	0.371	0.5
Yemen	0.520	2.0
Middle East Average	0.510	3.7
World Average	0.603	5.1

Source: Independence: Garriga (2016), Transparency: Dincer and Eichengreen (2014).

3.2 Fiscal Policy

Inflation is more often than not a reflection of severe imbalances in government finances. These imbalances are usually aggravated in conflict-affected countries for two reasons. On the one hand, the collapse in production during the conflict and the subsequent drop in tax revenues is not matched by an equal reduction of government expenditure (quite the opposite as a result of military spending) which has resulted in significant deficits. On the other, fiscal instability and imbalances have been historically the norm in most MENA economies as a result of the government's dependence on hydrocarbons, poor budgeting procedures, and short-term planning (Soto, 2019). As shown in Table 1.3, the government deficit exceeded 10 per cent of GDP in all the countries and government debt is extremely high in Libya and Syria, and somewhat uncomfortable in Iraq and Yemen. Table 1.5 indicates that expenditures in Iraq, Libya, Syria, and Yemen are heavily tilted towards military expenditures to the detriment of social investment. Total expenditure on education and health as a share of GDP is at par or below military expenditure in these economies, being twice as high as the world average and at the level in MENA economies (excluding high-income countries). The heavy cost of the military effort is also reflected in its relative importance in the government budget, being at least twice as high in conflict-affected Arab countries than the world average and also significantly higher than other fragile and conflict-affected countries. Thus, the relocation of resources can be sizable: according to SIPRI (2017), military expenditures doubled in Iraq and almost tripled in Libya in the five years that followed the Arab uprisings in contrast to the previous five years. Hence, there is a sizable potential peace dividend that can be used to finance social protection programmes, even if maintaining security requires substantial government resources (Davoodi et al., 2011).

The issue of restructuring government finances away from the military and towards welfare-improving programmes and the provision of public

Table 1.5 Structure of Government Expenditures (%)

	Education	Health	Military	Military
	As share of GDP			As share of Gov. Expenses
Iraq (2015)	–	3.4	5.3	12.6
Libya (2014)	–	–	11.4	10.8
Syria (2009)	5.1	3.5	4.0	15.1
Yemen (2014)	–	5.6	5.0	14.3
World (avg. 2010–2015)	4.7	9.5	2.3	6.3
MENA (avg. 2010–2015)	–	5.7	3.0	10.7

Source: World Bank Indicators database.

goods is complicated by the fact that the military obtains revenue not only directly from the government but in many cases also from their significant business interests. In several MENA economies, the armed forces control—and sometimes have a legal monopoly over—key industries, ranging from telecommunications to construction and housing projects (e.g., Egypt and Syria). While there is limited data available on the financial performance or the size of these entities, there is little doubt that they play a significant role in the economy. These companies also serve the interests of many high-ranking officials and regime figures who make money by acting as middlemen or suppliers and sub-contractors. This is, perhaps, one of the most delicate issues that fiscal reforms must deal with in the reconstruction process. As discussed in the section on microeconomic reforms, privatization and market liberalization are likely to affect military interests and, thereby, may jeopardize the peace process.

Another crucial element impinging on fiscal sustainability is the public debt. As expected, governments in post-conflict transitions are usually mired in public debt and, despite initial flows of foreign aid, must face the issue of balancing the budget to serve its obligations and lower the risk of default. Achieving sustainable debt levels, nevertheless, is a rather difficult feat because the costs of adjustment do not fall evenly among different groups of the population thus calling for conflict, and also because the timing of benefits may be incongruent with the available political space. Most options entail complicated trade-offs. In principle, sustained economic growth can reduce the pressure of financing a given stock of public debt and, while growth can prove elusive and slow in coming, it has been the main tool for achieving fiscal sustainability in many countries. Inflation has also been a popular tool to wipe out some of the (domestic) public debt, but it tends to fall disproportionately more on the poor. Foreign aid has also been used to reduce external debt but, as mentioned, at the risk of overvaluing the currency, reducing competitiveness, and penalizing investment and exports. Some countries have resorted to selling assets—for example, state-owned enterprises—which can be slow and politically sensitive if privatized firms increase prices to the public to cover costs. More coercive measures such as financial repression –a favourite option in Latin America—can provide much-needed short-term financing to the government but severely hamper long-term development by distorting the allocation of funds to investment projects and penalizing saving.

3.2.1 Fiscal Policy Reforms

Building or re-establishing fiscal institutions in post-conflict countries is an essential requisite for the conduct of a new fiscal policy in the post-conflict phase, one that should aim at strengthening fiscal solvency and sustainability (i.e., attaining sustainable levels of government deficits and debt), contributing to macroeconomic (or cyclical) stabilization (i.e., reducing fiscal policy pro-cyclicality or raising policy counter-cyclicality), and making fiscal policy design and execution more resilient to government corruption and private-sector lobbies. The principles of good governance –namely transparency, accountability, equal treatment, non-discrimination, integrity, competition, and predictability—are crucial not only for obvious economic reasons, but also because they impinge on the political and sociological aspects of the post-conflict transition. In particular, good governance and the notion of policy fairness tend to build support for the reforms and enhance social cohesion, lower political acrimony, and provide space for those foundational reforms that generally require substantial efforts in the short term but yield fruits only in the long run. In the case of public procurement—an area traditionally prone to corruption—these good-governance principles are of prime importance for the achievement of efficiency in resource allocation and also of integrity.

Reforms essentially entail a three-step process (IMF, 2004b): creating a legal and/or regulatory framework for fiscal management; establishing and/or strengthening the fiscal authority; and designing appropriate revenue and expenditure policies while simultaneously strengthening revenue administration and public expenditure management. The ultimate aim is to make fiscal policy and fiscal management effective and transparent. In particular, institutional reforms should seek to avoiding ad-hoc decision-making; promoting transparency in fiscal operations; ensuring a minimum level of revenue collection; and ensuring that spending patterns reflect government priorities. In some countries, an explicit mechanism for coordinating donor assistance is also necessary.

With the above in mind, we should like to draw attention to a few aspects of post-conflict fiscal policy. Specifically, reliance on government spending, as a fiscal stimulus, may not effectively serve the purpose of enhancing production and employment; this is likely to be the case when countries are highly indebted or if spending is financed through borrowing, leading to low if not negative fiscal multipliers with counterproductive effects on production. Indeed, in most studies, fiscal multipliers are found to be small in the MENA region (Ilzetzki et al., 2013). This raises doubts as to the usefulness of discretionary fiscal policy for short-term stabilization purposes.

Indeed, changes in the composition of government expenditure appear to be more significant in terms of stimulation effects. Most of the literature on the 'peace dividend' shows that most countries can encourage growth by decreasing military spending, which frees up resources for physical and human capital formation with the purpose of increased investment in health and education. Similarly, controlling corruption reduces the amount spent on public services, and so opens up further space for spending on social sectors. There is evidence that policies of social inclusion are particularly growth enhancing after a war (Collier and Hoeffler, 2002a).

Finally, it may be noted that modern fiscal management relies, in around a hundred developed and developing countries, on fiscal rules, that is, explicit restrictions that govern the conduct of fiscal policy. Reform of fiscal institutions and fiscal rules aims at avoiding four main biases in fiscal policy (Fatás, 2005): those that lead to fiscal policy volatility, to fiscal policy pro-cyclicality, to unsustainable deficits and budget plans, and to intergenerational unfairness. The imposition of rules and restrictions on fiscal authorities is called for in order to avoid welfare-decreasing equilibria arising from the decisions of discretionary policy-makers who favour short-term output stabilization over long-term debt sustainability (Wyplosz, 2005); and with the aim of constraining the actions of successor governments with different budgetary preferences (Alesina and Tabellini, 1990), or from asymmetric information between politicians and voters (Beetsma and Debrun, 2015).

Schmidt-Hebbel and Soto (2017) provide hard evidence of the effectiveness of fiscal rules in improving solvency and sustainability and reducing pro-cyclicality in both emerging and developed economies. Imposing fiscal rules and restrictions, however, may also have costs, derived from badly or over-narrowly defined rules and poorly structured and managed institutions. Excessively narrow rules without escape clauses may find fiscal policy straitjacketed when shocks of an unexpected kind or magnitude materialize (Cimadomo, 2012). Blind compliance with the rules during unforeseen events could have a considerable macroeconomic cost, forcing the policy-maker either to incur the latter or to suspend the rule. Therefore, if post-conflict countries face high levels of macroeconomic and budget volatility, they should refrain from adopting hard and fast fiscal rules and restrictions in order to preserve greater flexibility in fiscal policy discretion, but steps could be taken towards the implementation of fiscal rules, once revenue and expenditure stability is achieved.

Many fiscal rules feature explicit monitoring by an independent domestic agency, usually dubbed the 'fiscal council'. This is a permanent agency with a statutory or executive mandate to assess, publicly and independently of partisan influence, a government's fiscal policies, plans, and performance against macroeconomic objectives related to the long-term sustainability of public finances, short to medium-term macroeconomic stability, and other official objectives (Coletta et al., 2015).

The importance of the fiscal council cannot be overlooked and should not be perfunctorily dismissed in the case of post-conflict countries on the grounds that they are expensive to set up or that they produce information that is too sophisticated for the needs of the economy. If properly designed, such an institution provides for less arbitrary government decisions, greater social inclusion, and a more representative allocation of government funds. In addition, it can be made independent of the political cycle by design and be geared towards long-term goals, thus placing important intertemporal constraints on government policies.

3.1.2 Commodity Price Shocks

An external force affecting fiscal performance arises when taxes levied on exporting to volatile commodity markets—such as hydrocarbons—are the main source of government financing. Abundant resource receipts may induce currency volatility and real exchange rate distortions in the short term, hampering the financial and exporting sectors. In the long term, resource rents may hinder economic growth by encouraging rent-seeking and corruption; by lowering savings and capital formation to levels that do not compensate for the non-renewable character of the resource exported; by impeding diversification of the economy; and by supporting oligarchical government protected by a lack of transparency and the inability of the overall populace to have a say in how resource revenues are spent. Poor government and other unfortunate outcomes are also associated with the alleged curse of having oil deposits. Dealing with resource rents, therefore, is an important task of any reconstruction agenda. For an analysis of fiscal reforms and institutions that could improve fiscal management vis-à-vis resource dependence see Schmidt-Hebbel (2016).[3]

3.3 Exchange Rate Management

Empirical evidence suggests strong links between the choice of the regime and (fixed, floating, or managed) macroeconomic performance (Rogoff et al., 2004). As might be expected, there are conflicting views as to the superiority of the different regimes. It has been argued that pegging the exchange rate can lower inflation by inducing greater policy discipline and instilling greater confidence in the currency; however, it could lead to currency overvaluation and Dutch disease. Floating regimes, on the contrary, avoid overvaluation but can lead to excess currency volatility. Similarly, there are varying arguments concerning the effects of exchange rate policy on investment and growth.[4]

Furthermore, the choice of the exchange-rate regime cannot be isolated from the choice of the means of conducting monetary policy, from the issue of the credibility of the monetary authorities or even the inflow of foreign aid. To illustrate, evidence indicates that countries that have adopted IT in the context of a floating exchange regime have experienced a reduction in the pass-through from exchange rate changes to inflation, suggesting that a floating exchange regime does not present a significant threat to inflation control, nor has it resulted in increased (nominal or real) exchange rate volatility (Edwards, 2007). And in economies where, for whatever reason, the Central Bank lacks credibility or does not have sufficient reserves to operate convincingly in the market, there is little chance that a fixed exchange regime will survive a speculative attack against the national currency. Floating the currency would be better for practical reasons as well as a tool to progressively acquire a more solid reputation.

The conflict-affected countries in our study are endowed with important deposits of hydrocarbons (Bowman, 2011; Salisbury, 2011), but only Iraq and Libya are major oil exporters. The oil industries are important in terms of generating foreign currency and, more importantly, in terms of tax revenue for the government. Unfortunately, oil price volatility tends to induce high procyclicality in government finances and, thereby, in the economy. In turn, procyclicality hampers efficiency and penalizes long-term initiatives. Fluctuations in economic activity generate discontent.

The successful provision of a stable currency and the promotion of an efficient means of payment lend credibility to the state. And with respect to foreign aid, while evidence suggests that aid positively affects growth in the long term of any exchange regime, the indirect effects of currency overvaluation could hamper economic growth in countries with fixed or managed floating regimes (Elbadawi and Soto, 2013a). Given the centrality of tradable activities for post-conflict growth, an environment in which the currency is severely misaligned (typically overvalued) is not conducive to sustained growth in exports or the economy generally. Left to market forces, as is the case of floating exchange regimes, the combination of massive aid and currency overvaluation has a negative impact on growth.[5]

When choosing exchange regimes, post-conflict governments should be aware that deciding in favour of either a fixed, floating, or managed regime cannot take place in isolation from the existing conditions and characteristics of the economy, and that complimentary measures and institutions must be established to support the credibility and sustainability of any regime. A fixed exchange system would require massive central bank reserves and substantial fiscal discipline to be credible; in their absence, the progressive misalignment of the exchange rate will lead inevitably to stalled exports and growth and eventually to a currency crisis. A floating regime may isolate the currency from the fiscal stance, but it would require the development of instruments so that export industries can cope with currency volatility, and a firm hand to deal with speculative capital and aid inflows. To be credible, managed regimes will demand a significant institutional ability to restrain political interference and corruption.

3.4 Foreign Direct Investment

Given a shortage of domestic resources, the reconstruction of a country would need to rely on foreign resources additional to aid. One source of such funds is foreign direct investment (FDI). It is probably commonly agreed that FDI triggers technology spill-overs, assists human capital formation, contributes to international trade integration, helps to create a more competitive business environment, and enhances the development of enterprise (see Alfaro, 2017).[6] Although there is a consensus regarding the economic benefits of foreign direct investment, these are often viewed as being dependent on the recipient countries having reached minimum levels of institutional, financial, or human capital development.

Attracting FDI, nevertheless, requires the appropriate institutional set-up to provide investors with an environment that would permit them to conduct their business without incurring unnecessary risks, that is, one that provides for the registration of firms, the protection of private property, of minority shareholders, and a modern bankruptcy law (Lewarne and Snelbecker, 2004; Kusago, 2005).

Benefits, however, are not automatic consequences of FDI and the potential spill-over of benefits will be realized only if local firms have the ability and motivation to invest in absorbing foreign technologies and skills. It is important, furthermore, to recognize that not all forms of FDI are a priority for the economy. Crucially, any investment regime must recognize that foreign investment is part of the economic development in the reconstruction and peace-building process, and not an end in itself. Therefore, the FDIs to be encouraged are those that benefit the objectives of post-conflict reconstruction such as job-creation and the spill-over of knowledge or technology that benefits the host economy. It is important to keep in mind the point that attaining this objective may be more difficult in the case of oil-rich countries in that they tend to attract FDIs with limited transformative possibilities. Purely extractive industries (e.g., mining) usually provide limited opportunities for creating employment and links with the local economy and, in some cases, they may bring associated negative environmental and social impacts (Turner et al., 2008). This is a matter that needs to be addressed if recipient countries are to maximize their benefit from the inflows of FDIs.

4 Microeconomic Issues and Policies

The reconstruction of institutions at the microeconomic level is vital for sustainable development and, more importantly, for the appropriation of the benefits of development by the population (O'Driscoll, 2018). If successful, these reforms in turn increase the legitimacy of reconstruction.

In what follows we identify three key issues that need addressing in the economic agenda for reconstruction. First, the need to restore—and sometimes expand—property rights, so that security levels improve, and the returns on endeavours are accrued to their legitimate owners. Second, a proper delineation between the areas where private initiative is best allocated by market forces and those sectors where the market fails due to 'imperfections' such as natural monopoly power, informational asymmetries, and externalities. Third, the design of a proper regulatory setup for each type of market. The competition found in free markets will not fulfil its promise of development and welfare benefits unless adequate regulation and supervision are in place. Likewise, where the market fails, the intervention must be designed so that efficiency is preserved, and benefits accrue to the population and not to interest groups or those bureaucrats in charge of running state-controlled businesses. Anticompetitive behaviour is a direct threat to the creation of a viable new social contract.

4.1 Property Rights Reforms

The lack of property rights contributes to conflict which, in turn, usually jeopardizes property rights. This vicious circle is hard to break. Entrepreneurs will not invest if they foresee that their returns and property will be expropriated by the government or appropriated by other individuals. Similarly, when their property rights are protected, families and workers have the incentive to invest in housing as well as in education and training.

Leckie (2005), among others, identifies housing, land, and property (HLP) rights as a key challenge in all post-conflict countries and regions. Restoring rights to returning refugees and displaced persons, resolving ongoing disputes, re-establishing a rights registration system, protecting the rights of vulnerable groups and many other HLP issues invariably surface in post-conflict settings (IRFC and NRC, 2016).

The issue of restoring HLP rights becomes more acute in post-conflict economies where internal displacement and extensive destruction of housing call for an active reconstruction programme. HLP rights are not only indispensable to the peace process but also to economic development and poverty alleviation (Calderon, 2004; Galiani and Schargrodsky, 2010). With ill-defined or incomplete property rights, landowners need to expend their resources to defend their rights (e.g., guards and fences), so diverting their resources from more productive uses (Allen and Lueck, 1992). Well-defined property rights may improve access to credit because reliable information on an individual's ownership reduces transaction costs and the uncertainty that hinders the use of the property as collateral for credit (Deininger and Binswanger, 1999). Evidence collected in the Latin American and Asian economies indicates that entitled families substantially increase housing investment, reduce the household size, and enhance the education of their children relative to control groups (Lawry et al., 2014). Property rights are also important for reducing poverty through the slow process of increasing physical and human capital investment, helping to reduce poverty in the future.

Addressing these issues is an essential component of the peace-building process and an indispensable prerequisite for the rule of law. Setting up an HLP agency and providing it with adequate staff and resources is imperative in order to ensure that people's property rights receive the necessary institutional, political, and legal status. It is, nevertheless, important to design the new agency—or to transform existing ones—so as to instil modern management techniques, accountability, and efficiency.[7]

Advocates of formal titling, nevertheless, tend to ignore the limited capacity of central land administrations to establish titles or the difficulties in establishing decentralized institutions (Teyssier and Harris, 2012). Here, other institutional reforms play a decisive role and call for coordination. A registration system can be rendered ineffective by the absence of a judiciary system that is sufficiently accessible and impartial to allow actions by the state to be challenged effectively, by ineffective government institutions with overlapping mandates that may issue conflicting documents regarding the same property, or by unclear and contradictory policies that make enforcement unpredictable and costly (Deininger and Feder, 2009).

4.2 Market Liberalization and Regulation of Competition

The second key component of restructuring post-conflict economies relates to ensuring free but properly regulated markets. When successful, market liberalization benefit consumers via improved access, lower prices, and better quality of goods and services. For businesses, reforms significantly improve international competitiveness (Guasch and Hahn, 1999).

While the wave of reforms in the MENA region before the Arab uprisings helped to open up space for the private sector, the response was weak and performance lagged behind the rest of the world (Nabli et al., 2008). Keller and Nabli (2007) find that financial sectors remained feeble, trade liberalization was only partial (with continuing high protection levels), public ownership remained overwhelmingly high, and the regulatory framework and supportive institutions for private investment did not materialize. Youssef and Zaki (2019) note that while pro-market liberalization reforms were implemented in the 1990s, it was not until the 2000s that MENA authorities began to pass competition laws in order to improve the functioning of markets.

Without a proper regulatory setup, competition in a free market would not deliver its promise of development and welfare. Regulated competition promotes the use of more efficient methods of production, benefiting consumers with access to less expensive or better-quality goods and services. Unregulated competition, on the contrary, leads to abuse, rent extraction, and corruption. Reforms in regulation and supervision are thus indispensable components of the reconstruction agenda. But striking an adequate balance between economic freedom and state intervention is usually difficult and expensive to implement. These issues are more pressing in post-conflict MENA countries than elsewhere because, for historical reasons—compounded by years of conflict—the state enjoys an overwhelming advantage in terms of allocating resources and deciding what, when, and how production is to take place.

A transition from an administered to a market economy is essential to sustain growth, but there is considerable mistrust in the region regarding reform and many blame market liberalization for the rise of crony capitalism (Diwan et al., 2019). Reforms are unpopular when they entail the removal of subsidies or streamlining of the workforce at state-owned enterprises, which makes it difficult to judge the choice of reforms correctly (Arezki, 2019). Moreover, the unequal competition in markets dominated by state-owned enterprises deters private investment, reducing the number of available jobs and preventing countless talented youngsters from prospering.

The success of the reconstruction agenda depends crucially on engaging the private sector to provide for sustained growth, legitimate wealth accumulation, increased employment and wages, and increased productivity. But, for the private sector to fulfil its role, there needs to be a sufficiently level playing field. The four conflict MENA economies rank very low in the Doing Business set of indicators (Table 1.6) and there has been a marked decline since the onset of the conflicts following the Arab Spring. Almost all their backwardness is government related: the excessive number of procedures required for starting a business, sluggish and usually corrupt mechanisms to deal with construction permits, to register property, and pay taxes. These attest to a failed bureaucracy that needs deep and far-reaching reforms. These are compounded by often obsolete legal codes that do not provide for the protection of minority investors, costless enforcement of contracts, and operative insolvency procedures.

Table 1.6 Doing Business Indicators

	Iraq	Libya	Syria	Yemen
Ease of Doing Business in 2010 (out of 183 countries)	144	n.a.	132	109
Ease of Doing Business in 2017 (out of 212 countries)	168	185	174	186
Getting electricity	116	130	153	187
Getting credit	186	186	173	186
Paying taxes	129	128	81	80
Trading across borders	179	118	176	189
Starting a business	154	167	133	163
Dealing with construction permits	93	186	186	186
Registering property	101	187	155	82
Protecting minority investors	124	183	89	132
Enforcing contracts	144	141	161	140
Resolving insolvency	168	168	163	156

Source: World Bank's Doing Business Database.

4.2.1 Privatization and the Overwhelming Size of the State

Reconstruction reforms must also deal with government's involvement in and ownership of dominant firms or monopolies in key industries, such as infrastructure, construction, the financial sector, etc. Reforms should focus on identifying opportunities for the privatization of state-owned enterprises (SOEs) in industries where market failures are absent, for two main reasons. First and foremost, for efficiency considerations: the bulk of the literature concludes that, if properly carried out, privatization improves efficiency significantly and has important spillovers on the rest of the economy. Second, privatization can be an important source of revenue for resource-scarce post-conflict governments.

Infrastructure is crucial for generating growth and increasing competitiveness. Network utilities—such as electricity, natural gas, telecommunications, railways, and water supply—are usually state monopolies, providing extremely weak services, especially for poor people. Common problems include low productivity, high costs, bad quality, insufficient revenue, and shortfalls in investment. Recognizing the importance of infrastructure, many countries over the past two decades have implemented far-reaching reforms—restructuring, privatizing, and establishing new approaches to regulation.

The historical record of privatization in the region is, unfortunately, discouraging: privatization programmes have lacked a clear strategic focus, have been implemented on a stop-go basis, and in many cases, have resulted in the transfer of ownership without an accompanying transfer of state control (Page, 2003). The fear of redundancy has also slowed down privatization, particularly in the manufacturing sector. However, elsewhere privatization has been much more successful, and the lessons learned demonstrate how to properly design the process, reducing corruption and inefficiency; how to regulate privatized firms, so that efficiency gains accrue to the general public; and how to provide incentives for investment and development in privatized industries. Chong and López de Silanes (2005) and Estrin and Pelletier (2018) make a compelling case for the success of privatization in Latin America which has brought substantial benefits. However, they also caution that the manner in which privatization is carried out matters: transparency and homogeneity of procedures, speed, and moderation in pre-privatization restructuring lead to better outcomes and give less opportunities for corruption.

One final element in the privatization process is the continued control of key industries by the armed forces or their personnel in MENA. Privatization and market liberalization are likely to affect military interests and may, thereby, jeopardize the peace process, and it seems highly unlikely that officers in the military will respond to calls for divestment unless there is some form of compensation offered. This is a complicated issue both for peace agreements and for long-term development (Brömmelhörster and Paes, 2004), with no easy solutions.

4.3 Regulation and Interventions where Competition Fails

Under such certain conditions—collectively called market failures—competition does not allocate resources efficiently or guarantee their best social use. Government regulation can rectify these problems, as long as the cost of intervention does not exceed its potential benefit. In particular, government regulation can be less costly than a resort to litigation to solve disputes arising from any market failure (Glaeser and Shleifer, 2003). We now turn to two areas where markets fail because producers and/or consumers can act strategically and benefit systematically from distorting the price mechanism.

4.3.1 Anticompetitive Behaviour

Anticompetitive agreements (e.g., cartels), abuses by companies with a dominant market position, and mergers and acquisitions are damaging to reconstruction in several aspects. First, they hinder efficiency, reduce productivity, and hamper economic growth. Second, they benefit the owners of the firms at the expense of the general population. Because the former tend to be part of the elite, they generate popular discontent, undermining the political support for reconstruction. Third, because it is illegal, those involved in anticompetitive actions usually turn to corruption in order to hide their actions or avoid paying the cost.

From an institutional viewpoint, implementing antitrust policies is of the utmost importance for both economic and political reasons. On the economic front, there is abundant evidence of the pernicious effect of anticompetitive actions on economic growth, wages, incomes and welfare of the population, and on efficiency and adoption of new technologies. On the political front, abuse by companies is frequently equated with abuse by the elite and the ruling parties. When such abuse goes undetected, is not subject to sanctions, or is arbitrarily prosecuted, the legitimacy of the state and the political system is jeopardized.

Competition law, consumer protection regulations, and other government policies are highly developed in the EU, the United States, and many emerging economies. Adopting and adapting such regulations to the case of post-conflict economies ought to be a priority for the reconstruction agenda. In several countries, legal and even constitutional changes were required to give a wide range of inspection and enforcement powers to the authorities for investigating businesses, hold hearings, and instigating sanctions against crimes. Crane (2012) discusses the three defining elements of modern antitrust institutions: executive authority; technocratic administration; and judicial supremacy.

Market regulation deals with four main areas of market failure. First, *natural monopolies,* that is, those industries where the best social policy is to allow the presence of a single company. Reconstruction agendas should weigh the convenience of having state-owned companies with a properly regulated equilibrium price (and isolated from political pressures to set prices below marginal costs) or allowing private firms to operate a monopoly under a price-quality framework (Joskow, 2007). Second, *markets with significant externalities* for which reforms should propose a framework to ameliorate their ensuing problems. In particular, to deal with the political economy of the problem: because negative externalities impose a cost on third parties, industries tend to develop powerful lobbies to avoid paying such costs or compensating those affected (Aidt, 1998). Third, the problem of *missing markets* in post-conflict economies is pervasive: public goods are normally underprovided due to both fiscal constraints and the poor managerial abilities of public servants. Reconstruction agendas should identify areas where the private sector could provide these services (e.g., using PPP schemes, franchising, and BOT contracts). Fourth, reconstruction agendas must consider the political implications of *merit and de-merit goods*. Merit goods are those of which societies would prefer to have a supply beyond what strict cost-benefit analysis would provide (e.g., education, healthcare, environmental protection). De-merit goods, on the contrary, are those where society would like to penalize their consumption (e.g., tobacco, alcohol, gambling). In designing the reforms, the authorities ought to make an assessment of the political and economic willingness to pay for merit goods and, equally decisively, assess the ability of the government to tax de-merit goods not only to discourage consumption but also to collect revenue for financing reconstruction (e.g., infrastructure).

Finally, there exists the danger that regulators might be 'captured' by regulated companies and end up furthering the interests of the company at the expense of society (Armstrong and Sappington, 2006). Many factors increase the likelihood of capture: political interference and corruption, the lack of expertise and resources of the regulatory agency, the inability to block regulated firms from offering employment opportunities to regulators who have proved to be cooperative, regulated firms providing a sizable portion of the regulator's budget, etc. National regulatory agencies (NRAs) have recently been set up in several MENA countries. Abrardi et al. (2016) investigate their impact in twelve MENA countries (including Iraq, Libya, Syria, and Yemen) from 1990 to 2011. They find that inception of a regulatory agency has a positive impact on capacity growth, but the setup of the NRA is influenced by the quality of the institutional environment.

4.3.2 Organized Crime

Post-reconstruction efforts need to prevent organized (and unorganized) crime from monopolizing economic sectors and from creating a lawless environment that threatens legitimate businesses. This is important because the end of conflict usually brings an end—or at least a significant decline—to the profitability of a war economy. Participants in a war economy are armed, trained for violence, and display low-risk aversion. Therefore, if the situation is conducive, they can easily turn to organized crime. Organized crime hampers the quality of governance because, by corrupting, threatening, and otherwise compromising the integrity of public officials and institutions, it erodes the state's long-term ability to provide for the common good (Miraglia et al., 2012). The ability to deliver public goods is a key element in the reduction of the political, social, and economic fragility of the state. Organized crime is one cause of state failure.

5 Conclusions

Peace-building post-conflict presents formidable challenges at the political, economic, and sociological levels. In this chapter, we depart from the literature on post-conflict economic recovery which accepts the assumption that failed nation-states fail in their own unique way and that, accordingly, each reconstruction effort is unique.

While we recognize that idiosyncratic political, economic, and sociological elements play a role in post-conflict reconstruction, we think that reconstruction must deal with common challenges, such as establishing genuinely inclusive and democratic governance; repatriating human and financial resources, dealing with the donor community, reversing the deterioration of human development and security conditions, confronting the problem of the destruction of infrastructure, facing the increase in the numbers of people in need of social assistance; coping with large fiscal deficits; curtailing inflation; managing both external and public debt; or normalizing external trade previously disrupted by hostilities.

Our analysis of the reforms to be considered in an economic agenda for reconstruction is based on three premises, culled from the literature on post-conflict rebuilding and the experience of a large number of countries. First, in order to gain legitimacy and be sustainable, reconstruction policies should focus on achieving broad economic inclusion and reducing inequality, in addition to achieving substantial reductions in unemployment, especially among the young. Second, reconstruction policies should be primarily geared towards changing, improving or, even in an extreme case, eliminating altogether the pre-conflict institutional fabric of the country. Third, proposed economic reforms and policies ought to be in line with the establishment of a new form of social contract, implicit or explicit, that incorporates the principles of democracy.

Unlike that of other emerging regions, the experience of the MENA region in the reduction of unemployment is not encouraging because of the poor performance of the labour market. It calls for the corrective of a paradigm shift, whereby governments abandon the use of public employment as a key mechanism for generating political allegiance and allow the private sector to become the main source of income for working families governed by a regulatory framework that ensures conformity with the public interest.

Labour market reforms should be considered a crucial component of the reconstruction agenda.

Four areas of macroeconomic management are deemed crucial for the success of reconstruction programmes: inflation control, the exchange rate policy, fiscal policies, and the physical infrastructure and FDI. First, macroeconomic policies must establish new institutions necessary for a modern monetary policy framework, where inflation control is the sole task of an independent but accountable monetary authority, whereby it would be subject to a formal political procedure (e.g., by scheduling periodic hearings in Parliament to inform about the conduct of monetary policy). Second, government finances should prioritize programmes improving welfare and the provision of public goods above military expenditure. Reforms must lead to fiscal stability and responsibility whereby building or re-establishing fiscal institutions will aim at strengthening fiscal solvency and sustainability (i.e., attaining sustainable levels of government deficits and debt), contributing to macroeconomic (or cyclical) stabilization, and making the design and execution of fiscal policy more resilient against government corruption and private-sector lobbies. Since exchange rate regimes influence inflation, economic growth, investment, and productivity, we submit that the successful maintenance of a stable unified currency would lend credibility to the reconstruction process. Fourth, given the usual relative shortage of domestic resources, the financing of reconstruction would also have to rely on foreign resources. One important source is direct foreign investment (FDI). Attracting FDI requires the appropriate institutional setup to provide investors with a secure environment in which to conduct their operations free from unnecessary risks.

Beyond the initial impact of the peace dividend, macroeconomic structural reforms by themselves are insufficient to generate sustained improvements in welfare for the population. Reconstruction of institutions at the microeconomic level is vital for sustainable development and, more importantly, for the appropriation of the benefits of such development by the population. We identify a number of key microeconomic issues that would need to be addressed. They include firstly, restoring—and if necessary, expanding—property rights, to ensure that returns of their endeavours accrue to the legitimate owners and are not diminished through taxation by the government or those engaged in violence. Secondly, properly demarcating those areas best suited for private initiative distinct from those sectors where market failure occurs due to 'imperfections' such as the natural monopoly of power, informational asymmetries, and externalities requiring active public sector interventions. Thirdly, designing a proper regulatory structure for each type of market. Competition in free markets will not deliver on its promise of development and welfare unless adequate regulation and supervision are in place. Similarly, where the market fails, public sector intervention must be designed so that efficiency is preserved, and benefits accrue to the population at large and not to interest groups or bureaucrats in charge of running state-controlled businesses.

It is thus clear that once they have settled their civil conflicts, the challenges facing the four countries under study in the economic, political, and social dimensions of reconstruction are not only formidable but also closely intertwined in that the attainment of national peace and human prosperity goes beyond the provision of economic and social welfare to embrace the concepts of freedom and democracy.

Notes

1 In comparison, Latin American countries successfully transited from dictatorship to democracy without political unrest while having similar levels of inequality of conflict as has afflicted MENA countries, for example, Argentina and Uruguay, or much higher levels, such as Brazil or Chile, where Gini coefficients are in the range of 0.50.
2 In economies where the minimal institutional requirements for CBI are not available, an alternative policy to control inflation is to dollarize. But such an option may not be feasible or even necessary and the countries concerned should consider a political and economic strategy to secure minimal degrees of independence in their monetary policy in four key areas (institutional, operational, personal, and financial) (see Mersch, 2017). It may be noted that in addition to CBI, monetary policy is now conducted using inflation targeting (IT) schemes in over 65 countries in the world. Studies show that countries resorting to IT perform consistently better than the control group in terms of controlling inflation (Corbo et al., 2002). Evidence for the effectiveness of conducting a monetary policy using IT cannot be generally applied to conflict-affected countries where the institutional conditions for targeting inflation and/or allowing the currency to freely float are unlikely to be present, at least in the initial stages of reconstruction. It remains that If IT is deemed to be unviable, that a number of the institutional components of modern monetary regimes (transparency, independence, and accountability) should be adopted.
3 Countries affected by highly volatile commodity prices have set up sovereign wealth funds (SWF) as a mechanism to support their fiscal policies. Elbadawi et al. (2017) provide evidence, with emphasis on the MENA economies, that countries experience significantly less fiscal procyclicality when they have an SWF in place and that this effect acts independently of another fiscal institution such as fiscal rules or fiscal councils. Of the conflict economies, Iraq and Libya have already implemented oil revenue-based SWFs, but only the latter has accumulated significant resources. Syria and Yemen ought to consider implementing SWFs as medium-to-long term objectives for their fiscal policies.
4 For example, certain writings conclude that pegged regimes stimulate higher investment, but floating regimes lead to faster productivity growth (Ghosh et al., 1997). However, pegged regimes are associated with slower growth and greater output volatility (Levy-Yeyati and Sturzenegger, 2003). Elbadawi and Soto (2013a, 2013b) found evidence that in post-conflict countries the choice of exchange regime has no direct effect on overall GDP growth, and that free floats may have a negative effect on exports, and that fixed and managed exchange regimes tend to be associated with lower levels of inflation.
5 For this reason, it has been argued that aid commitments should be spread over time and increase gradually. It has also been suggested that aid might be more effectively used if delayed until capacity is restored. This is perhaps especially the case for project aid. Staines (2004), on the other hand, finds that the productivity of external assistance can be high in the initial post-conflict period when

governments are committed to following a sound macroeconomic strategy, particularly if assistance is provided for the budget in support of stabilization.
6 Estrin et al. (2017) conducted a meta-analysis of 175 studies and around 1100 estimates in Eastern Europe, Asia, Latin America and Africa from 1940 to 2008 and found that the macro-level effects are at least six times larger than the effects at the individual business level. They also find that benefits from FDI are substantially less dependent on development levels than previously expected.
7 Work along these lines is already in place in MENA economies. For example, NRC (2016) identifies the pressing needs of HLP in Syria and offers recommendations for action and remedy.

2 Grievances and Civil Wars
The State of the Literature

Cristina Bodea and Christian Houle

1 Introduction

There has been much research examining the reasons why some countries experience violent civil conflict. For a while, previous work eschewed rigorous evaluation of civil wars stemming from grievance and injustice, focusing instead on economic opportunity and greed (Collier and Hoeffler, 1998, 2004) or the characteristics of the state and the different facets of state capacity (Fearon and Laitin, 2003; Buhaug and Rød, 2006; Hendrix, 2010; Thies, 2010). For example, Fearon and Laitin write that they 'find little evidence that one can predict where a civil war will break out by looking for where ethnic or other broad political grievances are strongest' (Fearon and Laitin, 2003, p. 75). Similarly, Collier and Hoeffler note that 'a model that focuses on the opportunities for rebellion performs well, whereas objective indicators of grievance add little explanatory power' (Collier and Hoeffler, 2004, p. 587).

More recently, there has been a renewed interest in understanding how specific grievances can contribute to the onset of civil war, from the exclusion of particular groups from power to particular types of economic inequality (Ostby, 2008a,b; Wimmer et al., 2009; Cederman et al., 2011). These advances in studying the role of grievance are driven by the careful matching of the boundaries between ethnicity and inclusion in political power or understanding the way economic inequality is overlaid by social factors. The results from this more recent literature stand in stark contrast to the earlier conclusion that grievance has only a limited role in explaining the onset of civil war: both the political exclusion of ethnic groups and economic inequities between ethnic groups are contributing factors to civil wars.

This chapter reviews the studies that link grievance and civil war through political regime type and institutions, group relations, as well as society-wide and group-level inequality. We also discuss the role played by the presence of natural resources in the onset of civil war, and the overlap between political and economic inequities and natural resources.

The intersection of grievances and resource endowments is of particular importance for Middle East and North African countries. In this region,

DOI: 10.4324/9781003344414-4

ethnic and religious tensions, lack of a political participation and democracy, government controlled by sectarian parties and third-party support for authoritarian leaders have been important factors in the collapse of the social contract before the Arab uprising. Also, the discovery of oil has tended to aggravate pre-existing ethno-religious conflicts, political factionalism, and state weakness. Of countries in the region where the approach to the exploitation of natural resources has had a corrosive effect on civil peace, the four Arab countries featured in this volume include two rich oil exporters (Iraq and Libya), and another two oil producers (Syria and Yemen) with dwindling oil revenues that have strongly affected the ability of governments to provide public goods and quality services.

2 Democratic Political Institutions

One way to conceptualize average levels of grievance is to look broadly at regime type, in the expectation that political democracy is associated with both less repression and less discrimination, and therefore fewer grievances. That is, political institutions that allow freedoms and rights to large numbers of citizens should be associated with fewer individual and group grievances, and thus less civil conflict. The early literature has shown, however, that both strong democracies and strong autocracies experience the least civil conflict. For example, Muller and Weede (1990) find that overall political violence measured as death rate is significantly lower for regimes with either a high or a low capacity for repression. They argue that, at one end of this spectrum, severe repression inhibits mobilization and reduces the likelihood of success. On the other, the availability of peaceful avenues of political action renders rebellion unattractive. In the middle, intermediate levels of repression result in rebellion being more attractive than peaceful collective action.

This finding is replicated when the dependent variable is specifically coded as civil war onset, rather than political violence (Hegre et al., 2001; Fearon and Laitin, 2003). In this work, semi-democracies are weak, incoherent regimes mixing authoritarian and democratic features, in which repression still occurs and leads not just to grievances, but also to collective action that is facilitated by a relative political openness. Further, the survival of political institutions has been shown to be a feature of both consistent democracies and autocracies (Gates et al., 2006, p. 893). In this account, inconsistent regimes are unstable because of features that allow the elite to challenge the executive authority (very likely in an irregular fashion) and because both groups and individuals lack any incentive to support the democracy.[1] Most studies in this tradition that use political institutions as an explanatory variable employ the Polity scale ranging from –10 to 10 or a three-category measure (democracy, anocracy, and dictatorship) based on the Polity scale, or a binary measure identifying democracies versus autocracies (e.g., Cheibub et al., 2010).

Vreeland (2008), however, further challenges the notion that a focus on the political regime is the most useful way of identifying the role of grievance in the civil war onset. His work shows that correcting the degree to which measures of democracy may include indicators of political violence, makes the original finding of an inverted U-shape disappear.[2] Anocracies, having accounted for the fact that their coding includes indicators of violence, are not, on the whole, more prone to civil war. Rather, Vreeland finds that the increased risk of civil war, that arises when political participation involves extreme competition between groups, can be characterized as 'intense, hostile and frequently violent' (p. 402). This is supported by Bodea et al. (2017), who find that, in fact, only a small fraction of anocracies are linked to a higher risk of civil war: Among Polity defined anocracies, only partial democracies with factional politics increase the risk of civil war. These are countries with political factions that 'promote particularist agendas that favour group members to the detriment of common, secular and cross-cutting agendas' (Iraq, 1946-2013- Polity IV Regime Trends, p. 26). Similarly, Jones and Lupu (2018) also find that some anocracies see an increased risk of civil conflict. This result is contingent on the particular time period and, also, on the specific measure for civil conflict onset.

While capturing broad discontent, the political regime and political institutions remain an imprecise, average, measure of grievance. The results in this literature suggest that a focus on the politics of particular types of anocracies, and, in particular, on the group relations in those countries could be a more fruitful means of identifying the types of grievances leading to civil war. Nevertheless, in the context of this volume, increased corruption[3] and the inability of the governments to accommodate popular demands via the political system remain important concerns in particular Middle East and North African countries. In these countries, despite economic growth and improvement in welfare, conflict remains a possibility as long as civil and political rights remain contested.

3 Political Exclusion

Huntington (1968) suggests that modernization brings out new social groups with specific demands, and that, at least in some societies, the role of political institutions is to peacefully mediate these demands. Lijphart (1999) makes a similar point that rules can mediate the positions of contending groups. However, the power dynamics between social groups also conditions the kind of institutions that emerge in a society and thus can directly influence civil conflict. Work following Lipset and Rokkan (1967) suggests that political institutions reflect social cleavages, and that the independent effect of institutions should be limited. Huntington (1968) also suggests that underdeveloped societies experience a 'general politicization of social forces and institutions' (p. 194).

In the study of civil war, prominent scholars have found limited evidence for the idea that social diversity or social polarization are risks at the onset of civil war, emphasizing instead the material and geographic conditions that favour insurgency (Collier and Hoeffler, 1998, 2004; Fearon and Laitin, 2003). Others still stress the idea that social characteristics can explain civil conflict (Elbadawi and Sambanis, 2000; Sambanis, 2005; Reynal-Querol, 2002; and even Collier et al., 2009) and some find that diverse or polarized societies are more likely to experience ethnic civil war, or civil conflict more broadly (e.g., Sambanis, 2001; Reynal-Querol, 2002; Esteban et al., 2012). More recent work is focused on ethnic groups and the power relations between social groups, based on research and data by Wimmer et al. (2009). This work finds that exclusion from the government on ethnic criteria increases the risk of civil war (Wimmer et al., 2009; Cederman et al., 2010).

Closely related to arguments over whether social structure affects the degree of conflict in a society are questions about the exact nature of the relationship between these two phenomena. Ethnicity may matter mainly because of the number of interests that it generates, in which case indices of fractionalization should proxy well for the mechanism. Yet a more satisfying and sophisticated view endows ethnic groups with agency and strategy vis-à-vis each other and the state. Thus, in earlier work, it is argued that ethnic dominance increases the ability of, as well as the incentive of, the majority (group/s that make up 45–90 per cent of the population) to exploit minorities, and this increases the risk of civil conflict (Collier, 2001; Collier and Hoeffler, 2004). Also, based on rent-seeking models, the risk of civil conflict is argued to be higher when the distribution of social characteristics across a country's population is bi-modal and there is a high degree of social polarization, that is to say, situations in which two social groups are the same size (Esteban and Ray, 1994; Reynal-Querol, 2002).[4] These are, however, relatively narrow views of what may matter in the relationships between domestic ethnic groups that focus on their relative size. More broadly, Wimmer et al. (2009) argue that the state is a 'central object of and participant in ethnopolitical power struggles' and that '(ethnic) exclusion from state power and competition over the spoils of government' breeds ethnic conflict (Wimmer et al., 2009, p. 317). In this case, measures of fractionalization and polarization do not capture the relationship and antagonisms between the ethnic groups that have access to the state and excluded groups.

In an important development in the study of the relationship between violence and ethnopolitical conflict, Wimmer et al. (2009) introduce Ethnic Power Relations (EPR) data. This data records all politically relevant ethnic groups (regardless of minority/majority status) and their access to state executive power, as well as the intra-elite ethnic power dynamics. Their research shows that, controlling for political institutions (democracy, anocracy, autocracy), exclusion from state power leads to a higher risk of civil war in general (as well as fighting initiated by the excluded) and ethnic fragmentation of governmental power leads to infighting between elites. A large amount of the following literature uses the EPR data, finding support for the thesis that political exclusion or marginalization is linked to civil war.[5] The link between civil conflict and the access to power of ethnic groups is thus rich and robust. More recent evidence also tackles the charge that the institutional arrangements that govern the access to power of ethnicities are themselves a product of conflict. Wucherpfennig et al. (2016), thus, find that instrument an ethnic group's inclusion to power with the group's geographic location and the British/French identity of their colonial rulers. This identification strategy shows that ethnic exclusion is causally linked to civil war and that the effect is considerable.

4 Economic Inequality

Going back to Gurr's (1970) theory of relative deprivation, individuals' discontent with regards to their social situation was posited to generate social conflict. The use in early studies of individual-level inequality data, like the Gini coefficient, has shown that inequality has a little consistent effect on civil conflict. Most authors do not find a relationship between inequality measured in this way and civil war (Cramer, 2003; Fearon and Laitin, 2003; Collier and Hoeffler, 2004; Collier; Hoeffler and Rohner, 2009).[6] Some others argued that grievances are too prevalent and too common, so that they act as a background to civil conflict, but are not the causes or explanations for why latent discontent turns violent (Fearon and Laitin, 2003; Collier and Hoeffler, 2004). Houle (2016), on the other hand, explains that the lack of statistical significance is due to the fact that inequality in income has two effects that go in opposite directions, neutralizing each other. Houle identifies a direct effect on aggravating distributional conflicts and an indirect effect on increasing the size of the military, which plays a role in deterring the mobilization of groups, a necessary factor in the onset of civil conflict.

The lack of quantitative findings linking income inequality to civil war was a striking departure from the qualitative literature which linked the inequality of groups to conflict (Stewart, 2000, 2002; Sambanis, 2005). It also contradicts the many instances in which economic inequality or the lack of economic opportunities are known to have contributed to other forms of political instability. For example, while looking at the causes of the Arab Spring, Malik and Awadallah (2013, p. 296) note that 'Arab revolutions were fuelled by poverty, unemployment, and lack of economic opportunity'. Thus, recent work moved to match group-level inequality with social and geographical divisions with greater precision, displaying the strong influence of this horizontal inequality on the onset of civil war. In an early study, Ostby (2008) argues that civil wars are fought by groups, so it makes more sense to look at inequality between groups rather than individuals. Inequality that matches the boundaries that delineate ethnic group membership has the potential to increase both grievance and group cohesion and mobilization. Thus, for a sample of thirty-nine developing countries and using group inequality based on survey data, Ostby looks at the inequality between the two largest ethnic groups (along with asset ownership and educational opportunities) and finds that her measure of horizontal inequality indeed increases the risk of initiating the civil war.[7]

Cederman et al. (2011) further connect asymmetries in group income distribution with civil war. First, they distinguish between political and economic horizontal inequalities. They go on to argue that economic inequalities among groups can be transformed into grievances through a process of 'group comparison driven by collective emotions' (p. 481). Furthermore, such grievances increase group mobilization and the chance for violent collective action. Emotional social comparisons and resentment among groups thus contribute to mobilization and recruitment within groups, alongside other factors derived from group dynamics contributing to mobilization. Cederman et al. proceed to test their theory using spatial coding of wealth (G-Econ data) matched to ethnic group location (GeoEPR), as well as coding whether specific ethnic groups have links to rebel groups actively involved in fighting a civil war.[8] Their main data covers the years 1991–2005 and their analysis shows that both the exclusion of political groups from government and economic group inequities contribute to the onset of civil war.

5 Oil and Conflict Risk

In the early literature, natural resources were prominently linked to civil war, mostly as generators of the opportunity to rebel, not as contributors to or mitigators of motivation. Yet, the more recent literature suggests that resource exploitation may contribute to economic grievance and also be used by governments to strategically distribute patronage in order to limit concerns about unfair exploitation or to invest in the military with the clear objective of deterring rebellion.

The literature on the resource curse is very prominent, and it has been argued natural resources influence conflict through a number of channels (de Soysa, 2002; Fearon and Laitin, 2003; Ross, 2004a; de Soysa and Neumayer, 2005; Dixon, 2009; Lujala, 2010; Ross 2012). Two ground-breaking papers, Collier and Hoeffler (2004a) and Fearon and Laitin (2003), both show that wealth in natural resources increases the probability of civil war onset. Collier and Hoeffler (2004a) suggest that natural resources finance rebel groups and thus lower opportunity costs of embarking on rebellion. On the other hand, Fearon and Laitin (2003) emphasize the fact that oil producers tend to have a weaker state apparatus, which makes it difficult for their governments to sustain efficient conflict prevention, a conclusion supported by Humphreys (2005). In addition, Fearon and Laitin (2003), Englebert and Ron (2004), Fearon (2005), and Besley and Persson (2009) argue that natural resources swell the state's coffers, thus increasing the value of the state, making conflict over the 'prize' of the state more likely.

Oil production may also contribute to civil conflict by creating grievances over the unfair distribution of rents (Sorens, 2011; Ross, 2012). For example, oil-rich regions may have incentives to secede because of the perception of exploitation by the central government. Paine (2019) suggests that oil production generates economic grievances because the nature of oil production (capital intensive, geographically concentrated, largely immobile, and in the formal sector) incentivizes the governments to make locally unpopular tax decisions. Such grievances, contribute, in turn, to separatist conflicts in oil-rich regions.

The negative effect identified by the resource curse literature is probably related only to oil and not to other natural resources in general. Fearon and Laitin (2003) and Fearon (2005) find no robust support for the role of primary commodities in civil conflict onset. This view is supported by de Soysa and Neumeyer (2008) who demonstrate that even when looking at a wider range of natural resources, only hydrocarbons affect the onset of civil war. Finally, Ross (2004a) reviews fourteen quantitative studies of the resource-conflict link. He concludes that primary commodities as a whole cannot be robustly linked to either civil war onset or duration. Only oil-exporting countries seem to be particularly prone to civil war onset. This finding is supported by another meta-analysis conducted by Dixon (2009).

On the other hand, despite the prominent work linking oil and civil conflict, research has long suggested that oil might provide states with the resources for delivering public or private goods and stabilizing political regimes, be they democracies or dictatorships. A considerable body of work suggests that rents from natural resources can stabilize the state-society relationship (Mahdavy, 1970; Beblawi and Luciani, 1987; Smith, 2004; Basedau and Lay, 2009; Fjelde, 2009; Morrison, 2009; Bodea, 2012; Ross, 2012; Colgan, 2014; Bodea et al., 2016). Bueno de Mesquita et al. (2003) point out that government decisions on spending are strategic responses aimed at maintaining power. Regimes can offset oil-related or other conflict risks by generous and large-scale distributional policies and, as a result, grievances are less likely to emerge. A large security sector, financed by oil money, also helps to render rebellion more difficult.

Ross (2001) argues that oil wealth produces two mechanisms through which a government can provide goods that reduce the social pressures on itself. First, natural resource wealth allows the government to buy off citizens using low tax rates and patronage (a 'rentier effect'). The second is a 'repression effect': natural resources allow the government to strengthen the military and security forces in order to maintain order in society. Along the same lines, Smith (2004) and Morrison (2009) both show that natural resources or non-tax revenues tend to increase political stability by maintaining regime durability.[9] Ulfelder (2007) and Wright et al. (2014) also find that autocracy and individual autocratic leaders are more durable in countries rich in natural resources.

Following Ross, periods of volatile or reduced oil revenue due to low hydrocarbon prices, are of particular concern for the stability of resource-rich countries. The Arab uprisings occurred in such a context, where reduced revenue from natural resources limited the ability of the governments involved to buy political allegiance. Instead, when facing popular discontent, they were more likely to resort to brutal repression.

6 Horizontal Political and Economic Inequality, Oil and Conflict

Much of the work on group-level political and economic inequality and civil war is independent of the research on the role played by oil in explaining the same outcome. Yet, the most recent work is considering the potential overlap. We first describe the limited literature which finds that natural resources can aggravate the effect of political exclusion on civil war onset. We then focus more specifically on the potential joint effect of horizontal economic inequity—income and wealth inequality between ethnic groups—and oil production in a particular country. There we discuss the main points made by Bodea and Houle (2020) and give an overview of the argument. The next section details their key empirical findings.

The spatial distribution of natural resources vis-à-vis the political representation of ethnic groups is found to be a contributor to civil conflict. Basedau and Pierskalla (2014), for example, find that, in Africa, the geographical presence of oil and gas in regions populated by groups with a monopoly of power over the national political institutions reduces the risk of conflict. Also, Asal et al. (2015) argue that the presence of oil in an area populated by a specific ethnic group increases the likelihood of ethnic armed conflict if that group is excluded from power at the national level. Their findings suggest that while political exclusion is a risk factor at the onset of civil war, this risk increases sharply if oil resources are located in the settlement area of the excluded group. Related, Hunziger and Cederman (2017) address the potential endogenous nature of oil resources and argue that regional conflict stemming from oil is likely when the local population does not see the benefits of oil production, while bearing the costs. Their evidence shows that oil production in an area populated by marginalized ethnic groups increases the risk of secessionist civil war. At the same time, they show that oil production in other geographical areas is not of consequence.

Thus, the contingent effect of political inequality on oil has been studied (Basedau and Pierskalla, 2014; Asal et al., 2015; Hunziger and Cederman, 2017). Yet, there is little understanding of such conditional effects for the case of income and wealth-based horizontal inequality. Cederman et al. (2011) do not focus on whether groups residing in countries with significant oil resources face modified incentives and emotions that interact in any significant way with horizontal income inequality. Bodea and Houle (2020) find that oil wealth can broadly influence grievance, and the ability and willingness of groups to mobilize, two key points in Cederman et al.'s theoretical account. In particular, we suggest that two dynamics may be at play:

on the one hand, we argue that there is potential for oil resources to increase distributional conflict and, therefore, increase group-based grievance in countries where ethnic groups are distinguished by marked differences in income. On the other hand, we suggest it is likely that the availability of resources in oil-rich countries which can be invested in the military inhibits mobilization in the select group of oil-rich countries that spend significantly on their military.

How do natural resources, in particular oil, influence the effect of horizontal income inequality? Income and wealth inequality between groups generates an emotional reaction both to a perceived lack of resources for one group as compared to the other ones, or the requirement to redistribute to the poorer groups, perceived as less deserving. Oil revenue can compound such reactions and aggravate the distributional conflict when the state does not spend on public goods, directs patronage to privileged groups, and is viewed as a prize to be looted. Yet grievance from the unequal distribution of income and wealth is argued by Cederman et al. to contribute to mobilization for violent collective action. Oil resources can have a counter-effect on this mobilization. Oil resources invested in the military act as a deterrent to mobilization and therefore to civil war onset.

Bodea et al. (2016) demonstrate significant variations in how oil-rich states allocate resources, with regard to general government expenditure, welfare expenditure, and military expenditure. Bodea and Houle (2020) ask how oil revenues and spending patterns interact with inequality in increasing or mitigating the risk of civil war. Their findings show that there is a greater effect of horizontal income inequality in oil-rich countries and that, in these countries, high levels of spending on the military mitigate the effect of horizontal income inequality.[10]

7 Horizontal Economic Inequality, Oil and Conflict—Empirical Evidence

Bodea and Houle (2020) empirically demonstrate that the effect of horizontal economic inequality on civil wars is conditional on oil resources. Their analysis is based on the important study of Cederman et al. (2011), which finds that those ethnic groups experiencing a greater degree of horizontal inequality are more likely to instigate a civil war. The unit-of-analysis employed by Cederman et al. (2011), and Bodea and Houle (2020), is the ethnic group-year.[11] Their measure of horizontal inequality demonstrates the degree of inequality between the average member of a given ethnic group and the average citizen from the same country.[12] The dependent variable takes the value one if an ethnic group initiates a civil war in a given year. The measure used by Cederman et al. (2011) is taken from the UCDP/PRIO Armed Conflict Dataset, which uses a battle-related death threshold of twenty-five casualties. Their sample covers more than 6000 observations on 424 ethnic groups and 115 countries between 1991 and 2005.[13]

Bodea and Houle (2020) replicate the analysis of Cederman et al. (2011) but split the sample between oil-rich and oil-poor countries.[14] Oil-poor countries are classified as those with an oil income below the 50th percentile and oil-rich countries as those with an oil income at about the 50th percentile.[15] They find that horizontal inequality only increases the likelihood of civil war among the former. In oil-rich countries, ethnic groups with horizontal inequality levels at the 95th percentile of the distribution are about three times more likely to instigate a civil war than those with horizontal inequality levels at the 5th percentile. In oil-poor countries, ethnic groups with higher horizontal inequality levels are actually less likely to engage in civil wars, although the effect does not achieve statistical significance.

Bodea and Houle (2020) also investigate whether the presence of oil in an ethnic homeland conditions the effect of horizontal inequality on war. As discussed above, Asal et al. (2015) and Hunziger and Cederman (2017) find that political exclusion has a particularly strong effect on the civil war between groups who have oil in their homeland. Bodea and Houle (2020) test this possibility using Hunziger and Cederman's (2017) data on the presence of oil in each ethnic homeland. They find that horizontal inequality only increases the probability of war between groups in a land that has oil reserves. Among oil-producing ethnic groups, increasing horizontal inequality from the 5th to the 95th percentile would again increase the probability of war by about three times.

Above, we have also explained that in addition to increasing grievances, oil revenues can be employed by governments either to repress opposition with the help of a generously compensated military or to co-opt it by means of shared patronage. We should thus expect military and welfare spending to weaken the effect of horizontal inequality on civil war. Bodea and Houle (2020) test this argument and find that, among oil-rich countries, horizontal inequality only increases the probability of civil war in countries with low military spending and low total government spending.

Taken together, these findings suggest that oil production in fact magnifies the grievances engendered by horizontal inequality. There is thus an interesting parallel between political and economic horizontal inequality: Both are particularly consequential when they are reinforced by oil production. The results also imply that oil-rich countries that employ oil revenues to either repress or co-opt the population are less likely to experience conflict.

8 Conclusion

In this chapter, we have first reviewed the grievances-based literature on conflict, with a focus on studies looking at political institutions, political exclusion, and economic inequality. We then briefly discussed some of the main arguments of the greed-based literature, which is usually portrayed as the polar opposite of the grievance-based approach. While the latter focuses on the factors that *motivate* actors to initiate conflict, the former focus on those that create *opportunities* for conflict.

After discussing these two approaches, we posit that the effects of the variables associated with them may not be independent. In particular, we discuss the argument and empirical findings of Bodea and Houle (2020), according to which the effect of horizontal inequality (which is associated with the grievance-based approach) on civil war is conditional on oil resources (which is associated with the greed-based approach). Bodea and Houle (2020) show that horizontal inequality only increases the likelihood of civil war between ethnic groups situated in oil-rich countries. They also find that the effect of horizontal inequality in oil-rich countries is conditional on the level of military spending and total government spending: as military spending/total government spending increases, the effect of horizontal inequality weakens. This suggests that oil-rich countries that spend revenue from oil production on repression and/or co-optation are less vulnerable to civil war.

Taken as a whole, this review has shown that, contrary to what is argued in a considerable body of the literature, grievances do play an important role in explaining conflict. But the review also shows that grievance-based and greed-based explanations of civil conflict are not independent of one another. Greed-based factors, such as oil, can aggravate those grievances caused, for example, by political or economic inequality. Moreover, any grievances may not be sufficient for conflict. A group that has incentives to initiate a civil war may not do so if it does not have the opportunity to do so. As suggested by Mahler and Pierskalla (2015), oil income, or other factors that create openings for conflict, may serve as a 'catalyst' for the politicization of ethnicity.

The review also indicates several paths for future research. First, the conditional argument could be applied to other greed-based and grievance-based factors. For example, it is possible that ethnic exclusion has a stronger effect on the civil war in countries where the state has a limited capacity for action of any kind. In strong states, excluded groups may not be able to challenge the regime. Second, the earlier literature finds that horizontal inequality affects forms of violence other than civil war, such as coups d'etat (Houle and Bodea, 2017), the breakdown of democracy (Houle 2015), and state repression (Ye and Han, 2019). The effect of horizontal inequality on these alternative forms of violence may also be contingent on oil resources. Third, Bodea and Houle's (2020) study is almost exclusively quantitative. It would also be interesting to study specific country cases and see if the relationship is in fact driven by the mechanisms they propose. Such studies would also help to determine that the quantitative results point to a causal relationship. Mahler and Pierskalla (2015), for example, show that gas deposits have served as a catalyst for interethnic tensions in Bolivia. Further qualitative studies looking more directly at horizontal inequality would contribute significantly to the debate.

Notes

1 The inverted-U relationship between political institutions and civil war is also found in Smith (2004).
2 Peic and Reiter (2011) confirm this result, while Gleditsch and Ruggeri (2010) find support for the proposition that anocracies experience more civil war.
3 Fjelde (2009), in particular, shows that corruption increases the risk of civil war, even if this effect is mitigated by the presence of oil wealth.
4 This work refers both to ethnic and religious polarization (Reynal-Querol, 2002; Montalvo and Reynal-Querol, 2005; Basedau et al., 2011; Esteban and Mayoral, 2011). Of note 'ethnicity' includes, depending on the context, religious groups, linguistic groups or racial groups. For example, in the study of ethnic wars, Reynal-Querol (2002) examines both religious polarization and linguistic differences. Also, in Ethnic Power Relations data, 'ethnicity' depends on the context. In Canada it is based on language, in the US on race, and in many Middle East and North African countries it is based on religion. In many cases, 'ethnicity' depends on the most important cleavage in the country. In recent work, Houle (2019) shows that the nature of the cleavage does not really matter. Race, religion, and language all have similar effects, in that case, on ethnic voting.
5 Roessler (2011), however, has found that political exclusion reduces the likelihood that an ethnic group will stage a military coup.
6 A smaller group of authors finds evidence of a positive relationship between economic inequality and civil war onset (e.g., Boix, 2008; Baten and Mumme, 2013; Bartusevicius, 2014). However, most of these studies employ slightly different research designs. For example, Bartusevicius (2014) looks at the effect of inequality in educational attainment (not income or wealth inequality) on small-scale popular uprisings (not full-blown civil war). Moreover, Baten and Mumme (2013) focus on inequality in physical height. Other authors have also found that income inequality breeds other forms of political violence, beyond civil war. For example, Svolik (2012) and Houle (2016) show that income inequality affects military coups, while Griffin et al. (2020) find a positive relationship between relative deprivation and protests.
7 See also Sambanis and Milanovic (2009). Some have focused on regional inequality, including Ostby et al. (2009).
8 An ethnic group is coded as participating in civil war if 'a rebel organization expresses its political aims (at least partly) in the name of the group and a significant number of members of the group were participating in the conflict' (Cederman et al., 2011, p. 484).
9 Houle (2018a) argues that oil has a differential effect on the two stages democratic transition—authoritarian breakdown and the establishment of democracy. He finds that authoritarian breakdown is unaffected by oil, but that oil hurts the chances for the subsequent democratic transition.
10 To show that, among oil-rich countries, the effect of horizontal inequality depends on military spending, they split the sample between countries with either high or low levels of military spending. They classified countries as having high (low) military spending if their military spending is higher (lower) than the median. They find that horizontal inequality only increases the risk of civil war in countries with low levels of military spending. Of those with high levels of military spending, its effect is not statistically significant. They also show that their results are robust to the use of alternative thresholds.
11 Cederman et al. (2011) identify ethnic groups using the Ethnic Power Relations (EPR) dataset, which only includes politically relevant ethnic groups.
12 Cederman et al. (2011) estimate the wealth of ethnic groups using ethnic group settlement maps and data on the spatial dispersion of wealth in countries.

13 The analysis includes the same control variables as in Cederman et al. (2011). These controls include a series of ethnic group-level variables, such as the number of years since the group has been involved in a conflict, and country-level variables, like GDP per capita and the number of ethnic groups that are excluded from executive power.
14 Bodea and Houle (2020) measure oil/gas wealth with the indicator of oil and gas production per capita (logged) from Ross (2012).
15 They also show that the results do not depend on the particular cut-off point employed.

3 Power-Sharing and Peace-Building

Nicholas Sambanis

1 Introduction

Civil wars are 'sticky': once they start, they are hard to end. When they do end, there is a high risk the violence will recur within a few years.[1] What makes civil wars so sticky and so likely to restart? Is power-sharing the way to help end civil wars and build peace?

Seen through the prism of the bargaining model of conflict, the 'stickiness' of civil war is due to the difficulty of reaching a mutually enforceable settlement that could avoid the high costs of violence in adjudicating disputes over resources or power. The fact that a political conflict has turned violent suggests that it cannot be resolved via a mutually acceptable, self-enforcing bargain that avoids the resort to arms. In light of this, what explains the sharp decline in the prevalence of civil wars since the middle of the 1990s? That decline represents a structural break in the pattern of civil wars since 1945. Is that due to factors that enable the parties to negotiate more effectively and reach bargains that avoid or reduce the use of violence? Scholars have argued that the invigorated role of United Nations peacekeeping and peace-building since the end of the Cold War and the decline in interventions by major powers and proxy wars are partly responsible for the decline in the prevalence of civil war. Both developments are conducive to a more broadly collaborative environment in which the international community has promoted power-sharing solutions for ending civil wars. Power-sharing institutions increase the political inclusion and accommodation of minority groups and former rebels after a civil war, thereby reducing grievances that could fuel further violent conflict.

Recent studies that present comprehensive data on power-sharing show a sharp increase in all forms of power-sharing as the solution to civil war since the mid-1990s (Graham et al., 2017). Whereas until about the late 1980s most civil wars ended in military victory, negotiated settlements are now the most common way in which they terminate (Toft, 2010). These settlements are usually reached with the assistance of external actors, including multilateral institutions such as the United Nations (UN). UN peace missions have increased since the 1990s and their mandates have expanded in their scope

DOI: 10.4324/9781003344414-5

and in the degree to which they intrude into the political affairs of the host country (Doyle and Sambanis, 2006). Some form of political inclusion for all minorities and all groups involved in the fighting is now the usual goal of international intervention and this is reflected in the content of negotiated settlements after the civil war.

Power-sharing institutions are the means via which inclusion is achieved in post-war states. Yet it is not clear if these institutions are effective or under what conditions we should expect different power-sharing institutions to reduce the risk of war recurring. This review addresses that question and highlights gaps in the literature that future studies should address.

2 Measurement of Power-Sharing

Typically, the term power-sharing (P-S) has been used to describe the institutional mechanism for the distribution of nominal political power (e.g., cabinet positions) according to a fixed rule. That rule reflects the relative size of the groups involved or their relative power. This concept of P-S is due to Lijphart (1985), who argued that consensus-building via consociationalism should be the political system instituted in new democracies or divided societies in which majoritarian systems would be a poor choice. The concept of 'consensus' democracy is frequently used in reference to P-S systems that are centred on institutional rules which give all groups access to executive power. This implies that there are several kinds of systems that can qualify as P-S institutions, including proportional-representation (PR electoral systems, federations, or confederal systems, as long as all groups have in principle equal access to power. Some P-S systems give the power of veto over major executive decisions to all groups, whereas others achieve the goal of political inclusion via electoral means, designing electoral rules that ensure the representation of minority groups. Some P-S systems expand central authority whereas others foster decentralization/regional autonomy. At the core of the concept of P-S is that power will rely in different communities and that power allocation will depend on the principles of proportionality and autonomy (Lijphart, 1969, 1975; O'Leary, 2005).

The fact that there are many different ways that different societies can achieve the goal of inclusion and power-sharing implies that the category of P-S institutions is likely to be quite heterogeneous. Another consequence of the breadth of the concept is that empirical measures of P-S are likely to vary significantly across studies. Focusing on post-conflict cases, Fearon and Laitin (2008) code only nine cases since 1945 of power-sharing following civil war.[2] By contrast, Hartzell and Hoddie (2003), one of the first studies to explore the post-conflict implications of P-S, code over thirty instances of P-S institutions in the same period.[3] Cammett and Malesky (2012) review the same set of conflicts as Hartzell and Hoddie and extend the period covered to 2010, identifying fifty-three cases of P-S.[4] Mattes and Savun (2009) explore 46 cases of negotiated settlement coding 'fear-reducing' and 'cost-increasing' provisions in these settlements to assess the impact of power-sharing.

This brief comparison suggests that definitions and operational criteria for the coding of P-S vary widely. P-S is as much a process, as it is an outcome,[5] but more commonly, P-S refers to a set of institutional criteria for inclusion in policy-making.[6] P-S differs from the related concept of 'power-dividing' (Roeder and Rothchild, 2005) chiefly by the fact that P-S institutions usually include veto powers for every actor/group that is a member of the P-S coalition. Consociationalism (Lijphart, 1969, 1977) is an example of institutional P-S. However, such institutional features of power-sharing are not always present and in fact it is worth considering under what conditions any of the groups involved would push for a rigid institutional structure for sharing power. Nomikos (2017) addresses this question by distinguishing between electoral P-S (veto power arises from the possibility of electoral results that overturn an established regime;[7] these can include 'grand coalitions' or 'unity governments', which are the norm in post-conflict settings) and institutional P-S which divides positions that can be allocated to each party independent of elections.

Electoral P-S is the most common outcome of peace negotiations after a civil war when there are mainly two conflicting parties (seen in 76.5 per cent of all cases) and when there are multi-party negotiations with ethnic parties (88.5 per cent of all cases). Nomikos (2017) finds that in post-conflict countries with multi-party systems, institutional P-S is less likely if there is an ethnic majority group, and more likely the more unified the groups are. Nomikos (2017) also finds a positive and statistically significant association between institutional P-S and UN intervention, which is consistent with the earlier observation that the UN's increased involvement in peace-building has coincided with a spike in the use of P-S solutions. This type of P-S contributes to democratization by favouring the formation of larger ethnic coalitions, which is conducive to democratization.

A similar argument about the conditions under which institutionalized P-S will be pursued is developed by Bormann (2019). His research addresses the occurrence of 'oversized' ethnic coalitions, which he argues are formed when ethnic elites face intra-group competition and are uncertain about the stability of alliances formed with other co-ethnics. Under such conditions, these elites have incentives to include non-co-ethnics in broader coalitions.[8] Bormann questions the assumption that political institutions constrain elite behaviour; P-S need not promote post-conflict stability b/c conflict is simply displaced and now occurs within the governing coalition. He also perceives conflict risk as arising from any ethnic groups not included in the P-S coalition as they may mobilize in order to gain access to the governing coalition.

One of the most influential typologies of P-S used in empirical studies is Graham et al.'s (2017) three-way typology, distinguishing between 'inclusive, dispersive, and constraining' forms of power-sharing (pp. 688–689).

Inclusive arrangements 'mandate the participation of several parties of groups in particular offices or decision-making processes.... [they] place power broadly and jointly in the hands of multiple recognized groups'. Inclusive power-sharing distribute shares in the central government/policymaking to each party. They thereby make it more likely that policies will reflect a broader set of preferences. Lijphart's (1985) 'grand coalition' is an example of such an institution.

Dispersive arrangements 'divide authority among actors in a well-defined pattern (e.g., territorial decentralization) ... [they] limit the power of one faction over others through partitioning or devolution of political authority'.

Constraining arrangements 'limit the power of any actor and thus protect ordinary citizens and vulnerable groups against encroachment and abuse... [they] limit the scope of political authority to maximize citizens' autonomy'.

Though influential, Graham et al.'s (2017) typology is primarily inductive rather than theory-driven. They compile a list of nineteen power-sharing indicators (regime characteristics) in 180 countries from 1975 until 2010 and use factor analysis to load these characteristics on the three conceptual types that they consider distinct. It is worth exploring the merits of their typology in contrast to other possible ways of organizing and classifying cases. It is also worth exploring the accuracy of the coding for the given set of P-S types. Cursory inspection of the examples in Graham et al. (2017) reveals some coding problems. For example, one of the best examples of inclusive P-S on their list is Cyprus from 1975 to 2010. The 1960 constitution in Cyprus allocated Turkish Cypriots a significant share of power in government with executive privileges in excess of their relative population size. Technically, the 1960 constitution is still in effect today, which is why Cyprus is on its list as one of the best examples of inclusive power-sharing. However, Cyprus was partitioned in 1974 following a Turkish invasion and there is now a de facto independent Turkish Republic of North Cyprus that is not represented by the internationally recognized government of the Republic of Cyprus. With Turkish Cypriots having 'exited' and the de facto partition of Cyprus still in effect since 1974, this is hardly an example of inclusive power-sharing. One might argue instead that this is an example of dispersive power-sharing, albeit one in which power is not shared in a consensual manner.

Differences in the coding of power-sharing often account for significant discrepancies in empirical results in studies of the impact of power-sharing institutions. One important source of disagreement concerns the coding of constitutional provisions regardless of whether or not they are actually implemented. Some studies (e.g., Graham et al., 2017) code any rule in the book, whether or not they are not followed in practice. Others code only implemented arrangements.[9] Another source of disagreement over coding concerns whether macro-level variables should be coded (e.g., whether the country is federal) without regard to the 'functionality' of federal institutions. In some countries, such as Nigeria, administrative units cut across ethnic settlement patterns, so ethnic groups are not as functionally autonomous as they would be in countries where ethnic settlement patterns are roughly mapped on to administrative boundaries, as was the case in the former USSR (see Bormann, 2019). Thus, a given level of 'macro-level' power-sharing might have very different practical implications in different contexts. Other distinctions that have been drawn focus on the macro-level context of P-S institutions. Specifically, the interaction between P-S and regime type is important (Magaloni, 2008).[10]

To summarize, while there are many variations in definitions and measures of P-S, most empirical studies code P-S to reflect differences in institutional mechanisms of how to allocate power among social (usually ethnic) groups. A key distinction that can be drawn is between 'inclusive' and 'dispersive' power-sharing. Inclusive power-sharing refers to allocating access to the central government, while dispersive power-sharing refers to granting territorially concentrated groups policy autonomy. We rely on this typology for much of the discussion in the rest of this chapter.

3 Determinants of Power-Sharing

Under what conditions will different types of P-S be adopted? It would be useful to explore this question as a way that considers types of P-S that might be suitable for MENA countries that are emerging from conflict and where P-S is being considered. Determinants of P-S arrangements have not been studied extensively hitherto. Important arguments concerning this subject include—with varying degrees of support in the empirical literature (a) the power-balance and degree of internal factionalism determines whether P-S rules will be institutionalized; (b) the risk of setting precedents determines whether a state will make dispersive P-S concessions; and (c) the colonial history of a country shapes the type of P-S institutions they are likely to adopt.

3.1 Factionalism

A recent study by Nomikos (2017) tries to explain the differences in the degree of the institutionalization of P-S arrangements using the most comprehensive list of post-conflict cases of P-S compiled to date. The key argument is that the degree of the institutionalization of P-S depends on the nature of the challenges the elites expect to face in the post-conflict period. If the challenges to the elites are likely to be external to them (i.e., stemming from out-groups/the main wartime rivals), then an institutionalization of governance rules could help to guard against any backsliding by the opposing groups on commitments to share power. If, however, challenges are mainly internal to the group due to a high degree of factionalism, then institutionalized P-S is unnecessary and might even be undesirable. Thus, the balance of power at the end of a war is a key variable as is the degree of internal factionalism.

Nomikos (2017) finds that the probability of institutionalized P-S increases by 20–40 per cent when ethnic groups are unified rather than factionalized. He also finds that institutionalized P-S increases when the UN is involved in the peace process.

3.2 Precedent-Setting

An influential argument concerning the conditions under which governments are likely to make concessions on autonomy to ethnic groups is put forward by Walter (2006) who draws on the logic of the bargaining model in international relations theory. Focusing on concessions to autonomy (i.e. 'dispersive power-sharing'), Walter argues that governments are less likely to make concessions when they face many potential challengers who will be emboldened by the perception that the state is making concessions because it is weak. Walter (2006) tests this argument by regressing an ordinal variable measuring the degree of 'accommodation' (government concessions on cultural reform, autonomy, or independence) on the number of ethnic groups in the country as well as other empirical proxies of her reputation theory.[11] While the theoretical argument about reputation is plausible, a replication of Walter's analysis shows that there is no support for her empirical claims (see Sambanis et al., 2018). The number of ethnic groups in the country is not a good proxy for the argument about reputation and there is no negative and statistically significant correlation between the number of ethnic groups and a government's proclivity to accommodate demands for self-determination. Further research is needed to establish the conditions under which making concessions on autonomy is likely to be perceived as a weakness, and thus would increase the demands made by other groups in the country.[12]

3.3 Colonial Histories

A major source of data on power-sharing is the Ethnic Power Relations (EPR) dataset, which has been used in multiple studies on the consequences of patterns of ethnic group exclusion (see, especially, Wimmer et al., 2009; Cederman et al., 2010). These studies have analysed a number of outcomes, but the main focus is on the effect of political exclusion on the onset of violent conflict. Because of the apparent endogeneity of institutions of exclusion on factors that might also affect conflict risk, the best studies in this literature attempt to identify the effect of exclusion via instrumental variables regression (Wucherpfennig et al., 2016). Via those analyses, we get useful information on the determinants of political exclusion in first-stage regressions. Focusing on post-colonial states, Wucherpfennig et al. (2016) exploit the differences in colonial rule to explain differences in the ways that ethnic groups were represented in government at the time of independence. Via the path-dependent nature of institutional design, this exogenous advantage could be carried through to influence contemporary conflicts.

The effect of P-S institutions on the propensity for conflict could therefore be identified via instrumental variables (IV) regression using colonial history as an instrument under the assumption that colonial history does not affect conflict outcomes in other pathways that are not modelled. One could debate whether the instrument actually satisfies this exclusion restriction but for our purposes, this estimation strategy is useful because it provides a glimpse (even if only a partial one) of the determinants of inclusion out of a set of explanatory variables used in the first stage regressions of their IV model. Their analysis shows that the political inclusion of ethnic minorities is less likely in former British colonies but for larger ethnic groups is more likely. Other country-level variables, such as per capita GDP, population size, violence at independence, country size, and other geographic controls (e.g., distance of the group to capital; distance to the coast) that are often included as covariates in civil war models do not significantly affect the likelihood or otherwise of the inclusion of minority groups.

Missing from the first-stage regressions in Wucherpfennig et al. (2016) is a measure of the degree of ethnic difference or fragmentation at the country level. Given that P-S has been used extensively as a means of managing the conflicting interests and anxieties of ethnic groups in multi-ethnic states, it would be reasonable to control for country-level heterogeneity. Perhaps this is not crucial for African states, most of which are very ethnically diverse,[13] so we might not find much of a correlation between power-sharing and ethnic fragmentation. However, in other regions, high levels of ethnic fragmentation are taken into account in the design of federal or other decentralized systems (Weingast, 1995; McGarry and O'Leary, 2009). Moving beyond the degree of ethnic or cultural difference, it would also be important to control for the degree of power symmetry between the ruling group and its challengers because this is likely to affect the type of P-S, including the degree of institutionalization (see earlier discussion of Nomikos, 2017). In weak states with a considerable underlying risk of internal armed conflict, if the ruling group's power and the challengers' power are symmetrical, then the emergence of P-S is more likely. In countries where the ruling group is weak and is facing a strong rival, one could see repressive minority regimes and where both the rival and the ruling group are weak, unstable, violent, and exclusive regimes with no power-sharing (Roessler and Ohls, 2018).

Summarizing results from the available studies, a number of factors appear to influence the adoption of P-S institutions. P-S is more likely in ethnically diverse states, particularly those with a majority ethnic group; in post-conflict states, especially those where the UN has intervened to stop the violence; in states with prior exposure to democratic governance; and states where challengers are relatively strong. However, it is difficult to draw lessons that apply broadly across types of P-S since most empirical studies focus on a preferred definition of P-S. It is likely to be the case that differences in the type of P-S and the strength of different P-S institutions throughout the world are a function of differences in the relative size and strength of ethnic groups, the historical contingencies, and the particularities of each case. This literature is now ripe for a meta-analysis that could help to organize the many disparate findings regarding the correlates of different forms of power-sharing.

4 Consequences of Power-Sharing

What is the effect of P-S on the post-war risk of conflict recurrence and democratic stability? These are both distinct outcomes, though they are often connected. Democratic stability could be a function of the underlying risk of violent conflict (recurrence of war) in a post-war state. Indeed, a recurrence of war is the most common reason for democratic failure in post-war settings. Separatist claims by a group reneging on a pre-existing dispersive P-S arrangement is a key cause of democratic failure (Graham et al., 2017).

It was noted at the outset that the cross-country empirical literature on P-S is inherently limited by the fact that the causal effect of P-S on different outcomes cannot be identified due to the lack of a valid instrumental variable. Most studies treat P-S as an exogenous variable and do not discuss the plausibility of that assumption. Other studies recognize that P-S institutions are endogenous, but they are unable to address this problem except by adding a number of controls that reduce the risk of confounding and omitted variable bias.[14] Thus, any review of the empirical effects of P-S cannot preclude that established correlations in published studies might be subject to unknown sources of bias.

4.1 Democratic Stability

One of the primary motivations for promoting P-S as a solution to civil war is the idea that P-S promotes inclusion, which in turn contributes to democratization. Nonetheless, the effects of P-S institutions on democratization after the civil war have not been studied extensively. One exception is a prominent study by Graham et al. (2017), which provides an analysis that is likely to frame the next wave of studies on this topic. In light of the importance of that article, its focus is discussed below though with the caveat that this does not represent an exhaustive review of the relationship between power-sharing and democratization.

According to by Graham et al. (2017), the effects of P-S on democratic survival are heterogeneous and depend on the type. Their analysis is based on new data on their tripartite typology of power-sharing (inclusive, dispersive, and constraining). Their new data on P-S show clearly that all types of P-S have been increasing over time. Drawing on the theory of democratic survival, they estimate an empirical model of democratic stability, where the dependent variable is a binary indicator that denotes whether a country is still a democracy five years later. The analysis is conducted on a sample of democratic countries and the dependent variable is regressed on the institutional P-S variables mentioned above and several controls (per capita GDP level and rate of growth; population size; oil/fuel dependence; ethnolinguistic fractionalization; regime age; past democratic breakdowns in the country; irregular turnovers of power; and time-dependence controls). The study produces a broad range of new results, though the focus is only on differences between the effects of different types of institutions. Their key finding (p. 698) is that only a constraining P-S exerts a statistically significant and positive effect on the probability of democratic survival in the full sample.

In post-civil war settings, Graham et al. (2017) find that the only type of power-sharing that produces positive outcomes on democratic stability is 'inclusive'. This has important implications for policy design after ethnic wars since 'dispersive' power-sharing is often used as a way to bring the parties to the negotiating table. Without autonomy concessions, it is questionable whether ethnic or separatist wars would end in negotiated settlements. Key here is the interpretation of the coefficient for the interactive terms in the results of Graham et al., since they use an indicator variable for 'post-civil war states' that interacted with each type of P-S. The base term for the type of P-S gives an estimate of the effect of P-S in countries without any recent conflict, whereas the coefficients for the interactive terms assess the difference in the effects of P-S between post-conflict states and states without conflict. It is notable that, while inclusive power-sharing has a significant positive effect on democratic survival, dispersive power-sharing has a negative effect (Graham et al., 2017, p. 699).

The policy implications of these findings cannot be over-stated. The fact that the international community promotes both inclusive and dispersive P-S as solutions to ethnic war is premised on an assumption that both types are likely to produce positive outcomes. Democratization has been one of the primary stated goals of civil war interventions and an even more prominent motive in so-called FIRCs (forced regime transitions).[15] The mechanism underlying the discrepancy between the effects of dispersive and inclusive institutions is not clear.

This debate is far from settled, however. Much of the empirical literature is based on results that are not robust to using different datasets on conflict. Appendix Table 3.1 presents the results of a reanalysis of Graham et al. (2017), replacing the UCDP/ACD data on conflict used in their analysis with a new dataset on conflict by Sambanis and Schulhofer-Wohl (2019). The use of different data on conflict onset and duration results in a different set of countries and periods that are classified as 'post-conflict' and that change alone is enough to produce massive changes in the estimated impact of power-sharing. As we show in the appendix, it is possible to find substantial support for the claim that regional autonomy (i.e., 'dispersive' power-sharing) reduces the risk of post-conflict recurrence. Given the sensitivity of the results of Graham et al. (2017), it is fair to say that the jury is still out on the effects of P-S on democratic survival.

4.1.1 Power-Sharing and National Identification

A key channel through which power-sharing could affect the risk of secessionist conflict is via its impact on national identification. Does P-S strengthen national identification at the expense of ethno-sectarian identities, or vice versa? A strong national identity should be correlated with long-term democratic stability as well as a low risk of conflict recurrence.[16] Yet we do not know which types of political institution encourage national identification.[17]

One of the few large-N studies to make the connection between P-S institutions and democratization via the national identification mechanism is Elkins and Sides (2007). Their argument (p. 693) is that democratic consolidation depends on the ability of political institutions to create a strong, unifying identity that fosters allegiance to the state without limiting civil liberties. A strong sense of national identity can produce this kind of loyalty to the state, but not all states are equally good at fostering national identification. Democracies are thought to cultivate the allegiance of citizens to the state, but democratic institutions—especially elections—can actually exacerbate ethnic, religious, or other cleavages if leaders seeking to gain the allegiance of the members of their group, politicize group identities (Rabushka and Shepsle, 1972; De Figueiredo and Weingast, 1999). Electoral competition along ethnic lines can divide a nation, which can diminish the foundations of democratic stability.[18] Indeed, several authors argue that federal systems are ideally suited to maximize political stability because of the checks and balances that they create (Weingast, 1995). However, Elkins and Sides (2007) find no evidence that power-sharing institutions promote minority attachment to the state and so they question whether power-sharing really fosters inclusion in a meaningful sense.

Another promising study by Ray (2018) combines attitudinal data from the World Values Survey (2010–2012) and data from the Ethnic Power Relations (EPR) dataset to show that political inequality between ethnic groups (what we called 'exclusion' previously) significantly weakens the sense of national pride and national identification. This study demonstrates that support for ethnic separatism in divided societies increases due to the decline of group status (which occurs when ethnic groups are 'downgraded' in terms of their degree of inclusion). It follows that P-S could help to reduce the risk of separatist conflict by encouraging a sense of national identification in 'included' groups.

It might be that the effects of P-S on national identification depend on the type of power-sharing. Specifically, 'inclusive' power-sharing that brings peripheral minorities closer to the centre and gives them access to the designing of policy should minimize differences between minorities and the rest of the country, which would in turn result in stronger national identification.[19] By contrast, territorial or 'dispersive' power-sharing may have the opposite effect if it minimizes contact between ethnic groups. The more separate (autonomous) from the rest of the country these groups perceive themselves to be, the less likely it is they will consider themselves part of the nation.

The argument above could be made even more specific by stipulating the precise mechanism connecting P-S institutions to identities.[20] Yet even without a fully specified model, it is worth exploring the available data to see if there is any preliminary evidence in support of this argument. If there is, then we will have identified an important pathway—social identities— underlying the connection between P-S and democratic consolidation.

To test this argument, we need cross-county, over-time data on national identification as well as data on political and institutional changes that are consistent with the two types of P-S that we are exploring here (dispersive or inclusive power-sharing). While it is possible to use one of the sources of data reviewed above to capture P-S, cross-country data on national identification are harder to come by (Ray, 2018 is the closest antecedent to such a study). The Afrobarometer surveys constitute a possible source of data.[21] These surveys ask explicit questions about the strength of national identification relative to ethnic identification.[22] National identification is weaker in African countries than in Europe, North America, or other parts of the world. Tanzania is an outlier with extremely high levels of national identification (88 per cent of the population say they would choose to identify as Tanzanian first and foremost). Nigeria is at the opposite extreme, with just 17 per cent of the population indicating that they identify nationally. Out of 16 countries included in the 2008 wave of the Afrobarometer survey, only two have more than 60 per cent of the population identifying nationally (Tanzania at 88 per cent and South Africa at 64 per cent).

Cross-country analyses show that national identification is stronger in more economically advanced countries and among people who are more educated and are part of the formal economy (Robinson, 2014). Politically dominant groups (usually national majorities) are more likely to identify nationally, though ethnic homogeneity is negatively associated with national identification.

The extant literature has not explored differences in national identification as a function of regime characteristics. I provide an initial examination of this question based on joint work with Nils-Christian Bormann. Merging data on inclusion and changes to the status of groups over time with the Afrobarometer survey data, the issue of whether there are statistically significant differences between the level of national identification among powerless and discriminated groups as compared to among 'senior' or 'junior partners' in government is explored. We expect to find these differences consistent with results showing a correlation between ethnic exclusion and violent conflict. In Cederman et al.'s (2010) study of the effects of political exclusion on ethnic conflict, the key mechanism is that excluded groups are more likely to mount ethno-nationalist challenges to the state, which would indicate that they do not consider themselves part of the nation. Our analysis assesses an implied mechanism underlying theories of exclusion and ethnic conflict. In the appendix (see Appendix Figure 1) there is some evidence that discriminated groups identify nationally to a lesser extent than dominant groups, but we do not find any significant differences in national identification between powerless groups on the one hand and included groups ('junior partner' or 'senior partner'). This surprising null result is informative and should be explored further.[23] One limitation of this analysis is that it relies on data from a small number of surveys in conflict countries;[24] also small is the number of countries that have experienced changes in P-S institutions over time, especially among the sample of post-conflict countries covered in the Afrobarometer surveys.

One possible reason for the lack of an association between inclusion and national identification in the set of countries included in the Afrobarometer survey is time: according to democratic theory, democracy can induce attachment to the state, but this is a process that takes place in the long term. Attachment to the state and a corresponding weakening of other, competing, identities occurs when democracy becomes 'predictable' for citizens (Przeworski, 1991). A similar, though more nuanced, argument is made by Kevin Russell (2015), who sees identities and interests co-evolving over time as institutions help the citizens' expectations about the future to converge to produce a common standard. When the citizens can rely on the state to plan their future, their attachment to the rule of law and other state institutions grows; but this process takes hold over a long period of time with the citizens constantly updating their beliefs that the state is committed to strengthening national identity. An empirical observation that follows from this discussion is that transitions to democratic power-sharing should induce an increase in national identification but only over the long term. While the political inclusion of ethnic groups can potentially reduce conflict in the short term, we should not expect an immediate change in national identification. This analysis could be expanded by considering separately the effects of inclusive vs dispersive institutions while also addressing the earlier argument about long-term vs short-term effects. Next, I turn to the differences between dispersive and inclusive institutions with respect to the recurrence of war.

4.2 War Recurrence

Looking deeper into the causes of democratic breakdown, Graham et al. (2017) note that the primary reason in post-conflict states is the recurrence of conflict, either in the form of a new separatist conflict or a coup. Thus, to properly understand the dynamics of democratic stability in post-conflict states, we need to understand the risk of war recurring post-conflict, which is what we turn to next.

The main motivation for the use of power-sharing institutions is that they should reduce the severity of the commitment problem faced by former combatants during the implementation phase of a peace settlement

(Mattes and Savun, 2009). Some authors question this argument and argue that P-S cannot eliminate the commitment problem (Fearon and Laitin, 2008). Focusing on military power-sharing (integrating combatants in the military after a civil war), Glassmyer and Sambanis (2008) argue that these agreements are unlikely to resolve the commitment problem because they do not provide credible security guarantees; instead, they are used mostly as a way of providing former rebels with employment. A 'middle' position holds that P-S is effective if it arises from a victory (whether for the rebels or the incumbent government); by contrast, P-S, which is the result of a negotiated settlement, will be more unstable (Mukherjee, 2006).

The advantages and disadvantages of power-sharing institutions with respect to their ability to contain ethnic or nationalist conflict have been debated heavily and there is no consensus opinion in the literature. Two types of P-S institutions have been considered explicitly with respect to their potential to reduce the risk after a conflict of a return to violence: inclusive and dispersive power-sharing.

Dispersive P-S usually takes the form of agreements on autonomy. An autonomy settlement may be provisionally defined as one that grants a distinct form of territorial self-government short of sovereign independence, to a named population. Do such agreements produce long-term territorial stability, thereby reducing the incidence of secession, as many have argued? Or, by contrast, are autonomy agreements, especially asymmetrical autonomy agreements, the mechanism through which proto-states emerge that later bid for secession?

According to many scholars, autonomy agreements in multi-ethnic, especially multi-national, states are bound to fail. Ethno-federalism has 'a terrible track record' (Snyder, 2000, p. 327) and ethno-federal institutions are seen as prone to conflict and breakdown along ethnic lines (Brubaker, 1995; Bunce, 1999; Roeder, 2007). Philip Roeder, for instance, has argued the latter position (Roeder, 2007). In early work on this topic inspired by the collapse of Yugoslavia and its descent to war, Valery Bunce (1999) wrote that multi-ethnic federations will fail because, by virtue of granting ethnic groups and their leaders the symbols and institutions of statehood, they enhance their appetite for independence.

By contrast, other scholars have suggested that autonomy, defined as 'internal self-determination', should be promoted by the international community as the best way of reconciling self-determination and the territorial integrity of existing member-states of the UN.[25] There have been multiple studies of the effects of autonomy, described under multiple headings: partially independent states, federacies, national autonomy, territorial autonomy, and asymmetric autonomy, to name the most prominent.[26] A cautious defence of multi-national federations is developed by McGarry and O'Leary (2009). They argue that part of the reason that ethno-federalism has a bad track record is that 'failed federations were forced together ... [so] there was no possibility of genuine dialogue' between the parties (McGarry and

O'Leary, 2009, p. 9). They also point out (p. 15) that, if ethno-federalism was not perceived as a valuable, even necessary, political system, then it would not have been used by Leninist centralists in the USSR and Yugoslavia. Thus, they turn the question 'Why did ethno-federalism in USSR and Yugoslavia collapse?' on its head and they ask, 'Why did it last as long as it did?' and 'How was it able to unify ethnic groups and nations that were in the midst of a civil war?'[27]

Another argument that McGarry and O'Leary (2009, p. 9) put forward to explain the failure of ethno-federalism is that many such states are federal in name only and in fact collapse is a result of an effort to re-centralize.[28] Their evidence comes mainly from a qualitative review of a few historical case studies, including in-depth knowledge of the case of the Iraqi Kurds (O'Leary, 2018). Other studies use cross-country data on 'lost autonomy' to show that there is a positive correlation between ethnic groups whose autonomous status has been downgraded and the risk of violent conflict between those groups and the state (Sambanis and Zinn, 2006; Siroky and Cuffe, 2016; Germann and Sambanis, 2021).[29] Using expanded data on self-determination movements across the world as well as new data on revocations of autonomy status, Germann and Sambanis (2021) show that 'lost autonomy' indeed correlates with conflict escalation, but both violent and non-violent forms of conflict could result from efforts to regain autonomy. Germann and Sambanis (2021) point to the need to focus more closely on the process of conflict escalation to explain why some conflicts over self-determination remain non-violent and others do not. Lost autonomy, as coded by Germann and Sambanis (2021), occurs in about 11 per cent of all cases of violent claims for self-determination and 27 per cent of all non-violent claims for self-determination. In fact, very few groups (2.7 per cent of 14,745 group-years in their dataset) that have not lost autonomy make violent claims (Germann and Sambanis, 2021).

In the appendix (Appendix Table 3.2), we replicate the analysis in Germann and Sambanis (2021) to show the consistently positive association between lost autonomy and conflict over self-determination. This analysis uses data on self-determination movements from 1945 to 2012. Most of these movements are non-violent, yet most of the quantitative literature has focused on violent separatist conflicts and less is known about the correlates of non-violent separatist movements. Table 3.2 shows clearly that lost autonomy (which includes historical losses of autonomy) and autonomy downgrades are positively and significantly correlated with the onset of non-violent conflict over self-determination, while also controlling for other variables that have been shown to affect demands for autonomy, as well as region and country fixed effects. In further analyses, Germann and Sambanis (2021) use a two-step model that analyses conflict escalation from non-violence to violence and find that violent escalation is strongly correlated with ethnic exclusion from power. Recent autonomy losses are also associated with violent escalation, and they conclude that 'unless autonomy downgrades are reversed, conflicts are hard to resolve, and recurrence is likely even after a period of little or no violence' (p. 20). This analysis, therefore, suggests that reneging on prior dispersive power-sharing arrangements is a risk factor for conflict recurrence.

Prima facie support in favour of the argument that efforts to re-centralize explain the onset of violent ethnic conflict is also provided by Cederman et al. (2015), who use data from the Ethnic Power Relations database to study the consequences of 'downgrading' ethnic groups. Their study is based on an innovative new dataset that identifies all politically relevant ethnic groups in each country and codes access to power over time for all these groups during the decades since 1945. The dataset mentioned previously in the section on 'measurement' of power-sharing, focuses on the measures for 'inclusion' of ethnic groups. Cederman et al. (2015) analyse the effects of including ethnic groups in central government as well as the effects of granting concessions on autonomy or both. They find a negative correlation between inclusion and ethnic war onset (where war is defined as the onset of an internal conflict producing twenty-five or more deaths). A similar result is shown in respect of autonomy (Table 3.3 in Cederman et al., 2015, p. 362). These results are produced by models using different configurations of the data by Cederman and his co-authors,[30] thereby questioning a previous literature that offered 'supply-side' explanations of ethnic insurgency (studies that sought to explain the incidence of insurgencies by reference to opportunities for looting, rough terrain, and state weakness). These two sets of literature have opposing policy implications. For Cederman et al., granting regional autonomy increases the likelihood of peace, but there are catches: autonomy must be granted early on, and is best combined with inclusive power-sharing arrangements in the central or federal government.[31] By contrast, Fearon and Laitin (2003) place greater emphasis on strengthening/centralizing state power and achieving impartial government.

Despite these interesting new results, the debate on the effects of autonomy arrangements or inclusion is far from settled. One open question concerns the timing of autonomy concessions—are they effective only if granted before the conflict turns violent or can they be used as a means to end ethnic civil wars? The most developed set of quantitative tests of this question to date are by Cederman and co-authors, drawing on the EPR dataset. Thus, what follows builds on their study to explore some of the conditional effects of inclusion as a conflict resolution strategy.

4.2.1 *Exploring the Conditional Effects of Dispersive Power-Sharing*

One of the first papers to consider the effects of regional autonomy in different political contexts was Brancati (2006), who argued that concessions regarding decentralization can have a direct positive effect, reducing conflict by appeasing the desire of groups for self-governance, but also an indirect negative effect by empowering regional elites and spurring the growth of regional parties. The assumption here is that regional elites will want to claim more resources for themselves and will therefore utilize the apparatus of sub-national state institutions to heighten ethnic differences and mobilize support for ethnic conflict in pursuit of their own individual agendas. That argument pushes us to consider institutional strategies to limit the power of the elites, not only at the national, but also at the regional (sub-national), level.[32] Among others, Mattes and Savun (2009) argue that P-S institutions can be effective in constraining the of ability actors to renege on their previous commitments, thereby decreasing the insecurity felt by regional elites. Graham et al. (2017) note that not all P-S institutions have the same positive effect on peace and that constraining it has this kind of effect, particularly in post-conflict societies (Gates et al., 2016).[33] In their analysis, constraining institutions activates the 'protection mechanism', protecting individuals, not elites, from the abuses of power. We could synthesize the work reviewed above to consider whether there are P-S institutions that are effective at protecting regional/sub-national elites from an erosion of their power by the centre; and if so, we could consider whether these institutions are effective at reducing elite-driven demands for secession and conflict among regionally autonomous ethnic groups.

Dispersive institutions such as autonomy arrangements empower and co-opt regional elites. The logic behind creating such institutions is that they can give regional elites incentives not to challenge the existing order (Gandhi and Przeworski, 2006; Magaloni, 2008), but the elites are not constrained from discriminating against weaker, smaller groups or repressing their political rivals (Gates et al., 2016, p. 518). It follows that the internal ethnic make-up of autonomous regions is an important variable that can influence how well these arrangements work in practice, as is the degree of intra-group political competition. This conjecture could be explored further using a comparative case-study approach, but the cases should be chosen carefully to account for the confounding effect of other variables, including the degree of intra-group elite competition and other institutional features of autonomy arrangements. Such factors could combine with concessions on autonomy to produce different degrees of risk for incumbent regimes. Thus, arguments such as Walter's that are based on the logic of restricting concessions on autonomy so as to cultivate a reputation for strength would have to be modified to account for institutional differences across countries. For example, institutional arrangements that encourage cross-ethnic voting could be effective in reducing ethnic conflict and might translate into a lower risk of separatism by regional parties or provincial majorities.[34] It follows that granting more autonomy in such situations is less likely to be perceived as a sign of the state's weakness. Similarly, if there is a high level of intra-group political competition, regional elites should be less likely to organize a challenge against the state and they will have more incentives to improve relations between provincial majority and minority populations (cf. Wilkinson's 2004 study of electoral ethnic violence in India).

4.2.2 Effects of Power-Sharing in the Shadow of External Intervention

We now turn to an analysis of how external intervention in civil war shapes the impact of power-sharing. This analysis draws on joint work with Nils Bormann and Mark Toukan and departs from the observation that the success or failure of any negotiated settlement often requires external intervention to provide assurances to former combatants, address spoiler problems, and provide the resources and technical capacities for peace (Doyle and Sambanis, 2006). While the effect of the impartial multilateral intervention on post-war peace-building has been analysed extensively, much less is known about how the spectre of partial intervention affects the stability of post-war power-sharing. That is the key question addressed by Bormann, Toukan, and Sambanis (2019).

The international environment is a neglected factor in influencing the success or failure of autonomy arrangements after the civil war. In general, the great powers, today's P5 of the UN Security Council, the BRICS, or the G7, disown secession as a threat to regional or global stability. Yet it is not hard to find examples of hypocrisy in their conduct since 1945, or 1991. France and the UK, for instance, adopted different postures towards Biafra's attempted secession from Nigeria. Today, the Russian Federation opposes the secession of Kosovo/Kosova and Chechnya but recognizes the secession of South Ossetia and Abkhazia from Georgia, and oversaw, through force and the ballot box, the secession of Crimea from Ukraine and its subsequent annexation to the Russian Federation. The United States and the EU's policies on these subjects are the exact opposite of Russia's: they backed the secession of Kosova/Kosova while supporting the territorial integrity of Georgia and Ukraine. Elsewhere, South Africa, like many African states, opposes secession on the African continent, but South African diplomats supported South Sudan's departure from Sudan, as did Sudan's neighbours (Ethiopia, Uganda, Kenya, Tanzania). Turkey opposes secession in Iraq and Syria but upholds the (so-called) Turkish Republic of Northern Cyprus.

Recognizing the influence that great powers, regional hegemons, or meddlesome neighbours exert on the implementation and function of dispersive power-sharing, we note the conspicuous absence of any systematic research on the legacies of external intervention in civil wars. Bormann, Toukan, and Sambanis (2019) test whether the shadow of intervention (i.e., expectations created by the behaviour of external actors during the previous war) affects the stability of arrangements on territorial autonomy. Specifically, pro-rebel intervention provides groups with an 'outside option' that renders the government hostage to external interference, the more extensive the inclusion of former rebels. Separatist conflict is also more likely in the presence of external support for rebels who are granted concessions in the form of dispersive power-sharing.

To test this hypothesis, Bormann, Toukan, and Sambanis begin by replicating key results from Cederman et al. (2015), which show that territorial autonomy concessions only have a pacifying effect if they are offered prior to the conflict turning violent. Focusing on post-war cases only and dropping observations of group-years where there has not been war, we can explore this argument with reference to the correlation between agreements on territorial autonomy and war recurring. We drop cases where inclusion and autonomy were granted before the civil war since those cases cannot inform our discussion of power-sharing as a strategy to end wars and prevent their recurrence.[35] Appendix Table 3.3 reproduces the results of the analysis in Bormann, Toukan, and Sambanis (their Table 3.1). Column 1 replicates Model 1 in Table 3.3 of Cederman et al. (2015), showing that inclusive power-sharing has a significant effect in reducing conflict, while concessions on autonomy do not. Column 2 breaks down these P-S institutions into pre-conflict and post-conflict and recodes some of the Cederman et al. (2015) data to properly assign pre-conflict and post-conflict cases of power-sharing. When some coding data in Cederman et al. (2015) are corrected, we find that inclusive P-S helps to reduce the risk of conflict no matter when these P-S institutions are established, though only pre-conflict autonomy has a significant association with conflict and the association is positive (increasing conflict risk).

Bormann et al. take this model as a starting point and add variables measuring interventionism in the previous war (identifying all cases where there was any type of intervention during the last two years of a civil war). They distinguish between pro-rebel and pro-government intervention and interact the history of intervention with the inclusion and autonomy variables. They retain all other covariates from the original study (group size, federal systems, population size, per capita income, etc.). Their findings suggest that a history of intervention conditions the association between P-S and war recurring.

Specifically, controlling for intervention history, Bormann et al. find that the negative association between inclusive P-S and a risk of conflict remains strong while the coefficient of post-conflict autonomy depends on whether there was autonomy pre- or post-conflict and if there was intervention in the previous war. In cases with a history of intervention, regional autonomy for the rebels was associated with a higher risk of conflict resumption (see the coefficient of the interaction term between autonomy and intervention history in model 3). Yet inclusion also has the same positive coefficient, so we further disaggregate in model 4 the type of intervention, whether it is pro-rebel or pro-government. We find that the association between intervention and conflict resumption points in the opposite direction, depending on whether it is pro-government or pro-rebel (column 4). While the interactive effect between intervention and inclusive P-S is not robust to small specification changes in the model, we see (model 4) that the association between territorial autonomy and war risk is the opposite depending on whether intervention occurred on the side of the government (decreasing risk of war recurrence) or on the side of the rebels (increasing risk of war recurrence). In model 5, we see that the direct correlation of post-conflict autonomy with conflict recurrence is negative whereas the interaction between post-conflict autonomy and a history of intervention has a negative coefficient and this effect is clearly due to pro-rebel interventions (model 6). Seen through the prism of the bargaining model, this would suggest that the presence of an external backer for rebels makes them less likely to be satisfied with the level of inclusion or autonomy that the government is willing to offer. Such 'outside options' may make the post-war peace fragile, subject to unexpected changes in the balance of power between former rebels and government or to domestic political developments in the external sponsor that could lead it to become more interventionist.

These results are informative, though they are not conclusive. The mechanisms underlying these correlations are not yet clear. Is a history of pro-rebel interventions destabilizing because it makes the elites among rebel groups likely to make ever-increasing demands that the centre cannot keep accommodating? Or is the centre less likely to believe in the credibility of the former rebels' commitment to power-sharing given their 'outside options' provided by external backers? In either case, any exogenous change to the power balance between the government and former rebels could trigger a mutual suspicion that in turn could undermine the stability of power-sharing in the absence of mechanisms to make such agreements self-enforcing.

To identify the mechanisms underlying those correlations, comparative case studies will be very useful. Bormann et al. (2019) describe an approach to case-study design that provides process-tracing of different mechanisms while also exploring 'out of sample' cases (i.e., cases that are not included in the quantitative analysis either because they occurred outside the time period corresponding to the quantitative analysis or because the case was miscoded such that it was mistakenly excluded from analysis). Such cases do not contribute to the analysis of quantitative data and are therefore eligible for inclusion in the qualitative analysis design, which can explore whether the purported mechanisms underlie the intervention-autonomy instability nexus.

5 Conclusion

This chapter has provided a review of the literature on power-sharing after the civil war by identifying sources of ambiguity in the measurement of the concept of power-sharing; by identifying key correlates of power-sharing institutions; and by exploring open questions in the literature. Of particular relevance to the post-conflict transition of MENA countries that have suffered from civil war is the discussion of the consequences of power-sharing in section 4, where we have addressed the impact of power-sharing on post-conflict democratization as well as its impact on the risk of war recurring. We have shown that the literature is equivocal on these important questions as results of landmark publications on the topic are sensitive to small changes in the underlying data and measurement. We have also considered fruitful ways to enrich the literature on power-sharing by considering the mechanism of social identification as one potential pathway through which power-sharing can affect political preferences. We explored whether or not minority groups that are included in a government coalition are more likely to identify nationally and suggested this as a question that is worth further exploration. We also considered the role of external intervention in shaping post-conflict trajectories in countries with and without power-sharing. Our results suggest that intervention on behalf of rebel groups weakens the positive effect of inclusive or dispersive power-sharing institutions.

Appendix Table 3.1: Replication of Graham et al. (2017)

Graham et al. (2017) analyse the effects of three types of power-sharing agreements—constraining, dispersive, and inclusive—on democratic survival. They find that only 'constraining' power-sharing has consistently positive effects on democratic survival and that, in the subset of countries that have experienced 'civil war', inclusive power-sharing after the civil war also promotes democratic survival, whereas dispersive power-sharing has a negative effect. This analysis depends on identifying and coding all periods of internal armed conflict and in this replication, we focus on whether the results are sensitive to the coding of countries as 'post-conflict' or not. Specifically, they use the UCDP/PRIO dataset definition of conflict, which includes all countries that have experienced a conflict that has caused at least 1,000 cumulative deaths according to the UCDP/PRIO dataset.

Given significant ambiguities in the coding of civil war, an issue that is discussed in depth in Sambanis (2004), we replicate their analysis using different conflict data. We draw data from Sambanis and Schulhofer-Wohl (2019). We focus on Table 4 in the Graham, Miller, and Strøm article, specifically on how switching data sources changes results for the interaction term between the post-conflict indicator with each type of power-sharing institution. Results are shown below, in a Table reproducing results published in Sambanis and Schulhofer-Wohl (2019). There is a marked change in the estimated effect of dispersive power-sharing when we use different data on conflicts. The coefficient goes from negative to positive and significant using their three preferred model specifications. The magnitude of the effect of inclusive power-sharing also increases substantially and the effect of constraining power-sharing is attenuated becoming statistically insignificant in model 3. Thus, we find that both inclusive and dispersive power-sharing can help promote democratic survival (Appendix Figure 3.2).

Appendix Table 3.1 Replication of Graham et al. (2017)

	(1)	(2)	(3)	(4)	(5)	(6)
	Table 4 Model 1		Table 4 Model 2		Table 4 Model 3	
	ACD	SSW	ACD	SSW	ACD	SSW
Inclusive Power-sharing	−0.0648 (0.0771)	−0.0311 (0.0863)	−0.0534 (0.0933)	−0.00145 (0.111)	−0.145 (0.102)	−0.0529 (0.124)
Dispersive Power-sharing	−0.0128 (0.0941)	−0.0423 (0.0955)	−0.0669 (0.0966)	−0.0810 (0.0981)	−0.0841 (0.102)	−0.0971 (0.104)
Constraining Power-sharing	0.397*** (0.0839)	0.363*** (0.0818)	0.323*** (0.0925)	0.294*** (0.0894)	0.353*** (0.0973)	0.336*** (0.0952)
Post-Civil War (10 Years)	0.593*** (0.175)	4.814*** (0.651)	0.736*** (0.196)	4.799*** (0.671)	0.797*** (0.198)	5.481*** (0.707)
Inclusive ×x Post-Civil War	2.113*** (0.450)	18.80*** (2.033)	2.249*** (0.599)	18.98*** (2.134)	2.403*** (0.628)	22.25*** (2.360)
Dispersive × Post-Civil War	−0.440*** (0.162)	1.447** (0.682)	−0.452*** (0.166)	1.358** (0.671)	−0.489*** (0.166)	1.367** (0.694)
Constraining × Post-Civil War	0.250 (0.162)	0.577** (0.243)	0.309* (0.172)	0.493** (0.246)	0.383** (0.184)	0.424* (0.253)
Ethno-Linguistic Fractionalization	−0.489* (0.264)	−0.517* (0.275)	−0.538* (0.280)	−0.581** (0.290)	−0.375 (0.285)	−0.420 (0.293)
Regional Polity	0.0990*** (0.0173)	0.104*** (0.0183)	0.0981*** (0.0182)	0.101*** (0.0190)	0.0913*** (0.0189)	0.0944*** (0.0197)
GDP/capita (logged)	0.597*** (0.0789)	0.547*** (0.0805)	0.516*** (0.0958)	0.470*** (0.0926)	0.486*** (0.0938)	0.441*** (0.0907)
GDP Growth	0.00859 (0.0105)	0.00834 (0.0102)	0.00789 (0.00966)	0.00790 (0.00948)	0.00618 (0.0112)	0.00564 (0.0112)
Fuel Dependence	−0.0110* (0.00586)	−0.0206*** (0.00555)	−0.0113** (0.00557)	−0.0200*** (0.00526)	−0.0130** (0.00569)	−0.0214*** (0.00530)
Population (logged)	−0.0640 (0.0420)	−0.0380 (0.0413)	0.0114 (0.0455)	0.0282 (0.0453)	0.00895 (0.0456)	0.0241 (0.0447)
Past Democratic Breakdown	−0.211*** (0.0598)	−0.224*** (0.0614)	−0.197*** (0.0628)	−0.203*** (0.0643)	−0.182*** (0.0670)	−0.185*** (0.0676)
Democracy Age	−0.00468** (0.00234)	−0.00185 (0.00292)	−0.00783*** (0.00273)	−0.00504 (0.00316)	−0.00843*** (0.00259)	−0.00582** (0.00273)
Freedom House			2.017*** (0.411)	1.710*** (0.396)	1.861*** (0.424)	1.460*** (0.415)
Horizontal Constraints			−0.177 (0.398)	−0.0496 (0.392)	−0.157 (0.422)	−0.0817 (0.415)
Recent Regular Turnover					0.342*** (0.126)	0.278** (0.128)
Recent Irregular Turnover					−0.576*** (0.183)	−0.518*** (0.177)
Polity					0.0360 (0.0273)	0.0371 (0.0278)
Disruption					1.021 (0.756)	0.607 (0.807)
Constant	−2.578*** (0.844)	−2.384*** (0.867)	−4.401*** (1.019)	−3.915*** (1.024)	−4.434*** (1.040)	−3.835*** (1.028)
Years of Power-sharing Cubic Polynomials	Y	Y	Y	Y	Y	Y
Observations	2,181	2,181	2,137	2,137	2,124	2,124

Robust standard errors in parentheses
*** p<0.01, ** p<0.05, * p<0.1

Appendix Table 3.2 Multinomial Logit Regressions of Conflict on Lost Autonomy and Exclusion

	(1)	(2)	(3)	(4)	(5)
Ethnic Grievances:					
Exclusion	0.987**	0.960**	0.694*	0.004+	0.004
	(0.314)	(0.304)	(0.313)	(0.002)	(0.003)
Lost autonomy	1.098**	1.024**	0.806**	0.012***	0.013***
	(0.354)	(0.341)	(0.282)	(0.002)	(0.004)
Autonomy downgrade		2.064***	1.920***	0.065*	0.074*
		(0.454)	(0.487)	(0.027)	(0.032)
Group-level controls:					
Regional concentration	1.562***	1.554***		0.009**	
	(0.372)	(0.367)		(0.003)	
Relative group size	0.536	0.39	−0.479	−0.007	−0.01
	(0.668)	(0.0677)	(0.823)	(0.005)	(0.008)
Separatist kin $_{t-1}$	0.555**	0.587**	0.634**	0.008*	0.007*
	(0.202)	(0.200)	(0.234)	(0.003)	(0.004)
Regional autonomy	0.21	0.319	0.14	0.003	0.005
	(0.298)	(0.278)	(0.347)	(0.005)	(0.006)
Hydrocarbon reserves $_{t-1}$			0.667*		0.004
			(0.276)		(0.003)
Mountainous terrain			0.211		−0.002
			(0.356)		(0.004)
Noncontiguity			1.938**		0.021
			(0.746)		(0.021)
Country-level controls:					
ln(GDP per capita $_{t-1}$)	0.454*	0.441*	0.368	0.007	0.009+
	(0.215)	(0.218)	(0.242)	(0.004)	(0.005)
ln(country population $_{t-1}$)	0.339**	0.314**	0.286*	−0.005	−0.009
	(0.108)	(0.107)	(0.111)	(0.007)	(0.009)
Democracy $_{t-1}$	−1.068	−1.049	−1.785*	−0.021*	−0.02
	(0.749)	(0.714)	(0.784)	(0.010)	(0.013)
Federal state $_{t-1}$	0.526	0.512	0.607+	0.003	0.001
	(0.371)	(0.355)	(0.328)	(0.011)	(0.014)
Number of rel. groups	−0.034***	−0.033***	−0.033***	−0.000	−0.000
	(0.007)	(0.007)	(0.007)	(0.001)	(0.001)
Systemic Conditions:					
Cold War	−0.037	−0.062	−0.312	0.000	−0.002
	(0.326)	(0.334)	(0.364)	(0.004)	(0.005)
Region FEs	Yes	Yes	Yes	No	No
Country FEs	No	No	No	Yes	Yes
Only concentrated groups	No	No	Yes	No	Yes
No. of groups	686	686	528	686	528
No. of countries	140	140	121	140	121
Observations	23612	23612	18169	23612	18169

Notes: Models 1–3 include region dummies (not shown) and are estimated with logit regression. Models 4 and 5 include country dummies (not shown) and are estimated with OLS. All models include controls for time dependence and a constant (not shown). Standard errors clustered by country in parentheses. +$p<0.10$, *$p<0.05$, **$p<0.01$, ***$p<0.001$.

Power-Sharing and Peace-Building 89

Appendix Table 3.3 Reproducing Results from Bormann, Toukan, and Sambanis (2019) on the Effect of Territorial Autonomy on Post-conflict risk of War Recurrence

	Dependent Variable: Ethnic Territorial Armed Conflict Onset					
	(1)	(2)	(3)	(4)	(5)	(6)
Inclusion	−1.47***		−2.86***	−1.95***		
	(0.44)		(0.31)	(0.58)		
Autonomy	0.20		−0.69	−0.34		
	(0.29)		(0.47)	(0.44)		
Senior Inclusion		−1.94***			−1.46***	−1.64***
		(0.30)			(0.40)	(0.49)
Senior Autonomy		0.85**			0.62	1.11***
		(0.35)			(0.39)	(0.42)
Junior Inclusion		−1.27**			−2.70***	−1.73***
		(0.53)			(0.29)	(0.60)
Junior Autonomy		0.15			−1.17**	−0.78
		(0.30)			(0.53)	(0.49)
Intervention history			−0.41		−0.39	
			(0.33)		(0.33)	
Gov. intervention				0.39		0.33
				(0.33)		(0.32)
Rebel intervention				−0.63		−0.57
				(0.38)		(0.37)
Relative group size	0.99	1.02	0.01	1.18	−0.48	1.04
	(2.43)	(2.38)	(2.75)	(2.66)	(2.85)	(2.70)
Relative group size sq.	−4.12	−4.16	−3.11	−5.28	−2.40	−5.22
	(3.09)	(3.05)	(3.63)	(3.72)	(3.72)	(3.72)
Number of excl.	−0.02**	−0.02*	−0.01	−0.01	−0.002	−0.001
groups	(0.01)	(0.01)	(0.02)	(0.02)	(0.02)	(0.02)
Federal	−0.34	−0.34	−0.22	−0.12	−0.20	−0.16
	(0.33)	(0.34)	(0.32)	(0.31)	(0.31)	(0.14)
log gdp lag	0.07	0.08	0.10	0.20	0.12	0.23
	(0.10)	(0.10)	(0.12)	(0.14)	(0.13)	(0.14)
log population	0.25***	0.25***	0.23**	0.12	0.22**	0.14
	(0.10)	(0.09)	(0.09)	(0.09)	(0.09)	(0.09)
Ongoing conflict	0.57*	0.55	0.33	0.30	0.26	0.26
	(0.34)	(0.34)	(0.37)	(0.38)	(0.37)	(0.37)
Peace years	−0.15***	−0.15***	−0.19***	−0.18***	−0.18***	−0.16***
	(0.06)	(0.06)	(0.05)	(0.05)	(0.05)	(0.05)
Autonomy × intervention hist.			1.48**			
			(0.59)			
Inclusion × intervention hist.			1.84***			
			(0.53)			
Autonomy × gov intervention				−0.98**		
				(0.48)		
Inclusion × gov intervention				−0.13		
				(1.01)		
Autonomy × reb. intervention				2.60***		
				(0.87)		

(Continued)

Appendix Table 3.3 continued

	Dependent Variable: Ethnic Territorial Armed Conflict Onset					
	(1)	*(2)*	*(3)*	*(4)*	*(5)*	*(6)*
Inclusion × reb. intervention				0.34 (0.97)		
PC Inclusion × intervention hist.					2.15*** (0.64)	
PC Autonomy × intervention hist.					2.00*** (0.69)	
PC Inclusion × gov intervention						−0.21 (1.31)
PC Autonomy × gov intervention						−0.77 (0.54)
PC Inclusion × reb. intervention						0.76 (1.25)
PC Autonomy × reb. intervention						2.92** (0.83)
Constant	−5.22*** (1.37)	−5.23*** (1.35)	−4.64*** (1.25)	−4.66*** (1.25)	−4.84*** (1.33)	−5.13** (1.17)
Observations	1,989	1,989	1,694	1,694	1,694	1,694
Log Likelihood	−218.88	−218.66	−182.14	−180.05	−180.95	−179.40
Akaike Inf. Crit.	465.76	469.32	398.27	400.10	399.91	402.80

Notes:
*$p<0.1$, **$p<0.05$, ***$p<0.01$ Standard errors clustered on country.

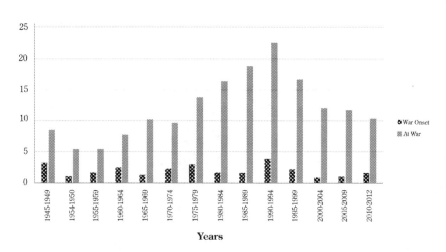

Appendix Figure 3.1 Global patterns of onset and prevalence of civil war by 5-year period; 1945–2012

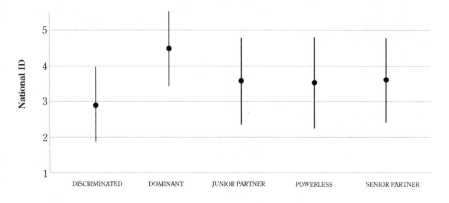

Appendix Figure 3.2 Strength of national vs ethnic identification by power status
Note: Afrobarometer data on national identification merged with EPR data on ethnic exclusion.

Notes

1 See Appendix Figure 1. Plotting the onset and overall prevalence of the civil war around the world from 1945 until 2012, we see no clear pattern in the onset of the civil war since 1945. Yet there is a steadily increasing prevalence of the civil war over that period until the early 1990s, followed by a sharp drop starting in 1995 after the end of a surge of new conflicts surrounding the collapse of the USSR. Data on civil wars are drawn from Sambanis and Schulhofer-Wohl (2019).
2 They code civil war outcomes as much as possible on the basis of whether the rebels achieved their end of taking control of the central government or the region they are fighting for, rather than on whether there was a formal 'negotiated settlement' or a 'truce' (p. 3). The nine P-S cases include the political deal that ended the period of '*La Violencia*' in Colombia in the late 1950s and the institutional arrangements that followed the end of Apartheid and white rule in South Africa and Rhodesia, respectively.
3 Their data ends in 1998. Another ten cases can be coded using the same criteria by extending coding to the period from 1999 to 2005. See Roeder and Rothchild, 2005 and PRIO/UCDP Peace Agreement Dataset.
4 Cammett and Malesky (2012) propose a new typological classification, distinguishing between closed-list PR, open-list PR, executive coalition, specialized veto rules, proportional civil service appointment rules, and forced legislative coalition. They also code P-S along a set of additional dimensions, including economic, territorial, and military. Glassmyer and Sambanis (2008) distinguish between political and military and political power-sharing and code some form of military power-sharing (integrating former combatants in the government military) in 30 per cent of all civil wars. Military power-sharing refers to agreement to integrate rebel groups into the military either by directly allotting positions (including in the officer corps) to former rebel groups, or by opening up enlistment possibilities to previously excluded groups (usually ethnic groups).
5 See Mukherjee (2006) on the impact that offers of political power-sharing can have during the negotiation of settlements for ending civil war.

6 In the context of post-war transitions, most studies of P-S usually refer to institutional outcomes that are codified in treaties. Yet the universe of cases of P-S is likely to be larger since power-sharing concessions are often necessary to end civil wars even in the presence of significant asymmetries of military power (where most analysts would code the war as ending in a 'victory').
7 McGarry and O'Leary (2009, pp. 692–693) explain in these terms their recommendation of a PR system for ethnically divided places like Iraq: a PR system is an assurance against one-party rule and against the likelihood of artificially constructing a majority in the legislature out of a plurality in the electorate.
8 Bormann explores the relationship between ethnic coalitions and civil war. He finds that they reduce the risk of territorial civil war but have no effect on conflicts over control of the central government.
9 Sambanis et al. (2018) code two versions of their autonomy concessions variable, one 'strict' list and a more 'lenient' one. The 'strict' list includes only fully implemented concessions though the lenient list includes any concessions announced by the state regardless of implementation status on the assumption that such announcements might actually impact group behaviour towards the state.
10 Magaloni (2008) explores the conditions under which power-sharing agreements between autocrats and members of the ruling elite are credible. This type of P-S is different from democratic P-S in that the focus is on including elites who can undermine the dictator's rule if excluded, rather than on including large segments of the population.
11 Other empirical proxies of the reputation theory include the economic or psychological value of the land under dispute. The key argument is that the higher the value of land the less likely governments are to accommodate the groups opposing them.
12 As Fearon (2003) shows, most countries in Europe and the Americas have one large group that comprises the majority of the population (often with a share of total population above 80 per cent). By contrast, most African countries have at least two large groups, with the size of the second largest group often around 40 per cent of the population.
13 However, given the appeal of the conceptual argument, it is worth considering if different empirical formulations of the argument have more predictive power. We return to this question in the conclusion, where we suggest a modification of Walter's argument that could be explored in the context of the case study project.
14 An exception is Wucherpfennig et al. (2016), who use an instrumental variable approach to estimate the causal effect of political exclusion.
15 On FIRCs, see Downes and Monten (2014).
16 The stronger the population's sense of national identity, the lower the probability of violence along ethno-sectarian lines, and vice-versa. For a model of this process, showing how countries can get stuck in high ethnic conflict and ethnic identification equilibria as compared to low-conflict and national identity equilibria, see Sambanis and Shayo (2013).
17 It is known that decentralization in and of itself need not produce consistent effects of national identification across countries. Miguel's (2004) comparison of Kenya and Tanzania makes this point clearly, exploiting variation in the provision of public goods and collective action across broadly similar areas of the two countries to argue that the higher degree of collective action observed in Tanzania is due to the nation-building policies of that government. Kenya, with a roughly similar degree of decentralization in local governance, produces markedly lower degree of collective action in ethnically heterogeneous areas due to the absence of concerted efforts by the central government to reduce the salience of ethnic and tribal identities.

18 Eifert, Miguel, and Posner (2010), analysing Afrobarometer data from over 35,000 respondents in several surveys in ten African countries finds that ethnic identities become more salient by exposure to political competition. The closer a survey is done to a competitive Presidential election, the more likely are respondents to identify ethnically.
19 Interestingly, no study I know of has considered if inclusion increases the national identification of included minorities while decreasing the national identification of majority groups, who pay 'heterogeneity costs' due to power-sharing.
20 The mechanisms underlying these effects on identification should be clarified. If, for example, social identification is assumed to be influenced by the degree of everyday contact between different groups, then the prediction outlined above would seem reasonable. If, however, group identification is heavily influenced by the rhetoric of its leaders or specific policies, then it is not clear if we should expect to find a difference in social identification when we compare inclusive and dispersive regimes.
21 http://www.afrobarometer.org/data [Accessed 4 March 2018].
22 The main question used by other studies to explore determinants of national identification is: 'Suppose that you had to choose between being a [Ghanaian/Kenyan/etc.] and being a [respondent's ethnic group, choosing among a list of groups pre-determined by Afrobarometer]. Which of these two groups do you feel most strongly attached to?'
23 It is possible that the EPR-based classification of groups into the different inclusion categories (e.g., 'junior partner' or 'powerless') is too coarse for our purposes. Take Nigeria, for example, where there is an agreement between the Christian South and Muslim North to alternate the presidency. EPR codes both Muslim and Christian groups as Senior Partners because of that arrangement. Yet the identity of the President might matter in shaping their co-ethnics national identification. There is an uptick in national identification for the Muslim Hausa in 2008 when there was a Muslim President in Nigeria relative to 2005 and 2012/13 when there was a Christian in office. The Yoruba, two thirds of whom are Christians and one third Muslim, show a similar, albeit weaker, pattern.
24 I also note that only about half of respondents in Afrobarometer surveys are matched to ethnic groups that are included in the EPR dataset, which is our source of data on inclusion. The EPR dataset only codes 'politically relevant' groups. An alternative approach would be to focus only on dispersive power-sharing, which could be coded for all individuals' ethnic group affiliations in the Afrobarometer surveys. This would entail additional coding of cases as there is currently no available dataset that codes regional autonomy or other forms of dispersive power-sharing for all ethnic groups in Africa.
25 Alan E. Buchanan, 2007 (2004, ch. 9).
26 See e.g., Nimni, 2005; Weller et al., 2008; Weller and Nobbs, 2010; Rezvani, 2014.
27 Although this argument is compelling, the acknowledgement that successful ethno-federalism should be consent-based begs the question whether it is the appropriate system to use in the aftermath of an ethnic war.
28 They cite the example of Nigeria, which 'is so centralized that it has been described as a "hollow federation"'.
29 There could be different mechanisms underlying the association between lost autonomy and outbreak of conflict. Siroky and Cuffe (2015) focus on recent cases of loss of autonomy and argue that groups that have lost autonomy recently are more likely to be politically mobilized with established group leaders and are therefore in a better position to mount a violent challenge against the state. Sambanis and Zinn (2006) draw on the literature on social movements to argue

that lost autonomy is a form of indiscriminate repression that can radicalize moderates and induce them to support the use of violence. Germann and Sambanis (2021) look not just at recent cases of lost autonomy, but also at historical autonomy that was lost during the de-colonization period and argue that lost autonomy represents decline in status that can generate resentment and support ethno-nationalist calls for regaining autonomy.
30 Wimmer, et al., 2009; Cederman, et al., 2010, 2013.
31 Cederman, et al., 2015; see also McGarry and O'Leary 2009.
32 An example is Cammett and Malesky (2012), who consider the impact of different electoral rules. They find that closed-list proportional representation (PR) systems promote stability by reducing the salience of 'greed' and 'grievance' motives for civil war. Close-list PR strengthens parties and adds checks on the executive while reducing incentives for personalistic voting.
33 The types of constraining institutions that they consider include judicial review; military legislator ban; freedom of religion.
34 On the use of electoral institutions and constitutional design to address this issue, see Horowitz (1985), chapters 14 and 15.
35 War recurrence data is from the ACD dataset. Recurrence is defined as the onset of a new round of conflict with 25 deaths or more per year. This is as in Cederman et al., (2015).

Part II
Country Studies

4 Causes, Consequences, and Future Directions of the Syrian Conflict

Nader Kabbani and Alma Boustati

1 Introduction

The Syrian conflict has been one of the most devastating and destructive wars of the twenty-first century. Since the start of the conflict in March 2011, over 600,000 people have been killed (SOHR, 2021). Around six million people, from a pre-conflict population of 22 million, have left the country as refugees (UNHCR, 2021). A further seven million people have been internally displaced. The United Nations' Economic and Social Commission for Western Asia (UN ESCWA, 2020) has estimated the economic cost of the conflict during its first eight years to be USD 442 billion. By 2014, at the conflict's peak, the regime had relinquished control of over two-thirds of the country and Syria had become the site for a plethora of competing political and military forces and fundamentalist groups, including a new, malignant, Islamic State.

Since then, with the support of its allies, Russia, Iran, and Iranian-backed militia, the regime has been able to regain control over the country's main cities and economic arteries. As early as 2017, the regime began encouraging factories to reopen and launched a bid to reconstruct the country. However, despite peace and reconciliation initiatives being pursued along multiple fronts, no political settlement has emerged. Indeed, the conflict continues to rage in parts of the country. Reconstruction has stalled as a result of the continued unrest, stifling international sanctions, and the predatory business practices of the regime. Rather than witnessing a period of reconciliation and economic growth, the current phase of the Syrian conflict has been characterized by continued violence, infighting within the regime and among its allies, severe social and economic pressures on the Syrian people, and a continuation of frayed relations with the outside world.

In 2020, the arrival of the coronavirus pandemic compounded the challenges facing the country. Covid-19 strained Syria's battered healthcare system and disrupted economic activity. Together with a financial meltdown in neighbouring Lebanon, the pandemic constrained the flow of remittances and humanitarian aid to the country and reshaped the priorities of donor countries. The successive blows to Syria's economy resulted in a precipitous

DOI: 10.4324/9781003344414-7

fall in the value of the Syrian Pound and led to further economic hardship, especially among displaced populations and refugees in neighbouring countries which were facing their own pandemic challenges. The financial strain also exposed fissures and discord in the regime, as the government struggled to secure the revenue needed to cover its mounting fiscal obligations. And yet, the challenges posed by the global pandemic and the financial crisis in Lebanon have also presented a new opportunity for the Syrian regime and the international community to explore a pragmatic political resolution to the conflict.

Syria today is at a crossroads; decisions made over the coming months by the regime and the international community will determine whether it begins the long, slow process of healing; enters a prolonged period of stagnation; or plunges once again into conflict. This chapter analyses key issues surrounding efforts to secure economic recovery and explores post-conflict alternatives that might promote peace and stability. Section 2 revisits the underlying causes of conflict. Section 3 reviews the conflict's economic and social costs. Section 4 discusses short- to medium-term approaches towards economic recovery and building peace. Section 5 concludes.

2 The Underlying Causes of the Syrian Conflict

Several alternative explanations for the causes of the Syrian conflict have been put forward. They include environmental factors, economic conditions, political exclusion, ethnic divisions, institutional weaknesses, and external meddling. Before discussing future directions for the country, it is important to understand what combination of these factors was responsible for the outbreak of the conflict.

2.1 Climate Change

Some analysts attribute the eruption of the conflict to economic grievances that were the result of climate change. The argument put forth is that the 2007–2010 drought caused mass internal migration—some 300,000 people migrated from the northeast to the south according to Selby et al. (2017)—and created economic and social pressures, including rising unemployment and food insecurity which, it has been argued, caused or contributed to the conflict (Gleick, 2014). This was exacerbated by mismanagement and poor policy responses to the drought, including unsustainable water-use practices and the neglect of rapidly growing and irregular urban peripheries fed through internal migration.

These explanations, however, have been met with doubt. Selby (2019) argues that Syria's pre–civil war agrarian crisis was caused more by long-term structural factors than drought-induced scarcity, primarily the collapse of Syria's oil rent-led model of development and the existence of an ethnically contested borderland and frontier zone in northeast Syria. According to

Selby et al. (2017, p. 232), 'For its advocates, this Syria-climate change thesis is powerful not so much for its own sake, but because it illustrates the chaos that may ensue as greenhouse gas emissions rise'. They go on to show that the severity of the drought and the migration patterns it triggered are not strongly correlated with the chronology and geography of the Syrian conflict. They claim that the migration patterns observed were more probably caused by economic liberalization than by severe drought. Indeed, it is difficult to argue that were it not for the drought the country would have avoided its descent into conflict.

2.2 *Economic Conditions and Economic Liberalization*

When Bashar al-Assad came to power in 2000, the government initiated a series of economic reforms to move the country away from a state-led economy and towards a 'social market economy' (Figure 4.1). Azmeh (2014) argues that with oil revenues declining, the model of a rentier-based political economy that the country had pursued since the 1960s was no longer affordable. Indeed, the state encouraged private and foreign direct investment and eliminated energy subsidies and guarantees for public sector employment. The government removed barriers to private sector entry for many industries and reformed some of the country's rigid regulatory frameworks. As with any process of economic liberalization, the impact of these policies is complex and controversial. Some groups were no doubt negatively affected even if overall economic conditions improved.

In macroeconomic terms, the state's policy of economic liberalization appears to have been successful and allowed for increased participation by the private sector. Between 1997 and 2007, nominal GDP per capita more than doubled while real GDP per capita increased by 15 per cent (World Bank, 2019b). Macroeconomic conditions were stable and foreign direct investment increased from 0.5 per cent of GDP in 2001 to 2.8 per cent in 2008. Between 2000 and 2009, the contribution of the private sector to GDP

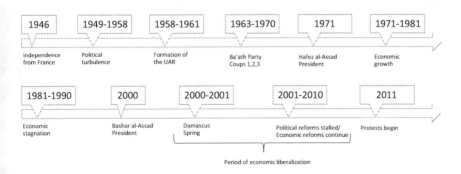

Figure 4.1 Overview of the Syrian context: timeline

increased from 36 per cent to 65 per cent and economic growth averaged 4.5 per cent per year (Syrian Central Bureau of Statistics, 2011).

Economic liberalization appeared to have contributed to lower poverty rates and less inequality (Devarajan et al., 2016). Poverty rates using the lower poverty line declined from 14.3 per cent in 1997 to 12.3 per cent in 2007 (Abu-Ismail et al., 2011).[1] Furthermore, the share of consumption among the poorest 20 per cent of households increased from 8.1 per cent in 1997 to 8.9 per cent in 2007, while the share of consumption among the richest 20 per cent declined from 41.8 per cent to 40.3 per cent. Multi-dimensional indicators of both poverty and inequality also showed significant declines between 1990 and 2010. Syria also fared well when compared to Arab countries with similar levels of development such as Egypt (UN ESCWA, 2016). Indeed, at the start of the conflict, Syria had a large and stable middle class. Finally, poverty rates declined in all rural and urban regions of the country, except for the drought-stricken rural northeast. Taken together, these results suggest that economic growth in Syria was largely inclusive and pro-poor.

Some research has suggested that an expanding youth population might increase the likelihood of domestic unrest and agitation for change, especially under stagnant economic conditions (Urdal, 2004). Syria prior to the conflict does not fit neatly into this characterization (see Figure 4.2). First, while the share of youth in the population in 2010 was high at 20.6 per cent, as compared to the global average of 17.5 per cent, the youth population had peaked a decade earlier in 2000 at 22.3 per cent and was actually in decline (UN Statistical Databases, 2019). Furthermore, while employment growth averaged only 1.3 per cent per year between 2000 and 2010 (SCBS, 2002–2010), less than the overall population growth rate of 3 per cent (UN, 2019), overall unemployment rates fell from an average of 11 per cent between 2001 and 2003 to 9.2 per cent between 2008 and 2010. Youth unemployment rates also declined from an average of 23 per cent between 2001 and 2003 to 20 per cent between 2008 and 2010 (SCBS, 2002–2010). Together with healthy average annual economic growth rates of 4.5 per cent, it would be a stretch

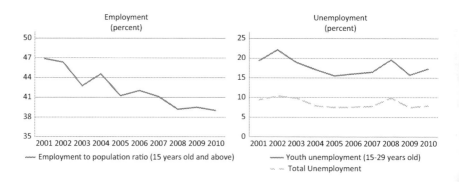

Figure 4.2 Main macroeconomic indicators

to characterize economic growth in Syria as stagnant. Indeed, weak employment growth was partly the result of a decline in the rates of female participation in the labour force (World Bank, 2017b). Female participation in the labour market fell from 22 per cent in 2001 to 14 per cent in 2010 (SCBS, 2002–2010), mainly in the rural areas of the country.

Some have argued that the 2008 global financial crisis and the resulting shocks to demand heavily affected the Middle East and North Africa (MENA) region and may have contributed to the uprisings (Lawson, 2018). While the global financial crisis did affect Syria, its economy was not as integrated into the global economy as other MENA countries, such as Tunisia and Egypt. As a result, the effects of the global financial crisis were weaker and dissipated faster than elsewhere in the region. Unemployment rates increased from 8.4 per cent in 2008 to 11.0 per cent in 2009 before settling back down to 8.5 per cent in 2010 (SCBS, 2002–2010). Also, annual economic growth remained above 4 per cent during this entire period (Devadas et al., 2019).

Yet, some communities benefited less from the economic reforms than others. Between 1997 and 2007, poverty rates fell more sharply in urban areas (21 per cent) as compared to rural areas (5.5 per cent). This may have caused rural communities to feel marginalized. Furthermore, evidence suggests that while poverty declined, vulnerability (based on the upper poverty line) increased slightly from 33.2 per cent in 1997 to 33.6 per cent in 2007 (Abu-Ismail et al., 2011). Studies suggest that it is actually vulnerable populations that are most likely to be involved in social unrest (Desai and Yousef, 2019). Moreover, while economic growth was inclusive, the cost of the economic reforms was most probably borne more heavily by the poorer sections of society. Household survey data tend to under-represent both the poorest and richest 2–3 per cent of households. As a result, they might not include rising inequality at the extreme ends of the income distribution. Goulden (2011) claims that inequalities in access to housing produced a socioeconomic crisis for those living in 'informal' settlements—particularly around Damascus—that may have sparked the civil unrest.

Thus, while overall economic conditions do not appear to have been the primary cause of the 2011 crisis, it is likely they were a contributing factor. A more fundamental cause was the lack of any significant reform in political governance. Indeed, early demands of the protestors were largely political, an issue to which we now turn.

2.3 Stalled Political Reforms and Rising Corruption

In contrast to economic reform efforts, political reforms remained stalled except for a brief period of openness from 2000 to 2001 when Bashar al-Assad first came to power. Indeed, among MENA countries Syria stands out more in terms of political than economic indicators. In 2010, Syria scored lower than the MENA average on political freedoms and higher on perceived corruption and distrust of government institutions in comparison to other Arab Spring countries (World Bank, 2017). While the pre-2011 economic indicators for Syria paint a positive or mixed picture, the political indicators were unambiguously negative.

Since the 1950s, the political situation in Syria can be characterized as an 'authoritarian bargain', a social contract present in practically all Arab countries (Desai et al. 2009; Assaad, 2014). Under this bargain, citizens tacitly agree to give up political rights in exchange for public services, benefits, transfers, and jobs. The bargain is sustainable in those countries blessed with natural resources which therefore derive a sufficient amount of rents to maintain their public benefits at an acceptable level. However, it can be unsustainable in countries with limited natural resources. Countries with declining natural resources, like Syria, Egypt, and Yemen were especially susceptible to social unrest since their governments had failed to meet their end of the bargain. The solution in such cases is either to grant the citizens greater political rights or to increase repression.

In the case of Syria, political reforms were under consideration even before 2000. However, the regime had not taken steps to initiate them. A key issue centred on Article 8 of the Syrian constitution which entrenched political power in the hands of the Ba'ath party and prevented the emergence of new parties to challenge it. Control of the political system allowed the regime to keep elections uncontested, control government institutions, and dominate professional associations. Together with its control of the military and the security forces, the regime's monopoly on political activity was the third element in its hold on power. However, as the regime gained influence over the business community it had an opportunity to loosen its grip on the political process without jeopardizing this hold. The delay in opening the political space arguably contributed to the initial unrest in early 2011.

As Safadi and Neaime (2017) argue, Syria's exclusionary political system along with its unflinching autocracy, weak governance structures, and the deteriorating social contract were determining factors in the uprising's outbreak and spread. Indeed, the demands of the protesters at the start were mainly political, including calls for greater democracy, justice, and freedom. Consistent with the idea of a deteriorating social contract, the Syrian government had been reducing access to public services, benefits, and employment since 2000, but had not compensated its citizens with an increase in political rights and freedoms. Instead, increased corruption and crony capitalism during the 2000s further eroded the ability of the state to keep its side of the contract.

Perceptions of corruption increased substantially between 2003 and 2011, at the same time as the government's main push to liberalize the economy was taking place (Transparency International, 2020). In 2003, Syria ranked 66th of 133 countries in terms of perceptions of corruption, outperforming many other countries in the MENA region including Egypt, Lebanon, Morocco, and Turkey. By 2010, Syria's rank had declined to 134th of 178 countries, falling behind these same countries and indicating a rising trend in corruption. Additionally, there was a persistence in over-regulation that allowed insiders to game the system (World Bank, 2017). As a result, the benefits of economic reform tended to flow to individuals who were politically connected and could circumvent restrictions and regulations. Increased corruption and cronyism arguably laid a foundation for the social unrest and ultimately the violent conflict that followed.

2.4 The Social Dimension

In contrast with the stalled process of political reform, the Syrian government began to loosen its tight control over the activities of the non-political civil society. Between 2000 and 2010, the number of registered NGOs tripled. The work of international organizations also expanded, and they began implementing projects outside the sphere of government control. For example, in 2000, the United Nations Development Programme (UNDP) launched the country's first microfinance project in Jabal al-Hoss, one of the poorest areas of the country. International organizations also began to directly support the work of civil society groups. Opportunities for social engagement increased. However, government-sanctioned civil society activity only dealt with social and economic issues; none of them addressed political issues, such as human rights (NGO Platform, 2011). In the end, it was in the political dimension that public grievances spilled over into unrest. When they did, there were no organizations that had both the legal standing and the grassroots legitimacy to engage the regime on behalf of the public.

Some analysts have pointed to sectarian divides as a possible cause of the conflict (Laborie, 2014). Syria is a Sunni-majority country that, since the 1970s, has been controlled by a group from the minority Alawite community. Even though there are lasting scars from the regime's conflict with the Sunni Muslim Brotherhood in the early 1980s, Philips (2015) argues that the 'ancient hatred' narrative does not make sense in the context of Syria. He contends that Syrian national identity shows surprising robustness when compared to other multi-sectarian states such as Lebanon or former Yugoslavia. Indeed, Syria contains a rich mosaic of ethnic groups, including Sunnis, Alawites, Kurds, Druze, Arab Christians, Armenians, Shi'as, and others. Azmeh (2014) points out that leading up to 2011, formerly clear-cut sectarian lines were becoming blurred. The composition of the new economic elite was multi-sectarian, composed of Sunnis, Alawites, and Christians; and interfaith and intersect marriages were becoming more common. The 'new' image of Syria had a secular identity. While there is no denying that the initial protests had a Sunni character, it is only one factor in a more complex narrative that is better understood through the lens of political frustration and class.

One sectarian dimension that came to play a major role during the conflict was the presence of a large Kurdish minority in the northeast parts of the country. The Kurds in Syria, as in neighbouring countries, faced repression and disenfranchisement. Under Bashar al-Assad, the Kurdish communities in Syria were given greater freedom and were allowed to organize and to teach their language but there was no serious attempt to change the status quo. This disenfranchisement culminated in riots in 2004, during which the regime met with a severe crackdown. When the events of 2011 unfolded, many young Kurds joined the protests, but most Kurdish leaders remained silent. This was in part due to a fear of repercussions as had occurred in 2004 and in part due to scepticism regarding any alternative (International Crisis Group, 2013).

Khashanah (2014) contends that the sectarian factor was created after the crisis had begun and advanced by external powers to achieve their geopolitical goals. Phillips (2015) calls the conflict 'semi-sectarian' and concludes that even though sectarian ties played a role in Syrian identity pre-crisis, they only translated into sectarian violence as a result of structural changes in economic, social, and political factors post-conflict. Sectarianism, rather than being a trigger, was deployed by parties in the conflict to fan the flames.

2.5 Weak and Inflexible Institutions

There is no denying that the 2012 uprisings in Tunisia, Egypt, and other Arab countries, as well as the initial success of those uprisings, created a popular momentum among young Syrian activists to push for political change (International Crisis Group, 2011; Azmeh, 2014). Had the uprisings in other Arab countries not occurred, the social unrest in Syria might not have transpired or unfolded the way it did. This so-called 'neighbourhood effect' was the spark that set alight the timbers of political frustration and resentment at the changes in economic conditions. However, why did the unrest in Syria grow and spread, but not in other Arab countries, such as Jordan, that were experiencing a similar kind of social unrest at the time? It was clearly Syria's heavy-handed security response to the evolving crisis that provided the combustible environment which allowed the unrest to grow and spread. In the early weeks of the unrest, the reaction of elements in the security apparatus to relatively minor acts of protests (such as spray-painting slogans and voicing economic grievances) was severe and disproportionate, including detention and mistreatment. This mishandling of the early stages of the protests created a desire for retaliation and fuelled anti-regime sentiment rather than, as presumably had been hoped, dissuading it.

As the civil unrest spread across the country the conflict became militarized, eventually intensifying into a civil war. This process was helped along by two factors. The first was the regime's increasing use of force and its refusal to yield to public demands, which created further outrage and a desire for retaliation. This led to a vicious cycle that slowly became violent. A second factor was the increasing intervention of external powers. As the conflict evolved and intensified, hundreds of Syrian factions emerged. Many were backed by external powers that sought to further their own political and economic agendas. They in turn weaponized sectarian divisions by backing sectarian militias and reinforcing the sectarian dimension of the conflict through the media.

There had been attempts to reform Syria's state institutions, including its security apparatus, before the crisis. Some of these were successful, but most failed. For example, to mitigate the economic effects of lower revenues from oil, the government reduced subsidies on heating oil and other products in 2010. To compensate, it introduced ration cards and a cash transfer programme. However, these programmes were poorly implemented. Another botched programme was an initiative to combat unemployment. As mentioned earlier, the government also failed to take action to address the drought that gripped the country from 2007 to 2010 (Gleick, 2014; Selby et al., 2017). A few initiatives were established outside existing public structures, such as the Syrian Commission for Family Affairs, but these lacked the authority to effect real change. In the end, the government demonstrated a lack of ability to implement real change in the public sector. More importantly, on the eve of the unrest, there were few reform-oriented institutions that it could rely on to deal with the evolving crisis. Instead, it turned to existing deep-state institutions to take charge, including the country's security forces.

In summary, our analysis suggests that the initial spark of the conflict in Syria was provided by the social unrest unfolding in the other Arab countries. This spark was given further oxygen through the mismanagement of the security response and was provided with the means to spread as a result of legitimate grievances, resulting from the disintegration of the governing social contract, which had not been placated by substantive political reforms. Finally, the conflict became militarized due to the heavy-handed regime response followed by the involvement of foreign actors both of which weaponized the sectarian divides of the country.

The above analysis holds important lessons for post-conflict stability and reconstruction of the country. First, the disintegration of the social contract was an important factor in the escalation and spread of the conflict. The future stability of the country must be based on a new or reaffirmed, inclusive and agreed upon, social contract that addresses legitimate economic and social grievances. Second, weak and inflexible public institutions were at the heart of the conflict's spread. As discussed below, these institutions remain weak and inflexible. Unless reformed and improved, they will be unable to deliver an effective post-conflict stability and reconstruction agenda. Third, the current reality is that foreign powers are a key part of the settlement of the conflict in Syria. Any sustainable peace arrangement would thus have to address their interests without impinging on those of the Syrian people.

3 The Economic, Social, and Political Costs of Conflict

Syria today is very different from the pre-conflict country of ten years ago. Indeed, it has undergone profound changes that have altered its social, economic, and political fabric. Understanding the conflict's impact is essential to identifying where to focus peace-building and reconstruction.

3.1 The Heavy Toll of Conflict

The first few months of the Syrian conflict were a time of popular protests and efforts by the regime to contain them. Few expected the conflict to turn into the ten-year civil war that has taken a devastating toll on Syria's social, economic, political, and institutional landscape. Internally displaced persons reached 6.7 million in 2020 (UN OCHA, 2021), creating great hardship and uncertainty for families and overwhelming the ability of the humanitarian agencies to respond. The outflow of refugees, estimated to have reached 5.7 million people by November 2021 (UN HCR, 2021), has placed a heavy burden on the neighbouring countries of Lebanon, Jordan, and Turkey which have hosted most of them.

By the end of 2019, the economic costs of the conflict had reached USD 442 billion (UN ESCWA, 2020); with the physical damage estimated to have been USD 118 billion and the losses from the lower economic output at USD 324 billion. Syria's nominal GDP plummeted from USD 59 billion in 2010 to 20 billion in 2018, a decline of 66 per cent (SCBS, 2011; SCBS, 2019). In addition, over the past ten years, the Syrian pound (SL), tumbled from SL 47 against the dollar in 2010 to SL 460 in 2018 and SL 620 for 2019 (SP Today, 2020). Prices of goods increased more than ten-fold between 2010 and 2018 (SCBS, 2019), while wages increased only four-fold (SCBS, 2019; SCBS, 2011), placing an onerous financial strain on households. By 2018, the median monthly salary of workers was between USD 80 and 90 (SCBS, 2019), not enough to meet even the basic needs of a family.

The Syrian pound has continued to fall, reaching SL 3,540 against the dollar in November 2021 (SP Today, 2021). To place this in context, accounting for salary adjustments, an employee earning 1,000 dollars per month in 2010 would make less than 20 dollars today, not even enough to put food on the table for their family. Not surprisingly, as people struggle to make ends meet and engage with a wartime economy, petty corruption increased and has become institutionalized across the country. Households have been forced to liquidate assets and supplement their income through other means, such as remittances, social assistance, and informal activities. Incidents of child labour and child marriage have also increased as household coping strategies have become increasingly desperate (UN OCHA, 2021).

By 2020, close to 90 per cent of the population lived below the poverty line, up from 80 per cent in 2019, and around 60–65 per cent are estimated to live in extreme poverty (UN OCHA, 2021). In addition, opportunities for work remain scarce. The economic situation in the country has been deteriorating, due to the lack of foreign investment, crippling international sanctions, the coronavirus pandemic, and a financial meltdown in neighbouring Lebanon. As a result, the unemployment rate in 2020 stood at 50 per cent

UN OCHA (2020), similar to what it was at the peak of the conflict in 2015 and up from an estimated 30 per cent in 2018 (SCBS, 2019).

International sanctions have stifled economic activity. Trade sanctions by the United States and the European Union have resulted in limited investment and contributed to economic hardship (Lund, 2019). Additionally, they also imposed financial sanctions on individuals and companies affiliated with the regime through travel bans and frozen assets (Walker, 2016). Altogether, the negative impact of these sanctions on the national economy has affected the civilian population as much as the regime associates and may even have strengthened the regime's hold on the country (Samaha, 2019).

3.2 Devastation Across Economic Sectors

All sectors of the Syrian economy witnessed large declines in output during the conflict. However, some sectors were hit harder than others. In terms of relative contribution to GDP, agricultural output fell from 18 per cent of GDP before the conflict to 14 per cent by 2018 (SCBS, 2011, 2015, 2019). The agricultural sector is arguably the main sector of concern, as it provides the most basic of commodities, food, in addition to employment and income. In the years prior to the conflict, the agricultural sector played a key role in the Syrian economy, accounting for 20 to 25 per cent of value added to the GDP and employing 26 per cent of the economically active population (World Bank, 2019a). As of 2016, as a result of the conflict, the agricultural sector had suffered an estimated USD 16 billion loss in damaged assets with an additional destruction of agricultural infrastructure, such as irrigation systems, estimated at USD 3 billion (FAO, 2017).

The contribution of manufacturing and mining to GDP fell from 22 per cent before the conflict to 13 per cent by 2018. This partly reflects a sharp decline in oil extraction in the eastern governorates of the country, which remain outside the control of the government. However, the manufacturing sector was also hit hard. In the pre-war period, Syria was a producer of textiles, pharmaceuticals, chemical products, and more. The conflict devastated the manufacturing sector. The dollar value of manufacturing output declined by 60 per cent between 2010 and 2018 (SCBS, 2011, 2019). Some factory owners were able to move their facilities to safer areas inside Syria (such as the coastal areas) or out of the country to Lebanon, Turkey, or Egypt. Many of those who remained saw their facilities destroyed or looted during the fighting, with multimillion-dollar equipment melted down to make artillery shells or to sell on the back market.

The total value added of private sector services remained steady in relative terms at 46 per cent of GDP (SCBS, 2011, 2015, 2019). Public services, such as health and education, also declined in absolute terms, but increased significantly in relative terms from 14 per cent of GDP in 2010 to 27 per cent in 2018. This is reflected in the employment figures; public sector employment increased from 30 per cent of total employment in 2010 to 44 per cent in 2018 (SCBS, 2011, 2019). Thus, the public sector has been serving as an employer of last resort for many families. The services sector has been hit hard by the departure of skilled workers who were able to find work in other countries. This brain drain has important implications for the country's post-conflict redevelopment prospects that we discuss in the next section.

3.3 The Social Impact of the Conflict

The Syrian civil war has created rifts in the country's rich tapestry of communities. The brunt of the conflict was borne by a few cities, towns, and villages, while other communities remained relatively unscathed. Most households saw their livelihoods evaporate, while a few benefited massively from the conflict. This is reflected in a visible new elite that has accumulated wealth and power during the crisis. A study of the impact of the conflict on social relations conducted by the Syrian Centre for Policy Research found that social capital declined across its three dimensions: networks, trust, and shared values, especially trust (SCPR, 2017).

Educational attainment also suffered. In 2020, an estimated 2.45 million children were out of school, one-third of the school-age population UN OCHA (2021). Roughly 40 per cent of school infrastructure had been damaged, destroyed, converted to shelters or was no longer accessible (Relief Web, 2017). According to a 2017 assessment, 52 per cent of 7th graders and 35 per cent of 8th graders could not read 2nd-grade reading material and 63 per cent of 7th graders and 46 per cent of 8th graders could not solve a 2nd-grade maths problem (IRC, 2017). Such low levels of educational attainment mean that many young people entering the labour force will only find work in low-skilled activities such as construction, manufacturing, and agriculture.

As the crisis took hold, the regime reversed many of the positive social changes introduced over the previous decade. It constrained civil society activity and limited international organizations to operating within specific regions and on specific projects. By contrast, in opposition-controlled areas, civil society groups, including local councils and newly created NGOs, experienced a massive increase in activity and support from donors, international NGOs, and UN agencies. However, it was difficult to institutionalize their work and introduce proper regulation and oversight. Furthermore, there was little that tied the initiatives in regime-controlled and opposition-controlled areas. Thus, the ability of civil society initiatives in opposition-controlled areas to transfer knowledge and experience to the rest of the country post-conflict remains uncertain.

3.4 The Political and Institutional Impact of the Conflict

While the Syrian conflict severely impacted the economy and eroded its social fabric, political institutions remained largely intact. Heydemann (2018b) argues that the patterns of economic governance in the civil wars underway in Libya, Syria, and Yemen exhibit significant continuity with pre-war practices. Civil wars do not represent a break from the past, rather institutions and norms persist as parties compete to seize power. Heydemann (2018b) notes that rebel areas have largely replicated the governing institutions of the regimes they seek to replace. Furthermore, opposition security institutions have tended to reproduce the political systems of the regime, including corruption, a lack of accountability, weak capacity, and cronyism. Thus, even if insurgents manage to secure some modicum of political control or power-sharing, they are unlikely to contribute to the development of an inclusive, participatory post-conflict political and economic order.

As the conflict evolved, central power and authority in regime-controlled areas became concentrated in the hands of a few key figures, while political authority was devolved to local centres, leading to the creation of fiefdoms of power and influence. Some local groups initially operated with impunity. However, as the conflict subsided new intra-regime fault lines emerged as the central authorities tried to reassert their control over the regions and local authorities sought to retain the privileges and autonomy they acquired during the conflict. In opposition-controlled areas, the presence of local councils elected by popular vote and their administrative units were unable to prevent local militias, many of which have a radical bent, from having effective control of administrative matters and decisions. This suggests a systematic divergence in the desired outcomes of development between governing bodies, such as elected representatives and ministries, and actual centres of power, whether on the side of the regime or of the opposition.

4 Post-conflict Recovery: Rebuilding Lives and Restoring Livelihoods

By the end of 2021, the Syrian conflict has yet to reach a final settlement. Still, the regime has survived the crisis largely intact and has regained control over the main commercial centres of the country. Barring unexpected developments, the regime will continue to consolidate its gains. While the regime will surely not acquiesce to a political transition after its military successes, the country's current economic difficulties create room for negotiation and possible compromise with the international community on issues of security, economic recovery, and governance. This section explores viable development pathways for moving forward in regime-controlled areas of the country. We discuss four issues that face Syria's post-conflict economic recovery: sources of finance; rethinking reconstruction; moving forward; and entry points for engagement.

4.1 Financing Reconstruction

As of 2019, estimates for the cost of rebuilding the country range from USD 250 billion to USD 400 billion (Daher, 2019a). Financing for reconstruction can come from three sources: the government, the private sector, and foreign donors. The Syrian government does not have the financial resources to cover these costs. The government's 2019 budget included only SL 443 billion (USD 450 million) for 'investment projects in liberated areas'. In addition, the state has other pressing financial obligations, including increasing the salaries of some 1,640,000 public sector employees (SCBS, 2019), the average value of which has declined to less than 20 USD per month; not enough to provide a family with even the most basic necessities. In addition, the state must contend with the public health and economic costs of the coronavirus pandemic as well as reduced remittances and flows of finance to the country. In terms of reconstruction, the regime has so far focused on rebuilding key infrastructure and commercial hubs and developing those areas that have remained loyal to it. It has so far neglected areas that rebelled, including the areas from where most of the refugees came from.

Financing for private sector-led reconstruction in Syria is limited. The dollar value of deposits in the Syrian banking sector fell from USD 29.8 billion in 2010 to USD 4.6 billion in 2016, a decline of 85 per cent (UN ESCWA, 2020). State-owned banks are saddled with large bad debt portfolios (Daher, 2019a). The financial meltdown in neighbouring Lebanon has also greatly affected the Syrian business community who came to rely on Lebanese banks for help to manage their businesses and as a place to secure their savings. International sanctions have dampened foreign investment potential. Expatriates are a potential source of finance. During the conflict, many Syrians quit their jobs, mothballed their businesses, and moved overseas. Some have done well financially. These expats might be willing to return and rebuild their homes, businesses, and communities, were the regime to offer assurances that their investments and families would not be at risk. Unfortunately, after promising indications to the contrary in 2017, the regime then reverted to predatory practices including setting arbitrary taxes, customs duties, fees, and fines on established and returning businesses. This has dampened interest in investment and, together with the sanctions, has moderated the bounce-back post-conflict that the authorities had expected to enjoy.

Foreign assistance poses its own challenges. Syria's allies, Russia and Iran, are looking to profit from, rather than financially support, reconstruction efforts. Syria's neighbours, Lebanon, Jordan, and Turkey hope to play a role in reconstruction but will not contribute funds. Their interests are in creating opportunities for businesses in their own countries and ensuring that Syrian refugees living in their countries are motivated to return home. The United States is unlikely to support reconstruction while Iran retains a military presence in the country. However, the regime is unlikely to reduce its strategic links with Iran, to which it owes its survival. Japan provides support through international organizations and will most probably continue to do so. These mainly involve training and building up abilities such as the UN's Training for All initiative (UNDP, 2019c).

Arab Gulf states may support reconstruction efforts, partly in the hope of weakening Iranian influence in the country and partly to check Turkish incursions in the north. Indeed, the UAE reopened its embassy in Damascus in 2018 and considered funding reconstruction efforts before pressure from the US caused it to drop its support. With oil prices recovering from historic lows in early 2020, Gulf states might consider supporting a wider effort to mobilize funds for reconstruction. However, they also face urgent requests for humanitarian and development assistance from across the region. Thus, their support will require some form of a political resolution to the conflict that is both acceptable to Western countries and that ensures that their support is not wasted.

The EU has a huge stake in the stability and security of its southern neighbour: continued conflict, insecurity, and economic hardship will motivate more Syrians to migrate and may create a breeding ground for radical elements. Indeed, between 2012 and 2019 the EU and its member states contributed over USD 13 billion to humanitarian relief for Syria UN OCHA (2020a), representing nearly half of all relief funding. This represents a huge investment and indicates the importance that the EU places on securing Syria's stability and security. The EU can provide support at three levels: funds for reconstruction, sanctions relief, and international recognition. But so far, the EU and its member states have been reluctant to do so. Its position is based on UN Resolution 2254 which states that the 'only sustainable solution to the current crisis in Syria is through an inclusive and Syrian-led political process... including through the establishment of an inclusive transitional governing body'. While the Syrian regime has in the past dismissed EU funding as unwanted and unneeded, its dire financial situation may lead it to re-evaluate this position. Compared to the alternatives, the EU member states, Japan and the Arab Gulf states, represent the most likely sources of funding for reconstruction.

4.2 The Dilemma of European and International Involvement

European governments are in a bind. On the one hand, they are loath to re-establish ties with a regime that has presided over one of the deadliest conflicts of the twenty-first century. Moreover, they worry that if they decide to engage without an inclusive political settlement or transitional process, this would serve mainly to secure the regime's hold on power while leaving unaddressed the underlying factors that led to the conflict. Regarding reconstruction, Van Veen (2019) argues that given the regime's return to an entrenchment and to clientelist economic policies, it is doubtful that any implementation modality can be found that would prevent the regime taking over any of the funds for reconstruction. This has led many analysts to advocate leaving Syria to its own devices until such time that there is a change of regime or a credible process of political transition (Heller, 2019). It has also been suggested that assistance should be limited to areas outside the regime's control, such as the de-escalation zones. However, this ignores the fact that the main economic hubs are under regime control. Furthermore, the regime has been slowly taking back more areas.

On the other hand, the EU has policy objectives that are difficult to advance if it does not engage with the regime. These include improving security, ensuring the safe return of refugees, and enhancing local governance (Asseburg and Oweis, 2017). Indeed, Barnes-Dacey (2019) points out that Europe's lack of engagement has limited its ability to have a meaningful role in developing a post-conflict agenda or creating an environment conducive to the return of the refugees. He also points out that sanctions have made it difficult for the country to rebuild on its own and reduce civilian suffering. Thus, disengagement comes at a high cost with consequences for the long-term stability of the country, its people, and its neighbours. While the EU has ruled out engaging in the effort at reconstruction until a comprehensive, genuine, and inclusive political transition is firmly under way, this position offers some flexibility in determining how far along with a transition the country must be before re-engagement begins. It also suggests flexibility in supporting economic recovery beyond reconstruction.

It is noteworthy that both the regime and the international community have so far focused primarily on the physical aspects of reconstruction. However, this view of reconstruction is problematic. Heydemann (2018a) argues that the regime has designed an intricate system to ensure that it controls every aspect of the reconstruction process. It is practically impossible to fund any reconstruction effort without some of the funds being channelled into the pockets of regime associates. For example, Law Number 10 of 2018 allows local governments to appropriate private property for the purpose of redevelopment. The international community, in turn, has balked at supporting reconstruction efforts that might enrich the regime, especially since the absence of a political settlement might lead to a resumption of fighting. The result has been a standoff that has prolonged the suffering of the Syrian people and delayed the return of refugees and displaced populations to their communities.

The international community thus faces a conundrum in Syria. Rebuilding homes, businesses, and communities devastated by the fighting will require international funding and assistance. However, given the regime's institutional lock on how reconstruction funds will be used, donors must explore alternatives to reconstruction financing. The solution is to realize that the concept of reconstruction itself has become a red herring, distracting from the more immediate and fundamental development issue of restoring livelihoods.

4.3 Rethinking Reconstruction

The heart-breaking images of Syrian communities destroyed by conflict cry out for a coordinated effort to *physically* rebuild and restore infrastructure and communities. For European donor counties, this recalls the experience of the Marshall Plan, the legacy of which continues in the work of institutions such as the International Bank for Reconstruction and Development and the European Bank for Reconstruction and Development. However, after World War II Europe had local capacities and institutions on which such reconstruction efforts could successfully be based. Imady (2019) notes that a prevailing fallacy is that countries devastated by conflict could rebuild if only they had the required resources. The lessons of Afghanistan, Iraq, and South Sudan, where corruption syphoned off financial resources, suggest otherwise. External financial resources are only effective when they build on local capacities and effective institutions. In countries devastated by war and crippled by weak institutions, this means starting small in order to build up local capacity. The main issue in cases like Syria is to identify local institutions to work with; in other words, entry points that are acceptable to both donors and the regimes (see Figure 4.3).

We pose that the way forward for foreign assistance to Syria is for all the parties concerned to realize that no one party can impose its first-best option. The Syrian regime will not be able to pick and choose among foreign donors interested in investing in the country. Western governments are not

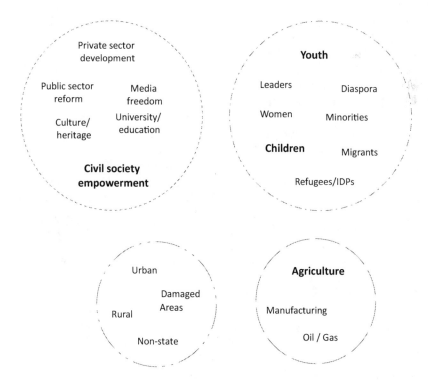

Figure 4.3 Entry points for post-conflict engagement

able to impose an inclusive political transition or any conditions that would weaken the regime's powerful hold on the country, especially now it has successfully re-established control over the key corridors and economic hubs in it (Dacrema, 2019). Only second-best options are realistically available, at least in the early post-conflict period. In this context, the EU will have to consider weaker conditions than they would have liked and should prioritize their top concerns, such as promoting security and stability, and ensuring a safe return for refugees. For the Syrian regime, even a basic economic recovery will require external funding and a relaxing of sanctions, both of which the EU is able to provide.

Pursuing second-best options in the short term does not mean compromising on the longer-term objective of achieving an inclusive and sustainable political resolution to the conflict. The EU can continue to insist that comprehensive reconstruction support remains contingent on Syria undertaking an inclusive political transition. In the meantime, it can support economic recovery efforts on specific projects. For example, Daher (2019a, 2019b) argues that sanctions should be reviewed and revised so as not to harm ordinary people and returnees. The EU can make assistance and sanctions' relief conditional on key targets such as the return of refugees under internationally monitored guarantees for their safety. Indeed, while 75 per cent of Syrian refugees in neighbouring countries expressed a desire to return home one day, over 95 per cent did not believe that conditions now were conducive to their safe return (UNHCR, 2019). Their main concern is safety and security. Securing their safe return requires a credible deal between the regime and the international community. Refugees also expressed concern over the availability of shelter, basic services, employment opportunities, and livelihoods (UNHCR, 2019) all of which require international financial support to secure.

When it comes to allies on the ground, the first point to note is that the Syrian regime is not homogenous. Some regime actors and associates want normalization of relations with the West. Others might wish the conflict and even the sanctions to continue, as this would allow them to continue to profit through black-market activities. The former group is comprised of reform elements that were sidelined during the conflict as well as other groups that have positioned themselves to take advantage of post-conflict economic opportunities. However, if opportunities are not forthcoming, these latter ones could go back to promoting conflict and instability.

At first glance, a natural partner for economic recovery might appear to be the private sector. However, Daher (2019a) notes that privatized reconstruction efforts tend to benefit those entities closest to a regime. He and others (Daher, 2019b), observe that the Syrian warlords are becoming integrated into the formal economy, moving money accumulated from illicit activities into property and investment. A 2016 Public-Private Partnership (PPP) Law allows the private sector to manage and develop state assets in all economic sectors, except oil. The law allows the regime's associates in the private sector to take control of the bulk of foreign investment flows. It is important to note that preventing the flow of all money to regime associates is not only impossible, but also undesirable. Part of an effective disarmament, demobilization, and reintegration (DDR) agenda is the reintegration of warring elements into the formal economy. Soldiers become workers. Warlords become businessmen. The problem is that there are associates of the regime who are positioning themselves to control the bulk of investment flows will leave little for ordinary citizens trying to rebuild their lives and livelihoods.

Government institutions are the traditional partner for economic recovery activities. However, the Syrian government is a target of Western sanctions. Indeed, in December 2019, the US extended sanctions further to cover any US or foreign entity supporting reconstruction by the Syrian government. Daher (2019a) persuasively argues that, because privatized reconstruction tends to benefit entities close to a regime, public institutions should be involved in planning and implementing reconstruction plans. Even though they are subject to regime authority, going through public channels would limit the opportunities for regime associates to enrich themselves and would enable the citizens to demand that there be a degree of transparency in these processes. The international community should identify public institutions that have the capacity and the (relative) independence to become effective partners. It will require a fair amount of trial and error to identify which institutions truly have the capacity to grow and transform. A key indicator will be their willingness to adopt strong monitoring and reporting systems to ensure at least a modicum of transparency and accountability.

This leaves two other channels through which donors can engage directly: international organizations and the NGO sector. Indeed, the international community is already engaged with both. Since 2012, UN agencies have operated in Syria through humanitarian response plans under agreement with the Syrian government. Their work evolved in response to the context and extended to such activities as rehabilitating schools and distributing food to families in need. They were joined in 2012 by the Office for Coordination of Humanitarian Affairs (OCHA) to help coordinate the humanitarian response, and the UN High Commissioner for Refugees to assist internally displaced people. Most UN agencies work in regime-controlled areas and some work in areas outside the regime's control. They undertake projects with donor funding, including from Western countries that refuse to deal directly with the regime. However, the regime has successfully limited the scope of their work to geographical areas and projects that it can approve. Furthermore, Asseburg and Oweis (2017) argue that no safeguards were devised as part of these projects to ensure the right of return for the original inhabitants or the halt of the falsification of public records. Such safeguards need to be adopted.

Similarly, international NGOs continue to operate inside the country, adjusting their programming to suit the context. These include the International Red Cross and Red Crescent and the Aga Khan Development Network. Many local NGOs also continue to operate. Whereas before the conflict there were around 1,200 registered NGOs, it is not clear how many remain active or how many new ones have appeared. Civil society remains the most independent channel through which aid can flow. The regime knows this and forces international and local NGOs to work through a handful of loyal organizations in order to ensure that funds do not reach areas or activities it wishes to deprive. The international community needs to identify which of these gateways it can work with. It could also agree with the regime on developing new gateways for assistance, such as a Social Redevelopment Fund, with an independent governance structure that is transparent and accountable to both the government and the donor community. Indeed, any donor assistance should be contingent on identifying dissemination channels that are transparent, accountable, and largely free of regime control or interference.

While it remains to be seen whether the Syrian regime or the international community would accept such compromises on a larger scale, it is important to note that small-scale initiatives already exist. The international community, including the EU, already supports projects in regime-controlled areas administered through international organizations, NGOs, and even public entities. The regime has allowed these projects a degree of autonomy, within clearly defined guidelines, in order to secure international support. It is possible to expand these channels to achieve development objectives acceptable to both sides. The Covid-19 pandemic has added a new dimension of urgency. The weak public health capacity of state institutions, the pandemic's disruption of economic activity, and the limited ability of neighbouring countries to support refugees have all led to widespread human suffering and a resurgence of violence and instability. This is the time to explore development projects and channels that go beyond the narrow concept of reconstruction and directly help people and communities rebuild their lives and livelihoods.

4.4 Restoring Livelihoods: Priority Areas

For the international community, the primary objective in Syria is arguably to enhance security and ensure the safe return of refugees. In this regard, it must identify entry points (sectors, partners, and projects) that are both acceptable to the regime and yet advance its own core objectives. An incremental approach is required. Priority areas for support should be identified through an analysis of the economic conditions and abilities of the country. Some have argued that Europe should start providing funds for rehabilitation projects in regime-held areas that could help prevent the collapse of essential public services, basically pursuing a more limited form of reconstruction (Crisis Group, 2019). We argue for a more sector-based approach. While a detailed analysis of this matter lies outside the scope of this chapter, we would like to suggest a few sectors based on our analysis above where economic recovery activities can be focused.

Revitalizing the agricultural sector should be a top priority as it will help reduce hunger and food insecurity. The agricultural sector contracted by 70 per cent between 2010 and 2018 and, according to available estimates, food prices increased over 3,000 per cent between 2010 and 2020. As a result, the national average food-basket amounts to 70 per cent of the average monthly family income (UN OCHA, 2021). More than 90 per cent of households spend more than half their income on food (FAO, 2017). Massive support is needed to rehabilitate farmland and rebuild the infrastructure necessary for agriculture to resume. Farmers need agricultural inputs (seed and fertilizer) and equipment to restart the agricultural cycle. Without external support, this may well be difficult given the lack of financing and the international sanctions (Walker, 2016; Lund, 2019). Revitalizing the agricultural sector will increase economic activity and employment in rural communities, helping refugees and IDPs to return home and rebuild their communities. Without any work undertaken to revitalize rural communities, returning refugees will tend to settle in urban areas regardless of where they came from originally (World Bank, 2019b). Finally, revitalizing the sector can help mitigate the risk of land being expropriated for reconstruction projects.

A second priority area is high-value-added industries. Private sector entities in value-added and skill-intensive sectors are less prone to regime capture. These include export-oriented manufacturing and high-tech services. However, legitimate enterprises have been reluctant to return and restart their operations. Sanctions have adversely affected the manufacturing sector (Walker, 2016; Lund, 2019). At the same time, the Syrian government has been overtaxing the private sector in order to cover public services and salaries. As a result, many struggling businesses have opted to close down at precisely the time when people need products and employment. The Syrian government and the international community should remove restrictions on productive sectors, as they will help to create jobs and improve the lives and livelihoods of ordinary people. The resulting economic activity can in turn reduce the incentive to migrate and can encourage refugees to return.

A third area is youth employment and training. This is a central component of disarmament, demobilization, and reintegration (DDR). While youth unemployment is estimated to have reached 70 per cent in 2017, businesses have been complaining of a lack of manpower as a result of the huge outflow of both skilled and unskilled individuals (Daher, 2019b). Similarly, a report by the FAO and the World Food Programme cited a shortage in farm workers as one of the challenges facing the Syrian agricultural sector. Youth (re)training and employment programmes can help the country meet these sector-specific labour shortages, spur economic activity, improve the lives and livelihoods of families, reintegrate the youth into the workforce, and reduce migration and illicit activities. Furthermore, training the young can take place both inside Syria and in neighbouring countries in preparation for their return to their communities.

International organizations are already undertaking a host of valuable, sector-specific initiatives inside regime-controlled areas of Syria. These include Training for All (UNDP, 2019) and a Smallholder Support Programme (FAO, 2020). Indeed, between 2017 and 2018, UNDP programmes alone supported close to 3 million people inside Syria with financial assistance totalling 83 million USD funded through grants from the EU, EU member states, Japan, and Switzerland (UNDP, 2019b). These programmes have so far tended to be small in scale and often focus on public sector capacity building. For example, most of the beneficiaries of the Training for All initiative are government employees, rather than unemployed youth. Still, these programmes do provide valuable support and they can serve as starting points for a sector-based economic recovery strategy.

None of the economic activities highlighted above are political in nature. Helping to revitalize the agricultural sector, promoting private sector development, and youth employment and training programmes, are all activities which both the regime and the international community can support Importantly, while they are not directly related to reconstruction; they will help to promote security and generate needed income that can assist families in rebuilding their lives and communities to independently undertake reconstruction projects. Finally, they can serve as entry points for developing programmes across other sectors, while at the same time promoting improved governance structures and trust.

5 Conclusion

The first part of this chapter reviews the explanations put forward regarding the underlying causes of the Syrian conflict. We find that economic conditions do not appear to have been the primary cause of the 2011 crisis, though it is likely they were a contributing factor. A more fundamental cause was the lack of significant political reform. Basically, the government failed to fulfil its side of the social contract in place since the 1970s, whereby the state would provide public benefits, services, and jobs in exchange for limited participation in politics. Dwindling government resources and increased corruption in the years prior to the crisis reduced the state's ability to keep its side of the bargain. That said, ultimately, the critical factor that ignited the crisis and let it spread was the mismanagement of the security response to the localized protests that in early 2011 mirrored public unrest in neighbouring countries. The heavy-handed security response allowed the social unrest to grow and spread, creating a desire for retaliation and fuelling anti-regime sentiment instead of dissuading it. As the conflict intensified, both sides of the conflict weaponized sectarian differences and opened the door to foreign intervention.

The second part highlights the economic, social, and political costs of conflict. Understanding the magnitude of these costs along with the profound socio-economic and political change brought about by the conflict is crucial to identifying where to focus peace-building and reconstruction. By the end of 2019, the degree of devastation resulting from the nine-year civil war was staggering: economic activity had declined by 65 per cent, one-quarter of the population had emigrated and another quarter had been displaced from their homes. The war created rifts in the country's rich tapestry of communities. The brunt of the conflict was borne by a few cities, towns, and villages, while other communities remained relatively unscathed. While the Syrian conflict severely impacted the economy and eroded the social fabric, political institutions have remained largely intact.

In the third part, we examine policy options for post-conflict security and economic recovery in Syria by focusing on entry points for international development actors and institutions. While, as of mid-2020, full normalization of relations and support for reconstruction efforts were not viable alternatives, non-engagement also comes at a high cost. We identified a viable path forward involving an iterative approach focusing on second-best options. Development assistance should target activities that restore livelihoods through entry points in selected economic sectors (e.g., agriculture, high value-added industries), thereby helping ordinary people to rebuild their lives and reduce the impetus to migrate. Donors and the regime would have to agree on mechanisms for vetting possible partners in the use of foreign aid, for monitoring progress and responding to violations of agreements. Such an iterative process can be used to test various channels of engagement and build on those that are effective, contributing to a virtuous cycle that can slowly promote improved development outcomes and governance structures in the country. The international community already supports projects in regime-controlled areas. In the short term, the focus can be on building on these activities. In the long term, the international community can continue to insist that full financial support for reconstruction and for sanction relief are contingent on Syria undertaking an inclusive settlement of the conflict.

In the absence of a viable settlement, this chapter argues for a less ambitious sector-based approach that would contribute to positive development outcomes in the short term, supported by process-oriented implementation mechanisms that would build institutional capacity and open the way for realizing more sustainable and inclusive outcomes in the long term. Indeed, the disastrous failures of recent efforts at state-building in Iraq, Afghanistan, South Sudan, and elsewhere, suggest that a more limited, iterative approach might actually lead to more positive outcomes. The current economic crisis in Syria, precipitated by the coronavirus pandemic and the financial meltdown in neighbouring Lebanon, have all created a sense of urgency as well as the opportunity to reach an agreement on a way forward. As of writing (mid-2020), it is difficult to imagine an inclusive and sustainable political settlement to the Syrian conflict. In the longer term, however, achieving lasting national peace and prosperity in Syria calls for a new social contract that embodies genuine and inclusive political governance.

Note

1 Poverty lines were derived using a procedure outlined in Ravallion (1998). First, for each household, the cost of purchasing its minimum caloric needs is estimated. Lower poverty lines are derived by adding to this amount spending on non-food items in households where *total expenditure* is equivalent to the cost of its minimum caloric needs. Upper poverty lines are derived by adding spending on non-food items in households where *food expenditure* is equivalent to the cost of its minimum caloric needs.

5 Conflict, Institutions, and the Iraqi Economy, 2003–2020

Bassam Yousif, Rabeh Morrar, and Omar El-Joumayle

1 Introduction

This chapter analyses the reasons behind the decline of Iraq's economy over the last decades, identifies bottlenecks and constraints that have hampered recovery, and offers remedies going forward. A country that at one time was a regional leader in terms of human capital and skills formation, with an advanced and effective medical system where care was provided free of charge, today faces problems in reconstruction and the provision of basic services, electricity, sanitation and, crucially, law and order. As the IMF (2004a, p. 34) has noted

> … after attaining middle income status in the 1970s, Iraq's nominal GDP per capita had dropped to about USD700 by 2002, and many of Iraq's human development indicators are now the lowest in the region.

Indeed, a traveller returning to this country after spending decades away would scarcely recognize it as the same country. Iraq's present circumstances have come about over decades of decline and are unlikely to be resolved easily or rapidly. In 1980, Iraq attacked Iran, initiating eight years of bloody conflict; and in 1990, it invaded Kuwait resulting in the 1991 Gulf war and debilitating economic sanctions. In 2003, an Allied invasion of Iraq toppled the dictatorship of Saddam Hussein. Since then and despite rising oil prices and hence revenues (until 2013), the state has failed to deliver basic services such as electricity and safe water, not to mention peace and security. As of 2014, Iraq has been experiencing budgetary difficulties induced by collapsing oil prices and exacerbated by an expanding public sector and internal conflict (a war with the Islamic State of Iraq and Syria, hereafter ISIS). This has further complicated longstanding problems of low investment rates and a poor quality of public services. These hardships need to be placed in the context of a long decline in human capabilities and institutions, including state institutions (Yousif, 2016), and are the result of frequent, sudden, and discontinuous institutional changes that have been affecting the country for decades (El-Joumayle, 2016).

DOI: 10.4324/9781003344414-8

2 Conceptual Foundations and Historical Background up to 2003

In this section, we first track the trajectory of Iraq's economy up to 2003 and the major economic and institutional issues it has been facing ever since. We focus on institutions and the capabilities of the government and take stock of their status after the prolonged conflict that afflicted Iraq in the 1990s and early 2000s. We then analyse the upheaval caused by the Allied forces' occupation and its aftermath of actions and outcomes, and finally put forward proposals for Iraq to move forward.

2.1 Long-Term Decline in Capabilities

Capabilities are the set of things that people are able to do or that one is able to choose (Sen, 1983). Knowledge and skills, health, and nutrition are important factors in the development process. Equally, expanding human capabilities is the ultimate objective of the development process, mediated by institutions. We follow Hodgson (1998) in defining institutions broadly to include organizations, in addition to Douglass North's definition of '*humanly devised constraints that shape human interaction*' (as quoted in Hodgson, 1998, pp. 179–180). Institutions can be formal, for example, humanly devised procedures, rules and laws, or informal, for example, customs, social capital, traditions, and others. While formal institutions may change rapidly, informal institutions are thought to be slower moving. Institutions may evolve slowly or change abruptly in times of war or revolution, in which case any institutional change is defined as 'discontinuous' (North, 1990). We contend that decline in formal institutions and capabilities, particularly those of the state, constitutes the most accurate way to understand Iraq's present circumstances.

Given this, two introductory points are pertinent. First, following Stewart and FitzGerald (2001a and 2001b), we contend that economies emerging from a period of prolonged conflict are unlikely to respond in the same way as they did during peace, in part because pre-conflict institutions may no longer function properly or may have been dismantled. Reconstruction policies would, therefore, have to account for the newly emerging domestic political alignments and existing (if imperfect) institutions rather than work against them. In particular, they should try to ameliorate existing horizontal inequalities to reduce the likelihood of a re-emergence of conflict (Stewart and FitzGerald, 2001b).

Second, we posit that political decisions taken in Iraq (comprising decisions to enter into conflict with neighbouring countries) and by external actors (following the 2003 Allied invasion), rather than any developmental strategy implemented by Iraqi governments prior to 2003, are what primarily account for Iraq's economic decline. This is because such decisions have induced discontinuous institutional changes that, more often than not, have proved harmful to development and economic growth (North et al., 2009). Thus, the Iraqi experience brings out the contrast between development as a concept or goal and developmental institutions as facilitators of that goal on the one hand, and political institutions as the enforcers of public policies, including critical decisions about war and peace, on the other. Development institutions devise rules, methods, planning, etc., all expanded and sustained by human capabilities and knowledge, including those in the public sector. These, in turn, relate to the notion of state capacity or effectiveness, which we define as the ability of the state to carry out its policies. In contrast, political institutions are responsible for formulating public policy. Distinguishing developmental from political institutions allows us to analyse their effects vis-à-vis the frequent discontinuous institutional changes that Iraq has experienced with deleterious effects on economic performance.

This view stands in contrast to the construction of an artificial dichotomy of activist versus minimalist state in economic strategy (see Yousif, 2016). We contest explanations of Iraq's economic decline that are based on rationales that emphasize Iraq's statist past as voiced by the Coalition Provisional Authority (CPA) (see Foote et al., 2004), the IMF (2004a) and post-Saddam Iraqi governments (IMF, 2004b). They have all located Iraq's poor economic performance in overly intrusive Ba'ath-era economic policies (1968–2003) and centralist planning. Economic planning actually preceded the Ba'ath party taking power in 1968, with the 'Development Board' established in 1950 to manage and plan the investment of the oil income. While we briefly discuss the inefficiency and waste associated with Iraq's statist economic policies, we postulate that they do not account for Iraq's developmental collapse: instead, discontinuous institutional changes brought about by actions of defective political institutions do. That is, in the main it is Ba'athi political, rather than economic, that is, institutional, policies, the internationally imposed economic sanctions, and the actions of the CPA that together account for Iraq's decline.

2.2 Oil Abundance and the Role of the State

Like other oil exporters, Iraq's central government has traditionally owned or controlled the production and export of oil and its revenues;[1] the state is consequently a central player in the economy since the 1950s. State involvement in oil economies tends invariably to be extensive in relation to GDP, despite variance in political and economic ideologies, for example, as in Saudi Arabia, Iran, Iraq, and Algeria. The central question thus concerns the nature of state involvement—what it does with oil revenues—rather than its share of the economy, which is inevitably substantial. Largely financed by oil revenues, an implicit social contract developed over time in Iraq whereby the state provided public goods, including education and health, as well as employment, particularly to better-educated workers, in exchange for political support. Oil has been seen as the main tool for diversifying economic activity, hence the large state investments in infrastructure and the non-oil economy since the 1950s (see Alnaswawi, 1994). The greater the state's capacity or effectiveness, the greater its ability to invest the income from oil and the more pronounced the effect on the economy.[2] According to Fukuyama (2013), higher levels of education, professionalism, and, to some degree, the autonomy of the state bureaucracy from political pressures tend to enhance state effectiveness. Human capabilities, more generally, are vital for the development process. The process that transforms human capabilities into development and economic growth that in turn contributes to still more expansion in capabilities is mediated by institutions: customs, laws, policies, political constraints and decisions, and processes.

This process of development or underdevelopment is usually multifaceted and rarely linear (Rodrik, 2005). We argue that it was probably rapid physical and human capital formation and steadily rising primary and secondary enrolment in education in the 1970s that strengthened Iraq's developmental structures and institutions. At the same time, there was poor political decision-making, which probably was a reflection of the declining political institutions and associated with the narrowing of the political space. And this, along with prolonged economic sanctions, eventually induced a severe decline in developmental structures and outcomes. By the 1990s, developmental institutions and state capacity had begun to atrophy, along with an economy-wide gradual loss in human knowledge and skills. Consequently, the experience of Iraq over the last four decades has been one of declining institutions, including, importantly, state institutions which are central to economic policy formulation and implementation, not to mention protecting property. This partly explains why rebuilding since 2003 has been difficult (see Yousif, 2016). Given the pervasive decline today, it is tempting to assume a generalized 'state/development' failure. We argue instead that it is the uneven development of political and developmental institutions that accounts for Iraq's decline.

2.3 Institutional Decline and the Social Contract

Iraq's long-term institutional decline ought not to be confused with a broken social contract or state failure. Problems with Iraq's social contract did not cause its institutional decline, which started in the 1970s, and one should be careful about making spurious causal connections about these. We show that the social contract in Iraq today, where the state provides increasing numbers of government jobs (with rising pay), along with some services to the population, as the primary ways to distribute oil revenues, is unsustainable for several reasons. First, the state is simply unable to provide sufficient jobs given Iraq's rapidly expanding labour force. Second, the provision of services and transfers to the population is constrained in terms of existing or projected revenues. Third, only a segment of the population (typically the better educated) is able to take advantage of government jobs. We locate the reasons for past conflict in defective or declining political institutions, not the social contract per se. In fact, the start of the Iran-Iraq war in 1980 occurred in the context of rising living standards, egalitarian income distribution, and political repression, rather than a social contract that was obviously in crisis.[3] This marked the start of deleterious discontinuous institutional change.

2.4 The Rise and Collapse of Development

During the 1970s, Iraq experienced both rising prices as well as increasing output and exports of its primary export (oil), with the result that oil revenues expanded from USD 1 billion in 1970 to USD 21 billion in 1979 (OPEC, 2005). The state, through its development apparatuses and the civil service, successfully transformed much of the revenue into investments in human and physical capital as well expanded private consumption, with investment growing faster than consumption (Yousif, 2012, 2016). This was facilitated by increasing levels of education and skills in society in general and, especially, in the public sector. Staff numbers at the Ministry of Planning, for example, rose from 639 in 1968 to 2,932 in 1976, many of them Western-trained technocrats (Savage, 2013). This reflected improved educational capabilities in Iraq as a whole, where literacy among 10-year-old and above rose from 30 per cent in 1965, to 47 per cent in 1977, and to 73 per cent in 1987 (Yousif, 2012).

At the same time, however, there was increasing state-sanctioned political violence with a perceptible narrowing of the political space. Political actions or decisions worked to undermine developmental institutions and eventually induced a decline in both those institutions and human capabilities. While a detailed analysis of the political institutions of this period is beyond the scope of this work, political actions, including the attack on Iran and later Kuwait, provide evidence of poor or declining mechanisms of decision-making. This coincides with a period of deteriorating rights and freedoms for most Iraqis. For Iraq, the Polity IV Country Regime measure, with a scale of 10 for most democratic to –10 for most repressive, declined from –5 to –7 during the 1970s and further to –9 in 1980 (see Polity, 2014). Likewise, Yousif (2012) utilizes an index of political freedoms and rights to illustrate the decline during the 1970s and 1980s.

There was a parallel narrowing within the political leadership itself during this period, with power increasingly concentrated in the hands of Saddam Hussein and his close associates and family (Davis, 2005; Yousif, 2012). This limited governing base made policy errors more likely and less reversible. While the causes of the Iran and Kuwait conflicts are complex, and we want to avoid over-simplification,[4] we contend that existing political institutions made policy mistakes more likely and corrective measures more difficult.[5]

The beginning of the Iran–Iraq war in 1980 interrupted oil exports, which recovered only gradually. Central government revenues declined, with the result that Iraq had to rely on foreign exchange reserves to finance the war, pay for imported goods, including food (sold to the public at subsidized rates), and carry out the state's ambitious investment plans. These multiple demands had exhausted reserves by 1983 and Iraq started to borrow heavily from its Arab neighbours and internationally; eventually, the government dropped its extensive investment plans (Yousif, 2012). Even so, there remained a commitment on the part of the state in the 1980s to pay for extensive social programmes, as part of the existing social contract: infant mortality, life expectancy, caloric consumption, immunization rates, the provision of safe water, and most education indicators continued to improve (at varying rates) even under war conditions (see Yousif, 2012).

Economic organizations and state institutions retained some degree of robustness, even though military priorities supplanted some development spending in the 1980s. State effectiveness was, and continued to be, central to Iraq's oil-producing economy, where the government provided a plethora of services, consumer and producer subsidies, and was responsible to a large degree for capital formation. A high level of professionalism and education, as well as a degree of bureaucratic autonomy, tend to promote state capacity (Fukuyama, 2013). Nevertheless, two opposing forces were influencing state effectiveness. On one hand, increased education and skills in the civil service and in society in general worked to expand effectiveness. On the other, there was rising politicization of the civil service (and society) after the 1970s, when the Ba'ath government started to undercut meritocracy in government service, instead favouring and promoting party members.[6] Nevertheless, state involvement in the economy and society and continuous gains in human capabilities[7] more than compensated for the political intrusion, implying that the government retained some degree of effectiveness in the 1970s and 1980s.[8]

The Iran–Iraq war (1980–1988) and the invasion of Kuwait (in 1990) were followed by two significant shocks, namely the 1991 war to eject Iraq from Kuwait and the subsequent comprehensive economic sanctions (1990–2003). We can quibble about whether these were internal or external shocks, brought about by Iraqi, US, or coalition decisions; from the perspective of the Iraqis, the distinction is immaterial. The 1991 war itself, especially the 42-day bombing campaign, while ostensibly intended to drive Iraq out of Kuwait, actually destroyed the country's civilian infrastructure, including power generation, oil and transport networks, and fertilizer, as well as iron and steel plants. Targets were deliberately chosen to 'amplify the economic and psychological impact of sanctions on Iraqi society' and if they were likely to need foreign expertise to repair them (Alnaswawi, 2002). The UN describes the economic and social consequences as 'near-apocalyptic results upon what had been, until January 1991, a rather highly urbanized and mechanized society' (quoted in Alnaswawi, 1994, p. 119). Moreover, comprehensive economic sanctions precluded rebuilding. Iraq's oil exports, prohibited under the sanctions, paid for a variety of items, including imports of food and medicine. In fact, the prohibition on export worked effectively to deny the ability to import, as the sanctions foreclosed access to international lending. Per capita GDP (at constant prices) declined by more than 50 per cent between 1990 and 1995 (UN Statistical Database, 2019). Among other reasons, the decline in incomes induced people to emigrate, notably those with higher levels of education and skills (Yousif, 2016), a process that would continue and possibly accelerate after the 2003 invasion, as discussed below. Based on UN data, Yousif (2016) calculates that Gross Fixed Capital Formation as a portion of GDP averaged only six per cent between 1991 and 2002, most probably less than the rate of capital depreciation and inadequate for rebuilding. Sanctions decapitalized Iraq, in human and physical terms, with dreadful implications for later reconstruction.

In prohibiting exports, the sanctions created a shortage of foreign currency, with the result that the value of the domestic currency plummeted with respect to foreign currencies, making imports (notably food and medicine) expensive. The public distribution system (PDS), which continues today, was set up to provide a basic level of consumption; the programme purchased (mostly) domestically produced grain at set prices, which was then rationed out to the population. Because Iraq was (and remains) a net importer of grain and lacked funds to import food, the PDS provided only a portion of the calorific requirements of the population. Malnutrition and a deterioration in water quality and the electricity supply along with a shattered infrastructure resulted in a spike in infant and child mortality. This had previously declined steadily during the 1970s and 1980s but then rose to 102 per thousand in 1999 (Garfield and Waldman, 2003). The Oil for Food Programme implemented in 1998 was supposed to improve humanitarian outcomes but was both too limited in size and too late to substantially reverse these trends (Cortright et al., 2002; Gazdar and Hussain, 2002). As Gordon (2012, p. 138) notes, by the time needed medical equipment imported under the programme had arrived 'there was often no longer adequate personnel to use it effectively'.

While the economy, society, and the civil service lost trained personnel, there was a concomitant decline in professionalism in the civil service, as corruption became the survival mechanism for many, gradually becoming a widespread and ingrained malaise. This, along with the withdrawal of the state from most of its traditional activities (except for the PDS) and increased reliance on what Tripp (2003) calls the 'shadow state', tracked the decline of the public bureaucracy. The consequences were severely weakened developmental institutions, reduced state capacity, and declining human capabilities—these were the initial conditions faced by US and allied forces when they invaded Iraq in 2003.

3 Occupation, Upheavals, and their Aftermath, 2003–2020

In March 2003, the United States and its allies invaded Iraq, overthrowing the Ba'athist regime (in power since 1968) and appointing the CPA to rule the country. The CPA, along with the international financial institutions (IFIs), quickly identified economically interventionist Ba'athist policies as the reason behind Iraq's economic decline, minimizing the adverse effects of conflict and economic sanctions (see IMF, 2004; Mahdi, 2007). With extensive powers to reconfigure Iraq's political economy, the CPA attempted reforms along free-market lines. However, it faced legal and political constraints; as its own officials recognized, an occupying power was restricted from selling Iraq's public assets. Without support for its reforms from the Iraqis, the CPA was concerned that a future Iraqi government might reverse them; hence proposals required Iraqi buy-in (Foote et al., 2004). While it held real power, the CPA was still obligated to consult with the Iraqi Governing Council, which it established in July 2003.

3.1 Coalition Provisional Authority policies

The CPA implemented some positive measures, such as sponsoring the writing down of Iraq's foreign debt, establishing an independent central bank, and introducing a new currency (Yousif, 2016). However, there was little recognition of the effects of decades of conflict and sanctions on markets and institutions and the imperfect ways that they functioned. Instead, the CPA's programme took the shape of extreme shock therapy, in the form of a rush to liberalize prices and markets with Eastern Europe as a model. The aim was to achieve allocative efficiency, encourage investment, notably foreign direct investment (FDI), thereby accelerating economic growth. CPA measures included allowing foreign firms to own assets in Iraq (except in the politically sensitive oil sector), a cut in corporate taxes, relaxation of foreign exchange restrictions, and implementing a low flat import tariff (Yousif, 2007, 2016).

In the political arena, orders 1 and 2 in May and August 2003, respectively, enforced de-Ba'athification and the dissolution of Iraq's armed forces (CPA, 2003). Together, these measures laid-off about 500,000 people, roughly 8–10 per cent of the labour force (Yousif, 2007). In terms of civilian work, de-Ba'athification resulted in the sacking of 30,000 civil servants, of which 15,000 were re-hired after winning their appeals against their redundancies; in addition, all army officers above colonel and 100,000 intelligence officers lost their jobs (Alaaldin, 2018). Thus, the disbanding of the army and de-Ba'athification made hundreds of thousands of trained military and intelligence personnel jobless and deprived the country of managerial and professional skills, inflaming insecurity and complicating rebuilding.[9]

The CPA substantially increased public sector wages in an attempt to appease the feelings of the population (Allawi, 2007). This move was in tension with the so-called neoliberal emphasis on efficient resource allocation as no one thought the wage rises reflected enhanced public sector productivity. Indeed, most of the increase in real GDP since 2004 is attributable to higher oil extraction, which employs less than two per cent of the labour force and not to leaps in Total Factor Productivity (TFP), as shown below (Figure 5.1).

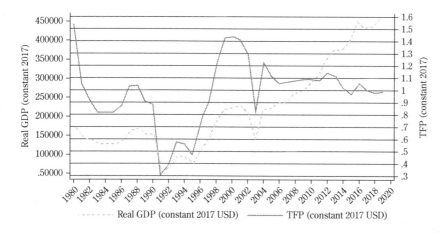

Figure 5.1 Total factor productivity and real GDP
Source: University of Groningen and University of California, Davis, Real GDP at Constant National Prices for Iraq, retrieved from FRED, Federal Reserve Bank of St. Louis: https://fred.stlouisfed.org/series/RGDPNAIQA666NRUG. December 2021. Total Factor Productivity at Constant National Prices for Iraq, retrieved from FRED, Federal Reserve Bank of St. Louis; https://fred.stlouisfed.org/series/RTFPNAIQA632NRUG. December 2021.

At the same time, the CPA put forward plans for the privatization of state-owned enterprises (SOEs), firms that nominally produced a wide variety of consumer and producer goods and employed roughly 500,000 workers.[10] Many of the SOEs were dilapidated or insolvent, and thus unattractive to investors. These brusque attempts at privatization incensed the public to such an extent that even the Iraqi Governing Council was unable to support the CPA's privatization initiatives. Consequently, the CPA abandoned its privatization plans in November 2003. It did not attempt to repair or rehabilitate SOEs, let alone ready them for privatization, and in fact denied them capital. Even so, the CPA continued to pay SOE workers, even though many SOEs were non-productive. (Henderson, 2005). This reinforced the notion that the SOEs should be subsidized regardless of output. Subsequent Iraqi administrations expanded both employment and pay in government service more generally, with the result that the public payroll consumed a growing share of public expenditure, as illustrated below (Figure 5.2).

3.2 Political Impasse and Insecurity

De-Ba'athification and the disbanding of Iraq's armed and security services placed large numbers of disgruntled men trained in violence on the streets.[11] At the same time, the CPA picked Iraq's Governing Council from among returning exiles, based on a system of ethno-sectarian apportionment whereby Sunni, Shi'is, Kurds, and other groups received set allocations. Alaaldin (2018) notes that the fall of the Ba'ath regime created an 'ideological and

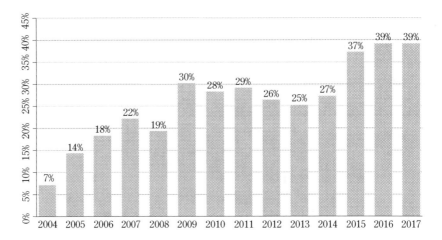

Figure 5.2 Wages and salaries as a proportion of public expenditure
Sources: World Bank (2018b).

political void' in addition to the security vacuum. This, along with the CPA's sectarian distribution, allowed ethno-sectarian and religious groupings to mobilize support based on sect as opposed to political ideology. Sectarian political groupings came to dominate specific government ministries, allocating jobs and other patronage to their supporters. As Al-Qarawee (2014) notes, some previously exiled political groups had little domestic support, so their viability depended on cultivating 'sectarianism and communal fears to create new constituencies'. Politics became polarized along ethno-sectarian lines, as cronyism and corruption characterized governance, a system that continues today (Kuoti, 2016; Herbert, 2018).

In this atmosphere of rising violence, sectarianism, and criminality, hitherto mixed neighbourhoods in Baghdad became virtually exclusively Sunni or Shi'a (Alaaldin, 2018). The figure below reports the number of civilian deaths resulting from violence and illustrates the extent of sectarian violence in the 2005–2007 period, when roughly 16,000–28,000 people died each year, that is, about 45–75 per day. The US invasion of Iraq is not to blame for the origins of Iraq's sectarianism, but the CPA's actions inflamed it (Figure 5.3).[12]

3.3 Brain Drain and Slow Reconstruction

Rising insecurity made rebuilding more difficult and costly. A number of factors were at work here. First, there was a high degree of waste and inefficiency that characterized US-led attempts at reconstruction (SIGIR, 2009). Second, insecurity was rife. Contractors and donors involved in reconstruction reported that providing security for capital projects often reached

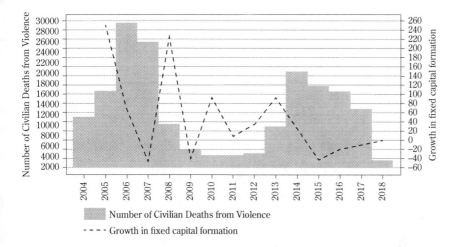

Figure 5.3 Violence and growth in fixed capital formation
Sources: Gross fixed capital formation: Calculated from World Bank data. https://data.worldbank.org/country/iraq?view=chart. Number of civilian deaths from violence is from Iraq's body count database. www.iraqbodycount.org/database.

30–50 per cent of the total cost (IMF, 2005). Finally, there was the continued loss of skills and capabilities, with a notable brain drain following the Gulf War in 1991 and a probably greater one after 2003 (Yousif, 2016). Sassoon (2011) explains in detail how post-2003 instability and violence provoked the large-scale emigration of physicians, academics, lawyers, and other professionals, depriving the domestic economy of their skills and expertise.

In Iraq, the state has historically had a pre-eminent role in terms of spending on investment (Yousif, 2012). It undertakes most capital spending, especially large-scale reconstruction projects, and accounted for roughly two-thirds of Gross Domestic Investment in 2013–2015 (World Bank 2017c). Hence, loss of skills, notably in the state sector, is bound to affect capital formation. For example, the technical capacity of the Ministry of Oil to monitor large contracts, and at the Ministry of Electricity expertise in various areas, ranging from engineering supervision to budgetary skills, has been lacking (USAID, 2012). A look at Iraq's emigrees explains why. According to one survey conducted by Fafo (2007) in Jordan (a major destination for Iraqi emigrants), 42 per cent of Iraqi women and 51.5 per cent of men over the age of 16, had at least a bachelor's degree—much higher than in Iraq and or elsewhere in the Middle East. Three-quarters of those surveyed arrived in Jordan after 2003, that is, in order to escape violence and insecurity (Fafo, 2007). As the World Bank (2017) has stated: 'the flight of educated Iraqis in search of better opportunities abroad has had and will continue to have severe negative long-term consequences for the Iraqi economy and for the education sector specifically'. Nor has the desire to

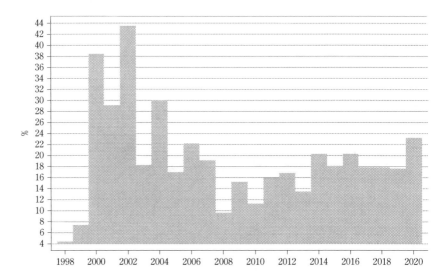

Figure 5.4 Gross capital formation as proportion of GDP
Sources: Gross fixed capital formation, % of GDP. Calculated from World Bank data. https://data.worldbank.org/country/iraq?view=chart.

leave abated. Acording to UNDP (2014), the desire to emigrate among Iraq's youth is 22.2 per cent nationally, it rises to 31 per cent in Baghdad and reaches 41 per cent for young males, all seeking better job opportunities and security.

For these reasons, capital formation has been low. As shown below, excluding 2004, gross fixed capital formation has hovered between roughly 10 and 23 per cent since 2003, mostly at or under 18 per cent—anaemic for a country recovering from decades of war and sanctions. According to Idris (2018), weak governance in Iraq is, at least partly, the result of emerging shortages in human capital, caused to some degree by the CPA policies post 2003 (Figure 5.4).

Both the US and Iraqi governments have engaged in investment spending. US capital spending would eventually rise to USD 60 billion, from an initial USD 20 billion, from 2003 to 2013. One-third of the USD 60 billion was spent on re-building and equipping Iraq's new security apparatuses, dismantled after the invasion in 2003. Much of the USD 60 billion investment fund was misspent, according to the Special Inspector General for Iraq's Reconstruction (CBS, 2013). The Iraqi government also invested in oil revenue. Until 2014, when collapsing oil prices created budgetary difficulties, the binding constraint on government capital spending was the availability of skills and expertise to manage and run public investment as well as violent conflict, rather than a lack of funding. Since 2003, the productive sectors of agriculture and manufacturing have mostly stagnated, partly due to

Figure 5.5 Value added by economic sector
Source: Own elaboration based on data from United Nations (UN), National Accounts and Main Aggregates Database (2021).

the slow repairing of dilapidated infrastructure; in contrast, the value of oil has been steadily rising, the result of higher production, as shown in Figure 5.5.

3.4 Oil Dependence

As shown below, oil production rose steadily after 2003, reaching a historic high of 4.9 million barrels per day in August 2019 (Paraskova, 2019). Oil generated more than 90 per cent of total revenues in the period 2013–2015 (World Bank, 2017), providing finance for social spending, capital and infrastructure spending, the PDS, and buttressing private consumption by paying the salaries of public workers.

Figure 5.6 illustrates how traditional money-metric macroeconomic measures can be misleading in an oil economy. Rising real GDP comes about when oil output rises, regardless of what happens to the oil price; together output and price determine nominal GDP and government revenues. Thus, paradoxically, rising oil output since 2014 is reflected in expanding real GDP, even as the war with ISIS and falling oil revenues created fiscal strain and hardship, leading to cutbacks in public investment. In fact, rising oil output was unable to offset collapsing oil prices and nominal GDP declined from 2014 to 2016. Thus, there is often little correspondence between nominal and real GDP and state revenues, and a rising real GDP can be a misleading indicator of future revenue collection (Figure 5.7).

For most of the post-2003 period, the central bank has managed to maintain price stability through a managed peg of about one USD to 1,200 Iraqi

134 *Bassam Yousif et al.*

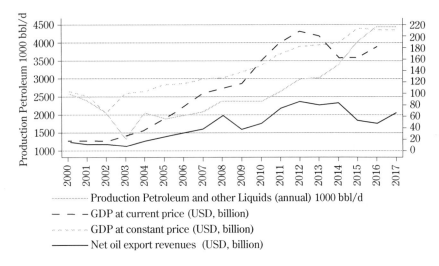

Figure 5.6 Oil and key macroeconomic variables

Sources: oil production and revenues: Calculated from U.S Energy Information. Petroleum and Other Liquids (annual) (1000 bbl/d): 1980–2018 production and consumption. https://www.eia.gov/beta/international/data/

GDP: Calculated from World Bank data about Iraq. https://data.worldbank.org/country/iraq?view=chart.

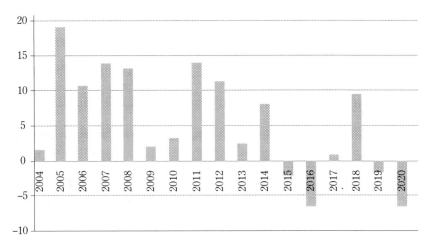

Figure 5.7 Fiscal balance, 2004–2020
Source: theglobaleconomy.com (2021).

Dinars (ID) and a liberal import regime. Price inflation was high in the aftermath of the invasion, in 2003 and for some years after, but prices have stabilized since 2008. An inflation rate in Iraq higher than that of the United States has increased the real effective exchange rate of the ID (IMF, 2017). However, the debilitated condition of key sectors, such as manufacturing and agriculture, and insufficient infrastructure and inputs (e.g., electricity) means that, in terms of import substitution and exports, they would respond only in a limited way to a nominal ID devaluation (IMF, 2017). On the other hand, devaluation would abruptly reduce the purchasing power of ordinary Iraqis, who rely on imports. Exchange rate stability is a notable factor in encouraging FDI, but so is security; FDI rose steadily after 2004, reaching a peak of USD 6 billion in 2013, but collapsed thereafter (World Bank, 2017). In late 2020 the Iraqi government devalued the Dinar by 23 per cent, primarily to reduce the dollar value of its fiscal deficit and hence international borrowing rather than to promote exports (Abu Omar and Al Ansary, 2020) (Figure 5.8).

3.5 *An Overstaffed and Under-Skilled Public Sector*

According to the World Bank (2017c), and not counting employees in SOEs, there has been a sharp rise in the number of people employed in the public sector: from 900,000 (or 22 per cent of all workers) in 2003 to more than 3 million in 2015 (or 42 per cent of the labour force). As shown earlier, the wage bill of public sector employees rose from 7 per cent of total government expenditure to 37 per cent in the same interval, financed by oil revenues. Some

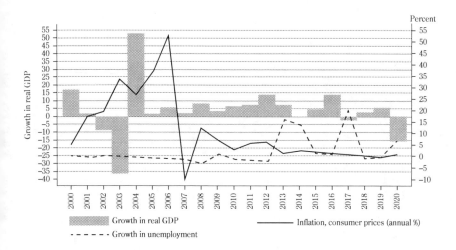

Figure 5.8 Real GDP, unemployment, and consumer prices
Source: GDP, Unemployment and Inflation: Calculated using World Bank data. https://data.worldbank.org/country/iraq?view=chart.

of this expansion is related to the need to hire personnel in the security and military fields, notably in reaction to the conflict with ISIS between 2014 and 2017. However, much of the hiring in the public sector is the result of nepotism or patronage exercised by sectarian parties that control certain ministries (World Bank, 2017), and is higher than the average in the MENA region (World Bank, 2018b). The result is that the public sector is both inefficient and overstaffed (Jiyad, 2015) (Figure 5.9).

Moreover, much of its expansion is unrelated to the logic of development or even to security priorities. Demands for more government jobs from the public at large, especially university graduates explain most of the rise in public sector employment (Jiyad, 2015). Iraq's budget law of 2019 offers a vivid example of this problem: of the projected spending of USD 111.8 billion (a 45 per cent increase over the preceding year), public sector salaries and wages take up USD 52 billion (Turak, 2018). Especially in times of expanding oil revenues, governments come under increasing public pressure to create more public sector jobs. This creates a permanent liability and leaves less money for other priorities, including investment and social spending, aggravating budgetary crises when oil prices decline later. Since 2014, a lack of funding has become a salient constraint on investment, in addition to the lack of capacity, skills, and expertise. The state has slashed its capital budget and even social spending has stagnated as a share of GDP, as shown above in low and declining health expenditure as a portion of all expenditures, the modest recovery since 2016 notwithstanding. The central government has exhausted the fiscal surpluses that accumulated in previous years and has

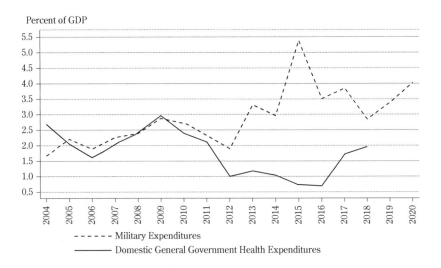

Figure 5.9 Military and health expenditures

Source: Own elaboration based on from World Bank data about Iraq. https://data.worldbank.org/country/iraq?view=chart.

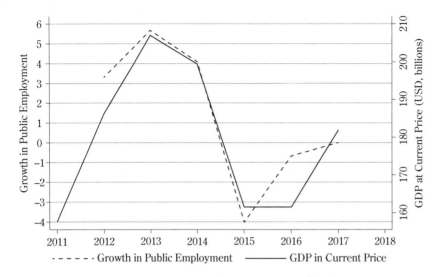

Figure 5.10 Growth in government revenues and jobs growth
Sources: Public employment, Al-Mawlawi (2018), Analysing Growth Trends in Public Sector Employment in Iraq.
GDP in current prices: Calculated using World Bank data. https://data.worldbank.org/country/iraq?view=chart.

increased its borrowing; public debt as a percentage of GDP was 32 per cent in 2014 and rose to 50.5 per cent in 2018 (IMF 2019a) (Figure 5.10).

Despite the rise in the number of people employed in the public sector since 2003, the capacity and efficacy of the public sector have probably declined, continuing a deterioration that started in 1990. We have noted the effects of the emigration of large numbers of skilled personnel. At the same time, political parties and their militias that control ministries have dispensed largesse in the form of public employment. Le Billon (2005) pointed out that the confluence of oil and political authoritarianism would leave Iraq vulnerable to corruption and mismanagement. Indeed, Transparency International's Corruption Perception index—a measure of corruption, as reflected in public opinion polling and the views of experts—has been low and declining since 2003, registering only marginal improvement in recent years (Table 5.1).

The World Bank has published Worldwide Governance Indicators since 1996 for over 200 countries and territories. These are six aggregate indicators: Voice & Accountability, Control of Corruption, Governance Effectiveness, Political Stability and Absence of Violence/Terrorism, and Rule of Law, five of which we show below. Although criticized for, among other things, bias towards investors and markets (see Arndt and Oman, 2008), it paints a similarly dim picture of stagnant or declining governance and rule of law. As Cordesman (2015, p. 6) notes, despite:

Table 5.1 Transparency International's Corruption Perceptions Index

Year	Rank	Countries Surveyed
2003	113	133
2004	129	145
2005	137	158
2006	160	163
2010	175	178
2014	170	174
2018	168	180
2019	162	180
2020	160	180

Source: Transparency International (2020).

> …the many claims the U.S. and Iraqi government have made since 2003, the World Bank is almost certainly correct in estimating that little or no progress has been made in the overall quality of governance since the fall of Saddam Hussein. A combination of fighting, political power struggles, sectarian and ethnic tensions and conflict, poor security and a tenuous rule of law, poor execution of all of the major functions of government from the local to national level, and the failure to develop and implement effective budgets and development plans have left a track record at least as bad as Saddam's authoritarianism and helped ensure a continuing state of civil conflict that has nothing to do with ISIS.

Indeed, according to Dodge (2013), ordinary Iraqis see successive post-2003 governments as having failed to meet their basic needs, including employment. There are also signs of declining faith in elections as a means of achieving popular demands the turnout in the 2018 parliamentary elections being only 44.5 per cent, a 40 per cent decline over the two preceding elections (Patel, 2018) (Figure 5.11).

3.6 Social Welfare and the Delivery of Public Services

The main welfare programme of note in Iraq is the public distribution system (PDS), which allocates essential food items, such as flour, rice, and sugar, to Iraqi households. The programme has had near-universal coverage, serving 99.4 per cent of poor, and 98.6 per cent of non-poor, Iraqis in 2018; for the poorest 10 per cent of the population it provides a subsidy equal to 30 per cent of their income (World Bank, 2018c). The in-kind nature and universality of the programme have raised concerns in the World Bank and in the IMF, which since 2003 has advocated a targeted cash scheme instead (IMF, 2003, pp. 20–21). Yet, the universality of the programme explains its huge popularity and successive Iraqi governments have found it difficult to

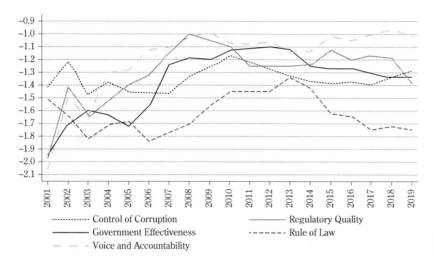

Figure 5.11 Governance indicators, 2002–2017
Source: World Bank, Aggregate Governance Indicators, 2011–2019. www.govindicators.org.

make substantial cuts in it; by contrast, Iraq's targeted Social Protection Net provided a cash benefit to only 11 per cent of the poor in 2012 (Alkhoja et al., 2016). Under IMF pressure to reform the programme, some high-earning public-sector employees have been excluded from the PDS (World Bank, 2017), but otherwise, all Iraqis, regardless of religion, sect, or class, are eligible to participate in this programme. In 2014, the programme consumed 1.8 per cent of GDP (World Bank, 2017) and was criticized as cumbersome as it involved procuring goods then reselling them at subsidized prices; however, it is one of the few programmes that has raised the welfare and income security of ordinary Iraqis.

In contrast, Iraqi public services have suffered from both low allocations and low project completion, aggravated by insecurity and limited skills. Electricity provision has been lacking since the 1990s and only recently, since 2014, started to improve (Al-Khatteeb and Istepanian, 2015), with power shortages severely hindering manufacturing. Security of course continues to be a concern: for example, in the war against ISIS, as of 2018 67,000 civilians have been killed (World Bank Group, 2018b) and 6 million people internally displaced between 2014 and 2017 (Iraq Humanitarian Response Plan UN HCR (2019). Waves of population dislocation and displacement since 2003, such as the sectarian war of 2005–2007 and the conflict with ISIS of 2014–2017, have caused a sharp rise in illiteracy among the youth, as demonstrated below. Internally displaced persons have had reduced access to education, especially in those areas affected by ISIS, with fewer parents sending children to school (Saadoun, 2018). Regarding health, life

Table 5.2 Illiteracy Rate in Iraq, (%)

Year	15 years and older	Ages 15 to 24
2000	25.95	15.20
2013	56.32	47.68
2018	49.86	43.66

Source: Own elaboration based on data from UNESCO (2019).

expectancy at birth actually declined slightly from 2000 to 2007 but has increased since then (FRED, 2019). The Institute for Economics & Peace (2018) estimates that in 2017 the economic cost of violence was 51 per cent of GDP (Table 5.2).

Much like capital formation in other sectors, investment in health and education has proved difficult to realize; by contrast, increases in salaries and staff have been easy to effect (World Bank, 2014a). The quality and reliability of education and health, and public services more generally, are low, and geographical coverage is poor. In one World Bank (2017) study, Iraq's public services scored roughly two-fifths of the average of Middle East and North Africa (MENA) countries on quality and 43 per cent on coverage.

3.7 Job Creation and Poverty

As in other MENA countries, Iraq faces insufficient employment creation in both the public and private sectors. Iraq has one of the youngest populations anywhere, half the population being under 19 years old (Bandiera et al., 2018), and the economy has found it hard to generate private sector jobs given the conditions of conflict and low levels of investment. Government administration, health, and education are mostly public in nature and employ most people, followed by construction, commerce, and agriculture, which are mostly private structures (Figure 5.12).

The number of people entering the labour force have been high, with the result that unemployment has remained high, albeit lower than its peak in the middle 2000s. Youth unemployment (between 15 and 24 years of age) stood at 16.6 per cent in 2018 (FRED, 2019). According to Iraq's 2012 Household survey, household poverty is dependent upon the sector in which a person is employed rather than whether they are working full or part-time; the agriculture and construction sectors are associated with higher levels of household poverty and public administration with a much lower rate (World Bank, 2017). This explains the public pressure that governments are under to provide more government jobs as well as the long queues for those jobs whenever they are available.

Even so, government jobs are an inefficient way of promoting general welfare and not enough jobs can be created to make a serious dent in poverty.

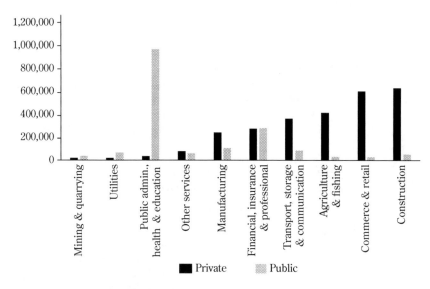

Figure 5.12 Employment by economic sector and employer
Sources: reprinted from World Bank (2018b).

Thus, in the context of rising oil revenues and real GDP from 2007 to 2012, 750,000 new jobs were created in Iraq, four-fifth of which were in the public sector; the main effect of this economic expansion however was that incomes for those employed were increased rather than jobs provided for the unemployed. Consequently, the corresponding decline in poverty, as measured by Headcount, was limited and indeed was reversed with the onset of conflict and violence in 2014 (World Bank, 2017). This all underlines the enormous insecurity that Iraqis experience and the high cost of violence.

This brings us back to our discussion at the start of the study, vis-à-vis the need for rebuilding to reinforce rather than go against prevailing political economies and the poor functioning of institutions and markets postconflict. Space does not allow for a detailed exploration, but the next section identifies the general parameters of solutions intended to (1) increase economic security for households, (2) reduce horizontal inequalities and hence the likelihood of conflict, and (3) allow investments in human and physical capital, and institutions, to recover.

4 Analysis and Recommendations

In the previous two sections, we first assessed the stance of institutions and government capabilities in Iraq following the prolonged decline of the past half a century, and then identified the strengths and weaknesses of the Iraqi economy vis-à-vis the pressing need to provide higher levels of welfare for the population and to set the economy on a path of sustainable development. In this section, we focus on identifying the potential risks that Iraqi society will face in the near future, including the damage caused by the Covid-19 pandemic, and provide suggestions for articulating government policies.

Given the current limitations in the capabilities of the state and in the face of the pressing need to provide a minimum level of welfare that, in turn, would achieve some political stability, we suggest a number of realistic reforms that we think could be instrumental in improving the current situation and that would give support to the discussion on a new social contract for Iraq.

4.1 Dangers and Opportunities of Oil Abundance

In the short to medium term, the immediate threat to Iraq's economy lies in either another collapse in oil prices or renewed conflict, especially one that affects oil exports. The Covid-19 pandemic, which we discuss below, illustrates this. Looking ahead, oil will continue to be the mainstay of Iraq's economy, providing funds to pay public employees, finance social spending, pay for public investment, and provide security. Iraq's oil reserves are sizable, estimated at 143 billion barrels or almost 10 per cent of known global reserves (IEITI, 2019). Although in dispute with other sources of authority, the central (federal) government still retains control of most of the oil revenue and will need to manage oil resources with care to maintain and increase output.[13]

Iraq's oil sector actually stands out as a notable example of success in the face of difficult circumstances: oil output has risen substantially since 2003 despite serious legal-political challenges and technical obstacles. But Article 112 of the 2005 Iraqi constitution is frustratingly ambiguous on the respective roles of central and regional governments in the management of oil resources (see Constitute, 2019). Attempts to resolve this uncertainty have largely failed, with the central government in Baghdad and the Kurdish Regional Government (KRG) engaging in contesting claims and actions about which governmental entity is allowed to explore, extract, and market oil. The KRG in fact enacted its own oil law in 2007 and has awarded about 50 extraction and exploration contracts (unrecognized by Baghdad) to international companies (Cordesman and Khazai, 2014), built oil export pipelines, and sold oil in international markets at a discount (which Baghdad regards as stolen oil). Unlike Baghdad's oil service agreements, these contracts are mostly production-sharing type arrangements. Oil policy in Iraqi Kurdistan has been murky, with the KRG unwilling to disclose who it sells oil to or other aspects of its operations, since Baghdad withdrew financial support for the KRG in 2014 (Osgood, 2018). This dynamic between Baghdad and the KRG has curbed oil exports and revenues.

The issue of control over oil is intertwined with Kurdish aspirations for independence, reflected in its vote for independence in 2017. Viewing the vote as illegal, the central government took control of Kirkuk (an ethnically diverse and oil-rich region) in response.[14] While most of Iraq's oil reserves lie outside the Kurdish region, Kurdish independence is not viable without Kurdish control over some of Iraq's oil. However, only 17 per cent of Iraq's oil reserves lie in northern Iraq (Cordesman and Khazai, 2014), only part of which the KRG controls. According to Article 140 of Iraq's Constitution, Kirkuk, which is presently not part of the KRG, is supposed to vote on whether to join the KRG or to remain within Iraq (Raheem and Rubaie, 2019); because of the sensitive implications of such a vote, it has not taken place. In reality, Baghdad fears making concessions over oil to the KRG, including control over exploration, extraction, and sale, for fear of encouraging regionalism elsewhere, notably in Basra where most of Iraq's oil is produced (Cordesman and Khazai, 2014). The thorny issue of the control of oil remains unresolved and Iraq presently operates under divergent oil management regimes, with the ever-present threat of conflict or violence.

In addition to the political, there are administrative and technical challenges. Cordesman and Khazai (2014) note that violence, sabotage, and poor infrastructure have all contributed to the limiting of Iraq's oil exports; engineering difficulties abound with water having to be brought inland to Iraq's southern oil fields from the Gulf, something which has proved difficult at times (see Shubbar, 2016). There is a need to improve oil marketing as Iraq is still using the same marketing techniques as in the 1970s and 1980s (al-Badran, 2017). These capacity issues will take investment and time to overcome but are complicated by factionalism and political deadlock in Baghdad.

4.2 The Centrality of the State and the Policy Landscape

Attempts to encourage the private sector notwithstanding, state-controlled oil revenues remain central to Iraq's economy. Thus, the question is not whether state involvement in the economy is substantial, but what form the involvement takes. In principle, there is no contradiction between an active state and a vibrant private sector. In the short to medium run, we advocate an expansion of the state and strengthening of its institutions rather than its withdrawal, although the ultimate objective of course is to encourage economic diversification and that requires significant private sector development.

Rodrik (2011) notes that there is no single method for achieving prosperity but that alleviating the binding constraints that hamper development is key. Countries following mainstream policies advocated by the Washington Consensus, he adds, have often fared worse than those that deliberately and strategically violated its precepts. Policy thus should be flexible, undogmatic, and experimental. Measures that reduce the odds of violent shocks occurring and that use and develop local institutions and resources ought to be favoured. Iraq has benefited from IMF technical assistance and World

Bank funding but should avoid formulaic policy pitfalls that at times emanate from IFIs.

Concerning the labour market, we contend that, first, the continued enlargement of public sector employment as a welfare programme is neither an efficient nor an egalitarian way to distribute oil revenues: the state is simply unable to employ the half a million Iraqi youths (Patel, 2018) that enter the labour market annually. Using the state in this way, Fukuyama (2013) suggests, also damages professionalism in the public sector and reduces state effectiveness. Ideally, hiring and wages in the public sector ought to be frozen, as Gunter (2018) advocates;[15] however, exceptions for essential personnel, as in health and education, would need to be made. This entails, second, developing alternative welfare programmes. We argue that Iraq eschew IMF calls, made since 2003 (IMF, 2003), to reform the PDS from an in-kind and comprehensive programme to a targeted cash scheme. IFIs have long had a preference for targeted as opposed to universal programmes, citing expense and the waste involved in providing benefits to the non-poor.

In contrast to IFI thinking, we view universal coverage as a potential benefit, especially as limited state capacity in Iraq makes identifying who is poor costly and difficult. Because of the numerous advantages in doing so, we instead suggest expanding the PDS into a basic cash income. First, the basic income scheme would use existing institutions built around the PDS, utilizing the latter's near-universal coverage, and require little in terms of additional capacity. Second, like the PDS, it would distribute oil revenues to all regardless of ethnicity, sect, or geographic location, reducing horizontal inequalities. Third, it would work to reinforce Iraq's political economy, where the public expects the state to distribute oil wealth equitably, strengthening the sense of nationhood. Fourth, such a scheme would also reduce pressure on the government to provide jobs. Fifth, a cash as opposed to an in-kind programme would reduce opportunities for corruption and inefficiency related to the PDS, vis-à-vis procurement and resale of goods, which is present even though the administrative cost of the PDS is modest.[16] A central intent of the proposal then is to enhance stability and allow investment and economic growth to proceed.

While space does not permit a detailed exploration of a basic income scheme, we provide a preliminary outline in three scenarios (see Van Parijs and Vanderborght, 2017). Extension of coverage might be gradual, starting with specific demographic groups and catering to circumstances (Standing, 2017). In the table below, scenario 1 represents a basic income of 25 per cent of GDP per capita, as Van Parijs and Vanderborght (2017) suggest; in 2020, the basic income would be USD 1,078 per person per annum. Scenario 2 represents 'Cost of Basic Needs', based on the result of the 2007 Household Survey; this translates into USD 732 per person per annum, USD 324 for food, and USD 408 for non-food items (Latif, 2015). Scenario 3, based on the World Bank's former poverty lines of USD 1.25 and USD 2 per day, implies a basic income of USD 456 and USD 720 respectively per person

Table 5.3 Basic Income: Three Scenarios (USD)

	2005	2010	2018
Gross domestic product (million current USD)	36,268	117,138	160,021*
GDP per capita (current USD)	1,343	3,808	4,301*
Scenario 1 One-fourth of GDP per capita		336	952	1,075*
Scenario 2 Cost of basic needs	732**		
Scenario 3			
World Bank Poverty lines of $1.25 per day			456
World Bank poverty line of $2.00 per day			720*

Notes:
* GDP estimated from UNCTAD (2021); population estimates based on Population Pyramid (2021).
** Scenario 2 is based on 2007 prices; scenario 3 is based on 2020 prices. One US $ = 1,254 ID in 2007. Sources: Population Pyramid (2021), UNCTAD (2021), Van Parijs and Vanderborght (2017), Latif (2015).

per annum, almost identical to the cost of basic needs in 2007. Based on Iraq's age structure data (see Population Pyramid, 2021), we estimate that extending USD 2 per day to every Iraqi would cost 16.7 per cent of GDP in 2020; targeting those between 20 and 34 year old costs 4.2 per cent of GDP (Table 5.3).

We ought to stress that we do not view this proposal as a panacea and do not downplay its costs. On its own, a basic income will not improve public services nor substitute for sector-specific policies (e.g., in agriculture or industry) (see Mirza, 2011). Although a rise in unearned income is supposed to increase leisure demand, a study of the effects of basic income on labour supply in Iran shows no reduction in supply (Salehi-Isfahani and Mostafavi-Dehzooei, 2018).[17] Establishing training and skills programmes for electricians, plumbers, etc., disrupted by internal and outward migration, ought to be pursued in unison in order to facilitate expanded investment rates (Gunter, 2013).

Parallel to labour market and income reforms, Iraq, among the least diversified oil exporters in MENA (IMF, 2019), should gradually diversify its sources of budget revenue away from its near complete dependence on oil; in 2013–2015 non-oil revenue, including income tax and other items, varied between 2.1 and 3.5 per cent of GDP (IMF, 2017). In addition to providing revenue, taxation helps to build a sense of accountability between the public and government, which is lacking in Iraq's reconstruction (Matsunaga, 2019).

A major obstacle to tax collection is Iraq's enterprise registration rules that are lengthy and complicated. According to the WorldBank (2019b), Iraq ranks 171 out of 190 in terms of 'ease of doing business' and 155 out of 190 for 'ease of starting a business'. Much of the private sector thus remains unregistered and untaxed, which adds to labour force informality. Iraq has medium to high levels of informality in comparison to other MENA countries. A quarter of economically active Iraqis are self-employed, and two-thirds do not have access to the pension system, both somewhat higher than MENA comparators; because of the decline in agricultural labour, only 2.6 per cent of the labour force is unpaid, lower than MENA comparators (Angel-Urdinola and Tanabe, 2012). Registration of employees might be facilitated by, for example, offering a tax holiday of a few years, instituting online registration, and making bank credit contingent on registration. Reducing informality and integrating businesses into the national pension system, will make the private sector more attractive as an employer, alleviating the political pressure on government jobs.

Concerning credit, a long overdue restructuring of state-owned banks is required over the longer term. As things stand, these banks lack sufficient capital and their ability to lend to small- and medium-sized firms, in principle significant generators of employment and output, is restricted (see IMF, 2017). Banks stay in business by charging for services and through buying and selling currency; they lend to SOEs, many of which are not viable commercially and overstaffed, which introduces a distortion in the credit market.[18]

4.3 The Covid-19 Pandemic and its Effects

The Covid-19 pandemic and ensuing world economic meltdown have aggravated Iraq's economic challenges and severely exposed its vulnerabilities. The pandemic has laid bare the country's dependence on oil. Lockdown and isolation instituted in industrialized countries have caused a collapse in the global demand for hydrocarbons and hence in oil prices and oil revenues— which account for almost all of Iraq's central government revenue and export earnings. The average price of Iraq's oil has declined from USD 64 per barrel in 2019 to USD 29 in early 2020. As a result, the World Bank (2020) estimates a deficit of 29 per cent of GDP for the planned 2020 budget, the financing of public sector salaries and pensions alone requiring an oil price of USD 58 per barrel. Iraq will have to resort to domestic borrowing for most of its needs and make deep cuts in spending, because grants and loans from international financial intuitions and foreign governments are likely to cover only a small portion of its financing needs.

Like other countries, Iraq has responded through workplace closures and restrictions on travel and gatherings (Ide, 2021). Informal sector workers have been more vulnerable to pandemic closures than those in the public sector; service sector workers, notably in transport, tourism, and hospitality have been worst affected (Jamal et al., 2020). In an attempt to lessen the economic damage, the Central Bank has tried to support households and small businesses by imposing temporary moratoria on interest and principal loan payments (World Bank, 2020), and the central government has started to make needs-based payments of ID 30,000 (roughly USD 25) to individuals (Jamal et al., 2020). While undoubtedly more will be needed to stimulate economic activity, these measures represent a reasonable, if limited, response to the Covid-19 pandemic conditions.

However, Iraq's difficulties in undertaking capital formation and the unsustainable rise in public employment have combined to complicate the fight against Covid-19. The continued expansion of the public sector—most recently in the autumn of 2019 when the central government authorised the hiring of an additional 500,000 government workers (a 17 per cent rise in state workers) in response to widespread youth protests (Hussein, 2020)—has squeezed central government finances. As shown earlier, low levels of public investment have left health structures weakened and still dilapidated from the effects of conflict and brain drain, although the fact of a population dominated by youth may moderate the effects of the pandemic. While these dire fiscal conditions may delay the implementation of a putative basic income scheme, one advantage of such a programme is that it is possible to apply gradually and selectively. Indeed, the Covid-19 pandemic has highlighted how rising public employment is an unviable safety net and illustrates the need for a more equitable distribution of public spending.

As the World Bank (2020) noted, Iraq requires a substantially larger stimulus package than the one the Iraqi government has enacted as of 2020. Over the next 6–12 months, actions to mitigate the effects of the pandemic might include the continuation or increase of government cash allocations to individuals, which to be sure is complicated because the government does not have an easy way of identifying who is poor or most needy. Reductions in salaries (especially of high earners) in the public sector might be a way to offset pressures on the budget in the short term, yet it might induce further brain drain and complicate the delivery of public services.

To summarize, the policies that we advocate can be applied selectively and strategically: vested interests in Iraq's bureaucracy or elsewhere may resist change because they benefit from the status quo, for example, as they receive bribes to expedite business registration. We contend that conflict and violence—not static economic inefficiency, per se—have acted as binding constraints on development. Hence, policies likely to reduce conflict, for example, the equitable distribution of oil rents in a basic income, ought to be prioritized.[19] In the longer term, repairing development capacity and institutions is vital, and there is a need for a body that assists in coordinating and overseeing public and private investment activities, as the Development Board did in the past (Al-Marsoumi, 2019).

5 Concluding Note

The protests that erupted in Baghdad and most of Iraq's southern provinces in the autumn of 2019 reflect popular frustrations at the high level of youth unemployment, dire public services, and chronic corruption. What we have attempted to do in this chapter is to give a context to this reality and explain why it has been difficult to escape it.

Iraq has been subject to multiple violent shocks, including wars, economic sanctions, invasion, civil war, and internal displacement. Eggertsson (2008) notes that negative external shocks are most destructive to developing countries because the rudimentary technology in these countries restricts their ability to respond to shocks. Likewise, North et al. (2009, p. 252) write:

> Over the last two centuries, sustained economic growth results from the reduction of negative shocks to social output rather than a marked increase in the rate of growth in years when output is growing.

Institutional decline along with loss of human and physical capabilities account for Iraq's lacklustre economic recovery; this decay is unlikely to be quickly reversed. We argue that the deteriorating political institutions and narrowing political space in the 1970s and 1980s, along with protracted economic sanctions in the 1990s resulted in the decline in developmental institutions and structures. Iraq's current social contract is unsustainable, but it wasn't obviously broken in the 1970s and 1980s when its institutional decline began. In other words, a broken social contract does not ultimately explain why institutions have been in decline for five decades or why the Iraqi government chose to engage in external and internal conflict. Reconstruction, notably under US occupation, sought to sideline the existing institutions and worked against the prevailing political economy; it neither constructed stable new institutions nor repaired existing but broken ones, aggravating conflict and establishing instead a fragile and fragmented polity. Subsequent Iraqi governments have not done better. The challenge—and it is a substantial one—is to encourage conditions where Iraq's human capabilities and institutions can develop.

We see a central role for the state in meeting this challenge and argue that this need not constrain the development of a vibrant private sector that is much needed. We argue also that a fairer distribution of oil resources is crucial; it is desirable in terms of fairness and because horizontal equality is likely to reduce the chance of conflict, so promoting capital formation and development. The present policy of distributing public sector jobs—often to the best connected rather than the most qualified—is both inequitable and unsustainable. Post-2003 politics based on ethno-sectarian apportionment has given power and voice to the political elites that claim to represent ethnicities, religions, or sects, and has disempowered the ordinary Iraqis that the elites claim to represent. Thus, 'power-sharing' among political elites does not necessarily empower ordinary Iraqis, but introduces bias, discrimination, and exploitation. Indeed, the frustrations of ordinary Iraqis, including much of the youth, at corruption and poor services represents a rejection of a political system that is based on partiality and cronyism. To meet the above challenge Iraq's power-sharing arrangement should emanate from a genuinely democratic and representative process that assures the accountability of the parties it comprises.

Notes

1 Before the nationalization of oil in 1972, Iraq received royalties from international oil companies rather than directly controlling oil sales. Central government control of revenues mostly continues today, although there is disagreement about who owns oil resources and revenues (regional versus central government) under the Iraqi Constitution of 2005 (see Constitute, 2019). Three main factors determine oil revenues: the quantities of exported oil, the trading price of oil on international markets, and the purchasing power of the USD vis-à-vis other currencies (Alnaswawi, 1994).
2 The Iraqi state can and has sub-contracted development work to private (national and international) firms. This still requires the government to identify priorities, establish rankings, and coordinate investments, viz. state capacity.
3 This relates to a shortcoming in the thesis that Acemoglu and Robinson (2012) have advanced in regard to how development is achieved, through 'inclusive' as opposed to 'extractive' institutions. Depending on how one defines these, Iraq's institutions, in for example 1980, might appear inclusive in many respects and extractive in others. Iraq's provision of free health and education and increasing levels of income is arguably economically inclusive, but its repressive political and security institutions were arguably extractive. The fact that Iraq invaded Iran in September 1980 is not in itself evidence that its institutions were in general extractive (or inclusive for that matter). One has to define such categories specifically and explain how the specific category of institution (e.g., extractive) generated (or ameliorated) social or international conflict; otherwise, it would be impossible to falsify the contention that institutions of a certain category cause conflict.
4 There were geo-political logics at work in Iraq's calculations: the Ba'ath leadership viewed revolutionary Iran as a threat to Iraq and to its own power; and Iraq had longstanding border and other disputes with Kuwait. Whether conflict provided a rational solution (i.e., cost minimizing) is another matter.
5 Sen (1983) noted that popular pressure for corrective actions regarding policy errors in pluralistic India have precluded the occurrence of famines, unlike in totalitarian China, even though in general terms China has done better than India in terms of improvement in nutrition.
6 The Ba'ath even created parallel (and often, secret) budgets to direct resources to particular priorities such as internal security (Savage, 2013).
7 Fukuyama (2013) actually argues that output measures like these are imperfect for gauging state effectiveness because they, for example, infant mortality, may improve as a result of technology and despite reduced governance. One measure of state capacity that is not accurately applicable to an oil economy such as Iraq is taxation. Accuracy and frequency of census data can serve as an alternative measure (Lee and Zhang, 2016). In this regard, it worth noting that while censuses were conducted at regular intervals in Iraq (usually every 10 years), the last census, of 1997, was partial and did not include the Kurdish region where the central government had no authority. Political impasse and instability have precluded the administration of a census since, though one is planned for 2020 (Kurdistan 24, 2019).
8 An interesting question that is beyond the scope of this study is whether expanded state capacity and effectiveness (at least in war and related activities) provided the Iraqi government with an impetus to engage in conflict that later destroyed capabilities.

150 *Bassam Yousif et al.*

9 To be fair, the CPA is only partly responsible for de-Ba'athification, as the Iraqi 'Higher National De-Ba'athification Commission' expanded the application of the policy. See Sissons and Al-Saidi (2013).
10 In addition, in 2003, 1,000,000 were employed in the Iraqi civil service as teachers, accountants, physicians, etc. (IMF, 2003).
11 For an exploration of the reasons or rationale of these policies, see Yousif (2007). It is not possible to view these actions as the result of ignorance or bad advice. According to Zinn (2016), US government officials, including those at the National Security Council, were aware of the potential risks of throwing hundreds of thousands of unemployed and armed young men onto the streets of Iraq's cities.
12 See Yousif (2010) for an exploration of this theme.
13 US and UK pressure for Iraq to de-nationalize and privatize its oil sector in 2006 and 2007 largely failed because of a popular backlash (Nalman, 2007; Muttit, 2012).
14 Kirkuk itself came under the control of Kurdish forces (fighting the Islamic State) in 2014.
15 Gunter (2018) calls for a hiring but not a pay freeze, probably in recognition of the political difficulties that a pay freeze would involve.
16 The program cost 1.8 per cent of GDP in 2013, of which 0.3 per cent was administrative (IMF, 2015) The IMF (2015) advocated reform of the PDS as the program creates 'distortions' to the extent that it purchases domestically produced wheat at double the price of imported wheat. But the price of imported wheat is itself distorted from heavy subsidization in producer countries and any saving in abrupt reductions of subsidies for wheat in Iraq would have to be compared against the decline in an already weakened agricultural sector.
17 Salehi-Isfahani and Mostafavi-Dehzooei (2018) argue that the basic income actually raised labour supply among service sector workers in Iran, because some credit-constrained service sector firms made use of the basic income to expand operations.
18 According to the (World Bank 2014), nonperforming SOEs have often received on an annual basis more funds than sectors such as health, education, water, and sanitation.
19 On binding constraints see Rodrik (2007).

6 Conflict, Peace-Building, and Post-Conflict Reconstruction in Yemen

Mahmoud Al Iriani, Hiba Hassan, and Irene Martinez

1 Introduction

Violent conflicts are by no means new to Yemen. For centuries, the country has been plagued with political and social instability. The current conflict is, however, the longest, bloodiest, and most destructive in Yemen's recent history. This chapter seeks to explore and understand the underlying causes of the conflict, including the presence of a weak state, economic deterioration, foreign intervention, corruption, and the marginalization of key local areas and groups. Our analysis also aims to correct some ubiquitous misconceptions found throughout the literature on the Yemeni conflict. We also seek to examine the dire consequences of the current conflict on the economy and the social fabric of the country and discuss the peace-building process and post-conflict economic reconstruction. Finally, we conclude with a summary of the findings and some policy implications.

2 The Road to Conflict

The weakening of the central state in Yemen and its eventual degradation has its roots in a plethora of factors that can in part be dated back to the arrival of the first Hashemite imam, al-Hadi, from Medina in 897 AD. Al-Hadi and later his descendants succeeded in preaching Zaydi Shiʿism in Northern Yemen and ruled the country intermittently (Knights, 2018).[1] In the early twentieth century, the Mutawakkilite dynasty, descendants of al-Hadi, seized power from the Ottomans and ruled Northern Yemen for half a century until they were expelled in 1962.

The revolution of September 1962 in North Yemen ousted the Mutawakkilite Imams and established the Yemen Arab Republic (YAR).[2] Subsequently, civil war broke out between the Republicans, with support from Nasser of Egypt, and the Royalists, backed by the Kingdom of Saudi Arabia (hereafter KSA), the Hashemite kingdom of Jordan, and covert support from Britain. In 1967, the Republicans lost the military assistance of Egypt in the wake of the Arab–Israeli war. Realizing the unending nature of the war, the two Yemeni combatants then resorted to dialogue, reaching a peace pact in

DOI: 10.4324/9781003344414-9

1970, which laid the ground for power-sharing arrangements in the newly formed government of the Yemen Arab Republic (in North Yemen). Meanwhile, South Yemen obtained its independence from Britain in November 1967 and established the Marxist 'People's Democratic Republic of Yemen' (PDRY). It then established a close relationship with the Soviet Union.

Brief intermittent conflict punctuated the relationship between the two new states. In 1990, the PDRY lost its Soviet support inducing Ali Salem al-Beidh, then leader of the PDRY, to approach the late president Ali Abdullah Saleh (Saleh) of the YAR seeking the reunification of Yemen. The two leaders announced the creation of the current Republic of Yemen (ROY) on 22 May 1990. The unification pact provided an arrangement of *equal* power-sharing, and Saleh became the president of the ROY while al-Beidh became the vice-president.

The equal power-sharing arrangement proved unsuccessful, and relations between the two leaderships deteriorated quickly.[3] The southerners accused Saleh of excluding them from executive decision-making and of leading an assassination campaign against senior southern officials (Williams et al., 2017). In 1994, North–South tensions led to a brief war and a failed attempt at violent secession by al-Beidh and other southern officials. The army and some Southerners loyal to Saleh were able to quell the attempt and expel secession leaders from the country. The central government in Sana'a regained control over all ROY territories, including the South.[4]

2.1 Spring 2011 Uprising

Following the war and the failed secession attempt in 1994, Saleh ruled the ROY with little opposition. However, in November 2005, an alliance of five major political parties formed the Joint Meeting Parties (JMP). This alliance declared its opposition to Saleh's plan to run for another term in the 2006 elections, as well as his preparations to groom his son to succeed him in power. Political tensions increased when the JMP called on Saleh to step down and announced its support for his rival in the 2006 elections. Nevertheless, Saleh won a new seven-year term despite signs of public discontent that led to the 2011 peaceful youth protests, one of the Arab Spring revolutions. The 2011 'Revolution of Change' was taken over by the JMP, notably by al-Islah party,[5] joined by other enemies of Saleh, including the Houthi movement, then located in the Sa'da governorate.

After a period of unrest, Saleh agreed to step down in exchange for complete immunity from prosecution under the terms of a GCC-brokered initiative. On 21 February 2012, VP Abd-Rabbuh Mansour Hadi was unanimously elected as president to lead a transitional government for two years, during which the international community brokered a National Dialogue Conference (NDC). The Conference prepared a document outlining a road map to peace and stability by means of establishing a federation of six districts in Yemen. The road-map was approved unanimously by participating delegates in NDC and a presidential panel in February 2014. Further, the NDC drafted a new constitution to be voted on shortly in a popular referendum. However, the Houthis and their new ally, Saleh, withdrew from the NDC agreement and announced their opposition to its proposed federal system, which they claimed would threaten the country's unity.

2.2 From Uprising to War

The rise of the Houthis began to gain momentum. In September 2014, the controversial decision of Hadi's transitional government to cut fuel subsidies led to massive hikes in fuel prices and resulted in public discontent (Williams et al., 2017). The Houthis supported the popular demonstrations that followed, and their leader Abdul Malek al-Houthi appeared on TV to request that fuel subsidies be reinstated (Feltman, 2018). They were also demanding a representative government that would reflect the seats allocated to political groups and independent activists during Yemen's NDC (Al Batati, 2015). Houthi armed groups advanced south from Sa'da and took control of the city of Amran, about 50 kilometres north of the capital Sanaʻa. The militant group then advanced on Sanaʻa and finally captured it on 21 September 2014, assisted by their former enemy Saleh who then also had control of most of the official armed forces.

Once the country was mired in a political deadlock, the situation escalated rapidly. In January 2015, the Houthis arrested the chief-of-staff and placed Hadi and his government under house arrest. When Hadi managed to escape to Aden on 21 February 2015, the Houthis announced the dissolution of the parliament and appointed a new Houthi-led presidential council. In March 2015, the Houthi–Saleh alliance advanced towards the city of Aden, prompting Hadi to flee to the KSA seeking help. Hadi's plea for assistance on arrival in Riyadh gave the KSA the opportunity to form the 'Arab Coalition', with the proclaimed aim of uprooting the Houthis and restoring the legitimate government.[6] The coalition began a military campaign, dubbed 'Operation Decisive Storm' in March 2015.

In the meantime, the capture of Sanaʻa by the Houthis and Saleh attracted local, regional, and international condemnation. In April 2015, the UN Security Council issued resolution 2216 imposing sanctions on individuals it said were undermining the stability of Yemen, naming the Houthis and Saleh. The Council also demanded that the Houthis withdraw from all areas seized and surrender military and security establishments, and all the arms they had captured. It also demanded that the Houthis cease all actions coming exclusively under the authority of the legitimate government and fully implement previous Council resolutions. Acting under Chapter VII of its Charter, the Council also called upon the Houthis to refrain from any hostilities or threats against neighbouring countries, release all political prisoners and individuals under house arrest or arbitrarily detained, and end the military recruitment of children (UN Security Council, 2015).

The coalition waged a massive air campaign against the Houthis and what remained of the government's forces. The situation continued to deteriorate, as witnessed by the seven-year ongoing war between the internationally recognized government backed by the KSA-led Arab Coalition and the new de facto Houthi government in Sana'a. Since then, the country has experienced an increase in the number and intensity of terrorist attacks, street protests, tribal clashes, and kidnappings, as well as growing tension in the South. In December 2017, the Houthis turned on and killed Saleh after he announced his intention to switch sides and join forces with the KSA-led coalition. The war continued with no victor, and in August 2019 tensions within the coalition surfaced when Hadi's government accused the UAE of helping the Southern Transitional Council (STC) to capture two southern governorates and force his government out of the temporary capital in Aden. In June 2020, the UAE assisted STC to capture the significant island of Socotra while the KSA forces on the island turned a blind eye. This development was the latest manifestation of the underlying tensions between the UAE and the KSA on the one hand, and the legitimate government's objectives in Yemen on the other.

3 Understanding the Roots of Conflict in Yemen

There is a prevailing perception in the political science literature that violent civil conflicts are related to one or more genuine grievances resulting from economic and social inequality, political repression, and ethnic and religious aspects (see the discussion in Bodea and Houle in this volume). However, Collier (2000) argues instead that economic analysis suggests that rebellion is more likely to be *a form of organized crime*, and rebels are not public-spirited heroes fighting against injustice. Once started, violence is promoted and continued when there are revenues to be made by warlords. The risk of civil war becomes higher when a country's resources and level of development do not match the elite's ambitions. The policy implications of this proposition are that if we neglect the economic dimensions of civil war, we miss substantial opportunities for promoting peace. Makdisi and Sadaka (2005) concluded that in the Lebanese civil war (1975–1990), religion rather than ethnic fractionalization was the main factor leading to the civil war. They point out that there is little evidence for the significance of economic factors. Still, economic factors could potentially explain the relatively long duration of the Lebanese war, a conclusion that agrees with Collier's.

In the case of Yemen, several writers have regarded the conflict as a sectarian war, but many indicators suggest otherwise. Most signs point to local political greed for power capitalizing on numerous existing grievances.[7] Even during the NDC, which was meant to come up with 'a new resilient social contract', only the Yemeni political elites and outside powers were present. The political elites and local groups, including those who presented their grievances during the NDC, made it clear that they aimed to seize more power and take control of the country's economic resources, rather than preaching sectarian principles. Yemen's mountainous terrain, tribal loyalties, and sectarian divide, as well as the destruction of the social contract by the Yemeni elites, were factors that played a significant role in creating a fertile environment for the current struggle to flourish. Furthermore, foreign powers are exploiting rifts between political groups and sponsoring some of them, in order to promote their own territorial and economic interests in the country's resources.

In what follows, we present some of the critical factors that paved the way for a power struggle in Yemen and a civil war that is likely to continue for the foreseeable future.

3.1 Geography

Geography plays a vital role in the foundation of Yemen's political economy, and the strategic location of the country has made it susceptible to regional and international influences that have nourished local competing political groups, contributing to its enduring political instability. Yemen lies on the Bab al-Mandab strait through which much of the world's oil shipments pass. It occupies around 528 thousand square kilometres on the southern end of the Arabian Peninsula. Its population in 2018 was estimated at a little over 30 million, 70 per cent living in rural areas. Only 3 per cent of the land is arable and the country has one of the lowest per capita fresh water supplies in the world. Yemen's water resources are very scarce, and much of Yemen's poverty is a result of acute water shortages. In the capital Sana'a, less than half the residents are connected to the main water supply, and tap water only flows intermittently in most major cities (Hincks, 2016). Trade has been vital for the country since ancient times notably under the kingdom of Sheba, sending spices and frankincense north to the Mediterranean world. Nowadays, trading ports such as Hodeidah, Aden, and Saleef are significant sources of revenue and are essential for the political control of the country (Easterly, 2018). The location of impoverished Yemen next to the oil-rich Arab monarchies means that the country has become a candidate for the role of poor backyard state of its wealthy neighbours.

3.2 Economic Factors

Before the recent conflict, Yemen was the Middle East's poorest country with overall weak economic and social indicators (Table 6.1). In 2012, about 44 per cent of the population was undernourished, with nearly five million requiring emergency aid (Hincks, 2016). According to the World Bank data, the indicators showed slight improvements in health, primary education, and the literacy rate during the last few decades. These improvements,

Table 6.1 Selected Economic and Social Indicators in Pre-conflict Yemen and MENA (2010)

Indicator	Yemen	MENA
Population (million)	24.4	325
GDP per capita (current USD)	1,283	2,000
HDI Rank	133	–
Percentage of the population below the poverty line	43	16.9
Percentage of urban population	31	58
Life expectancy at birth (Year)	63	71
Infant mortality rate (for every 1000 births)	78	27
Percentage of malnourished infants (under five years)	43	12
Percentage of Population with access to a safe water source	62	87
Health expenditures (% of GDP)	2.1	4.8
Adult literacy rate (%)	61	74

Source: World Bank (2019c)

however, were not enough to satisfy the aspirations of the Yemeni people for a better life, and certainly did not reflect the country's potential. The percentage of those below the poverty line increased, as well as the number of malnourished infants. The increase in GDP per capita resulted mainly from the influx of oil export revenues, which were used pro-cyclically. The significant oil revenues were primarily used to finance current expenditures, notably higher wages and salaries, which had negative consequences when crude prices later declined.

Not only was the economy performing relatively poorly, but it also showed low performance in almost all development-related indicators. As Figure 6.1 indicates, Yemen scored below the average of the MENA region in such indicators as economic reforms, governance, economic growth, and investing in people.[8]

Agriculture has been the main source of employment, providing around 55 per cent of jobs in 1991, but the real impact of agriculture on GDP was remarkably low at 24.2 per cent (Figure 6.2). The contribution of agriculture to GDP decreased to around 12 per cent in 2010. Before 2011, 69 per cent of the country's population was living in small, self-sufficient mountain villages, subsisting on agriculture.[9]

The incidence of poverty in rural areas was at 43 per cent, nearly twice as much as in the urban areas and growing continuously, but with marked regional differences in the level. The rural areas in the governorates of Saʿada, Hajjah, Amran, and Hodeidah were the poorest. Unemployment averaged 13 per cent in 2010 with almost 20 per cent unemployment among females and 22 per cent among the youth and is believed to have fuelled the public discontent that preceded the current conflict. Before the current conflict, the workforce in Yemen was mostly uneducated, informally employed, and male-dominated (ILO, 2015). The bulk of those employed worked either in

Conflict, Peace-Building, and Post-Conflict Reconstruction 157

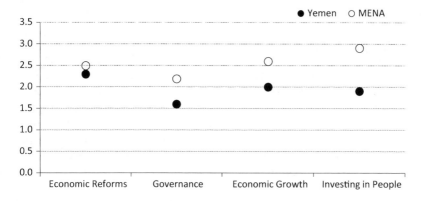

Figure 6.1 Pre-conflict development profile of Yemen (2010)

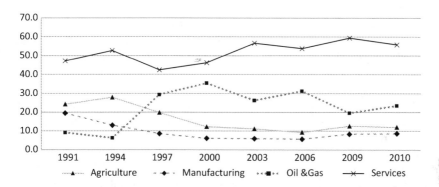

Figure 6.2 Pre-conflict contributions of economic sectors to Yemen's GDP (%)

agriculture or in wholesale and retail. Most of the employed workforce was engaged in 'own-use production', including subsistence foodstuff producers.

The long-standing structural weaknesses in the country's economy, particularly the lack of access to a stable source of fuel, electricity, along with increasing inflation and a high rate of unemployment had been continuously damaging the national economy and injuring the lives of people across the country, with a significant impact on those living in geographically unfavourable areas before the war. Some analysts have pointed to the weak economy, and the government's inability to provide badly needed services to ordinary citizens, to explain why it was grappling with the southern secessionists, the Houthi militant group, an al-Qaeda threat, and tribal issues (England, 2010). Public services had been deteriorating rapidly, partially due to falling public revenue for many years before the uprising. In addition to a weak economy, there was an evident lack of government presence throughout the country. Even before the current conflict, Yemen was plagued with violence between tribes over land and water, and a want of transparent processes for the settlement of disputes, negatively affecting prospects for any significant improvement in the economy.

3.3 Social Organization

One of the characteristics of the Yemeni state is the absence of formal institutional capacity due to the long-standing dominance of personal networks that bypass institutions and impede proper institutional development. Enforcement of the law was maintained, mainly through informal channels. The pre-conflict administrative system developed into a mix of corruption and elite dominance, which tended to provoke growing street protests, tribal clashes, terrorist attacks, and kidnappings, all of which signalled that there was state failure in Yemen. The country was also generally portrayed as a state on the verge of collapse, as it was running out of oil and, even more alarmingly, water. However, there are other dimensions that affect social grievances in the country. The anthropologist Paul Dresch argues that as early as the 1990s the traditional categories used to describe the Yemeni elite, such as merchants, shaykhs, officers, and modernists, had finally collapsed (Dresch, 1993). The Yemeni elites were defined as consisting of a set of classes, but these were never mutually exclusive and have become more fluid in recent years.[10]

Although Yemen has clear sea and land borders that may depict the country as a unit, the reality is that it is a segregated country with multiple regional power hubs. Socio-political groups and religious communities are comprised of tribes, governmental administrative units, political parties, and different religious communities. The structure of the tribes seems to be stronger in the North and to have more influence at the national level, unlike those in South Yemen which before unification pursued a policy of detribalization.[11] Thus, the difference in the tribal structure reflects the well-known divide of the country between North and South. Since the civil war of 1994, grievances among the Southerners led them to continuously express their desire for a separate state and these grievances resulted in the emergence of the Southern Peaceful Movement (SPM) in 2007. However, neither the North nor the South had stable socioeconomic systems or structures.

3.3.1 Exploring the Local

Responding to demands for the decentralization of authority, which rose after the 1994 civil war, the central government of Yemen issued the Local Authority Law (LAL) in 2000, as a blueprint for creating local councils in the country. Local authorities were technically allowed to make use of revenues obtained from utility bills and revenues from *zakat*.[12] However, since the final budgets were approved in the Parliament, the councils suffered chronic underfunding, which was an impediment to any significant developmental work by local district councils (al-Awlaqi and al-Madhaji, 2018). The effect of local councils on development gradually declined as, in the absence of a system of checks and balances, most councils wrongly allocated funds available for personal and political purposes.

Given an array of state levels in a large number of localities,[13] there was little coordination between public bodies, especially in the rural areas, which further damaged already collapsing public services (Mitchell, 2012). As of 2007, per capita public health expenditure was USD 11, and only 4.9 per cent of total government expenditure was allocated to health, much lower than in comparable countries (UNDP, 2008). Even the most impoverished households sought their medical care from private rather than public health facilities, as the government was failing to provide people with the health care they needed.

3.3.2 Urban Pressures

Demographic pressures have been a significant problem in the major cities of Yemen. Official sources estimate that the population of the capital rose from 135,000 in 1975 to over two million before the start of the conflict. The growth rate in smaller towns has also been rapid, averaging 10 per cent annually between the 1980s and the 2000s (Stadnicki, 2014). Informal settlement in Yemen's urban areas has grown by 229 per cent in the last two decades. In 2019, it was estimated that 70 per cent of urban residents live in informal settlements both in the national capital and in other regional capitals.[14] The government has been unable to secure essential services for most of the urban population, leading to further distrust and discontent. In the past, Qat production reduced rural-to-urban migration somewhat. Due to the war, migration changed, moving from war zones to safer areas, both urban and rural. If, in the future, higher levels of security are achieved, the pressure on urban centres will most likely increase as the rural-to-urban migration pattern returns.

3.4 Political Factors

The political system that developed after the unification in 1990 was layered onto a robust tribal structure, leading to a complex multilayered political structure. Despite the population differences between the Marxist PDRY and the traditionalist, free-market YAR,[15] a 50/50 power-sharing agreement was reached laying out the path for future disputes. Leaders pursued the integration of both former republics together with their tribes and sectarian and political diversities. Despite an initial appearance of democratic willingness, regional rivalry, along with an atmosphere of intense distrust between the leaders, led to the 1994 war, the attempt at secession, and the recent discontent in the South.

The electoral system in Yemen is based on a dual legislature. The Shura Council (Majlis al-Shura) has 111 members designated by the president, and the House of Representatives (Majlis al-Nawab) has 301 members chosen by plurality vote in single-member constituencies. Both houses sit for six-year terms and, until 2011, were controlled by the majority of Saleh's General People's Congress (GPC) party. Direct elections for a seven-year presidency term were first held in 1999 and another in 2006. Saleh was able to win both terms, discouraging any change in the accountability of officials or distribution of power. Saleh's patronage system benefitting from the dominance of the GPC in both the Shura Council and House of Representatives, was able to steadily modify the Constitution in order to permit him to run for re-election. This continuous exploitation and abuse of the electoral system enhanced the gradual deterioration of trust in the state and led to the popular uprising of 2011.

3.4.1 The Patronage System

Before the war, the patronage system was Saleh's favourite tool for maintaining his control over the country. Recognizing the strength of the social forces in Yemen, Saleh was known for avoiding exclusion or direct confrontation with opposing individuals and groups. Instead, his preferred tactics were cooption, compromise, and divide-and-rule, resulting in a relatively wide circle of clients who supported the regime. By the mid-2000s, the regime's dwindling resources as a result of the decline in oil revenues produced a change in the patronage system with a focus on resource distribution to selected individuals solely from Saleh's family. As a result, grassroots leaders in the North and South began to organize themselves to protest against the cuts in government handouts, undermining and marginalizing them and their territories.

In the meantime, the South experienced a wave of 're-tribalization' after unification. Southern leaders did not enjoy the financial and political support from Saleh afforded to their peers in the North, which was perceived as aggravating inequalities. There were some exceptions, including the frequent appointment of southern cabinet heads and various ministers loyal to Saleh. Economic exclusion also reinforced feelings of resentment and alienation in the South. Southern areas provided 80 per cent of Yemen's oil, but the bulk of revenues was monopolized by the government in Sanaʿa. This eventually contributed to the emergence of the SPM, with moderate demands regarding equality in employment, local decision-making, and greater control over the South's economic resources. Later, elements within the SPM, led by the STC, shifted to engage in secession from Yemen and the rebuilding of an independent 'South Arabia'.

Civil society was incapable of countering the actions of the regime, the result of this being an inability to ensure the democratic transition of power. Two essential barriers prevented civil society from forming an effective counterbalance to the regime. First, an inclination to rearticulate a system that encourages the continued dominance of the elite. The effectiveness and solvency of actors in the civil sphere, political activists, advocacy groups, newspapers, and professional syndicates, were derived mainly from their proximity to the leadership, which meant most civil society actors were, primarily, part of the regime. Second, the law, or more often the lack of its enforcement, prevented civil groups from pressuring the regime without risking penalties. Civil society was able to expand and slightly liberalize regulatory laws, but this did not result in a loosening of the regime's grip on power.

3.4.2 Rampant Corruption

In 2020, Yemen ranked 176 out of a total of 180 countries in Transparency International's Corruption Index, down by 8 per cent since 2012[16]. Corruption is deep-rooted in all Yemeni state institutions, with widespread partiality embedded in both the public and private sectors. Even before the outset of the 2015 war, the state was lacking in legitimacy because most of the country's 'economic benefits were redistributed among corrupt patronage networks' (Yemen Polling Centre, 2013). Not surprisingly, tax evasion was widespread, with tax revenue accounting for only 7.3 per cent of GDP in 2010. State institutions did not adequately protect the citizens or ensure security or justice. This weakness in the taxing and justice systems, combined with the inability of markets to provide adequate job opportunities, contributed significantly to the public discontent that preceded the outbreak of the Yemeni conflict. The war has aggravated the situation as security institutions and services in Houthi-controlled areas, and areas run by UAE-backed forces, operate without any accountability. Also, with the conflict, corruption has become pervasive in the customs' sector run by Houthis and the legitimate government, especially since levels of transparency have been extremely low.

3.4.3 The Interplay between Oil Rents, Sectarianism, and Political Institutions

As emphasized by rentier state theory, oil wealth influences the nature of the state and its relationship with society (Elbadawi and Makdisi, 2016). Oil resources in Yemen are relatively limited in comparison to those of neighbouring countries. However, it has been an essential commodity in the domestic economy for the last two decades. Between 2000 and 2009, the hydrocarbons sector, including refining, accounted directly for 20–30 per cent of Yemen's total gross domestic product (GDP), 80–90 per cent of its exports, and 70–80 per cent of government income (Salisbury, 2011). The energy sector was a valuable source of state revenue. However, due to the weakness of local checks and balances, and the lack of the enforcement of the international *Extractive Industries Transparency Initiative* guidelines, a large part of the oil revenue has been wasted by the regime helping the late President Saleh to preserve his power by means of patronage.

Even though sectarianism is not historically a feature of Yemen's religious culture, observers have noted a rising sectarian polarization originating from the use of the sectarian divide by politicians in their attempts to gain popularity and eventually rule the country. The Zaydi Houthis have implemented Shi'ite sectarian slurs from the conflicts in Syria, Lebanon, and Iraq in promoting their ambition to restore Hashemite rule in Yemen.[17] On the other hand, their *political* opponents have used popular slogans found in Wahabi, Salafi, and Muslim Brotherhood doctrine. Sects in Yemen are largely social categories and theoretical limits are defined in religious terms, but their relevance to politics derives primarily from political competition rather than actual doctrinal differences. Historically, sectarian slogans have been used by politicians to support their struggle to gain power. Recently, Saleh has allied with different religious groups, including the Muslim Brothers, the Salafis, and the Houthis. He was able to change sides easily through the patronage system he established, which was possible only by using the oil windfall that became available starting in 1986.

Before the introduction of Zaydism and Salafism, the Yemeni population followed the Shafi'i school of Sunni Islam. Currently, the Zaydis occupy most of the far northern areas of the country and constitute between 30 and 35 per cent of the population; the rest are Sunni Shafi'i adherents, and there is a small minority of Salafis. Since the spread of Zaydism, recurrent violent clashes have characterized the relationship between the followers of these sects. Some critical Yemeni groups, including many analysts, have presented the Zaydi and Salafi movements as intruding novelties, extraneous to 'authentic' Yemeni culture, brought from the KSA and Iran (al-Waday, 2017).[18]

3.5 Foreign Intervention

International and regional interventions in Yemen are nothing new. After the collapse of the Soviet Union and the unification of the two Yemeni states, the US gave more leverage to regional powers, specifically the KSA, to influence Yemeni politics. Following the 9/11 terrorist attacks and the KSA's link to them, the US increased its direct involvement in Yemen, helping the government to combat terrorist groups like al-Qaeda in the Arab Peninsula (AQAP) and ISIS, and waging drone raids on suspected terrorists in Yemen.

Since 2105, the violent war in Yemen has been propagated by a plethora of regional and international actors. While foreign influence has been more political than religious, the recent conflict between the KSA (and the West), and Iran, has resulted in the KSA introducing itself to the Sunni population of Yemen as the protector of Sunni Islam. Iran, on the other hand, is seen by the Houthi group as a nation standing up against the alleged injustice of the United States, Israel, and the KSA (Baron et al., 2016). The foreign policy of Iran in Yemen does not appear to have been a significant factor in

Yemeni affairs before the current conflict, even though Tehran had a long-established diplomatic presence in Sanaʻa. Tehran's policy seems to be based more on ideology rather than on theology. However, this does not inhibit the regime in Iran from using Shiʻism as a soft-power tool for organizing Shiʻites in the region and thus serve its agenda. The openness of certain Zaydi leaders towards Iran's foreign policy and Twelver Shiʻism gave Iran the means to develop its influence in Yemen.

While Iran's role in Yemen was negligible until recently, its neighbours in the GCC were actively engaged in the country's politics. GCC countries, notably the KSA, have long perceived Yemen as the weak link in the region—a possible source of instability in the Arabian Peninsula and along vital maritime routes. Of the GCC countries interfering in Yemen's affairs, the KSA undoubtedly stands out. The relationship between Riyadh and Yemen is a lengthy and twisted one. In Yemen, many citizens regard the kingdom to the north as a nouveau riche upstart that possesses disproportionate influence in the region, and the Saudis perceive Yemen as a troublesome and populous state in their own 'back-yard' which compels both attention and caution. The KSA has long advocated a policy of 'containment and maintenance'. 'Keep Yemen weak', as King ʻAbd al-Aziz allegedly advised his sons on his deathbed in 1953, reflects long-standing worries that a prosperous Yemen could form a significant threat to Saudi domestic security.[19] The Saudis are also wary of the collapse of a neighbouring state which, as the poorest and second-most-populous state in the Peninsula, could bring them a large influx of economic migrants (Salisbury, 2014).[20]

After the republicans prevailed in 1970 in YAR, Riyadh became, in the 1980s, a direct patron of both the Yemeni government and tribal and military chiefs, remunerating them with monthly stipends (Baron, 2019). This remuneration continued for most of the first 30 years of Saleh's regime, supporting Sanaʻa in its battle with the leftists during the 1970s and 1980s. While the stronger and wealthier neighbour was indeed providing economic assistance to YAR, it was also covering the country with schools that taught a curriculum based on Wahhabi Islam and which are politically and ideologically faithful to the ruling al-Saud. Meanwhile, the Houthis have developed a narrative of ideological opposition against Wahabi KSA. However, this was not always the case.[21] Later, ROY also became a target for Riyadh's counter-terrorism strategy when the country began to focus on tackling Islamic extremism. Yemen became the hub for al-Qaeda operatives fleeing from the KSA, and both the Saudi and Yemeni branches of the organization collaborated until their merger as AQAP in 2009.

The latest development in the standoff between the Yemeni government and the UAE was the massacre of the national army by UAE war jets on the outskirts of Aden. The Yemeni Ministers of the Interior and Transport claimed that the UAE warplanes supporting the STC launched 15 airstrikes targeting the army in the interim capital Aden and the city of Zanzibar, the centre of Abyan province.[22] The Yemeni Defence Ministry declared that the UAE airstrikes on government forces left more than 300 people dead or wounded. These developments reflect the fragile links between the Hadi government and Coalition members, namely the UAE and the KSA, and their divergent agendas.

The intervention by KSA and its allies in Yemen in March 2015 displayed a lack of a clear vision or strategy for achieving their declared goals. These goals were summarized as preventing the Houthis and their allies from ruling all of Yemen, reinstating the legitimate government, and preserve the security of the KSA and neighbouring countries. Only a month into the war, the KSA announced the end of the coalition's military operations 'Operation Decisive Storm' after it had attained its goals, and the launch of 'Operation Restoring Hope' to rebuild Yemen. However, after more than seven years of war, the legitimate government is still in exile, and the Houthis continue to control most of the highly populated areas of Yemen, including the capital Sana'a. The Houthi threat to the security of the KSA also appears to be more imminent, including Houthi attacks on Saudi airports and oil facilities.

Independent reports have documented that civilian targets and infrastructure in Yemen have endured a higher proportion of attacks by the coalition than Houthi military targets did during the first five years of the conflict.[23] Notably, Sa'ada, Ta'iz, and Sana'a, were most frequently targeted by Coalition airstrikes (Mundy, 2018). After the first few months of the war, which saw the liberation of most of the southern areas, there were almost no advances on the ground, and Houthis strengthened their grip on the areas they controlled. The Coalition showed no interest in liberating additional areas, save for capturing part of the western coastal region of the Hudaydah governorate by military forces loyal to the UAE. Instead, there have been increasing coalition airstrikes on the forces of the legitimate government which have been trying to advance into Houthi-controlled territories. The Coalition calls these strikes friendly fire. Some observers have pointed to the Coalition's lack of determination to restore the legitimate government and end the conflict. Keeping the country in chaos allows both the KSA and the UAE to take more control in the south, away from the legitimate government (Howard, 2018).[24]

4 The Legacy of a Failed Political Transition

The mismanaged unification of Yemen in 1990, and the several years of instability that followed, as well as the tribal structure, contributed to the country's lack of a strong central authority. Government control outside the major cities was minimal, leading several marginalized local groups to begin speaking up against the elite in Sana'a. Social discontent was used by competing political factions and by regional and foreign powers to serve their divergent agendas, resulting in the current conflict. Therefore, ending the conflict and healing the wounds it has created requires a long process of peace-building, followed by a comprehensive plan for social and political reconciliation and reconstruction of the economy.

4.1 Thwarted Path to Peace

It is common for states in a post-conflict phase to perceive federalism as a pathway to peace, leading to an inclusive government that incorporates previously marginalized voices. That was the perception among participants in the NDC who proposed a federal system motivated by the rooted Southern grievance and others and the need to decentralize Yemen. Also, hopes that decentralization would help rectify the political and social crises were among the reasons that spurred support by Yemenis for the proposed federal system (Williams et al., 2017). Yet, NDC representatives struggled to reach the necessary political consensus on the formation of federal regions, the distribution of power considering the location of natural resources, and social and political structures. Federalism, which was a major component of the transition plan, 'came to be viewed (by some) as a red herring and a symbol of division' (Williams et al., 2017, p. 10). The Houthis and their ally Saleh pulled out of the transition agreement at the conclusion of the NDC and denounced the proposed new constitution. The subsequent seizure of the country's capital, Sana'a, in 2015 by the Houthis and forces loyal to Saleh reflected the long-standing ambition of the two to win back control of the country.

However, Salisbury (2016) has attributed the failure of the transitional process between 2012 and 2014 to the mismatch between the needs of the Yemeni people and the priorities of the transition's foreign sponsors and the lack of accountability or transparency imposed on Hadi. Barakat (2016) claims that the political transition process set out by the Gulf Cooperation Council in 2011 failed to incorporate key sections of Yemeni society in the decision-making process, such as the southern separatist Hirak movement, the Houthis, and Yemeni youth and women. As a result, Hadi's transitional government was increasingly viewed as illegitimate and unrepresentative of the demands and concerns of the Yemeni people. Additionally, the reluctance to remove Saleh from the political scene may have contributed to the failure of the transitional period (Rashad, 2011), not to mention that it did not give the country the stability that had been predicted for it. Instead, it ensured the transition from 'one authoritarian leader to one who proceeded to monopolize power' (Salloukh, 2017, p. 48).

The UN Security Council confined its role during the transitional arrangement to issuing, but not enforcing, Resolution 2216 and sending special envoys to broker a long-awaited peace plan. Furthermore, Resolution 2216 paved the way for a catastrophic regional intervention by the Arab Coalition, which was unsuccessful in bringing the intended outcomes of peace and stability to Yemen. The international community watched the situation deteriorate as the Houthis and Saleh took over more regions and sent the government into exile. As with Syria and Libya, the Council started 'marathonic' peace moderation in Yemen, sending three successive yet unsuccessful special envoys since the start of the conflict: the Moroccan envoy Jamal Benomar, the Mauritanian envoy Ould Cheikh, and finally a British envoy Martin Griffith.

In light of the events that accompanied the work of the UN envoys in Yemen, and the historical failures of the UN in resolving violent conflicts in several other regions around the world, a breakthrough by the international community in brokering a peaceful end to Yemen's conflict is questionable. There is an increasing perception among Yemenis that the international community, represented by the UN and the major regional and international powers, has rather been instrumental in prolonging the conflict and preventing its conclusion. In a letter to the UN Secretary-General in May 2019, President Hadi criticized its special envoy to the country for what he called legitimizing the Houthis and treating them as a de-facto government, contrary to provisions of the Security Council resolutions, including Resolution 2216. For their part, the Houthis have charged the UN envoys with not considering their legitimate demands. Furthermore, the absence of the Arab League from the Yemeni crisis has also raised questions regarding the possible role of the major international powers in preventing the League from performing its expected role of finding a peaceful solution. Needless to say, the path to peace-building starts with the determination of the international community to enforce the Security Council resolutions and call for the various groups to lay down their arms and engage in a serious transitional peace process.

4.2 The Conspicuous Absence of the Central State

Prior to the crisis, the central government ruled the country through weak to non-existent institutions. At the onset of the 2015 war, the central state collapsed, but one cannot claim that it has completely disappeared. Today, state functions and security are being carried out by non-state actors, including militias, armed groups, and tribes. Political or local groups have emerged and created their own internal order. They established 'mini-states' to compensate for the absence of a central government. The Houthis formed their own cabinet, seized government facilities in the North, and carried out the role of the state. Secessionist groups in the South became more organized, particularly after the support they received from the UAE.

In general, and for all groups inside the country, overland trade continued. Despite the war, oil, weapons, food, medicine, and other goods continue to flow across Yemen financed by war money, but the majority of the population has few financial means for obtaining necessities. As such, dominating trade routes has become increasingly profitable for local actors, and control of customs' collection points has become a lucrative objective for all sides in the war.

Re-establishing a centralized Yemen is not a viable option without a strong and effective government capable of addressing fundamental problems and ensuring the fair distribution of resources. Furthermore, in the country's new reality, restoring central government is not likely to be a popular choice due to the perception among the people that in the past the central government mismanaged resources and brought about an absence of equality and justice. In addition, interest groups are likely to strenuously oppose any settlement that restores the central government's grasp on resources. These groups include profiteering armies, militias, and tribal groups who will lose their war-created incomes. Hence, the creation of a federal system, suggested by the NDC, with considerable economic autonomy for different regions, might be the most viable arrangement for a post-war Yemen.

5 Rebuilding Post-war Yemen

Poor pre-war economic performance, combined with devastating war damage to the physical capital and social fabric of war-inflicted countries, suggests that post-war reconstruction must be both a *nation and peace-building exercise*. From an economic standpoint, it was estimated that the resources required to bring the economies of the war-affected countries in MENA region back to 2010 levels might be in the order of two-to-three times each country's GDP (Devarajan and Mottaghi, 2017). However, in any war-devastated country, rebuilding the physical capital of the economy must be combined with building adequate institutions that will address the root causes of the conflict, facilitating social initiatives, and healing the country's wounds.

5.1 Political and Social Reconciliation

Most MENA countries have established similar social contracts. Rulers provided public sector jobs for their people, subsidized access to public services and basic foodstuffs, as well as energy, in return for loyalty and only limited political rights. In the 1980s, the shift to a market-based economy led many of the region's countries to reform economic subsidies and social assistance, but they made no changes to the political structures. Furthermore, governments in the region failed to encourage the development of a vibrant private sector, leading to 'soaring rates of unemployment' and popular uprisings (Larbi, 2016, p. 32). Countries with the weakest institutions and governance have been the most susceptible to violence and instability and the 'least able to respond to the internal and external stresses' (Barayani et al., 2011, p. 7).

In Yemen, the state often sought to consolidate its status by maintaining intertwined alliances between the social, political, economic, military, and tribal elites of the country instead of establishing a social contract with the people. These actions led to rivalry among the elites for control of state institutions and the country's resources, thus hampering the proper development of these institutions and resources. The 2011 uprising failed to remove the old elites, undermining any ability to initiate the reforms necessary (Larbi, 2016, p. 44). The post-uprising war has made Yemen's already fragile state institutions even less able to meet the most basic needs of the Yemeni people, further undermining state legitimacy. The failure of state institutions in the areas controlled by the Houthis and the Hadi government to assist people in the face of the recent Covid-19 pandemic is a striking example of how weak and inefficient these institutions are.

The presence of Hadi's internationally recognized government outside Yemen, particularly in Riyadh, and the reluctance of the coalition to permit Hadi and his government to return to Aden, has also contributed to decreased levels of state legitimacy. Civil servants in areas controlled by Hadi's government have received their salaries only intermittently over the past three years, while in the same period the civil servants who work in Houthi-controlled areas have not received any salary at all. The failure of state institutions to forge a relationship with the population has been evident in the reliance on international non-governmental organizations to deliver essential health, education, and humanitarian services. Although international organizations play a crucial role in providing vital needs in the wake of the violence, particularly in Houthi-controlled areas, they have further weakened the trust and the bond between citizens and the state.

5.1.1 New Social and Political Contract Needed

For a comprehensive political and social reconciliation in Yemen, what is needed is a new post-war social contract that puts an end to old policies and governance systems. Accountability and impartiality must be the core principles for a new negotiated settlement along with the establishment of inclusive political institutions. These institutions must emerge from 'a balanced increase in state capacity' and a distribution of power throughout society (Acemoglu and Robinson, 2016, p. 1). As such, the government can initiate this new social contract by demonstrating transparency in order to restore trust in government processes. Greater public participation and social dialogue are crucial at this stage, especially since expectations are low and government promises are no longer believed (Barayani et al., 2011).

A 2011 report by the World Bank argues that establishing legitimate institutions that can prevent repeated violence might take a generation. It states that *'even the fastest-transforming countries have taken between 15 and 30 years to raise their institutional performance from that of a fragile state'* (Barayani et al., 2011, p. 10). Therefore, Yemen needs a leadership oriented to rapid reform, one that commits to changing the old social contract followed by a phased economic reform process, nonetheless taking into consideration the fact that the effects of such reforms will not be felt for many years (Larbi, 2016). The role of civil society organizations is also critical, considering the ongoing violence that has prevented the government from performing its functions. Acemoglu and Robinson (2016) argue that pressure and demands by civil society are crucial because elites rarely create inclusive political institutions willingly. Yemen has strong local leaders across the country and a large number of registered civil society organizations that could be instrumental in the post-war reforms so long as they are free of the influence of the elites.

Furthermore, the development of a robust judiciary system and legislature that can truly restrain the executive authority is needed, because this can reduce the risk of renewed conflict. Starting the legislative process requires uniting the two parliaments, and two Central Banks in the Houthi-controlled capital Sana'a, and the legitimate government's temporary capital in Aden. Simultaneously, the new government should seek to develop a robust and vibrant private sector and competitive markets, seeking to embrace a more inclusive economy.

5.1.2 Growing Need for an Inclusive Power-Sharing Agreement

Sambanis (2019a) contends that negotiated settlements are the most common ending for civil wars and are usually reached with the help of external actors. Such settlements can be reached through power-sharing, where the inclusion of all segments of the society is achieved. Electoral power-sharing is considered the most common result of peace negotiations. And indeed, a power-sharing formula in Yemen does not seem a very far-fetched proposition despite the many obstacles. There is no doubt that Yemen is in dire need of frank and open negotiations that ensure long-term political and security provisions. Once the parties agree to come to the table, a negotiated settlement should include a power-sharing arrangement that 'grants all factions political and economic benefits roughly commensurate with their demographic weight' (Knights et al., 2019). However, considering the power-sharing arrangements in Iraq and Lebanon, which have failed to stabilize these two countries, religious sectarianism should never be a part of any future power-sharing agreement in Yemen.

For the past twenty years, Yemen's leadership has addressed political standoffs by signing informal power-sharing arrangements between tribes and regional groups in the absence of political institutions or a legal framework. Most of these agreements or understandings were short-lived or never implemented. At the same time, Western engagement in Yemen has been based on a state-building framework, mostly involving security. If the same pattern is adopted, it is highly likely that reconciliation will fail even if the current war ends, sowing the seeds of renewed conflict. Thus, the post-conflict phase must be based on inclusivity and accountability because bringing about sustainable peace in Yemen will require an inclusive political system that ensures the meaningful participation of marginalized actors. Furthermore, in order to begin reconstruction, an assessment of state institutions should be conducted after a ceasefire is reached.

Another challenge that threatens the transitional period is reforming the security apparatuses. Local communities in Yemen have been relying on local and self-created forms of security provision. This means that 'any single nationwide effort at security sector reform will need to contend with the weakened capacity and legitimacy of security services and decide whether or how to integrate these local security providers into the public system' (Yadav and Lynch, 2018). Likewise, the education system needs to be restored and reformed in order to promote long-term inclusion (Anderson et al., 2017, p. 2). In addition, both before and during the conflict, the KSA and the UAE created, built alliances with, and provided support to, groups in Yemen that operate outside the Yemeni government's sphere. Thus, for true state-building to be realized in Yemen, it will be necessary for the Yemeni government's backers to re-evaluate their involvement in the country (Ahmed and Al-Rawhani, 2018).

5.1.3 Prospects for a Lasting Peace

Due to the highly centralized nature of the previous government in Yemen, a new allocation of power in the country will pose a serious challenge. But this can be alleviated through a 'phased approach', which could involve drafting 'an interim constitution', thus giving the Yemenis adequate time to increase institutional capacity and carry out political and economic reforms (Williams et al., 2017, p. 18). This interim constitution may eventually be replaced by the permanent constitution that the NDC drew up. Besides, to restore its legitimacy the Yemeni government needs to re-create the bond between the state and its citizens, especially since it lacks a real presence on the ground. Restoring confidence requires a determined political will and readiness to revive the role of state institutions. Establishing national support for change through collaboration between the government and other sectors of society, as well as with regional powers and donors, and identifying the priorities and interests of the various communities, could be the starting point (Barayani et al., 2011, p. 12). The next stage should avoid the mistakes of the 2012–2014 transitional period. State institutions should undergo thorough reform to promote broad participation, transparency, and accountability. There might be a need in the post-conflict phase to propose a new candidate for interim president to lead the transitional period, a person who could win the support of Yemenis countrywide.

The post-conflict governance system in Yemen needs to recognize the de facto authority of local groups (Salisbury and House, 2018, p. 56). The UN Security Council will need to agree on a new resolution that can generate realistic approaches for future talks between the warring sides, without compromising the merits of Resolution 2216, a necessary prerequisite to prevent rewarding the seizing of power by force. A compromise that would give some sort of autonomy to different provinces identified by the NDC within a federal Yemen would be a viable option. This compromise, which will fulfil the demands for autonomy by Southerners and integrate the Houthis and others into the political system, while giving the tribes proper representation, should be encouraged by the international community. For instance, governors and officers elected by local tribes would make the tribes feel that they are genuinely represented.

Ultimately, and most importantly, pressure should be exerted on foreign and regional powers, including Iran, the KSA, and the UAE, which hold leverage over the Houthis and several other local groups, including various militias, to put an end to the ongoing war. There is no magic wand for transforming the current status quo into a fully functioning peace. However, future settlements should address the grievances of all local groups, and stop foreign intervention in Yemen's affairs, since otherwise Yemen risks renewed and endless wars in the future.

5.2 Rebuilding the Economy

The determinants of economic recovery in Yemen are more complex than mere good planning and adequate financial resources. The conflict has entered its fifth year with no signs of an imminent ending, and its damages are accumulating. The dire consequences of the conflict include the destruction of the country's meagre economic infrastructure and the displacement of millions of people. Indeed, the conflict has brought the economy to a complete halt. More importantly, it has created deep rifts in Yemen's social fabric, reanimated the long-forgotten sectarian divide, and destroyed the already weak structure of the state.

In addition to economic considerations, a host of interdependent pre-war challenges, effects of war, and post-war political, social, and security developments will determine the extent to which a satisfactory economic recovery in post-war Yemen is possible. Implementation of any well-designed economic plan may fail if political and social ills and security concerns are not addressed. New realities that arose due to the war must be considered. For example, while the war has devastated the economy and the livelihoods of most ordinary Yemenis, several groups and individuals have been able to build massive fortunes and are likely to resist any change to the status quo. Therefore, for any economic programme to succeed, it must take into consideration the ordinary citizens' needs as well as the concerns of influential groups and warlords who are likely to see their interests threatened by the establishment of peace. Not addressing such concerns will increase the probability of a relapse into violence and render any post-conflict macroeconomic policy ineffective.

5.2.1 Exacerbating the Humanitarian Crisis

The vicious fighting between the Houthis and the national army, supported by the Saudi-led coalition, has compounded the suffering of the Yemenis and dramatically aggravated the humanitarian crisis. According to the Yemen Data Project, a Yemeni group that monitors the war,[25] almost one-third of the Saudi-led coalition airstrikes have hit 'non-military' targets.[26] Attacks on civilians have also been blamed on the Houthis and other militant groups fighting for dominance, mainly the secessionist movement (STC), and several terrorist groups. Many state-run schools and other buildings have been occupied by the militants, and reports indicate that the Houthis have continued the forcible recruiting of child soldiers for front-line combat. Overall, the conflict in Yemen has created the world's worst humanitarian crisis in recent years. A report by the UNDP estimated that by the end of 2021 Yemen's conflict will lead to 377 thousand deaths—nearly 60 per cent of which are indirectly caused by the conflict[27]. The Covid-19 pandemic has worsened all aspects of the conflict, including the creation of yet more political chaos. Militant groups are likely to take advantage of the people's need for healthcare in the areas they control to tighten their grip on these areas.

The UN warned that an estimated 24 million people, amounting to 80 per cent of the population, need critical assistance and that 20 million people are food insecure (UNDP, 2019b). The UN's Integrated Food Security Phase Classification has confirmed the presence of pockets of 'catastrophic hunger in some locations, with 238,000 people affected' (Relief Web, 2019). Famine still looms at large, with 14.3 million people classified as being in acute need, including 3.2 million requiring treatment for acute malnutrition. More than 2 million people have been internally displaced, and 280,000 people have become refugees in other countries. In June 2019, UNICEF said that every two hours, one mother and six new-born babies die because of complications during pregnancy or birth. Aid organizations have also struggled to deal with the largest cholera outbreak ever recorded that has resulted in over 2.5 million suspected cholera cases between October 2016 and December 2020, including 3,981 related deaths. Since March 2015, fighting has destroyed more than 2,500 schools, and many families have enlisted their children as combatants in order to provide themselves with an income. UNICEF estimated at least 2,419 children were recruited in the fighting (UNICEF, 2019). It is estimated that as of 2019, the conflict has set back human development in Yemen by twenty-one years. It would go back an entire generation if the war were to end in 2022 (UNDP, 2019). As of 2019, the number of combat-related deaths had passed the 100 thousand mark, and it is estimated to have increased further by 60 per cent in the following two years (UNDP, 2021). Deaths indirectly caused by the war due to a lack of food, health services, and infrastructure have exceeded combat deaths by a large margin.

Yemen's dire food situation has been exacerbated further by the militant groups' frequent confiscation of food aid provided by international organizations[28] and the massive increase in food prices. Trade with the outside world has become more costly due to increased shipping costs and insurance premiums. The flow of imports has become slower due to the naval inspection and air blockade instigated by the Arab coalition. This combined

Conflict, Peace-Building, and Post-Conflict Reconstruction 173

with the loss of employment and income due to the war and the increase in food prices means the population has become unable to obtain necessary foodstuffs. Militant groups, including the Houthis and others belonging to the legitimate government, are in control of roads connecting ports with major cities in the North, leading to an unprecedented increase in the cost of food and medicine and an outbreak of contagious diseases like cholera and diphtheria. Throughout the war, the Houthis have been accused of torturing and killing journalists and critics, siphoning off aid supplies, using civilian infrastructure as a shield for military activity, and persecuting the country's Jewish and Baha'i minorities. The conflict has been placed among the most destructive conflicts arising since the end of the Cold War (UNDP, 2019).

Furthermore, as vicious war ravages Yemen, the Covid-19 pandemic is expected to take a heavy toll on the population. In particular, marginalized and displaced people are expected to be hit the most due to their poor access to health services. This will compound the already disastrous health and economic situation, reducing economic activity and increasing unemployment, leading to an increase in poverty levels. Local health authorities hesitated to confirm the spread of the Coronavirus in the country until 10 April 2020, almost six months after the first known case of the disease was reported in China. The Covid-19 crisis in Yemen has been accompanied by seasonal floods and outbreaks of other diseases like cholera, malaria, and dengue fever. CBS News reported that, in a pledging event for the humanitarian crisis in Yemen held in June 2020, UN humanitarian coordinator Mark Lowcock warned that Covid-19 is spreading rapidly in Yemen, making the situation catastrophic (CBS News, 2020).[29] Even though there were just 909 reported infections in Yemen up to 19 June 2020, there have been 248 deaths. The implied mortality rate is 27.3 per cent, which substantially exceeds the 5.8 per cent worldwide average. Because of Yemen's war-devastated health infrastructure, almost no testing for the virus is possible. The reported cases cover only areas controlled by the legitimate government. Hence, the number of infected individuals is believed to be much higher. The international community has started to respond to the Covid-19 crisis in Yemen by sending medical supplies, including virus-protection and testing materials. However, reports indicate that local militias have been confiscating the medical supplies that reach their areas of control and using such supplies for treating their members alone.[30] In general, the economic slowdown in donor countries because of the pandemic is likely to negatively affect their ability and willingness to provide much-needed assistance to Yemen.

5.2.2 New economic challenges

At the aggregate level, GDP experienced a negative rate of growth in real terms of almost 13 per cent during the 2011 uprising. It recovered between 2011 and 2014, with an annual average GDP growth rate of 3.6 per cent.

174 *Mahmoud Al Iriani et al.*

However, after the outbreak and escalation of violence in March 2015, the economy has again deteriorated sharply. The cumulative contraction in economic activity between 2015 and 2018 is estimated at approximately 40 per cent (World Bank, 2019d). The value of real GDP plummeted to USD 18.98 billion in 2018 compared to more than USD 43 billion in 2014 (IMF, 2019). As a result, real GDP per capita bottomed out at USD 668 in 2018, the lowest among countries of the MENA region and down from USD 1,309 in 2010 (Figure 6.3)[31].

Since the Houthis became the de facto authority in the capital city and most of the densely populated northern governorates, Hadi's government has lost the bulk of the tax revenues to the group.[32] Additionally, production and export of oil and gas have almost come to a halt, depriving Hadi's government of another vital source of revenue. The fiscal deficit since 2016 has led to major gaps in the operational budgets of basic services and unreliable payment of salaries in the areas under its control. Civil servants and pensioners in Houthi-controlled regions have not been paid salaries since mid-2016, which has severely compromised the population's access to essential services (Relief Web, 2019). Meanwhile, the Yemeni Rial experienced unprecedented depreciation amounting to more than 70 per cent between 2015 and 2020, further undermining purchasing power. These events have led to an apparent contraction in the economy as public and private spending declined substantially.

5.2.3 Estimating the Economic Costs of the Conflict

The global measurable economic impact of violence in 2017 alone was equivalent to 12.4 per cent of global GDP, or USD 1,988 per capita (Institute for Economics and Peace, 2018). At the local level, estimating the impact of

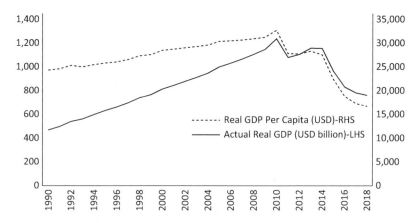

Figure 6.3 Actual real GDP and per capita GDP in Yemen, 1990–2018 (USD)

violence on the economies of conflict-plagued countries, and making those estimates available publicly, is essential for designing effective post-conflict reconstruction policies and deterring future conflicts.

Research on the effects of civil war on human lives and the economy of impacted countries is relatively new. Some of it discusses the determinants of violent conflicts, but not much considers their cost (Dunne and Tian, 2017).[33] The counterfactual approach has been popular among many of those who have attempted to estimate the cost of wars. This type of analysis compares observed values of economic variables during the conflict with their unobserved values in the hypothetical case of no conflict.[34] A simplified version of the counterfactual approach to estimate the economic impact of civil war may be presented as follows:

$$I = (Y|C=1) - (Y|C=0)$$

Where Y is real GDP, and I is the impact of the conflict on GDP, which is the difference between the actual Y with the conflict $(C=1)$ and what the value of Y would have been in the absence of conflict, or the counterfactual $(C=0)$. While $(Y|C=1)$ is observed, the counterfactual $(Y|C=0)$, is not known and must be estimated.

Our task is to come up with a reasonable estimate of $(Y|C=0)$. Several ways to estimate the counterfactual have appeared in the literature, with varying degrees of complexity. A popular way to estimate real GDP during the war in one country has usually been using data from other similar non-conflict countries during the period under investigation. In our case, we will rather use the out-of-sample forecast of real GDP as outlined in Box-Jenkins's univariate Autoregressive Integrated Moving Average (ARIMA) (Box and Jenkins, 1976). The ARIMA model uses the historical values of a single variable to forecast its future values. One advantage of this approach is that it requires no additional data other than the variable in question. ARIMA has been shown to sometimes outperform structural models in producing good-quality forecasts in the short term. Indeed, it has been shown that univariate ARIMA models are theoretically justified and can perform as well as the more complicated multivariate modelling techniques.

We may write an ARIMA model in the context of real GDP using the Box-Jenkins backshift operator (B) and extend it by adding the difference operator when the time series exhibits non-stationary behaviour (which is common in economic data series) (Pankratz, 1983). The resulting (ARIMA) model is:[35]

$$\phi_p(B)(1-B)^d y_t = \theta_q(B)\alpha_t$$

Where y_t is real GDP at time t, $\phi_p(B) = \left(1 - \sum_{i=1}^{p} \phi_i B^i\right)$ are the autoregressive parameters to be estimated, $\theta_q(B) = \left(1 - \sum_{i=1}^{q} \theta_i B^i\right)$ are the moving average parameters to be estimated, and d is the order of differencing. Finally, $\alpha_1, \alpha_2, ..., \alpha_t$ are a series of unknown random errors that are assumed to follow a normal distribution. This formulation essentially indicates that the observed GDP at time t depends on the previous values of GDP plus current and past random shocks. This model is also referred to as an ARIMA(p,d,q).[36]

Following Abadie and Gardiazabal (2003), Ali (2011), and Costalli et al. (2017), we use counterfactual analysis and ARIMA forecasting to estimate the economic cost of the conflict in Yemen fully realizing the limitations that data shortages impose on such analysis.[37] The actual performance of the economy during the war years 2015–2018 is compared with its expected (counterfactual) performance in the absence of war, obtained from ARIMA forecasting. The resulting measure of the economic impact of the conflict is assumed to reflect its overall direct, as well as indirect, effects on different sectors of the economy.[38] We used the Univariate Box-Jenkins (UBJ) three-stage model-building process to identify the best parsimonious forecasting model and provide short-term forecasts for real GDP in Yemen. UBJ is well documented in the literature and has been proved to provide reasonably robust forecasting models. To get our forecasts of real GDP, we used real GDP data in 2010 prices obtained from the World Bank's World Development Indicators (World Bank, 2019). The data extends from 1990 to 2018. The forecasted values are assumed to represent the values of real GDP in Yemen had there been no war (the counter-factual). The fitted model for real GDP growth in Yemen withstood identification, estimation, and forecasting tests, and performed reasonably well.

Figure 6.4 presents the actual real GDP (solid line) and estimated counterfactual real GDP, obtained from UBJ forecasts (dashed line). The forecast implies that if there were no war in Yemen, GDP would have continued to grow as depicted by the dashed line. The area between the solid and dashed lines represents the implied loss in real GDP due to the conflict, which is calculated to be around USD 86.6 billion. This estimate suggests that Yemen has lost the opportunity to increase its real GDP from about USD 31 billion in 2015 to a level close to USD 39 billion in 2018, an increase of about 26 per cent. This also implies that real GDP per capita would have increased from USD 908 in 2015 to about USD 1,428 in 2018, compared to an actual decline between the two periods, because of the war, to USD 668.

5.3 Post-war Economic Agenda

Reconstruction efforts ought to aim at compensating for the economic growth that would have been attained had the war not occurred. Compared to other conflict-ridden countries in MENA, Yemen's limited resources and pre-war poor economic development performance, as well as the devastating impact of violent conflict calls for even higher requirements than estimated. This implies that if peace in Yemen returns by the end of 2020, the

Conflict, Peace-Building, and Post-Conflict Reconstruction 177

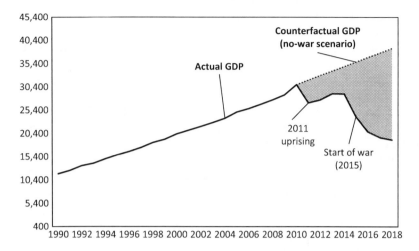

Figure 6.4 Actual and counterfactual GDP in Yemen, 1990–2018

economy must attain at least double the growth rates experienced before the war. Makdisi and Soto (this volume) have laid out a framework for the economic agenda to be implemented by the Arab countries affected by the 2011 uprising, which may be adopted in Yemen. Nevertheless, they stressed the need to design the reconstruction agenda to fit the particular needs of each country affected by the uprisings. Therefore, the reconstruction plan for Yemen must consider the country's unique political, social, and economic characteristics, the causes and the unique impacts of the conflict.

As a prerequisite to economic recovery, government institutions should be reformed in a way so as to have the ability to enforce law and order and deliver essential public services. However, empowering the private sector with minimal state interference is likely to significantly help in accelerating the recovery process. Government focus should be on enhancing the role of law and property rights, providing a healthy business environment through institutional capacity building, which encourages productive employment-creating investment and reduces the risk to business initiatives. The government should seek to promote private sector involvement in reconstruction efforts and search out the more inclusive benefits of economic recovery.

Of course, given the limited local natural, financial, and human resources, rebuilding war-torn Yemen requires additional support from regional as well as international communities. Nevertheless, for the strategy and policy for post-conflict recovery to survive in the immediate chaotic environment post-war and in the longer term, they ought to be designed with a significant contribution from local capacities. The reconstruction plan should also consider the pre-war institutions and those war-created ones which were, and still are, instrumental in creating tensions and conflict. In addition, for the reconstruction to assist in establishing legitimacy for the new authority, they must be economically and socially inclusive and result in immediate higher equality and employment.

Furthermore, any post-war reconstruction plans must consider both the lost opportunities due to the war as well as meet expanding population needs in the future. As indicated earlier, post-war reconstruction first requires the identification and evaluation of the damage that war has caused the economy. We have in the previous section provided a crude estimate of the real GDP loss due to the war, arguing that this estimate reflects the monetary value of the overall impact on the economy up to date. However, we have also indicated that there are future post-war losses that are not reflected in our estimate. In particular, educational opportunities lost due to the conflict, combined with losses to health services, are likely to affect an entire generation, leading to slower growth prospects in the future.

5.3.1 Macroeconomic Policies for Post-Conflict Recovery

Post-conflict economic performance in Yemen will be dependent on sound macroeconomic policies, which will facilitate the recovery of the economy and indeed speed it up. Given the pre-conflict lack of adequate and efficient monetary and fiscal institutions, the international community must take an active role in helping Yemen with reconstruction and development.

Recovery benefits are meant to be inclusive, and they tend to replace existing pre-war and war-created entities aimed solely at capturing rents from natural resources. This will most likely create discontent and resistance from influential groups, and persons who have been benefitting substantially from the absence of the state during the war, leading to what UNDP calls 'conflict trap' (UNDP, 2008), meaning that conflict may re-occur due to the new grievances. Therefore, it is crucial to consider such interests in post-war macro-policies. Effective policies should be implemented incrementally to alleviate any shocks associated with the resulting change in the economic environment. New policies should favour generating employment, in order to reduce further public discontent resulting from the loss of income-generating opportunities. After all, one of the seeds of the conflict was the high unemployment rate which has meant warlords could recruit thousands of unemployed individuals for frontline combat. Overall, post-conflict policies should prioritize reducing the risk of conflict re-occurring.

The post-war fiscal policy represents the government's management of public finances following a long and devastating war. Pre-war fiscal institutions and policies were performing chaotically. Revenue systems, particularly tax management and collection, were inefficient. Budgetary targets were rarely met, and the government budget was characterized by chronic deficits. Because of the war, the government's fiscal position has deteriorated further as tax collection has declined and spending on military operations increased. As a result, the government has resorted to inflationary financing.

The war has also been very detrimental to the pre-war suboptimal fiscal institutions that have the task of managing government fiscal policy and the macro-economy. This necessitates rebuilding and reforming fiscal institutions to provide efficient management of both revenue generation and spending. In the presence of the expected flow of reconstruction funds from international donors, setting some type of control mechanism will ensure the efficient use of such funds. Post-war fiscal policy must be constrained by sufficient fiscal rules to ensure acceptable fiscal behaviour on the part of the government and hence increasing international aid effectiveness. These rules typically aim at reducing fiscal policy pro-cyclicality and ensuring fiscal responsibility and public debt sustainability. Some rules include setting numerical limits on budgetary aggregates, deficits, and public borrowing. These rules should be enforced but also allow for some flexibility to deal with changing economic conditions, and without frequently changing any of the rules themselves.

Post-war monetary policy is important as well. Elbadawi and Soto (2010) have observed that the academic literature on policy has focussed on post-conflict financial institutions and aid effectiveness, and largely ignored the monetary regime and optimal exchange rate policy, despite their importance. Pre-war monetary institutions and policy in Yemen had been performing relatively acceptably. The Central Bank of Yemen (CBY) was to some extent successful in managing inflation through deploying various monetary policy tools, the exchange rate, and the financial and monetary systems in general. After the war started, the CBY continued its relatively successful management of the country's monetary policy. The exchange rate of the local currency remained relatively stable, close to the levels before the war, for about two years after the crisis started. Under the Houthis, CBY's foreign reserves were depleted and, consequently, its headquarters were relocated to the government's temporary capital Aden in late 2016. This move resulted in the creation of two different monetary institutions in Sana'a and Aden, weakening the conduct of monetary tools, which came under the control of the two adversaries. There has been a problem of liquidity shortages in local currency where banks became unable to satisfy withdrawal requests by depositors. The banking system, however, continued functioning despite being under pressure from the (two) financial authorities in Sana'a and Aden. Surprisingly, none of the local commercial banks have become insolvent, despite the tight liquidity.

Only the CBY in Aden is internationally recognized, but it controls a small fraction of the system. Despite financial support from the KSA of Aden's CBY, the local currency started depreciating. Nevertheless, the depreciation has been relatively moderate if compared to other war-torn countries. Even after the CBY in Aden began to lose control, the local currency lost only around 64 per cent of its value against the US dollar from the start of the war, compared to about 90 per cent and 67 per cent depreciation in the Syrian and Egyptian currencies during the same period, respectively. The

CBY's efforts to stop further currency depreciation sometimes resulted in temporary improvement in the exchange rate. Still, unless the CBY receives continuous foreign exchange income in the future it is expected that the local currency will continue to depreciate. Therefore, post-war reunification of the CBY in one central institution, responsible for managing monetary policy and regulating the country's banking system and the financial sector overall, is a necessary prerequisite for the financial sector to recover. The performance of the pre-war monetary policy was relatively acceptable but needed to be improved. Therefore, the post-war monetary policy should aim at enhancing pre-war practices and drafting new policies that ensure the stability of the economy and facilitate reconstruction efforts.

6 Conclusions

Even before the recent conflict, Yemen was the Arabian Peninsula's poorest and least developed country. Combined with a host of grievances from economic and social inequality, political exclusion, rampant corruption, religious politics, and overall weak institutions, this created an environment of instability across the country, which was exploited by local and foreign players to advance their own interests. Following the public uprising of 2011, traditional local powers made use of public discontent to serve their political ambitions, pushing the country into a vicious war. In addition, regional and foreign powers have been actively involved in Yemeni affairs turning the crisis into a proxy war.

The current violent conflict in Yemen is only the most recent among several major and minor conflicts that have plagued the country's history. However, resorting to modern weaponry by local and multiple foreign militaries has led to the creation of the worst humanitarian crisis in recent times. After more than seven years of war, Yemen's fragile state institutions have been unable to meet the most basic needs of the people. The Covid-19 pandemic will worsen the human crisis even more, taking a heavy toll on the population and calling for more involvement by the international community in providing badly needed assistance to the country's devastated health sector. However, the pandemic might still provide an added incentive for economic, political, and institutional reform.

Despite the presence of Hadi's government in the KSA, an apparent determination by the Arab Coalition to prevent it from conducting its functions inside the liberated territories, has led to the failure of state institutions to forge a relationship with the population in the part of the county the KSA controls. Also, the evident reliance on international official aid and NGOs to deliver essential assistance and services in the wake of the violence has weakened the trust and the bond between citizens and the state and contributed to decreased levels of state legitimacy.

Moreover, the conflict has probably reached a deadlock as there seems to be no possibility of a military victory by any side of the conflict. In addition, the international community has so far shown little will to broker an immediate and lasting peace. The security situation remains volatile, and violence between the two leading powers (the legitimate government backed by the Arab Coalition and the Houthis supported by Iran) does seem to be coming to an end in the near future. Furthermore, the noticeable rise of several Coalition-created local militias, particularly in the South, is likely to prevent the return of stability even if a peaceful settlement is reached between the two main parties in the conflict. The current lawlessness is expected to continue for the foreseeable future, including in the areas liberated from the Houthis. Even if the national civil conflict is settled, there is a risk that Yemen will continue to experience a series of smaller scattered conflicts fuelled by national and foreign actors, exacerbating the negative impact on the economy and the country.

Given that a military solution is unlikely, a negotiated settlement, with support from the international community, is the most promising scenario for ending the conflict. Such a settlement may be reached through political (but non-sectarian) power-sharing arrangements where the inclusion of all segments of society is guaranteed. Since electoral power-sharing is considered the most common result of peace negotiations after the end of a civil war, a power-sharing formula in Yemen, based on the National Dialogue Conference principles, does not seem that far-fetched despite the numerous obstacles to it. To achieve lasting peace and prosperity, Yemen can build on the outcomes of the National Dialogue Conference, an opportunity for political reconciliation that was lost when the state was dismantled in September 2014.

After a long-hoped-for settlement and the establishment of peace and stability in Yemen, the country is expected to go through an extensive phase of reconstruction. However, to succeed, a new social contract, acceptable to all parties in the conflict must be put in place in which political and social institutions are rebuilt to ensure a lasting national peace. Given the massive scale of war damage to the economy and society, the reconstruction of Yemen requires both regional and international efforts aimed at mobilizing adequate financial resources to achieve both urgent and long-term reconstruction goals. This in turn pre-supposes the achievement of peace and law enforcement throughout the county as one pre-requisite for the return of prosperity.

In turn, post-war macroeconomic policies should aim at correcting the pre-conflict mismanagement of the economy. A major task here is the rebuilding of fiscal and monetary institutions that would be capable of carrying out the required post-conflict fiscal and monetary policies as part of the overall reconstruction program aimed chiefly at reducing the risk of conflict re-occurring.

Notes

1 Although considered a branch of Shi'i Islam, the doctrinal gap between Zaydism and mainstream Sunni Islam is relatively narrow. Zaydis are sometimes referred

to as the Sunnis of the Shi'is and they make up a third of Yemen's population. There are substantial differences between the Shi'i Twelver Imami doctrine that is dominant in Iran and Zaydi Shi'ism.
2. The revolution of 1962 ousted the Imam but kept the Hashemite dynasty intact, sharing power with the republicans according to the 1970 peace pact. The Zaydi Hashemites claim that their descent from the prophet Muhammad grants them the exclusive right to rule Yemen.
3. The 50/50 power-sharing agreement ignored demographic and geographic realities. The YAR and PDRY had 4 to 1 population counts, and almost 1–1.75 of geographical area.
4. The military conflict lasted from 5 May to 7 July 1994.
5. Official name of the Muslim Brotherhood Movement in Yemen.
6. The coalition initially consisted of 12 countries, but only the KSA and United Arab Emirates (UAE) have actively engaged in the military operations. Also, a few thousand soldiers were sent to Yemen by the government of Sudan to engage in ground operations on behalf of the KSA.
7. Even though Houthis belong to the Zaydi sect, a branch of the Shi'a, it is observed that the two sides of the conflict include both Sunnis and Zaydis. Neither side of the conflict has officially claimed to be pursuing sectarian goals.
8. Based on a 1–5 scale, with 5 representing most advanced worldwide.
9. Despite the low productivity of traditional agriculture, the proliferation of Qat cultivation has provided rural areas with a good source of income, preventing any large movement of the population to urban areas (Qat is a cash crop produced and sold freely in Yemen. The fresh green leaves of Qat are chewed by Yemenis in social gatherings as a stimulant).
10. Yemen's traditional elite, which used to be composed of 'merchants, shaykhs, officers, and modernists', finally collapsed as, in recent years, each category in the elite began to assume the functions of other categories, Shaykhs becoming officers and doing business, officers engaging in business activities, and modernists allying with Shaykhs, etc.
11. However, detribalization in the South has not been very successful and lately the area has seen a strong revival of tribalism.
12. Zakat is an Islamic tax of 2.5 per cent on all types of assets, above a certain value, that have been withheld for an entire year.
13. According to Yemen's National Population Council, the country has more than 11,000 rural and urban settlements. They are assigned to 21 governorates (including the Sana'a municipality) that are subdivided into 333 districts that in turn are subdivided into 2210 sub-districts and then (as of 2001) into 38,284 villages (not settlements).
14. Informal settlements are localities with no urban planning or public services, and residents in these settlements are mostly poor migrants, neglected, lacking political connections, and formal representation.
15. The population of the two states at time of unification was estimated as 5 to 1 in YAR and PDRY, respectively.
16. To access Transparency International's Corruption Index for the year 2018, check https://www.transparency.org/country/YEM
17. The main slogan of the Houthis, called the Scream, reads 'God is great, death to America, death to Israel, curse on the Jews, victory to Islam'. The Houthis' capacity to transform their religious, political, and social identities, has enabled them to become one of the most influential political and social groups in Yemen. Not only did they speak to religious communities, but they also spread their power by bringing together the Hashemite-influential, mostly Zaydi families, who claim descent from the Prophet Muhammad. By taking on Hashemite

identity, they spread their influence beyond Houthi-controlled areas. Most notably, they brought the Twelver branch of Shi'i Islam from Iran to the Zaydi stronghold. The prominent Sa'ada-based cleric, Badreddine al-Houthi, as well as his sons Husayn and 'Abd al-Malik, studied the Twelver branch of Shi'ism in Qom, Iran.

18 A new nationalistic Yemeni movement called 'Yemeni National Movement' or 'Aqyal' has surfaced lately, with an announced objective of restoring the old Yemeni identity and heritage away from the current religious doctrines.

19 KSA's founding father and Imam Yahya went to war for the control of Yemen's northern provinces. Defeated, Imam Yahya was forced to sign the Ta'if Treaty in 1934 which gave KSA control over the Yemeni provinces of Asir, Jizan, and Najran (a total area of 235,000 square kilometres). The authenticity of 'Abd al-Aziz's advice is questionable but its sense seems to have been followed by KSA leaders for decades (see Salisbury, 2015).

20 Ironically, the very fewest Yemeni (or any Arab) refugees found their way to KSA, and the kingdom made significant efforts to completely seal its borders to them.

21 In the 1960s, Riyadh assisted the ousted Zaydi imam in his struggle to regain power from the nationalist republicans.

22 These comments are the latest in a series of statements by Hadi officials indicating that the UAE and KSA have deviated from the original Coalition objectives and become occupying forces.

23 A number of international organizations has documented violations against civilians by the coalition and other groups involved in the war. See for example this on report by Amnesty International, *Yemen: US-made bomb used in deadly air strike on civilians*, found at: https://www.amnesty.org/en/latest/news/2019/09/yemen-us-made-bomb-used-in-deadly-air-strike-on-civilians/

24 News reports indicate that KSA is in the process of building an oil pipeline extending to the Gulf of Aden through the coast of Al Mahara. UAE in its part is exerting more control of the vast Yemeni coasts along the Arabian and Red Seas, and Socotra Island.

25 Yemen Data Project reports in detail air raids by the Arab coalition, but very little is reported about violent attacks on civilians by the Houthis, STC, and other militias.

26 Of the coalition's 19,748 airstrikes to date, 6,295 hit 'non-military' targets in several governorates, with Sa'ada recording the highest number (1,650) as well as 6,729 raids hitting 'unknown targets'.

27 See UNDP (2019b).

28 Amid allegations that aid was being diverted for profit by the Houthi militant group, the World Food Programme (WFP) announced in June 2019 a partial suspension of food aid in the capital Sana'a after the Houthis rejected WFP plans to implement a biometric system to insure transparency of food distribution to those most in need.

29 Amid the pandemic-caused economic slowdown in donor countries, the conference came up with pledges of USD 1.35 billion, far short of the USD 2.41 billion target.

30 The Hadi government confirmed reports that the Houthis are reportedly commandeering WHO ambulances and diverting WHO-supplied Covid-19 materials to their military hospitals.

31 A recent UNDP report on the impact of war in Yemen projects that in the last six years the crisis has caused Yemen to miss out on USD126 billion of potential economic growth (UNDP, 2021).

32 Hadi's government claims that the land area controlled by the de facto Houthi authority is currently less than 25 per cent of the total area of Yemen. However, more than 70 per cent of the population of Yemen now live under the control of the group.
33 Due to data limitations, most of the current literature has used cross-country data. Examples of such literature include Venieris and Gupta (1986), Alesina and Perotti (1996), and Mauro (1995).
34 Costalli et al. (2017), Hoeffler and Reynal-Querol (2003) used cross-country data in their counterfactual analysis of the costs of war, while Brück (1997), Abadie and Gardiazabal (2003), and Ali (2011) analysed individual country data.
35 For more details on UBJ forecasting model, see Pankratz (1983).
36 For the formal derivation of the ARIMA (p,d,q) from the general ARMA (p,q) using backward shift operator, see Pankratz (1983).
37 The earliest known attempt to use counterfactual analysis appeared in a book by the economic historian Robert Fogel in 1962 (Fogel, 1962), and another attempt about 30 years later by sociologist Geoffrey Hawthorn (Hawthorn, 1991). Robert Cowley (1999) presented his series 'What If?' citing dozens of essays by historians or prominent writers about counterfactuals or 'how a slight turn of fate at a decisive moment could have changed the very annals of time'.
38 Since the conflict started, few attempts, including by international organizations including UNDP (2019), IRIS (2017), and Young (2017), have been provided to assess the economic costs of the current conflict in Yemen. Obviously, the war is still going on, and it is challenging to obtain reliable information and data about it, or to estimate the ever-changing costs.

7 Investigating the Libyan Conflict and Peace-Building Process
Causes and Prospects

Amal Hamada, Melike Sökmen, and Chahir Zaki

1 Introduction

The MENA region has been affected by cycles of conflict, be it armed intervention, inter-state conflict, or civil conflict. It experienced an increasing number of conflicts during the late 1970s and 1980s resulting from the Cold War era, when the superpowers and their allies fought and supported a broad range of wars and minor conflicts. While the second half of the 1990s was more peaceful than the first half, the next decade again saw violence in the region. Finally, since early 2011, MENA countries have experienced a wave of protests, uprisings, and demonstrations collectively referred to as 'The Arab Spring'.

Libya has been in continuous civil conflict since the Arab uprisings in 2011. Since then, it has suffered from recurring cycles of social, political, security, and economic crises that reinforce one another. This has led to increasingly weak state institutions and a deteriorating national economy, all of which have facilitated fragmentation, disunity, and the creation of fertile ground for continued violence and a war-driven economy. Despite national and international initiatives to achieve national reconciliation, Libya has been unable to turn its initial revolutionary success post 2011 into a transition to a stable and inclusive system. Indeed, political polarization escalated into an open armed confrontation in July 2014, leading to the establishment of parallel and rival governance structures (Tobruk and Tripoli) and making reunification a major challenge. Even with the current progress concerning presidential and parliamentary election taking place at the end of 2021 and the beginning of 2022 consecutively, doubts remain about the ability of the current government to achieve stability.

The last months of 2019 and early 2020 have brought increasing levels of threat that will complicate the situation in Libya. Regional competition between countries such as Egypt and Turkey is spilling over into the domestic politics of Libya, and the related military build-up is increasing the levels of violence putting all peace efforts at risk (Capasso et al., 2020). Moreover, the spread of the Covid-19 pandemic added more pressure on fragile state institutions and jeopardized the lives of Libyans in general.

DOI: 10.4324/9781003344414-10

Given the composition of its society, the stabilization of Libya requires the consolidation of peace between its politically polarized groups, by ensuring maximum inclusion in any peace process. Negotiated settlements are vital for preventing the toll of the conflict damaging the already fragile state institutions, the economy, and the depleting of Libya's financial reserves. That some local ceasefire agreements are already in place indicates that there is space for resolving disputes through dialogue.[1]

This chapter focuses on three major issues: (1) understanding the underlying causes of conflict, (2) identifying the potential peace-building efforts and political transitions in the post-conflict phase, and (3) proposing an economic agenda for post-conflict reconstruction. It presents an inclusive agenda of peace-building and economic reconstruction in line with the dynamics of the country. This agenda requires identifying priorities (e.g., political reconciliation), constraints (e.g., lack of transparency, lack of reliable and rigorous data), political challenges (e.g., the presence of powerful parallel governance structures and militias), and necessary resources (e.g., civil society actors, international cooperation), as well as economic challenges (economic diversification, macroeconomic policies, infrastructure, access to finance, trade policies, and investment climate).

The remainder of the chapter is organized as follows. Section 2 presents an overview of development prior to 2011 focusing on both economic and political dimensions. Section 3 explains why the conflict has been sustained. Section 4 analyses the economic cost of war. Section 5 shows how Libya can move from an exclusive to an inclusive model of development at both the political and economic levels. Section 6 concludes.

2 Overview of the Development Path Prior to 2011

2.1 Political Background

On the basis of our study of the political and socioeconomic map of Libya prior to 2011, we argue that three different elements have contributed greatly to the emergence of the conflict, its continuation, militarization, and the challenges facing reconciliation. These are the particulars of the state–society relationship, the absence of strong state institutions, and the militarization of tribes and the radicalization of Islamic groups. In order to examine these elements, we briefly review the birth and conformation of modern Libya.

In the Middle East in general a modern nation-state is a relatively new and controversial concept (Ayubi, 1996; Sika, 2014). Historically speaking, Libya did not have a legacy of central government control. Situated between the greater Maghreb and Egypt, the country historically served as a conduit for trade and pilgrimage from North Africa to the Arabian Peninsula. It had a social structure with a strong tribal presence in three locations: Cyrenaica, Tripolitania, and the Fazzan. Each of these three locations enjoyed relative independence and conflictual relations with colonial powers (British, French, and Italian). Libya gained independence from Italy in 1951 under the strong leadership of Muhammad Idris al-Mahdi al-Senusi, the prince of Cyrenaica, who inherited the leadership of the Senusi religious/Sufi movement that had a long history of fighting colonialism and playing the role of mediator between different tribes (Varvelli et al., 2017).

2.1.1 State-Society Relations

During his reign, al-Senusi, now the king, built his legitimacy on playing the balancing role between competing political and tribal forces and symbolizing the national identity of the new-born state (Golino, 1970). The discovery of oil in the late 1950s endowed the king with substantial resources with which to build new state institutions and, more importantly, to improve the living conditions of the small population (around 2 million) and thus increase the legitimacy of the regime. With oil revenues came rising hopes of prosperity, which materialized with a relatively fair distribution of wealth. Using oil revenues, the new monarchy was able to become the major employer, hiring 40,000 of the 160,000 Libyans in the workforce. By the end of the 1960s, Libya's economic growth was among the highest worldwide, reaching 20 per cent (Vandewalle, 1986). Revenues were also used to empower the state, which, in 1963, abandoned the federal system and drafted a new constitution for a unitary state. Nevertheless, there was increasing dissatisfaction with the regime of King Idris in two segments of society: the first included people who were influenced by the rising fever of Arab Nationalism in neighbouring states (mainly Egypt) and the second comprised of those concerned about high levels of corruption in the oil industry. But the political system was not able to deal with the increasing dissatisfaction. The monarchy was outdated, state institutions were not fashioned to reflect people's demands, and the ruling elite was isolated from society (Kawczynski, 2011).

In less than two decades, the Senusi dynasty was removed by the young Lieutenant Muammar Gaddafi in September 1969. Gaddafi, with the help of a group of young officers, led a successful military coup against the king who was travelling abroad in the summer. The coup soon received official recognition from the Arab and Western world and a new era started with 'free officers' taking control of the country and encountering very little resistance from the people, the elite, or the main tribes. Gaddafi had a different understanding of the role of the state (ideology, approach to the economy, and the role of the state) and, in 1973, decided to replace the old format of state institutions with the 'Jamahiriya'. The new format was supposed to promote popular engagement in politics and enable citizens to be part of the decision-making process rather than confining management to the upper levels of state institutions. Committees were formed from neighbourhoods upwards to the highest levels of the state. Concomitantly, and out of distrust of the old elite—university graduates and old technocrats—Gaddafi purged state institutions and created a new elite, with a different set of social and professional backgrounds, with which to manage the state. He dismantled the old network that was corrupt yet experienced in running state institutions, especially the oil industry. Detested in the beginning by Gaddafi and his entourage, the tribal structure of Libyan society nevertheless remained powerful. Gaddafi was able to destabilize the old power balance and force a new arrangement, whereby the marginalized and less powerful tribes allied with the state and forced other stronger tribes to follow their lead (Ladjal, 2016). The power of money (from oil), ideology (Arab nationalism), and force (intimidation) secured the new regime for more than four decades under Gaddafi and enabled him to progressively get rid of his colleagues from the free officers' movement. By 1977, Gaddafi was in full control.

It is important to note that the state–society relationship during the Gaddafi era worked in favour of the state at an expense to society. The Libyans remained totally dependent on both the state and the tribal system for protection and services. Civil society organizations representing the people and mediating between them and the state were traditional and mostly informal (e.g., councils of elders, and ad-hoc campaigns (Altai consulting for SJD\Libya, 2015)

2.1.2 Weak State Institutions

Tribalism was, and remains, the dominant organizational factor in Libyan society. King Idris tried to respect the tribal system and mirror the state institutions accordingly. With oil revenues came efforts to modernize and urbanize the young in society. National education was introduced in order to help create a new national identity, based on loyalty to the state rather than the tribe. The federal system adopted at the time of independence recognized and reinforced the power of the tribes and deepened the differences between the three main areas of Libya. Federalism was dropped in the early 1960s in favour of a unitary state. This should have induced a change in the power structure and state institutions. Yet, the ruling elite remained faithful to their original tribal affiliations and mobilized members from their own tribes to join the new ruling elite. In other words, tribal allegiances remained as important as they were before the coup of 1969 (Ladjal, 2016).

In the mid-1970s, Gaddafi started abolishing state institutions and laws, including Shari'a law, and replacing them with diffuse and dysfunctional entities based on his own ideology as described in the 'Green Book'. No laws, no bureaucracy, no professional occupations, just revolutionary entities fashioned as per the Green Book to manage state affairs and rule in society disputes (Green Book, 1975). According to Gaddafi's new ideology, the world had suffered enough from the failures of socialism and capitalism. Western democratic practices did not guarantee the rights of the people; rather, they isolated them in favour of a small elite controlling and manipulating the masses. He proposed a new universal theory where people would

Investigating the Libyan Conflict and Peace-building Process 189

restore their ability to make decisions and control economic affairs in their country. Rather than misrepresenting the will of the people in modern parliaments, popular committees were to be established in neighbourhoods to discuss and manage affairs. Gaddafi conceptualized tribes, parliaments, class, and political parties as destructive, misleading, with divisive effects on society. He stated, 'This new theory is based on the authority of the people, without representation or deputation. It achieves direct democracy in an orderly and effective form' (The Green Book, 1975, p. 22) (see Figure 7.1).

What was proposed as direct democracy turned into a one-man show. Gaddafi managed to get rid of most members of the Libyan Revolutionary Command Council, a twelve-person governing body that ruled the Libyan Arab Republic from 1969 to 1977. His relatives and tribe became his immediate entourage and the actual holders of power in the state. Oil revenues

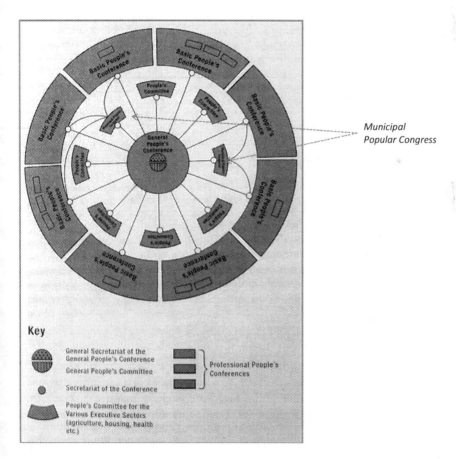

Figure 7.1 Gaddafi's conceptualization of popular conferences and people's committees
Source: The Green Book, p. 24.

were used to finance political and military adventures in Africa and Latin America, serving Gaddafi's dreams of ruling the world. Over the years, domestic economic conditions progressively deteriorated. What appeared to be an increasingly prosperous society with the discovery of oil in the 1950s, turned into a progressively poor society with a deteriorating infrastructure and public services.

The tribal system, by contrast, remained strong mainly for two reasons. The first is Gaddafi's reliance on tribes and tribal sheikhs to consolidate his power and compensate for the inability of the state to exert control over the masses. Following a simple patronage system, the government relied on the tribes for services and control and, in return, faithful tribal leaders enjoyed support from the state and secured high-level positions and revenue for themselves, their immediate families, and tribesmen. Second, the tribal system provided a sense of identity. With almost no state institutions and only the popular committees, the citizens were not able to develop a sense of loyalty that went beyond local communities, and the tribes remained the viable alternative in terms of identity and protection (Alshadeedi and Ezzeldine, 2019).

By the time the Arab Spring reached Libya and people decided to take to the streets in February 2011, the artificial facade of the Jamahiriyya fell to reveal the ugly truth of a stateless country. The tribe, which has always been present in serving and protecting the people and keeping the state running, became the working alternative to the failing Gaddafi regime. Thus, as emphasized in section 4, it is crucial for any reconstruction plan to stress the importance of restructuring tribal relations with the state and its institutions.

2.1.3 Militarization of Tribes and Radicalization of Islamic Groups

Before 2011, religion had a controversial role. At the political level, Gaddafi's Green Book presented a unique understanding of the role of Islam and the Shariʻa in public life, one that did not match any of the existing political and ideological agendas of Islamists in the region. On the other hand, Sufism had had a considerable influence on the people, and Islam provided a certain sense of identity when combined with Arab nationalism.[2] Nevertheless, Gaddafi's policies created a void that could not be filled with his particular ideological notions. With the failure and then the end of state institutions in guiding, serving, and protecting, people resorted to the tribes. The absence of the state gave opportunities for different Islamist groups to co-exist and operate at different levels of society.[3] The jihadists were the groups most threatening to the legitimacy and stability of the Gaddafi regime. Composed of young Libyans who were trained in Afghanistan and Iraq as part of al-Qaeda during the 1990s, they returned to Libya and were able to carry out a number of attacks against the regime.[4] A few years before the eruption of the 2011 revolution, Gaddafi decided to release jihadi prisoners in an attempt to defang the Islamists. This policy continued into the early stages of the conflict in 2011 and resulted in hundreds of radical Islamists being released from prison with no guarantee that they had distanced themselves from their original affiliations, nor any idea about their future alliances with the competing forces on the ground (Boucek, 2011). This decision, along with the failing of the state apparatus, reduced security conditions on the streets to total chaos. Reports at the early phase of the conflict revealed an increasing level of violence associated with Islamist groups against both local and international dignitaries, and various facilities (Wehrey, 2012).

Libya being in essence a tribal society, Gaddafi managed the tribes through a method of 'divide and rule'. During the early phases of the 2011 uprisings, he tried to use tribes to consolidate his rule and tried to purchase their support. A number of tribes remained loyal to the regime and misread the developments in the streets. This made them lose support and limited their influence over political developments in the aftermath of Gaddafi's demise. In the early phases of the conflict, Gaddafi also threatened to provide the tribes with weapons with which to embark on a civil war. This materialized later on, though not under Gaddafi's control, as smuggled weapons found their way to those tribes which developed their own militias and became involved actively in civil war.[5] A number of additional factors contributed to the increasing militarization of the tribes: failure of the state, intervention of the international community (e.g., France supported some of the militias), and the fragility of the transitional process. Demilitarization remains one of the main challenges for reconstruction.

Such militarization is coupled with ethnic fractionalization. Libya is characterized as having the highest level of ethnic fractionalization in the MENA region (see Figure 7.2).[6] Indeed, in Southern Libya, tribal groups have been in armed conflict with each other or with the national government

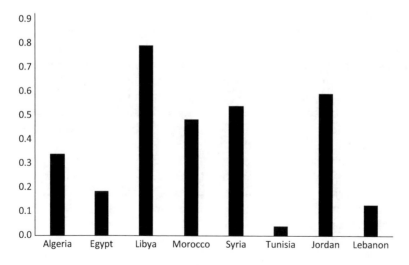

Figure 7.2 Indicator of ethnic fractionalization
Source: Alesina et al. (2003).[7]

192 *Amal Hamada et al.*

ever since the civil war. Tribal elements often shut down oil facilities as an instrument of negotiation, but this leaves many of those in the region who are dependent on oil for jobs in dire economic circumstances. Yet, it is not only ethnic groups and rival political factions that contribute to this state of affairs. ISIS formally established itself in 2014 and has carried out countless attacks ever since.

The recent health crisis raises many questions and challenges regarding the ability of the tribal system to respond to, contain, and fight Covid-19. The continuation of the war and the weakness of state institutions are increasing the importance of the tribes in protecting and serving their respective communities. Could the tribes make up for the inability of the state to meet the challenge of the current medical crisis? Do they have access to the resources and networks needed to perform such a task? In other words, how are tribal inter-alliances and relationships with local, regional, and international powers going to affect their ability to function and to respond to the current global crisis. Noteworthy, the current Libyan government led by Abdulhamid Mohammed Al-Dabaiba since March 2021 has pledged to provide vaccinations to Libyans in face of recent developments of the pandemic.

2.2 Economic Conditions Prior to 2011

Structural problems, from which the Libyan economy suffered at both the economic and social levels, contributed to the eventual onset of the conflict in Libya. They include state dominance, oil dependency, and high levels of unemployment.

2.2.1 State Dominance

One of the major issues in Libya is the dominant role of the state. World Bank data show that in 2010 the number of public employees was around 840,000, representing over 70 per cent of a total of 1,330,000 employees (see Figure 7.3). From a social perspective, this predominance of the state represents a tremendous degree of fragility in times of civil war as unstable or declining government revenues may easily mean that the income of the majority is in jeopardy. This significantly reduces the government's freedom of action when undertaking reforms.

The banking and finance system is also dominated by the public sector, and the extent and diversity of financial services it provided have been very limited, hindered by institutional weaknesses. The latter include the lack of a robust system of property rights, the absence of credit assessment information, the lack of competition, and state ownership.[8] Table 7.1 shows the degree of underperformance by Libya's commercial banking services in the period 2004 to 2017 relative to the average of the MENA region and upper-middle-income countries (UPC), which includes Libya when countries are classified according to GDP per capita. Domestic credit to the private sector

Investigating the Libyan Conflict and Peace-building Process 193

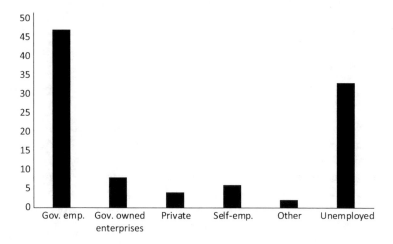

Figure 7.3 Labour Force by job status, 2010
Source: World Bank (2012).

Table 7.1 Financial Aggregates in Libya

	Libya	MENA	Upper Middle-income Countries
Commercial bank branches (per 100,000 adults)	11.0	12.8	13.4
Borrowers from commercial banks (per 1,000 adults)	128.2	145.1	196.6
Depositors with commercial banks (per 1,000 adults)	675.6	683.3	–
Domestic credit to private sector by banks (% of GDP)	16.2	46.8	80.9

Source: Own elaboration based on data from the World Development Indicators dataset.
Note: Figures are averages between 2004 and 2017.

by Libyan banks, a key variable to support sustained growth, represents only 34 per cent of the average of the MENA region and 20 per cent of the average in the UPC. As a result, the private sector efforts to invest and create employment have been constrained, undermining attempts to diversify the economy.

These structural weaknesses of the banking and financial system have been deepened by the introduction of a law banning interest-based financial transactions on 7 January 2013 by the Libyan General National Congress, in compliance with the Shari'a. This essentially bans interest on the financing of all civil and commercial transactions. The IMF's Article IV report of 2013 on Libya warned that this law may reduce access to credit for start-ups,

194 *Amal Hamada et al.*

entrepreneurs, and small and medium-sized enterprises, since lending by commercial banks may be interrupted which would negatively affect financial intermediation. Indeed, the adoption of this law was associated with, among other reasons, a decline in domestic credit to the private sector by banks from 27 per cent in 2014 to 17.6 per cent in 2018.

2.2.2 Oil Dependency

Libya's economic growth is highly dependent on fuel and hydrocarbons, which represent 97 per cent of merchandise exports (see Figure 7.4), the highest among oil exporters in the MENA region. Moreover, hydrocarbon activities represent 75 per cent of government receipts. As a result, oil price volatility renders the country's economic performance vulnerable and complicates fiscal management. While Libya had a sovereign wealth fund, called the Libyan Investment Authority (LIA), which was supposed to stabilize its public finances, Qaddafi and his family retained tight control over it from its establishment (Behrendt, 2011). Moreover, because of this political influence, the Security Council adopted the 1973-Resolution and imposed sanctions on the LIA in 2011. It argued that LIA is 'a potential international source of funding for [Qaddafi's] regime'. Clearly, the lack of transparency, accountability, and good governance affected the performance and the effectiveness of this fund from an economic perspective.

The importance of oil revenues, coupled with a relatively small population, has made Libya the country with the highest GDP/capita in Africa since the 2000s, although its oil rent/capita (Figure 7.5) and GDP/capita (Figure 7.6) are lower than the less-populous Gulf Cooperation Countries (GCC).

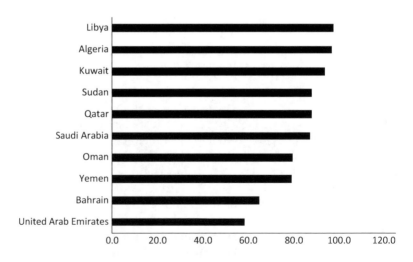

Figure 7.4 Fuel exports (% of merchandise exports)
Source: Own elaboration based on data from the World Development Indicators.

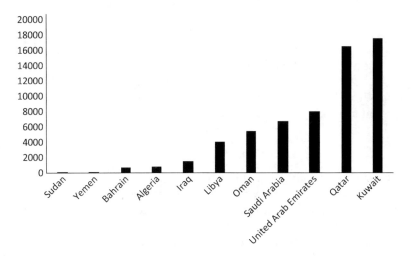

Figure 7.5 Oil rents per capita (current USD), average 2000–2017
Source: Own elaboration based on data from the World Development Indicators.

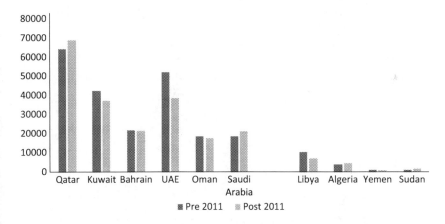

Figure 7.6 GDP/per capita of oil exporters in the MENA region, (USD)
Source: Own elaboration based on data from the World Development Indicators.
Note: Pre-2011 is an average over the period 2000–2010 and post-2011 is an average over the period of 2011–2018.

At the sectoral level, the share of agriculture in GDP is negligible (with the main products being wheat, barley, dates, groundnuts, cattle). In 2017, it contributed only 1.3 per cent to the GDP and employed around 11.2 per cent of the economically active population. The industrial sector is highly dependent on hydrocarbons with the petrochemical industry representing 63.8 per cent of the GDP and employing 25.4 per cent of the active population the same year (according to the World Development Indicators dataset).

196 *Amal Hamada et al.*

Services accounted for 34.9 per cent of GDP and employed 63.2 per cent of the labour force.

Thus, the overwhelming position of oil production coupled with the dominance of the state at both the financial and employment levels had two implications: first, it hindered the development of the manufacturing and agriculture sectors leading to a poorly diversified economy. Second, it negatively affected the emergence of a dynamic private sector capable of investing in and producing manufactured goods.

2.2.3 High Levels of Unemployment

The Libyan labour market, similar to most of the other MENA countries, has suffered from chronically high levels of unemployment and, since 2004, it has had the highest unemployment rate in the region (Figure 7.7).

The problem becomes more acute for the youth and women. Average youth and female unemployment rates in the period between 2000 and 2019 were around 48 per cent and 25 per cent, respectively (see Figures 7.8 and 7.9). Combined with existing ethnic fractionalization, these high rates of unemployment were one of the main factors that led to an unstable political equilibrium and rendered Libya one of the most fragile states of the region. Indeed, while Libya's index of state fragility was low before the Arab Spring of 2011, it increased substantially afterwards when compared to other countries in the region (Figure 7.10).

In a nutshell, the initial economic (oil dependency, high unemployment, and state dominance) and political conditions (weak institutions, tribalism,

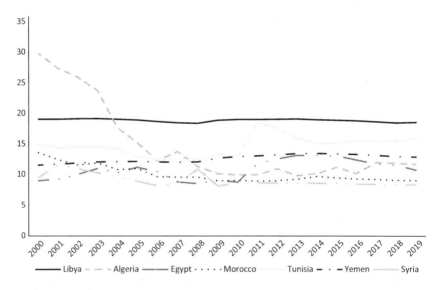

Figure 7.7 Unemployment rates (%), 2000–2020
Source: Own elaboration based on data from the World Development Indicators.

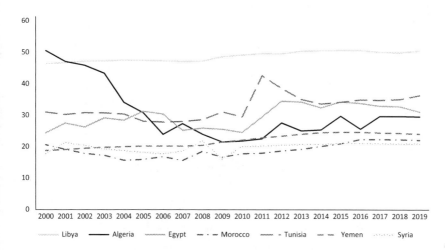

Figure 7.8 Youth unemployment rates (%), 2000–2019
Source: Own elaboration based on data from the World Development Indicators.

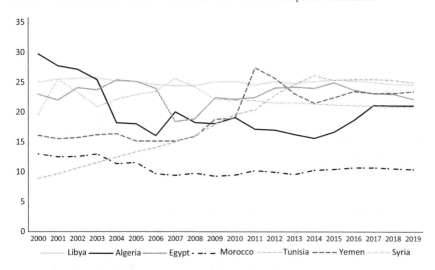

Figure 7.9 Female unemployment rates (%), 2000–2019
Source: Own elaboration based on data from the World Development Indicators.

and militarization) increased the fragility of the country making the conflict very likely to materialize, as will be shown in the next section.

3 Why Has the Conflict Persisted?

While some of the conflict dynamics in Libya are structural problems common to most of the countries that experienced the Arab Spring, other

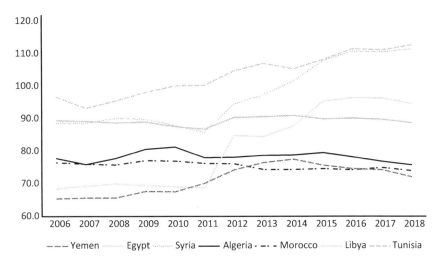

Figure 7.10 Fragile state index
Source: The Fund for Peace.
Note: The FSI is an aggregate index of 12 indicators to measure risk and vulnerability in 178 countries. It includes cohesion, political, economic, and social indicators. A rise in the indicators represents a worsening of the country's situation. Each index ranges from 10 (the worst situation) to 1 (the best situation). The global index ranges from 120 (the worst situation) to 12 (the best situation).

elements are specific to the Libyan context. This section analyses the dynamics that have sustained conflict in order to understand which potential set of policies and actions will or will not lead to a peaceful settlement and a sustainable post-conflict transition.

3.1 Government and the Lack of a Central Authority

Aside from the rooted divisions along ethnic and tribal lines, current political divisions play a great role in preventing the success of a political process aiming to build a functioning and centralized state. The UN supported peace negotiations amongst rival groups and managed to produce the Shkirat Agreement in December 2015. This agreement rests on four main principles: ensuring the democratic rights of the Libyan people; the need for a consensual government based on the principle of separation of powers, oversight, and balance between them; the need to empower state institutions; and respect for the Libyan judiciary and its independence (Libyan Political Agreement, 2015, p. 2). The agreement increased international support for and the recognition of the Government of National Accord, yet it did not help consolidate their rule. The lack of a central authority constitutes a pervasive malaise.

The UN-supported and internationally recognized Government of National Accord (GNA) is based in Tripoli, while a parallel administration, the House of Representatives, is based in Tobruk. At the same time, the so-called Libyan National Army (LNA) is based in Beyda and Benghazi under the leadership of Khalifa Haftar while the Libyan Army loyal to the GNA is based in Tripoli, all claiming authority in their respective zones of influence. Some towns and tribes allied with Haftar due to the GNA's lack of military power, while others allied with the LNA in order to have leverage against their rivals (Wehrey, 2019). Each party, thus, mobilized in collaboration with local militias and radical Islamic groups. One example of the damaging impact of political fragmentation is the country's Coronavirus response: the argument by anti-Haftar circles that any funding to tackle Covid-19 sent by the GNA to Haftar-controlled areas would fund their arms, prevents local authorities in Eastern Libya cooperating with the GNA on their Covid-19 response (Badi and Eaton, 2020).

The UN-brokered ceasefire deal signed between the LNA and GNA on 23 October 2020 was seen as a move towards increasing political talk between the different parties.[9] While the endorsement of a national unity government on 10 March 2021 and a planned presidential election for 24 December 2021 and 24 January 2022 increase the prospect of peace, the registration of divisive figures such as Haftar and one of Muammar Gaddafi's sons, Saif al-Islam Gaddafi, as presidential candidates risk this prospect, as they have support among rival segments of the population.

Lack of a central authority is further compounded by the eight-month-long oil blockade—closure of oil fields and ports—implemented by the Haftar-led LNA in 2020 and which cost close to USD 10 billion in oil revenue.[10] In July 2020, after the LNA, the GNA, and the state-owned National Oil Corporation (NOC) had reached an agreement through UN mediation to reopen oil terminals and restart production, the LNA reversed the negotiations on 11 July stating they would only allow a reopening once there was a mechanism set up to distribute revenues fairly across Libya. While pro-Haftar circles claimed that the Libyan Central Bank only used the oil revenues for the benefit of the GNA, the NOC claimed that the UAE had ordered Haftar and the LNA to reimpose the blockade. As previous attempts have shown, oil has the potential to bring rival powers to the negotiation table for unification talks, but the intention to drain one another economically by cutting access to oil not only hampers any attempts at peace agreements and government building but has a collateral impact on the capacity for providing services, on governance, and on the economy. The formation of a national unity government in March 2021 ahead of a planned presidential election has brought a measure of stability, attracting back companies such as France's TotalEnergies SE, Italy's Eni SpA, and Shell for investment in energy projects.[11]

An increased foreign presence and military support on the ground backing the GNA and Haftar's LNA, driven mainly by Russia, Turkey, Egypt, the UAE, and France, have given more incentives to the GNA and Haftar to make use of hard power as well as the continuation of parallel governments dominating their respective zones of influence. That each side is encouraged to take up arms unless a settlement can be reached on their terms hampers any attempt at unification or at forming a government.

So long as it persists, political fragmentation in Libya will continue to sustain lasting violence, making it difficult to achieve a comprehensive peace settlement. It is noteworthy that this political fragmentation is abused and supported by external powers (both regional and international) which add to the complexities of the situation on the ground as will be elaborated in the sections below.

3.2 Security

Given the lack of a centralized government or security apparatus, the environment of competition between different groups and actors, both big and small, amplifies insecurity. With local militia groups aligning with political actors, many, if not all, have turned into criminal networks with links to businessmen and public officials (World Bank, 2019a).

Policing has also been heavily affected in this environment. The police were already a neglected institution prior to the Arab Spring because of Gaddafi's rule favouring the intelligence apparatus over the establishment of a police force. Political fractures have prevented the establishment of a centralized police force to this day (Salem and Kadlec, 2012). Informal and localized policing carried out by ethnic, religious, and tribal groups at the state or town level have to a large extent replaced the already weak official policing bodies. The increasing level of militarization jeopardizes peace talks and attempts at rebuilding the state (Boserup and Collombier, 2018).

3.3 War Profiteering and Corruption

Armed conflict and civil war sustain negative incentives, particularly for those operating in security in Libya, to profit from this context. While smuggling was controlled and limited to the activities of favoured tribes and groups during the Gaddafi era, the fall of the regime created a power vacuum, producing open competition over smuggling routes and conflict between competing groups mainly defined along ethnic, tribal, and urban-based lines. The smuggling business has also expanded the protection market and generation of taxes from the movement of goods between territories under the control of certain groups. Hence groups that provide protection also become directly involved in smuggling (Eaton, 2018). The same competition between local actors is recreated in the state bureaucracy as well, where appointments have in various cases been based on patronage. Furthermore, profiteering from the war in Libya sustains the political influence and authority of many of the security personnel. As a result, establishing a unified and central government or security apparatus becomes extremely difficult, since the security personnel benefit from an absence of stability.

3.4 International Actors

While international actors officially welcome the transition process in Libya, some have contributed to the fragmentation of Libya's political system by trying to build strategic alliances with different local elements to promote their own interests. The recent developments in the Mediterranean region are just the latest manifestation of the role played by regional and international actors.[12]

For European countries, irregular migration from the Libyan coast to Europe and the fight against local ISIS militias have been priorities, together with the EU endeavour to build an effective government. As such, the EU is one of the main backers of the UN-sponsored GNA. At the same time, individual European countries, for example, Italy and France, have been pushing their own agendas mainly with regard to energy contracts in Libya.

The Turkish military intervention in January 2020 in support of the GNA turned the tide of Haftar and the LNA's offensive to seize Tripoli, ongoing since April 2019, and this was initially followed by internationally supported efforts to implement a ceasefire in Libya. Yet Turkey is using its support for the GNA to continue a series of proxy wars in the region against its regional rivals, mainly Egypt, the UAE, and Saudi Arabia; to push back against Greece and Cyprus' so-called efforts to exclude it from hydrocarbon projects in the Mediterranean; and as a form of display against supporters of Haftar. This further escalates conflict in a country in which none of the countries involved back down as part of a high-risk but high-return zero-sum game.

3.5 Migration

Economic migration was a common phenomenon in Libya long before the eruption of the civil war, although the composition of migrants has changed since 2015. The conflict has led to a surge of migrant smuggling mainly from sub-Saharan Africa. According to the International Organization for Migration (IOM) Displacement Tracking Matrix from July-September 2021, there were more than 610,000 migrants in the country, with a high regional concentration in western Libya, particularly Tripoli. The number of migrants is decreasing consistently since the start of the Covid-19 pandemic, but the unemployment rate among migrants (20 per cent) is still higher than pre-pandemic levels (17 per cent in February 2020) ("Migrant Report July-September 2021", 2021).

Besides losses in human capital, mass displacements of population have also been recorded both in the country and across borders. According to the IOM's Internally Displaced Persons (IDP) and Returnee Report from

July-September 2021, there were close to 200,000 IDPs in Libya. Since the ceasefire agreement signed in October 2020, there has been a continuing decrease in the number of IDPs ('UN OCHA 2021b', p. 104). According to UNHCR's Libya update from November 2021, there were more than 640,000 IDP returnees and more than 42,000 registered refugees and asylum-seekers in the country. Libya is not a signatory to the 1951 Refugee Convention, which means there is no formal refugee protection. Given the extremely dire conditions in detention centres in Libya (Human Rights Watch, 2018), social distancing measures and access to healthcare for IDPs and migrants have become even more difficult during the Covid-19 pandemic.

To sum up, the lack of a centralized and stable government or security apparatus and the surge of corruption in Libya are some of the political factors driving the conflict. The benefit- and ideology-driven international involvement and the inability to manage the movement of people greatly amplify the current conflict.

4 The Economic Costs of the Conflict

Conflicts typically lead to an immense amount of damage: losses in infrastructure and human capital, and deteriorating health and living conditions. Furthermore, the costs of a civil war persist long after the war is over.[13] In what follows we provide an assessment that helps to visualize the magnitude of the reconstruction programme and the financing needs of the post-conflict situation.

4.1 Macroeconomic Costs

As a result of the conflict, GDP growth declined significantly and became negative between 2013 and 2016, as shown in Figure 7.11. It reached also – 31.3 per cent in 2020 with the decline in oil and the COVID-19 pandemic. In cumulative terms, GDP per capita decreased from USD 31,735 to 5,378 in 2016 but recovered slightly to USD 11,187 in 2018. This decline is chiefly attributable to the decline in the hydrocarbon sector that has been jeopardized by the armed conflicts, especially around the main oil fields and terminals in the Sirte Basin. Indeed, in a country where the primary source of income is oil production, this damage affects the entire economy. According to data from the World Bank, the fall in hydrocarbon exports in 2011 led to a budget deficit of 15.4 per cent of GDP and a sharply reduced current account surplus. Oil production was around one million barrels per day in the first five months of 2018 before collapsing to only 0.7 million barrels per day in June. Average oil production was 1.6 million barrels per day before the revolution. Oil facilities suffered severe damage during the conflict. The Libyan National Oil Corporation estimated that, by 2018, damage to oil fields and terminals stood at USD 180 billion or three times the GDP of 2018 (Figure 7.12).

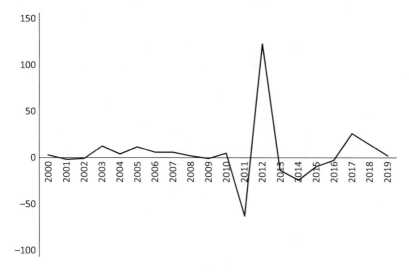

Figure 7.11 GDP growth in Libya (%), 2000–2020
Source: Own elaboration based on data from World Development Indicators.

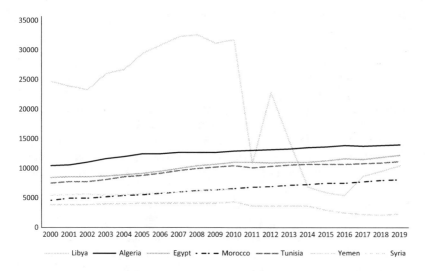

Figure 7.12 GDP per capita in PPP, constant USD of 2011, 2000–2019
Source: Own elaboration based on data from the World Development Indicators.

4.2 Human Capital Cost

Human casualties are estimated at nearly 16,126 deaths and 42,633 injuries between 2011 and 2017, comprising 1 per cent of the population. According to Daw et al. (2019), the overall mortality rate was 2.7/1000 population, and the injury rate was 7.1/1000. At the gender level, the overall male-to-female ratio of mortality and injury was 4.4:1. If age is taken into consideration, it is worthwhile noting that 42.3 per cent of casualties were between 20 and 30 years old and 26.4 per cent aged between 31 and 40 years. These figures show that the cost of the conflict has disproportionately affected young people, which in turn has had a negative impact on the structure of the labour force.

Moreover, according to UN OCHA (2021c), 1.3 million (circa 20 per cent of Libya's total population) people are in need of vital humanitarian assistance, of which 37 per cent are children. 316,000 school-aged children and 10,000 teachers are estimated to be in need of educational support (ibid 52). By the end of 2020, at least 287 schools (6 per cent) had been damaged or destroyed and only 19 per cent of enrolled school-aged children had access to services that respond to the Covid-19 pandemic, such as remote learning, necessitated by the closure of schools in 2020 (UN OCHA 2020a, pp. 65–66).

4.3 Infrastructure and Access to Services

The pre-existing problems regarding infrastructure and access to services have multiplied with the eruption of the civil war. Difficulties in recruiting people for work in services and infrastructure have resulted in a very slow improvement in conditions, if any.

Additionally, the militarization of health facilities and humanitarian aid has affected working conditions negatively, mainly because they became the targets of armed groups. As a result, outbreaks of communicable diseases such as malaria, polio, and tuberculosis have become increasingly common, particularly in migrant-detention centres. While there is a great need for mental health services, they are extremely limited (Massiah et al., 2018). A chronic shortage of electricity caused by damaged networks, a lack of maintenance and fuel, and a chronic shortage of water are recurring structural problems. Large parts of the country experience power cuts because of generation shortfalls and network problems.

According to UN OCHA (2021b), Libya's health system was close to collapse in 2020; 3,5 million people lacked consistent access to primary and secondary health services, including 1,2 million needing severe assistance. More than half of the healthcare facilities that were functioning in 2019 had closed, mainly because of security threats, insufficient national and health sector funding as well as high rates of Covid-19 infection among staff and patients (ibid.).

The needs of the Libyan health system have been well documented by the World Health Organization (WHO) but no monetary estimation of the costs is available. In 2011, the WHO launched a programme to rebuild the Libyan health system. However, repeated emergencies since then have not allowed a proper recovery of public sector services. The Ministry of Health has continued to rely on support from the WHO to access essential medicines. Provision of primary health care, especially for communicable diseases among migrants and refugees in detention centres, has become a major challenge.[14]

As of the end of August 2021, Libya had received a total of 3,847,790 Covid-19 vaccines and had administered 1,100,976 doses of vaccine (14.82 doses administered per 100 population) ('Libya Health Response' 2021, p. 6). While there had been a declining trend in infection rates at the national level, community transmission has still been ongoing in all districts in the country, and case and death numbers remain very high, with almost 309,000 confirmed cases and almost 4,250 deaths cumulatively by the end of August 2021 (ibid., p. 1).

It is important to note that the number of beds and hospitals per 1,000 people is higher in Libya than in other countries in the Middle East (see Figure 7.13). Nevertheless, the health infrastructure remains fragile.

5 Moving from Exclusive to Inclusive Development: A New Social Contract

We have argued in this chapter that the type of state-society relationships that governed Libya before 2011 greatly contributed to the progressive deterioration and subsequent breakdown of institutions. The old social contract relied heavily on the power of the state in terms of economic resources and security as well as on its policy of 'divide and rule' as a means of controlling the different tribes. The ongoing civil war, with limited prospects for ending in the near future, has added further problems to social cohesion and hampered the ability of Libyan society to achieve peace and rebuild the country.

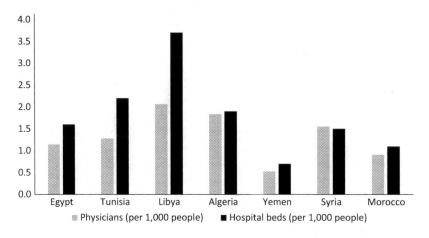

Figure 7.13 Number of physicians and beds per 1000 people, 2014
Source: World Development Indicators.

The Libyan conflict will eventually be settled. We submit that only a new social contract could pave the way for sustainable development in the post-conflict era. Such a contract, in our view, should include three major dimensions: (1) a politically inclusive agenda, (2) an equitable economic reconstruction process, and (3) an end to militarization. However, this best-case scenario will clearly be impeded by spoilers in the short term. This is why we first discuss the spoilers and opportunities in the short term and identify the main features of this scenario. We next show how international actors can have an impact on the development of the Libyan conflict. Finally, we present the main structural and stabilization policies required to achieve the economic new social contract.

5.1 The New Political Contract

5.1.1 Reconstruction: Opportunities and Spoilers

The main spoilers for an inclusive model for reconstruction can be summarized as: (a) a contested transition process; (b) the lack of social cohesion; (c) a persistent security and economy vacuum; (d) the lack of transparency and accountability of public institutions; (e) a fragmented and non-diversified economy; (f) volatile international oil prices and frequent interruptions to domestic oil production; and (g) fragmented international engagement (World Bank, 2019).

The potential for growth and development, social resistance against sectarianism, and important resources, such as oil and a young population, are opportunities to be considered when building an inclusive model for post-conflict reconstruction in Libya (World Bank, 2019). It is also worth noting that the initial Arab Spring protests were against authoritarianism and called for greater freedom, participation, rights, justice, and inclusion. This is a positive sign in terms of the possibilities of grassroots, inclusive peace-building in Libya.

Transition to democracy should include two tracks: follow international experiences in democratic practices; and plan for a long-term project of building democratic values to integrate with education and culture. Current efforts to hold national elections would be a big step in terms of democratization, particularly if they can be combined with an effort to adopt a new democratic constitution and a comprehensive plan for reconstruction.

Reconstruction means building new state institutions and reconciling different social groups, keeping in mind there is no simple economic agenda for achieving full reconstruction. Since there is little consensus among national and international actors on how to tackle the conflict in Libya, reconstruction remains a challenging issue. International involvement in reconstruction in many cases can come with expectations of economic, political, and ideological returns. So long as the new social contract does not have local and grassroots engagement, international involvement might act as a spoiler.

Non-state actors (e.g., militia groups and tribes) are usually motivated to affiliate with the state, not only for access to more resources but also to consolidate political power in their zones of influence. This could be an opportunity if a central government can reach out to non-state actors and cooperate in providing access to services and security. The high social standing of tribal leaders can be used as a positive factor in pushing for state reconstruction. This can be achieved through convincing the tribal leaders to recognize and support the peace process and act as informal forces in accord with a central government (Fraihat, 2011). In the meantime, as long as Libya undergoes a process of political transition without any form of centralized government, communication and reconciliation with strong non-state actors such as the tribes will be necessary to maintain peace. Were a post-conflict reconstruction process to be dominated by certain groups, this would probably result in its distortion, if not in failure. Hence, pushing for mediation between all the groups concerned is part of the institutional reconstruction. It has been argued that, so far, the record of Libya in the transitional justice needed for reconstruction has proved selective and lacking in comprehensiveness (Kersten, 2015).

Given the decentralized nature of governance in Libya and the role of local power holders (be it tribes, militia, city-states, etc.), it is wrong to assume that it would be possible to disrupt their influence in the near term. As such, even if certain power holders might refuse to disarm, lasting peace would not be possible without maximum inclusion, especially if they are players with the ability to veto agreements. Setting up individual negotiations with those who refuse to disarm or providing international guarantees for the conditions agreed have been some of the strategies used in other peace-building contexts.[15] Should a certain player insist on refusing to disarm as part of peace negotiations, excluding them from the peace process is an option; yet the more politically influential the player is the more this is likely to have a negative impact on the stability of the peace process.

5.1.2 A Feasible Peace-Building and Reconstruction Scenario

An ideal scenario for reconstruction is an inclusive settlement where the power is balanced and shared. The Skhirat Agreement might serve as a good background for such a scenario. In this scenario, all parties included agree on the conditions for rebuilding the state, and for the bureaucracy to become meritocratic. Hence the political settlement has a high probability of surviving, but this scenario is hard to achieve in practice, and the UN-supported agreement has failed to establish itself and help the transitional period. The worst-case scenario is one where the settlement ends up being exclusive, where it is the minority of the elites that are involved in state-building, and the system is clientelistic. This type of settlement becomes constantly threatened internally and externally, by excluded elites and other parts of the society (Elbadawi et al., 2019). As a result, we will look at an interim reconstruction scenario in Libya, which considers the opportunities and spoilers, and works towards achieving a realistic settlement.

In this scenario, all parties in Libya should manage to facilitate dialogue and some level of cooperation firstly on security, e.g., on the militias, and then on governance. Once dialogue is established, groups that undermine the settlement process need to be targeted politically by all actors involved in this process, in order to reduce their legitimacy.

Accountability is an important component of the settlement. The settlement process in this scenario will include setting up an independent body that investigates violations of rights and law at all levels. Since such a settlement process is likely to include multiple actors, accountability that applies to all parties will give these parties more political legitimacy in the eyes of Libyan society.

The process will first and foremost focus on peace-building and reconstruction at the local level. Given that grassroots' social movements have changed the political landscape in Libya before, for example, during the Arab uprisings in 2011, the power of social groups and civil society will not be ignored by the parties to the settlement process in this scenario. Civil society organizations will be expected to play a growing role in the settlement process.

Even though there have been elections in Libya since 2011, the people's approval of democratic norms has been mostly replaced by the need for stability and an end to the violence (BTI Libya Country Report, 2018). As such, reaching at least a necessary minimum of stability and political settlement is a precondition for a constitutional referendum or national elections. Until then, a transition government that is accountable to the rule of law will, in this scenario, govern the country. Here, support from the international community for reconciliation in the short term and preparation for elections in the longer term can be an impetus to the settlement process.

Two more processes need to be integrated into this scenario: the first one is the integration of women at all levels of the peace-building and reconstruction process. According to UNSCR 1325, women have to be included in all processes of conflict resolution and state-building, which has not happened in the case of Libya. Women need to be represented at talks around political and economic issues. The second one is fact-finding commissions investigating human rights' violations. Throughout the world, democratic transition has not succeeded without the integration of these commissions and the integration of their outcomes in the constitutional and legal framework of state-building.

5.1.3 Migration and International Involvement

Libya will continue to be a transit country attracting migrants from neighbouring countries. Even as part of a broader reconstruction model, refugee repatriation will be a challenging issue. In the short term, providing access to basic services, security, and legal protection for refugees and IDPs is a starting point. In terms of healthcare, developing a national policy, increasing human resources, and improving infrastructure are necessities, but the availability of funding is a decisive factor in the quality of healthcare, especially in the short and medium term. The context of the global pandemic and its impact on the refugees and IDPs is still to be revealed; nevertheless, there are many reports on the deteriorating conditions in refugee and IDP camps and the crisis within a crisis they are dealing with. The consequences of this health crisis require not only more funds but also better-trained medical staff, better infrastructure, and medical coverage, which conflict-afflicted Libya lacks.

Regarding international involvement in Libya, the agendas of international actors in Libya have been context-specific. This issue aside, the UN has put an immense effort into unifying Libya's state institutions. Preventing the National Oil Corporation from selling crude oil on the international market, for example, played an important role in Haftar's agreement to allow oil revenues to flow through Tripoli (International Crisis Group, 2018).

As much as support from the international community in terms of institution-building and mediation is an extremely useful resource, taking decisions based on loyalties or favours to specific international actors can reinforce corruption and favouritism in the Libyan state bureaucracy as well as the energy sector. Hence, institutional decisions regarding governance and economy should favour the Libyan state and society above anything else. This would greatly benefit from transparency and open competition. Supporting local authorities at the expense of the central state and not adapting to the Libyan context can cause much unintentional damage.

5.2 The Way Forward for the Libyan Economy

Analysing the post-conflict recovery of Lebanon, Kuwait, and Iraq, Sab (2014) finds that the speed of recovery differed significantly across these countries. It depends on the economic and institutional development of the country, the structure of the economy (oil versus non-oil), the duration of the war, and engagement of the international community. The GDP growth recovers faster in oil-exporting countries as compared to oil-importing ones, as the oil sector can recover rapidly after the civil war. However, the political situation in Libya remains uncertain, adding an extra layer of complexity to the conflict.

5.2.1 Sources of Growth: Between Distortion and Volatility

Before proposing recommendations for the Libyan economy, it is important to analyse its production structure and what are the sources of growth. Figure 7.14 presents the structure of GDP by sector. Obviously, it is chiefly dominated by industry (related to fuel and refineries) with a modest share

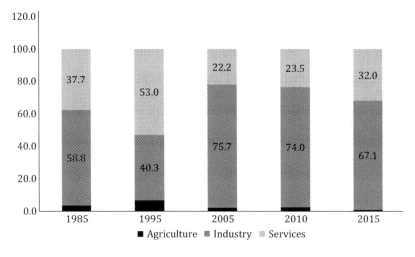

Figure 7.14 GDP composition by expenditure (%)
Source: UN Statistics.

for services and a negligible share for agriculture. Given that the industrial sector is capital-intensive, it does not help to generate jobs. Second, in terms of sources of growth, Figure 7.15 shows that the growth rate of physical capital experienced a significant decline whereas that of human capital and labour were relatively stable (Bhattarai and Taloba, 2017). Thus, more recently, both human capital and labour have contributed to growth more than material capital has. This is important for the way forward, as the recovery might be lengthier given the large human capital losses that were previously presented.

Third, growth was and is still closely correlated to oil prices. Indeed, Figure 7.16 a and b show that oil prices and GDP display almost the same trends and that oil rents are significantly correlated to GDP growth. This is why the latter is highly volatile in Libya when compared to other oil-abundant countries (like Algeria) or other regions (see Figure 7.17). Finally, labour productivity has also been declining (Figure 7.18).

Two preconditions are indispensable for the reconstruction of the Libyan economy. First, forming better institutions by neutralizing the militias and re-establishing the rule of law is crucial. The second precondition for any economic recovery is to rebuild the main infrastructure destroyed in the war zone, including transport infrastructure, sanitation, telecommunications, schools, public buildings, and hospitals. Indeed, despite its oil wealth, before 2011 Libya did not manage to build an adequate infrastructure that would support private sector investment and growth or attract foreign direct investment (FDI). As a result of the conflict, most of the infrastructure was destroyed. This damage has led to reduced connectivity, higher

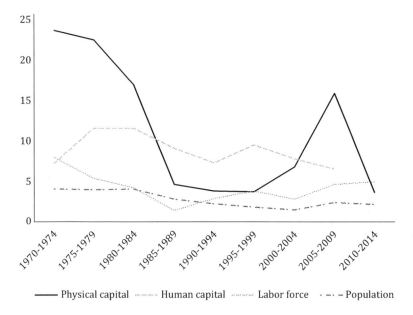

Figure 7.15 Growth rates in input factors per five-year periods in Libya (1970–2014)
Source: Own elaboration based on data by Bhattarai and Taloba (2017).

transport costs, and disruptions in supply chains and networks. Restoring damaged infrastructure is a priority in order to attract FDI for the manufacturing sector and for the tourism industry. In fact, the latter could regrow once there is some stability and adequate infrastructure. Furthermore, reconstruction will give the opportunity to improve the education and health systems and to modernize infrastructures. This, in turn, will contribute in the long term to developing trade and tourism, and to attracting FDI.

In what follows, we present reforms at three levels, stabilizing, institutional, and structural, that we believe should be implemented if Libya is to pursue a successful post-conflict recovery once a political settlement has been reached.

5.2.2 Institutional Reforms

As discussed in Section 2, weak institutions are the main problem affecting the Libyan economy. There is a clear need to enhance transparency, especially throughout the public sector. Data compilation remains weak, and responsibilities are spread over several agencies. The compilation of many key indicators has been interrupted by the conflict and has not been restored. The reconstruction of the state after the civil war represents a unique opportunity to foster transparency and accountability.

212 *Amal Hamada et al.*

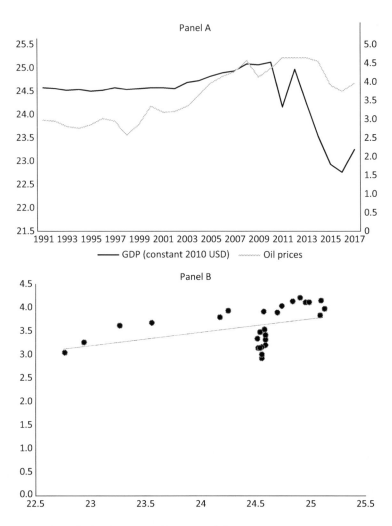

Figure 7.16 Correlation between oil rents and GDP
Source: Own elaboration based on data from the World Development Indicators.

The role of civil society is crucial in the reconstruction process. Civil society suffered from structural problems during the Gaddafi era that rendered its role almost non-existent. During the post-Gaddafi period of conflict, new civil society organizations were quickly working to establish common ground for engaging and networking. Though not well grounded, new civil society organizations such as the Forum for Democratic Libya (FDL) managed to build natural networks of tribal and ethnic affiliations to launch a limited social dialogue around the constitution (Geha, 2016). As such, supporting civil society should be a priority on the agenda of international aid donors. The current health crisis is putting more pressure on civil society

Investigating the Libyan Conflict and Peace-building Process 213

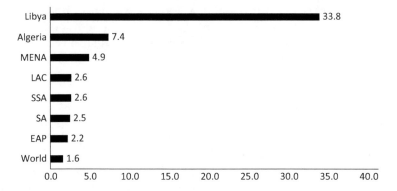

Figure 7.17 GDP growth volatility
Source: Own elaboration based on data from World Development Indicators.
Note: Volatility is measured as the standard deviation of GDP growth rates for each country/region.

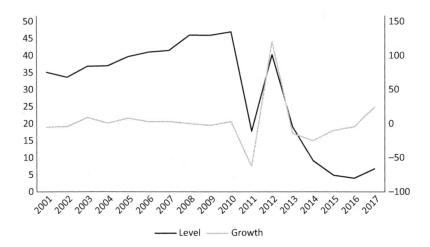

Figure 7.18 Labour productivity
Note: Authors' elaboration using UN statistics.
Level: Labour productivity calculated by dividing real GDP per employed person.
Growth: Annual growth rate of real GDP per employed person (GDP constant 2010 USD) (%).

organizations; in addition to their work in peace-building, they are working with local communities to spread necessary health information, to provide vital supplies such as gloves, masks, and sanitizers, and with doctors to network and provide them with assistance (CSPPS, 2020).

At the legal level, the IMF advises the Libyan government to adopt an Anti-Money Laundering and Combating the Financing of Terrorism (AML/CFT) law in line with international standards, and to devote resources to its effective implementation. The aim of this programme is to deprive the militias and armed groups of finance, by limiting illicit financial flows, and to support the recovery of stolen assets. In addition to this, efforts should be exerted to reform the security sector, to fight corruption, and restore order and the rule of law.

5.2.3 Structural Reforms

In order to build a strong post-conflict economy and reduce the reliance of the economy on capital, oil, and its associated industries, the Libyan economy should address three main issues: establishment of a more vibrant private sector, economic diversification, and finally SMEs' development and access to finance. It is important to note that, using a simple simulation with a 5 per cent of employment elasticity, when economic growth is 2 per cent, around 2000 jobs will be created. This number increases by 1.2 per cent and by 3.1 per cent when the GDP growth-rate reaches 5 per cent and 10 per cent respectively. Hence, even with a high economic growth rate, the private sector will not be able to reduce unemployment under the current scheme. This is why structural reforms are crucial to generate more jobs.

First, to have a more dynamic and vibrant private sector, the Libyan state might delegate some of its activities to the private sector and should foster the development of SMEs through investments. Policies to enhance the business environment and develop infrastructure form a part of these investments. However, the development of the private sector is not possible given a weak banking sector. Banks are not intermediating effectively and suffer from the presence of the government in the sector as well as the lack of an enabling legal environment. The banking system suffers from several further problems, such as the lack of a robust system of property rights, the absence of credit assessment information, the lack of competition, and government ownership. Finally, the law prohibiting interest introduced in 2013 in compliance with Shari'a law has to be revisited since it significantly hinders the development of new ventures.

Second, in terms of economic diversification, it is important to note that hydrocarbons have long dominated the Libyan economy, accounting for more than 70 per cent of GDP, more than 95 per cent of exports, and approximately 90 per cent of government revenue. A strand of the literature on oil-abundant countries has put forward the 'resource curse' theory, showing that resource abundance is associated with poor development outcomes (Gelb, 1988). Led by Sachs and Warner (1995), empirical work showed that resource-abundant countries have slower growth than resource-poor countries (Collier and Goderis, 2007). This is why, in order to benefit from the oil revenues, the Libyan government must diversify the economy and introduce effective political reforms, accompanied by a strong system of political checks and balances. This would trigger reform in macroeconomic institutions in general and fiscal institutions in particular, that would improve the management of natural resources, achieve more savings, and implement more effective public spending programmes.

Third, in order to boost SMEs, financial-sector intermediation is also necessary. This will help increase access to finance for all firms and especially small and medium-sized enterprises. This should have two consequences: first, a sector not based on hydrocarbons will be developed; second, SMEs will be able to generate jobs in the short term. Indeed, according to the World Bank dataset, youth unemployment was 44.43 per cent on average between 1991 and 2016. SMEs must also be connected to larger and foreign firms to guarantee their sustainability. Therefore, while promoting FDI, the government should attract them to the manufacturing sector in order to generate greater added value and create more jobs. A transfer of resources to more productive and higher value-adding sectors will be an important determinant of sustainable and labour-intensive growth, which will help to attract more FDI to sectors with strong job-creating potential.

5.2.4 Reforms for Macroeconomic Recovery

In principle, Libya does not need financial resources but rather technical support to enhance the management of the abundant revenues drawn from its natural resources, and to consolidate the budget, thereby contributing to a stable macroeconomic recovery. Some policies have already been set up to stabilize macroeconomics variables. In September 2018, the Libyan government approved a programme of economic reform under which fuel subsidies were to be reduced. This measure was enforced in October 2019, when the price rose from 0.15 to 0.85 Libyan dinars (USD 0.6) per litre, which is also the production cost.

The government also devalued the Libyan dinar in order to eliminate the considerable gap between the official and parallel exchange rates. These reforms ought to be complemented by other budget reforms. Government expenditure is skewed towards wages and subsidies, which undermines the fiscal stance and reduces the opportunity for spending on human capital and infrastructure. There is also a need to redesign the regressive energy subsidies that generate damaging externalities for the environment. The fiscal space can then be used to implement conditional cash-transfer programmes targeting the poorest households. Successful transitions implemented in Latin America (Mexico, Brazil) or the MENA region ('Takaful and Karama' in Egypt) may serve as models for Libya.

The monetary policy also needs reform. It is important that the Libyan dinar reflects its real value. Despite the recent devaluation, there is still a significant difference between the official exchange rate, fixed at LYD 1.3 to one USD, and the black-market rate, which in 2018 fluctuated at around LYD 6–7 per USD. Furthermore, the government imposed a service fee of 184 per cent on the official exchange rate for all foreign currency purchases (commercial or personal transactions). This led to the creation of a second official exchange rate of 3.90 LYD/USD which, according to the government, would help lower the black-market exchange rate. Nevertheless, the latter remained as it was. Ensuring easier access to foreign currency through the official banking system rather than the black market will help reduce such a gap.

In a nutshell, while the first and the second sets of reforms will help the Libyan economy improve its current structure, the last set of reforms shall enhance the macroeconomic management of the country.

6 Conclusion

Since the Arab uprisings in 2011, Libya has endured sustained civil conflict with varying degrees of intensity and recurring bouts of social, political, security, and economic crises that, frequently, have reinforced one another. This has weakened state institutions and the economy, thereby facilitating fragmentation, disunity, and dysfunctionality, creating a fertile ground for the growth of violence and a war-driven economy. Even though some progress has been achieved through national and international initiatives, Libya has so far been unable to turn its initial post-2011 revolutionary success into a process of transition to a stable and inclusive economic and political system.

Libya continues to lack a unified territorial structure and state institutions have not been able to achieve legitimacy in the eyes of the population. There is a lack of coordination between different levels of government and a widespread lack of transparency. Tribalism and ethnic divisions sustain (and profit from) insecurity. High levels of violence, a non-functioning security apparatus, and extremism enhance the conflict. In terms of the economy, oil dependency with its negative impact on the growth of other sectors, high inflation, the growth of the shadow economy and the black market, a fragile macro-economy, lack of trust, and unemployment are some of the most difficult challenges the country is facing. The exclusion of the youth and women from participation in public life and a crisis of migrants, refugees, and IDPs are large-scale societal issues. These vulnerable groups are impacted more by the Covid-19 pandemic. Indeed, with prevention measures and curfews, unemployment is rising, and this affects the food security of migrants, refugees, women, and informal workers (IOM, 2020). In terms of foreign policy, religious/ideological proxy wars and oil rivalries have exacerbated the conflict, while international peace initiatives have not succeeded because of the reliance on a one-size-fits-all approach to peace promotion as well as the effects of the economic interests of individual states in Libya.

According to Sambanis (2019b), power-sharing institutions increase political inclusion and the accommodation of minority groups and former rebels after the civil war, thereby reducing grievances that could fuel further violent conflict. Moreover, he argues that, in this context, an institutional mechanism for the distribution of nominal political power (e.g., cabinet positions) according to a fixed rule could be applied. The concept of inclusive power-sharing in Sambanis' study applies to the Libyan case. In line with this argument of inclusive power-sharing that produces positive outcomes for democratic stability, we claim that in the case of Libya, an ideal reconstruction scenario is where all parties are included in the process and share in the goal of rebuilding the state. Yet, we claim that this scenario is hard to achieve in practice and has previously failed in Libya. This is why we suggest that an inclusive power-sharing model can start out by facilitating dialogue and some level of cooperation initially on more pressing issues such as providing security and then moving on to governance. This model of power-sharing will work only if the reconstruction process is not dominated by certain groups, and there is an effort to include all the involved parties in the peace process. Adding these to the inclusive power-sharing model may reduce the risk of a return to violence.

In a nutshell, reconstruction requires building new state institutions and a new economy. We recognize that there continues to be little consensus among both national and international actors on how to tackle the conflict in Libya, and hence reconstruction remains a challenging endeavour. Nonetheless, the authors submit that the basis for any enduring settlement is a new social contract that would comprise at least the following three dimensions: (1) an inclusive political regime approximated by a substantive democratic arrangement, (2) an equitable economic reconstruction and (3) an end to the militarization of the militias.

Notes

1 Nevertheless, in the second half of 2020, we witnessed an increased tension between Libyan fractions supported and reflected in the increased intervention by Turkey and potentially Egypt. Yet, the government established early 2021 took the responsibility of leading the process of re-building state institutions and put an end to the civil war.
2 Some scholars argued in the late 1990s that Militant Islam did not have a chance in Libya for several reasons; namely Qaddafi's imposed ideology and the legacy of the Senusi movement. For example, see Deeb (1996).
3 The political map of Islamists in Libya is very complicated. Most of the population are conservative Muslims, nevertheless there was a broad range of political Islamist groups varying from Salafi groups affiliated with Saudi Arabia, Muslim Brotherhood, Sufi apolitical groups, and jihadis affiliated to al-Qaeda and Bin Laden. Some of these groups include sub-groups that overlap with different political affiliations and vary in degree of militarization.
4 For example, see Farouk study on the jihadis in Libya.
5 For the role of the tribes in forming the political map in Libya see CSDS (2019)
6 The main ethnic groups in Libya include Berber, Tuareg and Tebu. Though ethnicity and tribe intersect, the former was downplayed during Gaddafi reign in favour of the latter. After the fall of the regime, these three main ethnic groups, along with others, started demanding full recognition as ethnic minorities. For further details see Kohl (2014).
7 It should be noted that these authors relied on different years for each state depending on the availability of data. For Libya, data is for the year 1995.

8 Government banks, as well as other state-owned enterprises, operate under an implicit guarantee from the state that they will not go bankrupt. This, in turn, softens discipline and lowers the standard of business practices, hampers management and profitability and makes entities prone to corruption and political interference. For an international comparison, see Cornett et al. (2010).
9 For details on the peace agreement, see: https://www.crisisgroup.org/middle-east-north-africa/north-africa/libya/b80-fleshing-out-libya-ceasefire-agreement
10 See: https://www.dw.com/en/libya-haftar-plans-to-lift-8-month-oil-field-blockade/a-54981299
11 See: https://www.reuters.com/markets/commodities/exclusive-shell-eyes-return-libya-with-oil-gas-solar-investments-2021-11-30/, https://www.bloomberg.com/news/articles/2021-11-22/total-eni-eye-billion-dollar-oil-gas-solar-projects-in-libya
12 See different official and media statements made by the two countries related to political developments in Libya: https://www.egypttoday.com/Article/2/79297/Egypt-will-not-stand-idle-while-Turkey-intervenes-in-Libya, https://www.washingtonpost.com/world/turkeys-parliament-authorizes-troop-deployment-to-libya-as-proxy-war-escalates/2020/01/02/b97d35a8-2d6d-11ea-bffe-020c88b3f120_story.html, https://www.bloomberg.com/news/articles/2020-01-02/egypt-warns-against-turkish-military-interference-in-libya
13 According to Collier, by the end of a civil war, the economy is on average almost 15 per cent poorer than it would otherwise have been, and the mortality rate is higher due to diseases and the collapse of the health system.
14 For 2019, the WHO estimates the health sector funding requirements at USD 37.9 million for this year.
15 For more information on disarmament in peace processes see Stedman (2000) and Cunningham (2013).

Concluding Remarks

Samir Makdisi and Raimundo Soto

Scholarly writings have referred to the 'exceptionalism' of the Arab region, meaning the general persistence of autocracy in the Arab countries in contrast to progress towards democratic governance in other regions of the world, a matter confirmed by well-known democracy indicators. This exceptionalism, however, is confined to the political sphere. At the economic and social levels, the Arab region has made steady progress in line with, if not ahead of, other developing regions. Human Development Indices for the region reflect significant progress over the two decades prior to 2011, though tapering in the subsequent years on account of its ongoing conflicts. To the extent that we adopt an all-encompassing notion of development (sustainable economic growth with democracy), then the Arab region has fallen behind other regions in forging its development path. The failure of socio-economic development in the region to prompt a significant move towards genuine democratic governance has been cited as a counter manifestation of the modernization hypothesis, admittedly controversial among scholars of development.

Irrespective of the hypothesis that best conforms to the Arab region's development since World War II (essentially socio/economic development without democracy), it remains the case that two major characteristics set it apart from most other emerging regions, namely chronic conflicts and oil wealth (with related foreign interventions), that to a large degree, explain its pattern of development. While the specific impact of oil wealth on sustaining autocracy has recently been under some dispute it has generally been held that the combined influence of oil and conflict has not only helped maintain authoritarian rule in the region prior to 2011 but has since continued to counter the unleashing of potentially significant democratic changes.

The Arab uprisings of 2011 reflect, to a large extent, the ultimate failure of a development strategy to promote a new, more inclusive, and democratic social contract. While protests and political turmoil swept the entire region, only Tunisia managed to move forward along a democratic path despite underlying domestic political tensions and economic difficulties. Egypt reverted to autocratic rule while the four countries under study remain, as of mid-2021, subject to multifaceted conflicts sustained by Arab and foreign intervention, the Syrian and the Yemeni being the most vicious and intense and inviting, at one point (along with Iraqi conflict) an onslaught by fundamentalist groups.

In the introduction, we articulate several common economic, political, institutional, and social factors that underlay the 2011 uprisings: high levels of youth unemployment, perceptions of inequality, aspirations for political reform, and social fractionalization. The country studies also bring out additional but important country-specific triggers. They include a rising middle-class aspiring for greater freedom (Syria); the deleterious effect of foreign interventions (Iraq); increasing tribal divisions and their militarization along with foreign intervention (Libya); and tribal divisions motivated by both political and economic greed (Yemen).

Whatever their causes, once resolved, the uprisings provide these four countries with the opportunity to initiate their own transformation guided by two major objectives: establishing a genuinely inclusive and democratic political system of governance and restructuring the economy to reverse its past trends and promote steady growth in physical and human capital.

The promise of such a transformation notwithstanding, the remaining overhanging influence of Arab authoritarianism renders uncertain a move in the direction of genuine democratic governance, as demonstrated by the contrasting examples of the two other countries that experienced the uprisings, Egypt and Tunisia. This uncertainty, we have to keep in mind, is governed by two opposing influences. On the one hand, despite any resolution of the ongoing conflicts, oil wealth and outside interventions (intra-Arab and foreign), could continue to sustain varying forms of authoritarianism in the region[1] and/or foster chronic, low-intensity struggles (as in Yemen) that put a heavy toll on social cohesion, institution building, investment, and economic growth. On the other hand, modernizing influences associated with economic development, reflected in growth in real per capita income, rising levels of education, technological advances, etc., are also at work tending to promote, among other factors, democratic forms of governance. These competing influences will shape the yet-to-be-determined post-conflict phase of the countries under study, as well as the region as a whole. The more modernizing influences become entrenched, the stronger the democratic trend.

The political and economic challenges that Arab countries in conflict will face after their conflicts recede are staggering and will require a colossal effort on their part to make peace sustainable and economic reforms successful. Looking beyond the eventual settlement of their on-going conflicts, this volume has endeavoured to identify the conditions that would govern their post-conflict paths to sustained national peace and development. The thematic chapters provide three pivotal overall insights. The first is that political greed (e.g., abuse of power and corruption on the part of the governing authorities and privileged classes) leading to socio-economic grievances (induced by economic and wealth inequality, extreme poverty, high unemployment, etc.) underlay the Arab conflicts, creating the conditions for state failure. Hence the second insight at the political level that 'inclusive' power-sharing institutions (which mandate the participation of several parties in decision-making processes) are key to post-conflict national peace and democratic stability; and the third, that focuses on the main goal of post-conflict reconstruction as being the elimination altogether of the prewar institutional fabric of the countries in conflict, effecting a major shift in the developmental ideology and operations of the political system. Two major objectives of this shift would be achieving wider economic inclusion and reducing inequality as well as generating increasing employment opportunities; and equally, aligning economic reforms and policies with the establishment of a new form of social contract, whether implicit or explicit, that would reflect the attributes of democratic governance.

In line with the thematic studies and looking beyond the eventual settlement of any ongoing conflict, the case studies assert that if national peace and equitable development are to be sustained the old (pre-conflict) social contract, based on autocratic rule, marked government intervention, weak institutions, a considerable degree of public employment, and unsustainable transfers to the population would no longer be a viable option. Instead, a new social contract would have to be put in place; one that would reflect socio-economic inclusivity, institutional reform, and democratic political governance which will ensure equitable power-sharing and accountability; otherwise, the seeds of conflict will remain. In consequence, the direct role of the state in the national economy will diminish, though the specifics of its transformation could differ from one country to another depending in part on the relative importance of natural resources such as oil in the economy. In contrast, the regulatory functions of the state are expected to be further developed to assure the proper functioning of the emerging post-conflict state and economy.

In parallel, the case studies identify major economic reforms to be implemented as an integral part of the post-conflict development phase. Each country has its own specific concerns in this regard, for example, a more efficient management of oil resources and a more vibrant private sector in Iraq and Libya, a more equitable regional distribution of development expenditure in Syria, and a more efficient enforcement of property rights in Yemen, especially after its expected re-unification. At the same time, these countries face common post-conflict economic challenges at the structural, economic, and institutional levels. They include, among others, the issue of economic diversification, control of inflation, raising employment levels, husbanding fiscal expenditures, controlling corruption, and implementation of transparent policies. Some of the case studies point out that reaching these goals may not be feasible in the period immediately following the settlement of the conflicts. Rather a more gradual route might have to be traversed starting with political arrangements that initially may not be fully democratic but with sustained development would evolve into genuine democratic institutions as, for instance, in the case of South Korea. Failure to carry out major economic reforms, it should be stressed, could lead to the disruption of the desired or intended political change towards genuine democratic governance and, at worst, a return to various forms of open or disguised autocratic rule.

The fulfilment of such aspirations is subject to at least two major conditions, external and domestic respectively. The former is whether ongoing or potential conflicts in the region, including the long-standing Arab/Israeli conflict and the Iran/Gulf rivalries, are justly resolved. Otherwise, the pretext for actual or even potential conflict would always serve the objective of the 'autocratic' governing classes which is to maintain power.

We are aware of the ambiguity of what 'just resolution' might imply; whatever form it might take we interpret it to mean the elimination of the identifiable root causes of the conflict, as the case studies do with respect to each of the four countries, thereby opening the door for a peaceful post-conflict phase with a growing potential for the region to move along a democratic path. Oil wealth, whose potency has declined with the drop in its world price, and any remaining fundamentalist influences that feed on conflict would not be able, we believe, to counter this trend. And any potential destabilizing foreign interventions would be unlikely to succeed.

But removal or neutralization of disruptive external factors is not sufficient in itself for peace. Equally if not more important, are domestic readiness and the ability to learn the lessons of the civil conflict as the countries concerned prepare to move forward. Foremost is the need, as has already been emphasized, to create a new national condition that would prevent the recurrence of domestic conflicts, i.e., basically the establishment of democratic political institutions that seek wider economic inclusion and lessen inequality. Domestic peace agreements provide a window of opportunity for reforms and transformation, but they may not be long-lasting. Implementing them with determination would enhance the prospects for the successful adoption of a comprehensive agenda of economic and political reform.

A final word: though unlikely, it is possible that the conflicts in the four countries will yet persist for many years to come. If so, this would not simply imply an enduring non-fulfilment of the above conditions for their sustained national peace and development but possibly a future breakup of their present political entities, a disastrous outcome, discussion of which, however, lies beyond the scope of this volume.

Note

1 Articulated by North et al. (2009) as societies governed by 'limited access orders'.

Bibliography

Aarts, P., P. van Dijke, I. Kolman, J. Statema, and G. Dahhan (2012): 'From Resilience to Revolt: Making Sense of the Arab Spring', WODC Rapport 2119 University of Amsterdam, Department of Political Science.

Abadie, A. and J. Gardiazabal (2003): 'The Economic Costs of Conflict: A Case Study of the Basque Country', *The American Economic Review*, 93 (1): 113–132.

Abrardi, L., C. Cambini and L. Rondi (2016): 'Investment and Regulation in MENA Countries: The Impact of Regulatory Independence', in A. Rubino, M. Teresa Costa Campi and V. Lenzi, ed., *Regulation and Investments in Energy Markets. Solutions for the Mediterranean*. Academic Press.

Abu-Ismail, K., A. Abdel-Gadir, and H. El-Laithy (2011): 'Poverty and inequality in Syria (1997–2007)', UNDP, Arab Development Challenges Report, 15.

Abu Omar, A. and K. Al Ansary (2020): 'Iraq's Currency Devaluation May Not Be Enough to Salvage Sinking Economy', *Bloomberg*. https://www.bloomberg.com/news/articles/2020-12-24/iraq-s-devaluation-may-not-be-enough-to-salvage-sinking-economy, accessed December 21/12/2021.

Acemoglu, D. and J.A. Robinson (2006): *Economic Origins of Dictatorship and Democracy*. Cambridge: Cambridge University Press.

Acemoglu, D. and J.A. Robinson (2012): *Why Nations Fail: The Origins of Power, Prosperity and Poverty*. New York: Crown.

Acemoglu, D. and J.A. Robinson (2016): 'Paths to Inclusive Political Institutions', in J. Eloranta, E. Golson, A. Markevich, and N. Wolf, eds., *Economic History of Warfare and State Formation*. Singapore: Springer, pp. 3–50.

Acemoglu, D., S. Naidu, P. Restrepo, and J.A. Robinson (2014): 'Democracy Does Cause Growth', NBER Working Paper No. 2004 March.

Achcar, G. (2017): *Morbid Symptoms: Relapse in the Arab Uprising*. Stanford, CA: Stanford University Press.

Adam, C., P. Collier, and V.A.B. Davies (2008): 'Post Conflict Monetary Reconstruction', *The World Bank Economic Review*, 22 (1): 87–112.

Ahmed, E. and O. al-Rawhani (2018): *The Need to Build State Legitimacy in Yemen*. Sana'a Centre for Strategic Studies, September.

Aidt, T.S. (1998): 'Political Internalization of Economic Externalities and Environmental Policy', *Journal of Public Economics*, 69: 1–16.

Aidt, T.S. and G. Leon (2016): 'The Democratic Window of Opportunity', *Journal of Conflict Resolution*, Peace Science Society (International), 60 (4): 694–717.

Al-Awlaqi, W. and M. al-Madhaji (2018): *Local Governance in Yemen Amid Conflict and Instability*. CARPO. White paper prepared by the Sana'a Center for Strategic Studies, in coordination with the project partners DeepRoot Consulting and CARPO – Center for Applied Research in Partnership with the Orient. Sana'a, Yemen.

Bibliography

Al-Badran, F. (2017): 'A Look into the Future of Marketing of Iraqi Oil.' (in Arabic): Iraqi Economists Network. www.iraqieconomists.net/ar/2017/04/21/ ‏/فاضل-علي-عثمان-البدران-نظرة-مستقبلية

Al-Batati, S. (2015): 'Who are the Houthis in Yemen?' *Al Jazeera*. Retrieved December 20, 2018, from https://www.aljazeera.com/news/middleeast/2014/08/yemen-houthis-hadi-protests-201482132719818986.html

Al-Khatteeb, L. and H. Istepanian (2015): *Turn a Light on: Electricity Sector Reform in Iraq*. Policy Briefing #15, Foreign Policy at Brookings, Brookings Doha Center.

Al-Marsoumi, N. (2019): 'An Initial Reading of the Construction Board Law.' Iraqi Economists Network. www.iraqieconomists.net/ar/2019/09/19/ ‏/نبيل-جعفر-المرسومي-قراءة-أولية-في-مشر

Al-Mawlawi, A. (2018): Analysing Growth Trends in Public Sector Employment in Iraq. https://blogs.lse.ac.uk/mec/2018/07/31/analysing-growth-trends-in-public-sector-employment-in-iraq/, accessed 15/05/19.

Al-Qarawee, H.H. (2014): *Iraq's Sectarian Crisis a Legacy of Exclusion*. Carnegie Endowment for International Peace. processed, April.

Al-Waday, H. (2017): A Pure and Fixed Identity Threatened by Annihilation. Retrieved from Al-Madaniya: https://almadaniyamag.com/2017/07/09/2017-7-9-a-pure-and-fixed-identity-threatened-by-annihilation/

Alaaldin, R. (2018): 'Sectarianism, Governance, and Iraq's Future', Brookings Doha Center Analysis Paper # 24, November. Brookings Doha Center Analysis Paper.

Alesina, A., and R. Perotti (1996): 'Income Distribution, Political Instability, and Investment', *European Economic Review*, 40 (6): 1203–1228.

Alesina, A. and G. Tabellini (1990): 'A Positive Theory of Fiscal Deficits and Government Debt', *The Review of Economic Studies*, 57 (3): 404–414.

Alesina, A., A. Devleeschauwer, W. Easterly, S. Kurlat and R. Wacziarg (2003): 'Fractionalization,' *Journal of Economic Growth*, 8 (2): 155–194.

Alfaro, L. (2017): 'Gains from Foreign Direct Investment: Macro and Micro Approaches', *The World Bank Economic Review*, 30 (Supplement 1): 2–15.

Ali, H. (2011): *Estimate of the Economic Cost of conflict: A Case Study from Dharfour*. Doha: Al Jazeera Centre for Studies.

Alkhoja, G., R. Neman, and S. Hariz (2016): *Social Safety Nets in Iraq: Reform in a Time of Fragility, Conflict and Violence*. World Bank MENA Knowledge and Learning, no. 161. Washington, DC: The World Bank.

Allawi, A. A. (2007): *The Occupation of Iraq: Winning the War, Losing the Peace*, Yale University Press, 544 pages, New Haven, CT

Allen, D. and D. Lueck (1992): 'Contract Choice in Modern Agriculture: Cash Rent versus Cropshare', *Journal of Law and Economics* 35 (2): 397–426.

Alnaswawi, A. (1994): *The Economy of Iraq: Oil, Wars, Destruction of Development and Prospects, 1950–2010*. London: Greenwood.

Alshadeedi, H. and N. Ezzeldine (2019): 'Libyan Tribes in the Shadow of War and Peace', Netherlands Institute of International Relations. CRU Policy Brief, February.

Altai Consulting for SJD\Libya (2015): *Libya Civil Society Mapping*. http://www.altaiconsulting.com/wp-content/uploads/2017/06/Libya-Civil-Society-Mapping-Altai-Consulting-SJD-PUBLIC-.pdf

Alvaredo, F., L. Assouad, and T. Piketty (2017): 'Measuring Inequality in the Middle East, 1990–2016: The World's Most Unequal Region', WID. Word Working Paper Series, No 2017/16.

Amat, F., A. Arenas, A. Falcó-Gimeno, and J. Muñoz (2020): 'Pandemics Meet Democracy: Experimental Evidence from the COVID-19 Crisis in Spain', mimeo, University of Barcelona – IPERG.
Amin, M., R. Assaad, N. al-Baharna, K. Dervis, R.M. Desai, N.S. Dhillon, A. Galal, H. Ghanem, C. Graham, and D. Kaufmann (2012): *After the Spring: Economic Transitions in the Arab World.* Oxford: Oxford University Press.
Anderson, D., Balderas, A., Bro, A., Davis, A., Doyle, A., Eder, T., Hincks, L., Hollister, R., Hubeny, R., Shafi, N., and L. Thurm (2017): *Rebuilding a Unified Yemen Emerging from the Rubble.* Institute for the Study of Diplomacy, Georgetown University.
Angel-Urdinola, D.F. and K. Tanabe (2012): 'Micro-Determinants of Informal Employment in The Middle East and North Africa Region', World Bank Social Protection and Labor Discussion Paper 1201.
Arampatzi, E., M. Burger, E. Ianchovichina, T. Röhricht, and R. Veenhoven (2018): 'Unhappy Development: Dissatisfaction with Life on the Eve of the Arab Spring', *Review of Income and Wealth*, 64 (1): 80–113.
Arezki, R. (2019): 'Tearing Down the Walls of Vested Interests in the Middle East and North Africa', *Middle East Institute*, blog November 18.
Armstrong, M. and D.E.M. Sappington (2006): 'Regulation, Competition and Liberalization', *Journal of Economic Literature*, 44 (2): 325–366.
Arndt, C. and C. Oman (2008): 'The Politics of Governance Ratings', Maastricht Graduate School of Governance, Working Paper 2008/WP003, April.
Asal, V., M. Findley, J. A. Piazza, and J. I. Walsh (2016): 'Political Exclusion, Oil, and Ethnic Armed Conflict', *Journal of Conflict Resolution*, 60 (8), 1343–1367.
Assaad, R. (2014): 'Making Sense of Arab Labor Markets: The Enduring Legacy of Dualism', *IZA Journal of Labor and Development*, 3: 6. https://doi.org/10.1186/2193-9020-3-6
Asseburg, M. and K.Y. Oweis (2017): 'Syria's Reconstruction Scramble', *Syria Studies*, 9 (2): 15–30.
Ayubi, N.N. (1996): *Overstating the Arab state: Politics and Society in the Middle East.* London: Bloomsbury.
Azmeh, S. (2014): 'Uprising of the Marginalised: A Socio-Economic Perspective of the Syrian Uprising', LSE Middle East Centre Paper Series 6. London: LSE.
Badi, E. and T. Eaton (2020): 'Libya's Gen. Hifter Declared Military Rule Last Month. That hasn't Happened', *The Washington Post Monkey Cage*. Access date: 24 May 2020.
Bandiera, L., V. Chandra, J.C. Fosque, J. Von Der Goltz, T. Peterburs, N. Piffaretti, J. Saba, and C. Wheeler (2018): *Jobs in Iraq: A Primer on Job Creation in the Short-Term (English).* Washington, DC: World Bank Group.
Barakat, S. (2016): Is there a Path to Peace in Yemen? Brookings Institute. Retrieved June 7, 2019, https://www.brookings.edu/blog/markaz/2016/04/26/is-there-a-path-to-peace-in-yemen/
Baranyi, S., P. Beaudet, and U. Locher (2011): World Development Report 2011: Conflict, Security, and Development. *Canadian Journal of Development Studies / Revue canadienne d'études du développement*, 32 (3), 342–349.
Barnes-Dacey, J. (2019): 'Geo-Politics of Reconstruction: Who Will Rebuild Syria and Pay for It?' in Eugenio Dacrema, Valeria Talbot, and Paolo Magri, ed., *Rebuilding Syria: The Middle East's Next Power Game?* Milan: Ledizioni LediPublishing.

Baron, A. (2019): Foreign and Domestic Influences in the War in Yemen. The Proxy Wars Project. Retrieved from Virginia Tech Publishing: https://doi.org/10.21061/proxy-wars-baron

Baron, A.B., A. Cummings, S. Tristan, and M. al-Madhaji (2016): 'The Essential Role of Local Governance in Yemen', *Sana'a Centre for Strategic Studies*.

Barro, R.J. and D.B. Gordon (1983): 'Rules, Discretion and Reputation in a Model of Monetary Policy', NBER Working Paper No. 1079.

Bartusevicius, H. (2014): 'The Inequality-Conflict Nexus Re-Examined: Income, Education and Popular Rebellions', *Journal of Peace Research*, 51 (3): 35–50.

Basedau, M., G. Strüve, J. Vüllers, and T. Wegenast (2011): 'Do Religious Factors Impact Armed Conflict? Empirical Evidence from Sub-Saharan Africa', *Terrorism and Political Violence*, 23 (5): 752–779.

Basedau, M. and J. Lay (2009): 'Resource Curse or Rentier Peace? The Ambiguous Effects of Oil Wealth and Oil Dependence on Violent Conflict', *Journal of Peace Research*, 46 (6): 757–776.

Basedau, M. and J.H. Pierskalla (2014): 'How Ethnicity Conditions the Effect of Oil and Gas on Civil Conflict: A Spatial Analysis of Africa from 1990 to 2010', *Political Geography*, 38: 1–11.

Baten, J. and C. Mumme (2013): 'Does Inequality Lead to Civil Wars? A Global Long-Term Study Using Anthropometric Indicators (1816–1999)', *European Journal of Political Economy*, 32 (C): 56–79.

Beblawi, H. and G. Luciani (eds) (1987): *The Rentier State*. London: Croom Helm.

Beetsma, R.M.W.J. and X. Debrun (2015): 'Are Fiscal Councils Effective?' CBR Conference on Rethinking Fiscal Policy after the Crisis, Bratislava, 10–11 September.

Behrendt, S. (2011): 'Sovereign Wealth Funds in Nondemocratic Countries: Financing Entrenchment or Change?' *Journal of International Affairs*, 65 (1): 65–78.

Besley, T. and T. Persson (2009): 'The Incidence of Civil War: Theory and Evidence', Discussion Paper EOPP/2009/5, STICERD, London School of Economics.

Besley, T. and T. Persson (2011): 'The Logic of Political Violence', *The Quarterly Journal of Economics*, 126 (3): 1411–1445.

Bibi, S. and M. Nabli (2010): 'Equity and Inequality in the Arab Region', ERF Policy Research Report 33, Cairo.

Bhattarai, K., and A. Taloba (2017): 'Source of Growth in Libya: Is MRW Model Still Applicable for an Oil Based Economy?', *Advances in Economics and Business*, 5 (12): 670–682.

Blanco, F.; D. Emrullahuand, and R. Soto (2020): 'Do Coronavirus Containment Measures Work? Worldwide Evidence', Policy Research Working Paper No. 9490. World Bank, Washington, DC.

Bodea, C. (2012): *Natural Resources, Weak States and Civil War: Can Rents Stabilize Coup Prone Regimes?* The World Bank.

Bodea, C. and C. Houle (2020): 'Horizontal Wealth Inequality and Oil – Is There a Contingent Effect?' Working Paper, Michigan State University.

Bodea, C. and I.A. Elbadawi (2007): 'Riots, Coups and Civil War: Revisiting the Greed and Grievance Debate', Policy Research Working Paper; No. 4397. World Bank, Washington, DC.

Bodea, C. and I.A. Elbadawi (2008b): 'Political Violence and Underdevelopment', *Journal of African Economies*, 17 (Suppl_2): 50–96.

Bodea, C., I.A. Elbadawi, and C. Houle (2017): 'Do Civil Wars, Coups and Riots Have the Same Structural Determinants?' *International Interactions*, 43 (3): 537–561.

Bodea, C., M. Higashijima, and R.J. Singh (2016): 'Oil and Civil Conflict: Can Public Spending Have a Mitigation Effect?' *World Development*, 78: 1–12.
Boix, C. (2008): 'Economic Roots of Civil Wars and Revolutions in the Contemporary World', *World Politics*, 60 (3): 390–437.
Bol, D., M. Giani; A. Blais, and P.J. Loewen (2021): 'The Effect of COVID-19 Lockdowns on Political Support: Some Good News for Democracy?' *European Journal of Political Research*, 60 (2): 497–505.
Bormann, N.C. (2019): 'The Origins of Ethnic Power-Sharing Coalitions: How Uncertainty Fosters Cooperation', *Journal of Politics*, 81 (2):471–486.
Bormann, N.C., L. E. Cederman, S. Gates, B.A. Graham, S. Hug, K.W. Strøm, and J. Wucherpfennig (2019): 'Power-sharing: Institutions, Behavior, and Peace', *American Journal of Political Science*, 63 (1): 84–100.
Bormann, N.C., N. Sambanis, and M. Toukan (2019): 'Outside Options: Power-sharing in the Shadow of External Intervention After Civil War', Unpublished manuscript.
Boserup, R.A. and V. Collombier (2018): 'Militarization and Militia-tization Dynamics of Armed Group Proliferation in Egypt and Libya', Menara Working Papers No. 17. October.
Boucek, C. (2011): 'Islamist Terrorists in Libya', *Carnegie Endowment for Peace*. https://carnegieendowment.org/2011/05/11/islamist-terrorists-in-libya-pub-43951
Boughzala, M. and S. Ben Romdhane (2017): 'Tunisia: The Prospects for Democratic Consolidation', in I.A. Elbadawi and S. Makdisi, ed., *Democratic Transitions in the Arab World*. Cambridge: Cambridge University Press. doi:10.1017/9781316687000
Bowman, S.A. (2011): 'Regional Seismic Interpretation of the Hydrocarbon Prospectivity of offshore Syria', *GeoArabia*, 16 (3): 95–124.
Box, G., and G. Jenkins (1970): *Time Series Analysis: Forecasting and Control*. San Francisco: Holden-Day.
Brancati, D. (2006): 'Decentralization: Fueling the Fire or Dampening the Flames of Ethnic Conflict and Secessionism?', *International Organization*, 60 (3): 651–685.
Brömmelhörster, J. and W.C. Paes (2004): *Military as an Economic Actor: Soldiers in Business*. Gordonsville: Palgrave Macmillan.
Brubaker, R. (1995): 'National Minorities, Nationalizing States, and External National Homelands in the New Europe', *Daedalus*, 124 (2): 107–132.
Brück, T. (1997): Macroeconomic Effects of the War in Mozambique. QEH Working Paper Series No. 11 (QEHWPS11), Queen Elizabeth House, University of Oxford.
Brückner, M. and A. Ciccone (2011): 'Rain and the Democratic Window of Opportunity', *Econometrica*, 79 (3): 923–947.
BTI (2018): '2018 Libya Country Report'. https://www.bti-project.org/en/reports/country-reports/detail/itc/lby/ity/2018/itr/mena/
Buchanan, A.E. (2007): *Justice, Legitimacy, and Self-Determination*. 2nd ed. Oxford: Oxford University Press.
Bueno de Mesquita, B., A. Smith, R. Siverson, and J. Morrow (2003): *The Logic of Political Survival*. Cambridge, MA and London, UK: MIT Press.
Buhaug, H. and J.K. Rød. (2006). Local Determinants of African Civil Wars, 1970-2001, *Political Geography* 25(3): 315–335.
Bunce, V. (1999): *Subversive Institutions: The Design and the Destruction of Socialism and the State*. Cambridge: Cambridge University Press.

Bibliography

Calderon, J. (2004). 'The Formalisation of Property in Peru 2001–2002: The Case of Lima', *Habitat International*, 28(2): 289–300.

Cammet, M. and I. Diwan (2013): 'Conclusion: The Political Economy of the Arab Uprisings', in A. Richards and J. Waterbury, ed., *A Political Economy of the Middle East*. 3rd ed., New York: Westview Press.

Cammett, M. and E. Malesky (2012): 'Power-sharing in Post-conflict Societies: Implications for Peace and Governance', *The Journal of Conflict Resolution*, 56 (December): 982–1016.

Campante, F.R. and D. Chor (2012): 'Why Was the Arab World Poised for Revolution? Schooling, Economic Opportunities, and the Arab Spring', *Journal of Economic Perspectives*, 26 (2): 167–188.

Capasso, M., J. Czerep, A. Dessì, and G. Sanchez (2020): Libya Country Report, EU-LISTCO (Europe's External Action and the Dual Challenge of Limited Statehood and Contested Orders). Available on the following link: Libya Country Report – Cidob www.cidob.org › content › download › version › file.

CBS (2013): Much of the $60B from U.S. to rebuild Iraq wasted, special auditor's final report to Congress shows. https://www.cbsnews.com/news/much-of-60b-from-us-to-rebuild-iraq-wasted-special-auditors-final-report-to-congress-shows/, accessed 7/4/19.

CBS News (2020): As war and COVID-19 ravage Yemen, $1.35 billion in international aid isn't nearly enough. Here's why. https://www.cbsnews.com/news/yemen-war-and-coronavirus-international-aid-isnt-enough-and-this-is-why/

Cederman, L.E., A. Wimmer, and B. Min (2010): "Why Do Ethnic Groups Rebel? New Data and Analysis." *World Politics* 62(1): 87–119.

Cederman, L.E., K.S. Gleditsch, and H. Buhaug (2013): *Inequality, Grievances and Civil War*. Cambridge: Cambridge University Press.

Cederman, L.E., N. Weidmann, and K.S. Gleditsch (2011): 'Horizontal Inequalities and Ethnonationalist Civil War: A Global Comparison', *American Political Science Review*, 105 (3): 478–495.

Cederman, L.E., S. Hug, A. Schädel, and J. Wucherpfennig (2015): 'Territorial Autonomy in the Shadow of Conflict: Too Little, Too Late?' *American Political Science Review*, 109 (May): 354–370.

Chaturvedi, S. and S. Saha (2019): *Manufacturing and Jobs in South Asia: Strategy for Sustainable Economic Growth*. 1st ed. Singapore: Springer.

Cheibub, J.A., J. Gandhi, and J.R. Vreeland (2010): 'Democracy and Dictatorship Revisited', *Public Choice*, 143 (1–2): 67–101.

Chong, A. and F. Lopez De Silanes (2005): *Privatization in Latin America. Myths and Reality*. Series: Latin American Development Forum, The World Bank and Stanford University Press, Washington: DC.

Cimadomo, J. (2012): 'Fiscal Policy in Real Time', *The Scandinavian Journal of Economics*, 114 (2): 440–465.

CCPPS (2020): *A Polarised Nation during a Global Pandemic: the Libyan Predicament*, Civil Society Platform for Peacebuilding and Statebuiliding.

Coletta, G., C. Graziano, and G. Infantino (2015): 'Do Fiscal Councils Impact Fiscal Performance?' Government of the Italian Republic (Italy), Ministry of Economy and Finance, Department of the Treasury Working Paper No. 1.

Colgan, J.D. (2015): 'Oil, Domestic Conflict, and Opportunities for Democratization', *Journal of Peace Research*, 52 (1): 3–16.

Collier P. (2000): 'Rebellion as a Quasi-Criminal Activity', *The Journal of Conflict Resolution*, 44 (6): 839–853.
Collier, P. (2001): 'Implications of Ethnic Diversity', *Economic Policy*, 16 (32): 128–166.
Collier, P. and A. Hoeffler (1998): 'On Economic Causes of Civil War', *Oxford Economic Papers*, 50 (4): 563–573.
Collier, P. and A. Hoeffler (2002a): 'Aid, Policy, and Growth in Post-Conflict Societies', Policy Research Working Paper no. 2902, Development Research Group, The World Bank, Washington DC.
Collier, P. and A. Hoeffler (2004): 'Greed and Grievance in Civil War', *Oxford Economic Papers*, 56 (4): 563–595.
Collier, P., A. Hoeffler, and D. Rohner (2009): 'Beyond Greed and Grievance: Feasibility and Civil War', *Oxford Economic Papers*, 61 (1): 1–27.
Collier, P., A. Hoeffler, and M. Soderbom (2004): 'On the Duration of Civil War', *Journal of Peace Research*, 41 (3): 253–273.
Collier, P. and B. Goderis (2007): 'Commodity Prices, Growth, and the Natural Resource Curse: Reconciling a Conundrum', Economics Series Working Papers WPS/2007-15, University of Oxford, Department of Economics.
Collier, P., L. Elliot, H. Hegre, A. Hoeffler, M. Reynal-Querol, and N. Sambanis (2003): *Breaking the Conflict Trap. Civil War and Development Policy*. Oxford: Oxford University Press.
Constitute (2019): Iraq's Constitution of 2005. https://www.constituteproject.org/constitution/Iraq_2005.pdf?lang=en.
Corbo, V., O. Landerretche, and K. Schmidt-Hebbel (2002): 'Does Inflation Targeting Make a Difference?' in N. Loayza and R. Soto, ed., *Inflation Targeting: Design, Performance, Challenges*. Santiago: Central Bank of Chile, pp, 221–269.
Cordesman, A. (2015): 'Trends in Iraqi Violence, Casualties and Impact of War: 2003-2015', Centre for Strategic and International Studies, Burke Chair in Strategy, working draft.
Cordesman, A. and S. Khazai (2014): Iraq in Crisis. Center for Strategic and International Studies. Washington, DC: CSIS, Center for Strategic & International Studies; Lanham, MD: Rowman & Littlefield publis0gers.
Cornett, M.M., L. Guo, S. Khaksari, and H. Tehranian (2010): 'The Impact of State Ownership on Performance Differences in Privately-owned versus State-owned Banks: An International Comparison', *Journal of Financial Intermediation*, 19: 74–94.
Cortright, D., A. Millar and G. Lopez (2002): 'Smart Sanctions in Iraq: Policy Options', in D. Cortright and G. A. Lopez, ed., *Smart Sanctions: Targeting Economic Statecraft*, pp. 201–224.
Costalli, S., L. Moretti, and C. Pischedda (2017): 'The Economic Costs of Civil War: Synthetic Counterfactual Evidence and the Effects of Ethnic Fractionalization', *Journal of Peace Research*, 54 (1): 80–98.
Cowley, R. (1999): *What If? The World's Foremost Historians Imagine What Might Have Been*. New York City: Berkley Books.
CPA (2003): CPA Official Documents. https://govinfo.library.unt.edu/cpa-iraq/regulations/, accessed 4/5/19.
Cramer, C. (2003): 'Does Inequality Cause Conflict?' *Journal of International Development: The Journal of the Development Studies Association*, 15 (4): 397–412.

Crane, D.A. (2012): 'A Neo-Chicago Perspective on Antitrust Institutions', *Antitrust Law Journal*, 78 (1): 43–65.

CSDS (2019): 'The Tribe's Role in Shaping the Libyan Political Scene', Center for Strategic and Diplomatic Studies, http://www.csds-center.com/article/دور_القبيلة_في_تشكيل_المشهد_السياسي_الليبي

Cunningham, D.E. (2013): 'Who should Be at the Table? Veto Players and Peace Processes in civil war', *Penn State Journal of Law & International Affairs*, 2 (1); United Nations Peacekeeping, Disarmament, Demobilization and Reintegration (DDR).

Dacrema, E. (2019): 'Syria in the New Middle East: The Fate of a War-Torn Country', in E. Dacrema and V. Talbot, ed., *Rebuilding Syria: The Middle East's Next Power Game*. Milan: Ledizioni LediPublishing.

Daher, J. (2019a): *Surpassing the War Economy in Syria; the Different Scenarios at Hand*. Beirut, Lebanon: The Asfari Institute for Civil Society and Citizenship.

Daher, J. (2019b): 'The Paradox of Syria's Reconstruction', Carnegie Middle East Centre.

Dang, H. and E. Ianchovichina (2018): 'Welfare Dynamics with Synthetic Panels: The Case of the Arab World in Transition', *Review of Income and Wealth*, 64 (1): 114–144.

Davis, E. (2005): *Memories of State: Politics, History and Collective Identity in Modern Iraq*. Berkeley: University of California Press.

Davoodi, H., B. Clements, J. Schiff, and P. Debaere (2001): 'Military Spending, the Peace Dividend and Fiscal Adjustment', *IMF Staff Papers*, 48 (2): 290–316.

Daw, M.A., A. H. El-Bouzedi, and A. A. Dau (2019): 'Trends and Patterns of Deaths, Injuries and Intentional Disabilities within the Libyan Armed Conflict: 2012–2017', *PloS One*, 14 (5): e0216061.

de Figueiredo, R.J.P. and B.R. Weingast (1999): 'The Rationality of Fear: Political Opportunism and Ethnic Conflict', in B. Walter and J. Snyder, ed., *Civil Wars, Insecurity, and Intervention*. New York: Columbia University Press.

de Soysa, I. (2002): 'Paradise is a Bazaar? Greed, Creed, and Governance in Civil War, 1989–99', *Journal of Peace Research*, 39 (4): 395–416.

de Soysa, I. and E. Neumayer (2005): 'False Prophet, or Genuine Savior? Assessing the Effects of Economic Openness on Sustainable Development, 1980–99', *International Organization*, 59 (3): 731–772.

de Soysa, I. and E. Neumayer (2008): 'Disarming Fears of Diversity: Ethnic Heterogeneity and State Militarization, 1988–2002', *Journal of Peace Research*, 45 (4): 497–518.

Deeb M.K. (1996): 'Militant Islam and its Critics: The Case of Libya', in J. Ruedy, ed., *Islamism and Secularism in North Africa*. New York: Palgrave Macmillan, pp. 187–197.

Deininger, K. and H. Binswanger (1999): 'The Evolution of the World Bank's Land Policy: Principles, Experience and Future Challenges', *The World Bank Research Observer*, 14 (2): 247–276.

Deininger, K. and G. Feder (2009): 'Land Registration, Governance, and Development: Evidence and Implications for Policy', *World Bank Research Observer*, 24 (2): 233–266.

del Castillo, G. (2008): *Rebuilding War-Torn States: The Challenge of Post-Conflict Economic Reconstruction*. Oxford: Oxford University Press.

Derviş, K. and C. Conroy (2019): How to renew the social contract, Brookings Institution OP-ED, Tuesday, June 25, 2019.

Desai, R.M., T. Yousef, and A. Olofsgård (2009): "The Logic of Authoritarian Bargains", Economics and Politics 21(1): 93–125.
Desai, R.M. and T.M. Yousef (2019): 'The Vulnerable Class and Support for Violence in the Arab World', in R. Alaaldin, F.S. Fasanotti, A. Varvelli, and T.M. Yousef, ed., *The Rise and Future of Militias in the MENA Region*. Milan: Ledizioni LediPublishing, pp. 1–138.
Devadas, S., I.A. Elbadawi, and N. Loayza (2019): 'Growth after War in Syria'. Policy Research Working Paper WPS 8967, The World Bank. Washington, DC.
Devarajan, S. and E. Ianchovichina (2018): 'A Broken Social Contract, Not High Inequality, Led to the Arab Spring', *Review of Income and Wealth*, 64 (1): 5–25.
Devarajan, S. and L. Mottaghi (2016): *MENA Quarterly Economic Brief, January 2016: The Economic Effects of War and Peace*. Washington, DC: The World Bank.
Devarajan, S. and L. Mottaghi (2017): 'The Economics of Post-Conflict Reconstruction in Middle East and North Africa', *Middle East and North Africa Economic Monitor* (April): Washington, DC: World Bank.
Devarajan, S., L. Mottaghi, Q.T. Do, and M. Abdel-Jelil (2016): 'Syria: Reconstruction for Peace', Working Paper 104577. MENA Economic Monitor. Washington, D.C: World Bank.
Dincer, N.N. and B. Eichengreen (2014): 'Central Bank Transparency and Independence: Updates and New Measures', *International Journal of Central Banking*, 10 (1): 189–259.
Diwan, I., A. Malik, and I. Atiyas (2019): *Crony Capitalism in the Middle East: Business and Politics from Liberalization to the Arab Spring*. Oxford: Oxford University Press.
Diwan, I., M. Cammett, A. Richards, and J. Waterbury (2015): *A Political Economy of the Middle East*. 4th ed., Edited by M. Cammett, I. Diwan, A. Richards, and J. Waterbury Boulder, CO: Westview Press.
Dixon, J. (2009): 'What Causes Civil Wars? Integrating Quantitative Research Findings', *International Studies Review*, 11 (4): 707–735.
Dodge, T. (2013): "State and society in Iraq ten years after regime change: the rise of a new authoritarianism", *International Affairs*, 89(2): 241–257.
Downes, A. and J. Monten (2013): 'Forced to Be Free: Why Foreign-Imposed Regime Change Rarely Leads to Democratization', *International Security*, 37 (4): 90–131.
Doyle, M. W., and N. Sambanis. (2000): 'International Peacebuilding: A Theoretical and Quantitative Analysis,' *American Political Science Review*, 94 (4): 778–801.
Doyle, M. W. and Nicholas Sambanis. (2006): *Making War and Building Peace: United Nations Peace Operations*. Princeton, MJ: Princeton University Press.
Dresch, P. (1993): *A Modern History of Yemen*. Cambridge: Cambridge University Press.
Dunne, J.P., and N. Tian (2017): 'Conflict and Fragile States in Africa', Working Paper Series N° 274, African Development Bank, Abidjan, Côte d'Ivoire.
Easterly, G. (2018): 'Before 2014: Yemen's Economy before the War', The Yemen Project.
Eaton, T (2018): *Libya's War Economy: Predation, Profiteering and State Weakness*. London: Chatham House.

232 Bibliography

Edwards, S. (2007): 'The Relationship Between Exchange Rates and Inflation Targeting Revisited', in Frederic S. Mishkin and Klaus Schmidt-Hebbel, ed. *Monetary Policy under Inflation Targeting*, Series on Central Banking, Analysis, and Economic Policies, vol. 11. Santiago: Central Bank of Chile.

Eggertsson, T. (2008): *Imperfect Institutions: Possibilities and Limits of Reform*. 4th ed. Ann Arbor: University of Michigan Press.

Eifert, B., E. Miguel, and D. Posner (2010): 'Political Competition and Ethnic Identification in Africa', *American Journal of Political Science*, 54 (2): 494–510.

El Ouardani, H. and S. Makdisi (2018): 'Autocracy, Democracy and Populism with Reference to Tunisia', *ORIENT*, 4: 70–76.

El-Joumayle, O. (2016): 'Economic Growth, Abrupt Institutional Changes and Institutional Policies: The Case of an Oil-exporting Country', *International Journal of Contemporary Iraq Studies*, 10 (1–2): 105–137.

Elbadawi, I.A., B. Fallah, M. Louis, S. Makdisi, J. Youssef, R. Albinyana, and S. Tumen (2019): 'Repatriation of Refugees from Arab Conflicts: Conditions, costs and scenarios for reconstruction'. FEMISE Euromed Report 2019.

Elbadawi, I.A. and N. Sambanis (2000): 'Why are There So Many Civil Wars in Africa? Understanding and Preventing Violent Conflict', *Journal of African Economies*, 9 (3): 244–269.

Elbadawi, I.A. and R. Soto (2010): 'Exchange Rate and Monetary Policy for Sustainable Post-conflict Transition', Working Paper 392, Instituto de Economía, Pontificia Universidad Católica De Chile.

Elbadawi, I.A. and R. Soto (2013a): 'Aid, Exchange Rate Regimes and Post-conflict Monetary Stabilization', ERF Working Paper Series #751, Cairo, Egypt.

Elbadawi, I.A. and R. Soto (2013b): 'Exchange Rate Regimes for Post-Conflict Recovery', ERF Working Paper Series #748, Cairo, Egypt.

Elbadawi, I.A. and R. Soto (2014): 'Resource Rents, Institutions and Civil Wars', *Defence and Peace Economics*, 26 (1): 89–113.

Elbadawi, I.A. and S. Makdisi (2011): *Democracy in the Arab World: Explaining the Deficit*. London: Routledge.

Elbadawi, I.A. and S. Makdisi (2016): *Democratic Transitions in the Arab World*. Cambridge: Cambridge University Press.

Elbadawi, I.A. and S. Makdisi (2021): 'The Sustainability of GCC Development Under the New Global Oil Order', in G. Luciani and T. Moerenhout, ed., *When Can Oil Economies be Deemed Sustainable?* Singapore: Palgrave Macmillan, p. XXI, 365.

Elkins, Z. and J. Sides (2007): 'Can Institutions Build Unity in Multiethnic States?' *American Political Science Review*, 101 (November): 693–708.

England, A. (2010): 'Al-Qaeda Exploits Failures of Weak State', *Financial Times*, Retrieved April 2, 2019, from http://www.ft.com/intl/cms/s/0/7f0db11c-f895-11de-beb8-00144feab49a.html#axzz4BNNxVOAw

Englebert, P. and J. Ron (2004): 'Primary Commodities and War: Congo-Brazaville's Ambivalent Resource Curse', *Comparative Politics*, 37: 61–81.

Englebert, P. and D.M. Tull (2008): 'Postconflict Reconstruction in Africa: Flawed Ideas about Failed States', *International Security*, 32 (4): 106–139.

Economic and Social Commission for Western Asia (ESCWA) (2014): *Survey of Economic and Social Developments in the Arab Region 2013-2014*, ISBN: 978-92-1-128374-7

Esteban, J. and D. Ray (1994): 'On the Measurement of Polarization', *Econometrica*, 62 (4): 819–851.

Esteban, J. and D. Ray (2008): 'On the Salience of Ethnic Conflict', *American Economic Review*, 98: 2185–2202.

Esteban, J. and D. Ray (2011): 'A Model of Ethnic Conflict', *Journal of the European Economic Association*, 9 (3): 496–521.

Esteban, J. and L. Mayoral (2011): 'Ethnic and Religious Polarization and Social Conflict', Working Papers 528, Barcelona Graduate School of Economics.

Esteban, J. L. Mayoral, and D. Ray (2012): 'Ethnicity and Conflict: Theory and Facts', *Science*, 336 (6083): 858–865.

Estrin, A. and A. Pelletier (2018): 'Privatization in Developing Countries: What are the Lessons of Recent Experience?' *The World Bank Research Observer*, 33 (1): 65–102.

Estrin, S., R. Bruno, and N. Campos (2017): 'The Benefits from Foreign Direct Investment in a Cross-Country Context: A Meta-Analysis', CEPR Discussion Paper 11959.

Fafo Institute for Applied International Studies (2007): 'Iraqis in Jordan: Their Numbers and Characteristics.' http://www.unhcr.org/47626a232.html

Fatás, A. (2015): 'The Agenda for Structural Reform in Europe', CEPR Discussion Papers 10723, C.E.P.R. Discussion Papers.

Fearon, J.D. (2003): 'Ethnic and Cultural Diversity by Country', *Journal of Economic Growth*, 8 (2): 195–222.

Fearon, J.D. (2005): 'Primary Commodity Exports and Civil War', *Journal of Conflict Resolution*, 49: 483–507.

Fearon, J.D. (2011): 'Governance and Civil War Onset,' World Development Report 2011 Background Paper, World Bank, Washington, DC.

Fearon, J.D. and D.D. Laitin (2003): 'Ethnicity, Insurgency, and Civil War', *American Political Science Review*, 97 (1): 75–90.

Fearon, J.D. and D.D. Laitin (2008): 'Civil War Termination', Presented at the Annual Meetings of the American Political Science Association, Chicago.

Federal Reserve Economic Data (FRED) (2019): https://fred.stlouisfed.org/

Feltman, J. (2018): The Only Way to End the War in Yemen. Foreign Affairs. Retrieved May 10, 2019, from Foreign Affairs website: https://www.foreignaffairs.com/articles/yemen/2018-11-26/only-way-end-war-yemen

Fjelde, H. (2009): 'Buying Peace? Oil Wealth, Corruption and Civil War, 1985–1999', *Journal of Peace Research*, 46: 199–218.

Fogel, R. (1962): 'A Quantitative Approach to the Study of Railroads in American Economic Growth: A Report of Some Preliminary Findings', *Journal of Economic History*, 22 (2): 163–197.

Food and Agriculture Organization of the United Nations (FAO) (2017): *Counting the Cost Agriculture in Syria after Six Years of Crisis*. Rome: Food and Agriculture Organization of the United Nations.

Food and Agriculture Organization of the United Nations (FAO) (2020): 'FAO Launches Smallholder Support Programme to Improve Business-oriented Agricultural Skills for Youth and Women', 10 January 2020. http://www.fao.org/emergencies/fao-in-action/stories/stories-detail/en/c/1257290/

Foote, C., W. Block, K. Crane, Keith and S. Gray (2004): 'Economic Policy and Prospects in Iraq', *Journal of Economic Perspectives*, 18 (3):47–70.

Fraihat, I. (2011): 'Imperatives for Post-Conflict Reconstruction in Libya', *Brookings*. Conflict Trends, 2011 (4): 3–10.

Fukuyama, F. (2013): 'Commentary: What is Governance?' *Governance: An International Journal of Policy, Administration and Institutions*, 26 (3): 347–368.

Gaddafi, Muammar (1975): *Green Book*, processed.

Galiani, S. and E. Schargrodsky (2010): 'Property Rights for the Poor: Effects of Land Titling', *Journal of Public Economics*, 94 (9–10): 700–729.

Gandhi, J. and A. Przeworski (2006): 'Cooperation, Cooptation and Rebellion Under Dictatorship', *Economics and Politics*, 18 (1): 1–26.

Garfield, R. and R. Waldman (2003): *Review of Potential Interventions to Reduce Child Mortality in Iraq*. Basics II Report, Office of Health and Nutrition of the Bureau for Global Health, Washington DC: US Agency for International Development (USAID).

Garriga, A.C. (2016): 'Central Bank Independence in the World: A New Dataset', *International Interactions*, 42 (5): 849–868.

Gates, S., B.A.T. Graham, Y. Lupu, H. Strand, and K.W. Strom (2016): 'Power-sharing, Protection, and Peace', *Journal of Politics*, 78 (2): 512–526.

Gates, S., H. Hegre, M.P. Jones, and H. Strand (2006): 'Institutional Inconsistency and Political Instability: Polity Duration 1800–2000', *American Journal of Political Science*, 50 (4): 893–908.

Gazdar, H. and A. Hussain (2002): 'Crisis and Response: A Study of the Impact of Economic Sanctions in Iraq', in K.A. Mahdi ed., *Iraq's Economic Predicament*. Reading UK: Ithaca Press.

Geha, C. (2016): *Understanding Libya's Civil Society*. Middle East Institute. https://www.mei.edu/publications/understanding-libyas-civil-society

Gelb, A. (1988): *Oil Windfalls: Blessing or Curse?* New York: Oxford University Press (for the World Bank).

Germann, M. and N. Sambanis (2021): 'Political Exclusion, Lost Autonomy, and Nonviolent Conflict', *International Organization*, 75 (1): Winter.

Ghosh, A., J.D. Ostry, A. Gulde, and H.C. Wolf (1997): 'Does the Exchange Rate Regime Matter for Inflation and Growth?', mimeo, International Monetary Fund.

Gingerich, D. and J.P. Vogler (2020): 'Pandemics and Political Development: The Electoral Legacy of the Black Death in Germany', mimeo, University of Virginia.

Glaeser, E.L. and A. Shleifer (2003): 'The Rise of the Regulatory State', *Journal of Economic Literature*, 41 (2): 401–425.

Glassmyer, K. and N. Sambanis (2008): 'Rebel-Military Integration and Civil War Termination', *Journal of Peace Research*, 45 (3): 365–384.

Gleditsch, K.S. and A. Ruggeri (2010): 'Political Opportunity Structures, Democracy, and Civil War', *Journal of Peace Research*, 47 (3): 299–310.

Gleick, P.H. (2014): 'Water, Drought, Climate Change, and Conflict in Syria', *Weather, Climate, and Society*, 6 (3): 331–340.

Golino, F.R. (1970): 'Patterns of Libyan National Identity', *Middle East Journal*, 24 (3): 338–352.

Gordon, J. (2012): *Invisible War: The United States and the Iraq Sanctions*. Harvard University Press, https://doi.org/10.2307/j.ctv1mvw86c.

Goulden, R. (2011): 'Housing, inequality, and economic change in Syria', *British Journal of Middle Eastern Studies*, 38 (2): 187–202.

Graham, B.A.T., M.K. Miller, and K.W. Strom (2017): 'Safeguarding Democracy: Powersharing and Democratic Survival', *American Political Science Review*, 111 (4): 686–704.

Grawal, S. (2021): 'Ten years in, Tunisian Democracy Remains a Work in Progress', *Brookings Institutions Blog*. https://www.brookings.edu/blog/order-from-chaos/2021/01/22/ten-years-in-tunisian-democracy-remains-a-work-in-progress/

Griffin, J.D., de Jonge C.K., and V.X. Velasco-Guachalla (2020): 'Deprivation in the Midst of Plenty: Citizen Polarization and Political Protest', *British Journal of Political Science*, 51 (3), 1080–1096.

Guasch, J.L. and R.W. Hahn (1999): 'The Costs and Benefits of Regulation: Implications for Developing Countries', *The World Bank Research Observer*, 14 (1): 137–158.

Gunter, F. (2013): *The Political Economy of Iraq: Restoring Balance in a Post-Conflict Society*. Cheltenham, UK: Elgar Publishing.

Gunter, F. (2018): 'Immunizing Iraq against Al-Qaida 3.0', *Orbis*, 62 (3): 389–408.

Gurr, T. (1970): *Why Men Rebel*. Princeton: Princeton University Press.

Hartzell, C. and M. Hoddie (2003): 'Institutionalizing Peace: Power-sharing and Post-Civil War Conflict Management', *American Journal of Political Science*, 47 (April): 318–322.

Hawthorn, G. (1991): *Plausible Worlds: Possibility and Understanding in History and the Social Sciences*. Cambridge: Cambridge University Press.

Healy, A. and N. Malhotra (2009): 'Myopic Voters and Natural Disaster Policy', *American Political Science Review*, 103 (3): 387–406.

Hegre, H. and N. Sambanis (2006): 'Sensitivity Analysis of Empirical Results on Civil War Onset', *Journal of Conflict Resolution*, 50 (4): 508–535.

Hegre, H., T. Ellingsen, S. Gates, and N.P. Gleditsch (2001): 'Toward a Democratic Civil Peace? Democracy, Political Change and Civil War, 1916–1992', *American Political Science Review*, 95: 33–48.

Heller, S. (2019): 'Don't Fund Syria's Reconstruction', *Foreign Affairs*, August 14, 2019. https://www.foreignaffairs.com/articles/syria/2017-10-04/dont-fund-syrias-reconstruction

Henderson, A.E. (2005): 'The Coalition Provisional Authority's Experience with Economic Reconstruction in Iraq.' United States Institute for Peace. USIP report 138.

Hendrix, C. (2010): 'Measuring State Capacity: Theoretical and Empirical Implications for the Study of Civil Conflict', *Journal of Peace Research*, 47: 273–285.

Herbert, S. (2018): Who are the elite groups in Iraq and how do they exercise power? Knowledge, evidence and learning for development (K4D): GSDRC Helpdesk Report.

Heydemann, S. (2018a): 'Beyond Fragility: Syria and the Challenges of Reconstruction in Fierce States', in *Middle East Studies*. Northampton, MA: Faculty Publications, Smith College.

Heydemann, S. (2018b): 'Civil War, Economic Governance and State Reconstruction in the Arab Middle East', *Daedalus* 147 (1): 48–63.

Hincks, J. (2016): 'What You Need to Know About the Crisis in Yemen', *TIME*, https://time.com/4552712/yemen-war-humanitarian-crisis-famine/

Hinnebusch, R. (2016): 'The Sectarian Revolution in the Middle East', *R/evolutions: Global Trends and Regional Issues*, 4 (1): 120–152.

Hlasny, V. and S. Al Azzawi (2019): 'Asset inequality in the MENA: The missing dimension?' *The Quarterly Review of Economics and Finance*, 73: 44–55.

Hodgson, G. (1998): 'The Approach of Institutional Economics', *Journal of Economic Literature*, 36 (1): 166–192.

Hoeffler, A. and M. Reynal-Querol (2003): 'Measuring the Costs of Conflict', Unpublished Working.
Horowitz, D. (1985): *Ethnic Groups in Conflict*. Berkeley: UCAL Press.
Houle, C. (2015): 'Ethnic Inequality and the Dismantling of Democracy: A Global Analysis', *World Politics*, 67: 469–505.
Houle, C. (2016): 'Why Class Inequality Breeds Coups but not Civil Wars', *Journal of Peace Research*, 53 (5): 680–695.
Houle, C. (2018a): 'A Two-Step Theory and Test of the Oil Curse: The Conditional Effect of Oil on Democratization', *Democratization*, 25 (3): 404–421.
Houle, C. (2018b): 'Does economic inequality breed political inequality?' *Democratization*, 25 (8): 1500–1518.
Houle, C. (2019): 'Religion, Language, Race and Ethnic Voting', *Electoral Studies*, 61: 1020–1052.
Houle, C. and C. Bodea (2017): 'Ethnic Inequality and Coups in Sub-Saharan Africa', *Journal of Peace Research*, 54: 382–396.
Howard, R.T. (2018): 'Anything but Straight-Forward: The Saudi Agenda in Yemen', *RUSI News Brief*, 32 (2). Available at https://rusi.org/explore-our-research/publications/rusi-newsbrief/anything-strait-forward-saudi-agenda-yemen
Huber, J.D. and L. Mayoral (2019): 'Group Inequality and the Severity of Civil Conflict', *Journal of Economic Growth*, 24 (1): 1–41.
Human Rights Watch (2018): 'Libya: Events of 2018'. https://www.hrw.org/world-report/2019/country-chapters/libya
Humphreys, M. (2005): 'Natural Resources, Conflict and Conflict Resolution: Uncovering the Mechanisms', *Journal of Conflict Resolution*, 49: 508–537.
Huntington, S.P. (1968): *Political Order in Changing Societies*. New Haven and London: Yale University Press.
Huntington, S.P. (1991): *The Third Wave: Democratization in the Late Twentieth Century*. London: University of Oklahoma Press.
Hunziker, P. and L.E. Cederman (2017): 'No Extraction Without Representation: The Ethno-Regional Oil Curse and Secessionist Conflict', *Journal of Peace Research*, 54 (3): 365–381.
Ianchovichina, E., L. Mottaghi, and S. Devarajan (2015): 'Inequality, Uprisings, and Conflict in the Arab World', *Middle East and North Africa Economic Monitor*, (October): Washington, DC: World Bank.
Ide T. (2021) "COVID-19 and armed conflict", *World Development*, 140: 105355. doi: 10.1016/j.worlddev.2020.105355.
Idris, I. (2018) Inclusive and Sustained Growth in Iraq, K4D Helpdesk Report. Brighton, UK: Institute of Development Studies
ILO (2015): *Yemen Labour Force Survey 2013-14*, International Labour Organization, Regional Office for Arab States, Beirut, Lebanon .
ILO (2021): *ILO Labour Database*. www.ilostat.ilo.org, accessed 30/12/2021.
Ilzetzki, E., E.G. Mendoza, and. C. Végh (2013): 'How Big (Small?) are Fiscal Multipliers?' *Journal of Monetary Economics*, 60 (2): 239–254.
Imady, O. (2019): 'The Weaponization of Syria's Reconstruction', *Syria Study*, 11 (1): 6–21.
IMF (2003): *Iraq: Macroeconomic Assessment*. Washington, DC: International Monetary Fund.
IMF (2004a): Iraq: Use of Fund Resources—Request for Emergency Post-Conflict Assistance—Staff Report; Press Release on the Executive Board Discussion; and

Bibliography 237

Statement by the Executive Director for Iraq. IMF Country Report No. 04/325. International Monetary Fund, Washington, D.C.

IMF (2004b): 'Rebuilding Fiscal Institutions in Post-Conflict Countries', mimeo, Fiscal Affairs Department, International Monetary Fund.

IMF (2005): Iraq: Statistical Appendix. Report No. 05/295. Washington DC, August International Monetary Fund, Washington, D.C.

IMF (2012): 'Libya Beyond the Revolution: Challenges and Opportunities', International Monetary Fund, Washington, D.C.

IMF (2013): 'Libya, 2013 Article IV Consultation'. IMF Country Report No. 13/150. International Monetary Fund.

IMF (2015): Iraq: Selected Issues. Report No. 15/236. August International Monetary Fund, Washington, D.C.

IMF (2017): Iraq Staff Report for Article IV Consultation. International Monetary Fund, Washington, D.C.

IMF (2019a): Iraq: Selected Issues, IMF Country Report No. 19/249. International Monetary Fund, Washington, D.C.

IMF (2019b): World Economic Outlook, April 2019 Update. Washington, D.C.: International Monetary Fund.

International Crisis Group (2011): *Popular Protest in North Africa and the Middle East (VI): The Syrian People's Slow-Motion Revolution.* 108. Middle East and North Africa. Damascus and Brussels: International Crisis Group.

International Crisis Group (2013): *Syria's Kurds: A Struggle Within a Struggle.* Middle East Report 136. Erbil: International Crisis Group, Brussels, Belgium.

International Crisis Group (2018): 'After the Showdown in Libya's Oil Crescent'. Report No. 189. Brussels, Belgium.

International Rescue Committee (IRC) (2017): 'Syria's Education Crisis: Once-Thriving Classrooms Gutted by War.' International Rescue Committee. https://www.rescue.org/article/syrias-education-crisis-once-thriving-classrooms-gutted-war

IOM (2019): "IDP and Returnee Report Round 24 – Libya Mobility Tracking", Displacement Tracking Matrix (January–February 2019)

IOM (2020): *Living and Working in the Midst of Conflict: The Status of Long-term Migrants in Libya*, International Organization For Migration, Geneva, Switzerland.

UNHCR (2019): 2019 Iraq Humanitarian Response Plan, United Nations High Commissioner for Refugees, New York.

Iraqi Extractive Industries Transparency Initiative (IEITI) (2019): https://eiti.org/iraq, accessed 7/11/19

IRFC and NRC (2016): *The Importance of addressing Housing, Land and Property (HLP) Challenges In Humanitarian Response.* Mimeo prepared by the Norwegian Refugee Council and The International Federation of Red Cross and Red Crescent Societies (IFRC) for the Round table on The importance of housing, land and property (HLP) rights in humanitarian response, held in Geneva on 2nd March 2016, Publisher: bo.hurkmans.

IRIS (2017): *Yemen Six Month Economic Analysis Economic Warfare and the Humanitarian Context.* Mimeo by the Humanitarian Foresight Think Tank of the Institut de Relations Internationales et Stratégiques (IRIS), Paris, France. IRIS.

Bibliography

Jamal, M., E. Munir, F. Al-Saffar, F. Habib, S. Sallam, H. Ramadani, and A. Riyad (2020): Surviving the COVID-19 Crisis: Preliminary Findings of the Economic Impact on Iraq, KAPITA, Baghdad, https://www.iraq-businessnews.com/2020/06/02/major-new-report-on-economic-effects-of-covid-19-in-iraq/

Jiyad, S. (2015): 'The Employment Crisis in Iraq', al-Bayan Center for Planning Studies. http://www.bayancenter.org/en/2015/04/105/

Joffé, G. (2011): 'The Arab Spring in North Africa: Origins and Prospects', *The Journal of North African Studies*, 16: 507–532

Jones, C.I. and P.J. Klenow (2016): 'Beyond GDP? Welfare across Countries and Time', *American Economic Review*, 106 (9): 2426–2457.

Jones, Z.M. and Y. Lupu (2018): 'Is There More Violence in the Middle East?' *American Journal of Political Science*, 62 (3): 652–667.

Joskow, P.L. (2007): 'Regulation of Natural Monopoly', in A.M. Polinsky and S. Shavell, ed., *Handbook of Law and Economics*, Amsterdam: Elsevier North-Holland, vol. 2, pp. 1227–1348.

Karabarbounis, L. (2011): 'One Dollar, One Vote', *The Economic Journal*, 121 (553): 621–651.

Karakaya, S. (2016): 'Ethno-political Organizations in the Middle East: When Do They Opt for Violence?' *Politics and Religion*, 9: 332–363.

Kawczynski, D. (2011): *Seeking Gaddafi: Libya, the West and the Arab Spring*. Hull: Biteback Publishing.

Keller, J. and M.K. Nabli (2007): 'The Macroeconomics of Labor Market Outcomes in MENA over the 1990s: How Growth Has Failed to Keep Pace with a Burgeoning Labor Market', in Mustapha Nabli, ed., *Breaking the barriers to higher economic growth: Better governance and deeper reforms in the Middle East and North Africa*. Washington DC: World Bank.

Kersten, M. (2015): 'Transitional Justice without a Peaceful Transition - The Case of Post Gaddafi Libya', Center for Research on Peace and Development (CRPD) Working Paper No. 38.

Khan, A. (2007): 'Growth, Employment and Poverty: An Analysis of the Vital Nexus Based on Some Recent UNDP and ILO/SIDA Studies', United Nations Department of Economic and Social Affairs, Working Paper No. 49.

Khashanah, K. (2014): 'The Syrian Crisis: A Systemic Framework', *Contemporary Arab Affairs*, 7 (1): 1–21.

Klassen, S. (2018): 'Poverty, Inequality, and the "Arab Spring"', *Review of Income and Wealth*, 64 (1): 1–4.

Knights, M. (2018): 'The Houthi War Machine: From Guerrilla War to State Capture' *CTC Sentinel*, 15 (8): 15–23.

Knights, M., Pollack, K., and Walter, B. (2019): 'A Real Plan to End the War in Yemen', *Foreign Affairs*. Retrieved May 2, 2019.

Kohl, I. (2014): 'Libya's Major Minorities. Berber, Tuareg and Tebu: Multiple Narratives of Citizenship, Language and Border Control', *Middle East Critique*, 23 (4): 423–438.

Kuoti, Y. (2016): 'Exclusion and Violence in Post-2003 Iraq', *Journal of International Affairs*, 69 (2): 19–30.

Kurdistan 24 (2019): Iraq says long-overdue census to begin in 2020. https://www.kurdistan24.net/en/news/5489b44e-4b95-4544-8ed8-b5a4e8f4eaf5, accessed 24/06/2019.

Bibliography 239

Kusago, T. (2005): 'Post-conflict Pro-poor Private-sector Development: The Case of Timor-Leste', *Development in Practice*, 15 (3–4): 502–513.
Kydland, F. and E. Prescott (1977): 'Rules rather than Discretion: The Inconsistency of Optimal Plans', *Journal of Political Economy*, 85 (3): 473–492.
Laborie, M. (2014): "Syria: War, Sectarianism and Chaos', chapter 3 in *Geopolitical Overview of Conflicts 2013*. Madrid: Secretaría General Técnic, Ministerio de Defensa de España, 396 pages
Ladjal, T. (2016): 'Tribe and State in the History of Modern Libya: A Khaldunian Reading of the Development of Libya in the Modern Era 1711–2011', *Cogent Arts and Humanities*, 3 (1). DOI: 10.1080/23311983.2016.1183278.
Larbi, H. (2016): 'Rewriting the Arab Social Contract: Towards Inclusive Development and Politics in the Arab World', Harvard Kennedy School, Belfer Center for Science and International Affairs, Study Group Report.
Latif, H. (2015): 'Social Protection and Safety Nets in Iraq. Technical Report - a Regional Study of Social Protection and Safety Nets in the Middle East and North Africa', The World Food Programme (WFP): The Centre for Social Protection at IDS.
Lawrence, A.K. (2016): 'Repression and Activism among the Arab Spring's First Movers: Evidence from Morocco's February 20th Movement', *British Journal of Political Science*, 47: 699–718.
Lawry, S., C. Samii, R. Hall, A. Leopold, D. Hornby, and F. Mtero (2014): 'The Impact of Land Property Rights Interventions on Investment and Agricultural Productivity in Developing Countries: A Systematic Review', *Campbell System Reviews*, 1. DOI: 10.4073/csr.2014.1
Lawson, F. (2018): 'Re-visiting the Political Economy of the Syrian Uprising', in R. Hinnebusch and O. Imady, ed., *The Syrian Uprising: Domestic Origins and Early Trajectory*. London and New York: Routledge, pp. 77–91.
Le Billon, P. (2005): 'Corruption: Reconstruction and Oil Governance in Iraq', *Third World Quarterly*, 26 (4): 679–698.
Leckie, S. (2005): 'Housing, Land and Property Rights in Post-Conflict Societies: Proposals for a New United Nations Institutional and Policy Framework', Legal and Protection Policy Research Series, PPLA/2005/01, UN HCR.
Levy-Yeyati. E. And F. Sturzenegger (2003): 'To Float or to Fix: Evidence on the Impact of Exchange Rate Regimes on Growth', *American Economic Review*, 93 (4): 1178–89.
Lewarne, S. and D. Snelbecker (2004): 'Economic Governance in War Torn Economies: Lessons Learned from the Marshall Plan to the Reconstruction of Iraq', USAID, The Services Group (TSG).
Libyan Political Agreement (2015): https://unsmil.unmissions.org/sites/default/files/Libyan%20Political%20Agreement%20-%20ENG%20.pdf
Lijphart, A. (1969): 'Consociational Democracy', *World Politics*, 21 (2): 207–225.
Lijphart, A. (1975): *The Politics of Accommodation: Pluralism and Democracy in the Netherlands*. 2nd ed. Berkeley: University of California Press.
Lijphart, A. (1977): *Democracy in Plural Societies: A Comparative Exploration*. New Haven: Yale University Press.
Lijphart, A. (1985): 'Power-sharing in South Africa', Policy Papers in International Affairs No.24. Institute of International Studies. Berkeley: University of California: 137–171.

Lijphart, A. (1999): 'Australian democracy: Modifying Majoritarianism?' *Australian Journal of Political Science*, 34 (3): 313–326.

Lipset, M.S. and S. Rokkan (1967): *Party Systems and Voter Alignments: Cross-National Perspectives*. Toronto: The Free Press.

Lujala, P. (2010): 'The Spoils of Nature: Armed Civil Conflict and Rebel Access to Natural Resources', *Journal of Peace Research*, 47 (1): 15–28.

Lund, A. (2019): 'Briefing: Just How "Smart" Are Sanctions on Syria?' *The New Humanitarian*. https://www.thenewhumanitarian.org/analysis/2019/04/25/briefing-just-how-smart-are-sanctions-syria

Magaloni, B. (2008): 'Credible Power-Sharing and the Longevity of Authoritarian Rule', *Comparative Political Studies*, 41 (4–5): 715–741.

Mahdavy, H. (1970): 'The Patterns and Problems of Economic Development in Rentier States: The Case of Iran', in N.A. Cook, ed., *Studies in Economic History of the Middle East*. London: Oxford University Press, pp. 428–467.

Mahdi, K. (2007): 'Neoliberalism, Conflict and an Oil Economy', *Arab Studies Quarterly*, 29 (1): 1–20.

Mahler, A. and J.H. Pierskalla (2015): 'Indigenous Identity, Natural Resources, and Contentious Politics in Bolivia: A Disaggregated Conflict Analysis, 2000–2011', *Comparative Political Studies*, 48 (3): 301–332.

Makdisi, S. and R. Sadaka (2005): 'The Lebanese Civil War, 1975–90', in P. Collier, and N. Sambanis, ed., *Understanding Civil War: Evidence and Analysis*. Washington, DC: World Bank, Vol. 2, pp. 59–86.

Malik, A. and B. Awadallah (2013): 'The Economics of the Arab Spring', *World Development*, 45: 296–313.

Margalit, Y. (2019): 'Political Responses to Economic Shocks', *Annual Reviews in Political Science*, 22: 277–295.

Martins, P. (2013): 'Growth, Employment and Poverty in Africa: Tales of Lions and Cheetahs', Background paper for the World Development Report 2013, The World Bank.

Massiah, E., M. Abdalla, and K. Garber (2018): 'Is There a Doctor in the House? The Challenge of Primary Health Care in Libya'. *Brookings*. https://www.brookings.edu/blog/future-development/2018/12/10/is-there-a-doctor-in-the-house-the-challenge-of-primary-health-care-in-libya/

Matsunaga, H. (2019): The Reconstruction of Iraq after 2003: Learning from Its Successes and Failures. MENA Development Report Series. Washington, DC: World Bank. doi:10.1596/978-1-4648-1390-0.

Mattes, M. and B. Savun (2009): 'Fostering Peace after Civil War: Commitment Problems and Agreement Design', *International Studies Quarterly*, 53 (September): 737–759.

Mauro, P. (1995): 'Corruption and Growth', *The Quarterly Journal of Economics*, 110 (3): 681–712

McGarry, J. and B. O'Leary (2009): 'Must Pluri-National Federations Fail?' *Ethnopolitics* (Special Issue: Federalism, Regional Autonomy and Conflict), 8 (1): 5–26.

Mersch, I. (2017): 'Central bank independence revisited', Keynote address at the 'Symposium on Building the Financial System of the 21st Century: An Agenda for Europe and the United States', Frankfurt am Main, 30 March 2017.

Miguel, E. (2004): 'Tribe or Nation? Nation-building and Public Goods in Kenya versus Tanzania', *World Politics*, 56: 327–362.

Miraglia, P., R. Ochoa, and I. Briscoe (2012): 'Transnational Organised Crime and Fragile States', OECD Development Co-Operation Working Papers WP5/12, OECD, Paris, France.
Mirza, A. (2011): 'General Observations on Johnny West's Article.' Iraq Economists Network. www.iraqieconomists.net/ar/2011/10/29/د-على-مرزا-م-لاحظات-عامة-حول/ مقالة-جوني/ accessed 19/1/2020.
Mishkin, F.S. and K. Schmidt-Hebbel (2007): 'Does Inflation Targeting Make a Difference?' in F. Mishkin and K. Schmidt-Hebbel, ed., *Monetary Policy under Inflation Targeting*, vol. 11. Chile: Banco Central de Chile, pp. 291–372.
Mitchell, R. (2012): 'What the Social Sciences Can Tell Policymakers in Yemen', *The Middle East Journal*, 66 (Spring): 291–312.
Montalvo, J. G. and M. Reynal-Querol (2005): Ethnic Polarization, Potential Conflict, and Civil Wars. *The American Economic Review,* 95 (3): 796–816.
Morrison, K. (2009): 'Oil, Nontax Revenue, and the Redistributional Foundations of Regime Stability', *International Organization*, 63: 107–138.
Mukherjee, B. (2006): 'Why Political Power-Sharing Agreements Lead to Enduring Peaceful Resolution of Some Civil Wars, but Not Others?' *International Studies Quarterly*, 50 (June): 479–504.
Muller, E.N. and E. Weede (1990): 'Cross-National Variation in Political Violence', *Journal of Conflict Resolution*, 34 (4): 624–651.
Mundy, M. (2018): *The Strategies of the Coalition in Yemen War: Aerial Bombardment and Food War.* Tufts University. Somerville, MA: World Peace Foundation.
Muttit, G. (2012): *Fuel on the Fire: Oil and politics in Occupied Iraq.* New York: New Press.
Nabli, M. and M.A. Veganzones-Varoudakis (2004): 'How Does Exchange Rate Policy Affect Manufactured Exports in MENA Countries?' *Applied Economics*, 36 (19): 2209–2219.
Nabli, M., C. Silva-Jáuregui, and A.F. Aysan (2008): 'Political Authoritarianism, Credibility of Reforms and Private Sector Development in the Middle East and North Africa', *Revue d'Economie du Développement*, 16: 5–36.
Nalman, R. (2007): 'Poll: Iraqis Want National Oil Companies to Develop Iraqi Oil', *Huffington Post.* https://www.huffpost.com/entry/poll-iraqis-want-national_b_59483, accessed 6/11/19.
NGO Platform (2011): Mapping Civil Society Activity in Syria. Conducted by Istishari Investment and Economic Consulting for UNDP NGO Platform Project. October 2011.
Nimni, E. (2005): *National Cultural Autonomy and Its Contemporary Critics.* London: Routledge.
Noel, J.R. ed. (2005): *From Power-sharing to Democracy: Post-conflict Institutions in Ethnically Divided Societies.* Toronto: McGill-Queens University Press, pp. 3–43.
Nomikos, W. (2017): 'Why Share? An Analysis of the Sources of Powersharing', Unpublished manuscript, Yale University.
North, D.C. (1990): *Institutions, Institutional Change and Economic Performance.* 16th ed. New York: Cambridge University Press.
North, D.C., J.J. Wallis, and B.R. Weingast (2009): *Violence and Social Orders: A Conceptual Framework for Interpreting Recorded Human History.* New York: Cambridge University Press.

Bibliography

NRC (2016): 'Briefing Note: Housing Land and Property (Hlp) In the Syrian Arab Republic', Briefing Note, (May): Norwegian Refugee Council.

O'Donnell, G. (1973): *Modernization and Bureaucratic Authoritarianism: Studies in South American Politics*, Berkeley, CA: Institute of International Studies.

O'Driscoll, D. (2018): 'Good Practice in Post-Conflict Reconstruction', University of Manchester, mimeo. 02 November 2018.

O'Leary, B. (2005): 'Debating Consociational Politics: Normative and Explanatory Arguments', in Sid J.R. Noel, ed., *From Power Sharing to Democracy: Post-Conflict Institutions in Ethnically Divided Societies*. Montreal: McGill-Queen's Press. pp. 3–43.

O'Leary, B. (2018): 'The Kurds, the Four Wolves and the Great Powers', *Journal of Politics*, 80 (1): 22–36.

OECD (2008): *Concepts and Dilemmas of State-building in Fragile Situations: From Fragility to Resilience*. Paris: OECD.

OPEC (2005): *Annual Statistical Bulletin 2004*. Vienna: Organization of Petroleum Exporting Countries.

Orabi, F. (2013): 'Jihaddis in Libya During Qaddafi', Al-Misbar Studies and Research Center, September 16. https://www.almesbar.net/-القذافي-عهد-في/-ليبي-في-الجهاديون ا

Osgood, P. (2018): 'Selective Transparency: Things You can't See about KRG Oil', *LSE Middle East Centre Blog*. https://blogs.lse.ac.uk/mec/2018/04/25/selective-transparency-things-you-cant-see-about-krg-oil/

Østby, G. (2008a): 'Inequalities, the Political Environment, and Civil Conflict: Evidence from 55 Developing Countries', in F. Stewart, ed., *Horizontal Inequalities and Conflict: Understanding Group Violence in Multiethnic Societies*. Houndmills, UK: Palgrave Macmillan, pp. 136–159.

Paasonen, K. and H. Urdal (2016): 'Youth Bulges, Exclusion and Instability: The Role of Youth in the Arab Spring', *Conflict Trends*, Policy Brief 3. Peace Research Institute Oslo (PRIO), Norway.

Page, J. (2003): 'Structural Reforms in the Middle East and North Africa', in P.K. Cornelius and K. Schwab, ed., *The Arab World Competitiveness Report 2002–2003*. New York: Oxford University Press.

Paine, J. (2019): 'Economic Grievances and Civil War: An Application to the Resource Curse', *International Studies Quarterly*, 63 (2): 244–258.

Pankratz, A. (1983): *Forecasting with Univariate Box-Jenkins Models*. New York: John Wiley and Sons.

Paraskova, T. (2019): 'Is OPEC's No. 2 Finally Cutting Production?' *OilPrice.com*. https://oilprice.com/Energy/Crude-Oil/Is-OPECs-No-2-Finally-Cutting-Production.html, accessed 29/09/2019.

Patel, D.S. (2018): 'How Oil and Demography Shape Post-Saddam Iraq', Middle East Briefs # 122, Crown Center for Middle East Studies, Brandeis University.

Peic, G. and D. Reiter (2011): 'Foreign-Imposed Regime Change, State Power and Civil War Onset, 1920–2004', *British Journal of Political Science*, 41 (3): 453–475.

Phillips, C. (2015): 'Sectarianism and Conflict in Syria', *Third World Quarterly*, 36 (2): 357–356.

Pissarides, C. and M.A. Véganzonès-Varoudakis (2006): 'Labor Markets and Economic Growth in the MENA Region', *Contributions to Economic Analysis*, 278: 137–157.

Poast, P. and J. Urpelainen (2015): 'How International Organizations Support Democratization: Preventing Authoritarian Reversals or Promoting Consolidation?' *World Politics*, 67 (1): 72–113.
Population Pyramid (2021): Iraq Population Pyramid. https://www.populationpyramid.net/iraq/2020/, accessed 10/10/2021.
Przeworski, Adam (1991): *Democracy and the Market: Political and Economic Reforms in Eastern Europe and Latin America*, Cambridge: Cambridge University Press.
Przeworski, A. (2015): 'Economic Inequality, Political Inequality, and Redistribution', Working Paper, Department of Political Science, New York University.
Quandt, W. (2020): 'Why did Egyptian Democratization Fail? Fourteen Experts Respond', in A. Hawthorne and A. Miller, ed., Project on Middle East Democracy, Washington, DC.
Rabushka, A. and K.A. Shepsle (1972): *Politics in Plural Societies: A Theory of Democratic Instability*. Columbus, OH: Charles Merrill.
Raheem, Y. and A. al-Rubaie (2019): 'Tensions rekindle in Iraq's oil-rich Kirkuk,' https://thearabweekly.com/tensions-rekindle-iraqs-oil-rich-kirkuk
Rashad, M. (2011): 'Yemen's Saleh Signs Deal to Give Up Power', *Reuters*. Retrieved April 27, 2019, from https://www.reuters.com/article/us-yemen/yemens-saleh-signs-deal-to-give-up-power-idUSTRE7AM0D020111123
Ravallion, M. (1998): 'Poverty Lines in Theory and Practice'; LSMS Working Paper no. 133, World Bank, Washington D.C.
Ray, S. (2018): 'Ethnic Inequality and National Pride', *Political Psychology*, 39 (2): 263–280.
Relief Web (2017): 'Education in Syria: Battling against School Attacks, Lost Teachers and Book Shortages - Syrian Arab Republic.' Relief Web. https://reliefweb.int/report/syrian-arab-republic/education-syria-battling-against-school-attacks-lost-teachers-and-book
Relief Web (2019): Yemen: Humanitarian Needs Overview, https://reliefweb.int/report/yemen/yemen-2019-humanitarian-needs-overview
Remmer, K.L. (1993): 'The Process of Democratization in Latin America', *Studies in Comparative International Development*, 27: 3–24.
Reynal-Querol, M. (2002): 'Ethnicity, Political Systems, and Civil Wars', *Journal of Conflict Resolution*, 46 (1): 29–54.
Rezvani, D.A. (2014): *Surpassing the Sovereign State. The Wealth, Self-Rule, and Security Advantages of Partially Independent Territories*. Oxford: Oxford University Press.
Robinson, A.L. (2014): 'National versus Ethnic Identification in Africa: Modernization, Colonial Legacy, and the Origins of Territorial Nationalism', *World Politics*, 66 (4): 709–746.
Rodrik, D. (2005): 'Growth Strategies', in P. Aghion and S. Durlauf, ed., *Handbook of Economic Growth*, Vol. 1A. Amsterdam: Elsevier North-Holland, pp. 967–1014.
Rodrik, D. (2007): *One Economics, Many Recipes: Globalization, Institutions and Economic Growth*. Princeton: Princeton UP.
Rodrik, D. (2011): *The Globalization Paradox: Democracy and the Future of the World Economy*. London: Norton.

Roeder, P.G. (2007): *Where Nation-States Come From: Institutional Change in the Age of Nationalism*. Princeton: Princeton University Press.

Roeder, P.G. and D. Rothchild (2005): *Sustainable Peace: Power and Democracy after Civil Wars*. Ithaca: Cornell University Press.

Roessler, P. (2011): 'The Enemy Within: Personal Rule, Coups, and Civil War in Africa', *World Politics*, 63 (2): 300–346.

Roessler, P. and D. Ohls (2018): 'Self-Enforcing Powersharing in Weak States', *International Organization*, 72 (2): 423–454.

Rogoff, K.S., A.M. Husain, A. Mody, R. Brooks, and N. Oomes (2004): 'Evolution and Performance of Exchange Rate Regimes', International Monetary Fund Occasional Paper 229, Washington, DC.

Rørbæk, L.L. (2019): 'Religion, Political Power, and the "Sectarian Surge": Middle Eastern Identity Politics in Comparative Perspective', *Studies in Ethnicity and Nationalism*, 19 (1): 23–40.

Ross, M. (2001): 'Does Oil Hinder Democracy?' *World Politics*, 53: 325–361.

Ross, M. (2004): 'What Do We Know About Natural Resources and Civil War?' *Journal of Peace Research*, 41 (3): 337–356.

Ross, M. (2012): *The Oil Curse: How Petroleum Wealth Shapes the Development of Nations*. Princeton, NJ: Princeton University Press.

Rosset, J., N. Giger, and J. Bernauer (2013): 'More Money, Fewer Problems? Cross-Level Effects of Economic Deprivation on Political Representation', *West European Politics*, 36 (4): 817–835.

Rotberg, R. ed. (2003): *When States Fail Causes and Consequences*. Princeton: Princeton University Press.

Rougier, E. (2014): 'Fire in Cairo: Authoritarian-redistributive Social Contracts, Structural Change and the Arab Spring', Cahiers du GREThA (2007–2019) 2014-22, Groupe de Recherche en Economie Théorique et Appliquée (GREThA).

Ruiz Pozuelo, J., A. Slipowitz, G. Vuletin (2016): 'Democracy Does Not Cause Growth: The Importance of Endogeneity Arguments', Department of Research and Chief Economist, Inter-American Development Bank.

Russell, K. (2015): 'Shared Plans or Shared Power? Rule of Law Paths in New Democracies', PhD Dissertation, Yale University.

Saadoun, M. (2018): Why has Illiteracy Rate Gone in Iraq? A Report for Al-Monitor: The Pulse of the Middle East, December 9, 2018. https://www.al-monitor.com/pulse/originals/2018/12/iraq-illiteracy-education-culture.html#ixzz5z3V3msRj, accessed 21/10/19.

Sab, R. (2014): 'Economic Impact of Selected Conflicts in the Middle East: What Can We Learn from the Past?' IMF Working Paper 14,100, Middle East and Central Asia Department, Washington, DC: International Monetary Fund.

Sachs, J. and A. Warner (1995): 'Natural Resource Abundance and Economic Growth', NBER Working Paper 5398. Cambridge, MA.

Safadi, R. and S. Neaime (2017): 'Syria: The Painful Transition Towards Democracy', in I. Elbadawi and S. Makdisi, ed., *Democratic Transitions in the Arab World*. Cambridge: Cambridge University Press, pp. 184–208.

Salehi-Isfahani, D. and M. Mostafavi-Dehzooei (2018): 'Cash Transfers and Labor Supply: Evidence from a Large-Scale Program in Iran', *Journal of Development Economics*, 135 (November): 349–367.

Salem, P. and A. Kadlec (2012): 'Libya's Troubled Transition'. Carnegie Middle East Center. https://carnegie-mec.org/2012/06/14/libya-s-troubled-transition-pub-48511

Salih, K.E.O. (2013): 'The Roots and Causes of the 2011 Arab Uprisings', *Arab Studies Quarterly*, 35 (2): 184–206.

Salisbury, P. (2011): 'Yemen's Economy: Oil, Imports, and Elites', Middle East and North Africa Program Paper MENA PP 2011/02, Chatham House.

Salisbury, P. (2014): 'Yemen Capital Hit by Anti-government Rallies'. *Al Jazeera*. Retrieved May 17, 2019, from, http://www.aljazeera.com/news/middleeast/2014/08/yemen-houthis-rally-oust-government-20148181241479887O.html

Salisbury, P. (2015): 'Yemen and the Saudi–Iranian 'Cold War'', Chatam House Research Paper, February.

Salisbury, P. (2016): *Yemen: Stemming the Rise of a Chaos State*. London: The Royal Institute of International Affairs, Chatham House.

Salisbury, P. and C. House (2018): 'Marshalling Order in Yemen: How Reconstruction Will Make or Break the Post-War Order', *The Politics of Post-Conflict Reconstruction*, 56.

Salloukh, B.F. (2017): 'Overlapping Contests and Middle East International Relations: The Return of the Weak Arab State', *Political Science and Politics*, 50 (3): 660–663.

Samaha, N. (2019): 'The Economic War on Syria: Why Europe Risks losing', *European Council on Foreign Relations*, 11 February 2019, https://www.ecfr.eu/article/commentary_the_economic_war_on_syria_why_europe_risks_losing

Sambanis, N. (2004): 'What Is A Civil War? Conceptual and Empirical Complexities of an Operational Definition', *Journal of Conflict Resolution*, 48 (6): 814–858.

Sambanis, N. (2005): 'Conclusion: Using Case Studies to Refine and Expand the Theory of Civil War', in *Understanding Civil War: Evidence and Analysis*, ed. P. Collier and N. Sambanis. Washington, DC: World Bank, 299–330.

Sambanis, N. (2019a): 'Power-sharing and Peacebuilding. Conflict, Post-conflict Transition, and Peace-building in the Arab Region', *Economic Research Forum*: 2–34. ERF Working Paper No. 1396. Cairo: Economic Research Forum.

Sambanis, N. (2019b): Power-sharing and Peace-building. Unpublished Manuscript.

Sambanis, N. and A. Zinn (2006): 'From Protest to Violence', Unpublished paper, Yale University.

Sambanis, N. and J. Schulhofer-Wohl (2019): 'Sovereignty Rupture as a Central Concept in Quantitative Measures of Civil War', *Journal of Conflict Resolution*, 63 (6): 1542–1578.

Sambanis, N., M. Germann, and A. Schädel (2018): 'SDM: A New Dataset on Self-Determination Movements with an application to the Reputational Theory of Civil War', *Journal of Conflict Resolution*, 62 (3): 656–686.

Sambanis, N. and M. Shayo (2013): 'Social Identification and Ethnic Conflict', *American Political Science Review*, 107 (2): 294–325.

Santayana, G. (1905): *The Life of Reason: Reason in Common Sense*. New York: Charles Scribner's Sons.

Savage, J.D. (2013): *Reconstructing Iraq's Budgetary Institutions: Coalition State Building after Saddam*. New York: Cambridge University Press.

Schmidt-Hebbel, K. (2016): 'Fiscal Institutions in Resource-Rich Economies: Lessons from Chile and Norway', in I. Elbadawi and H. Selim, ed., *Understanding and Avoiding the Oil Curse in Resource-Rich Arab Economies*. Cambridge: Cambridge University Press.

Schmidt-Hebbel, K. and R. Soto (2017): 'Fiscal Rules in the World', in *Rethinking Fiscal Policy After the Crisis*, L. Ódor (ed.). Cambridge: Cambridge University Press, pp. 103–138.

Schmitter, P.C. and T.L. Karl (1991): 'What Democracy is and is Not', *Journal of Democracy*, 25: 114–120.

Sedik, T.S. and R. Xu (2020): 'A Vicious Cycle: How Pandemics Lead to Economic Despair and Social Unrest', IMF Working Paper WP/20/216, October 2020.

Selby, J., O.S. Dahi, C. Fröhlich, and M. Hulme (2017): 'Climate Change and the Syrian Civil War Revisited', *Political Geography*, 60: 232–244.

Selby, J. (2019): 'Climate Change and the Syrian Civil War, Part II: The Jazira's Agrarian Crisis', *Geoforum*, 101 (May): 260–274.

Sen, A. (1983): 'Development: Which Way Now?' *The Economic Journal*, 93 (372): 745–762.

Servén, L. (1999): 'Macroeconomic Uncertainty and Private Investment in Developing Countries: An Empirical Investigation', The World Bank Policy Research Working Paper 2035.

Shubbar, B. (2016): 'On the Consequences of Poor Planning and Negligence in Oil Service Contracts on the Future Development of the Oil Industry in Iraq—Sea Water Injection Project', Iraqi Economists Network. www.iraqieconomists.net/ar/2018/03/11/د-قراب-ق-ش-رَبُش-ح-لوح-ت-تاعبت-ءوس-التخطي-طو-ا/, accessed 22/1/2020.

Sika, N. (2014): 'The Arab State and Social Contestation'. Beyond the Arab Spring: the Evolving ruling bargain in the Middle East, pp. 73–98.

SIPRI (2017): Military Expenditure Database, downloaded from https://sipri.org/databases/milex

Siroky, D.S. and J. Cuffe (2015): 'Lost Autonomy, Nationalism and Separatism', *Comparative Political Studies*, 48 (1): 3–34.

Sissons, M. and A. Al-Saiedi (2013): 'A Bitter Legacy: Lessons of de-Baathification in Iraq.' International Center for Transitional Justice. https://www.ictj.org/sites/default/files/ICTJ-Report-Iraq-De-Baathification-2013-ENG.pdf, accessed 21/09/2019.

Smith, B. (2004): 'Oil Wealth and Regime Survival in the Developing World, 1960–1999', *American Journal of Political Science*, 48 (2): 232–246.

Snyder, J. (2000): *From Voting to Violence: Democratization and Nationalist Conflict*. New York: W.W. Norton.

Sorens, Jason (2011): 'Mineral Production, Territory, and Ethnic Rebellion: The Role of Rebel Constituencies', *Journal of Peace Research*, 48 (5): 571–585.

Soto, R. (2019): 'Policy Goals, Fiscal Institutions and Macroeconomic Management in the United Arab Emirates', in K. Mohaddes, J. B. Nugent, and H. Selim, ed, *Macroeconomic Institutions and Management in Resource-Rich Arab Economies*, Oxford University Press, pp. 356–426 .

SP Today (2020): US Dollar / Syrian Pound Historic Data. https://sp-today.com/en/currency/us_dollar, accessed 25/05/2020.

Special Inspector General for Iraq Reconstruction (SIGIR) (2009): Hard Lessons: The Iraq Reconstruction Experience. US Government Printing Office.

Stadnicki, R. (2014): 'The Challenges of Urban Transition in Yemen: Sana'a and Other Major Cities', *Journal of Arabian Studies*, 4 (1), 115–133.

Staines, N. (2004): 'Economic Performance Over the Conflict Cycle', Working Papers Series, 04/95, IMF, Washington, DC.

Standing, G. (2017): *Basic Income: And How We Can Make It Happen*. London: Penguin Random House.

Bibliography 247

Stedman, S.J. (2000): 'Spoiler Problems in Peace Processes', in P. C. Stern and D. Drukman, Commission on Behavioral and Social Sciences and Education, ed., *International Conflict Resolution After the Cold War*. Washington, DC: The National Academies Press, pp. 178–224.

Stein, H. (2016): 'Africa and the Great Recession: The Dynamics of Growth Sustainability', in P. Arestis and M. Sawyer ed., *Emerging Economies During and After the Great Recession*. International Papers in Political Economy Series. London: Palgrave-McMillan, pp. 77–115.

Stewart, F. (2000): 'Crisis Prevention: Tackling Horizontal Inequalities', *Oxford Development Studies*, 28 (3): 245–262.

Stewart, F. (2002): 'Horizontal Inequalities: A Neglected Dimension of Development', QEH Working Paper Number 81, Queen Elizabeth House, University of Oxford.

Stewart, F. and V. FitzGerald (2001a): 'Introduction: Assessing the Economic Costs of War', in ed. F. Stewart and V. FitzGerald, *War and Underdevelopment: Volume 1: The Economic and Social Consequences of Conflict*. New York: Oxford University Press.

Stewart, F. and V. FitzGerald (2001b): 'The Cost of War in Poor Countries: Conclusions and Policy Recommendations', in *War and Underdevelopment: Volume 1: The Economic and Social Consequences of Conflict*, ed. F. Stewart and V. FitzGerald. New York: Oxford University Press, pp. 225–245.

Svolik, M. (2012): *The Politics of Authoritarian Rule*. Cambridge: Cambridge University Press.

Syrian Center for Policy Research (2017): 'Social Degradation in Syria: The Conflict Impact on Social Capital.' June 2017. https://www.scpr-syria.org/social-degradation-in-syria/

Syrian Central Bureau of Statistics (SCBS) (2002–2010): Annual Labor Force Surveys for years 2002 through 2010. Damascus, Syria.

Syrian Central Bureau of Statistics (SCBS) (2011): Statistical Abstract 2011. Damascus, Syria.

Syrian Central Bureau of Statistics (SCBS) (2015): Statistical Abstract 2011. Damascus, Syria.

Syrian Central Bureau of Statistics (SCBS) (2019): Statistical Abstract 2019. Damascus, Syria.

Syrian Observatory for Human Rights (SOHR) (2021): 'Total Death Toll | Over 606,000 People Killed across Syria since the Beginning of the "Syrian Revolution", Including 495,000 Documented by SOHR', June 1. https://www.syriahr.com/en/217360/

Syrian Pound Today (SP Today) (2021): https://sp-today.com/en/, accessed 05/12/2021.

Tarrow, S.G. (1994): *Power in Movement: Social Movements and Contentious Politics*. Cambridge: Cambridge University Press.

Teyssier, A. and S. Harris (2012): 'Can Land Policies be Reformed without Transforming Land Institutions? The cases of Madagascar and Benin', 2012 Annual World Bank Conference on Land and Poverty.

Thies, C. (2010): 'Of Rulers, Rebels, and Revenue: State Capacity, Civil War Onset, and Primary Commodities', *Journal of Peace Research*, 47 (3): 321–332.

Tilly, C. (2003): *The Politics of Collective Violence*. Cambridge: Cambridge University Press.

Toft, Monica Duffy (2010): 'Ending Civil Wars: A Case for Rebel Victory?', *International Security*, 34 (4): 7–36.

Transparency International (2020): Corruption Perceptions Index (CPI) data for Syria 2003–2010. Accessed: July 2020. Berlin, Germany.

Tripp, C. (2003): 'Iraq: Political Recognition and Social Action,' *Social Science Research Council Items*, 4 (1): 9–15.

Tucker, V. (2012): 'Divergence and Decline: The Middle East and the World after the Arab Spring', mimeo. Washington, DC: Freedom House.

Turak, N. (2018): Iraq's massive 2019 budget still fails to address reform needs, experts say. A report for CNBC. Published WED, JAN 30, 2019. https://www.cnbc.com/2019/01/30/iraqs-massive-2019-budget-still-fails-to-address-reform-needs.html, accessed 21/10/2019.

Turner, N., O. Aginam, and V. Popovski (2008): 'Post-Conflict Countries and Foreign Investment', Policy Brief No 8, United Nations University.

Tzifakis, N. (2013): 'Post-Conflict Economic Reconstruction', in W.F. Danspeckgruber, ed., *Encyclopedia Princetoniensis: The Princeton Encyclopedia of Self-Determination*. Princeton: Princeton University, Liechtenstein Institute on Self-Determination.

Tzifakis, N. and C. Tsardanidis (2006): 'Economic Reconstruction of Bosnia and Herzegovina: The Lost Decade', *Ethnopolitics*, 5 (1): 67–84.

UCDP (2020): *UCDP/PRIO Armed Conflict Dataset*, Version 20.1, Uppsala Conflict Data Program, Department of Peace and Conflict Research, Uppsala University.

Ulfelder, J. (2007): 'Natural-Resource Wealth and the Survival of Autocracy', *Comparative Political Studies*, 40 (8): 995–1018.

UN Security Council (2015): Resolution 2216: Adopted by the Security Council at its 7426th meeting, on 14 April 2015. Retrieved on 21 October 2019.

UN Statistical Databases (2019): National Accounts—Analysis of Main Aggregates. https://unstats.un.org/unsd/snaama/, accessed 17/06/2019.

UNCTAD (2021): UNCTSAD Statistics. https://unctadstat.unctad.org/EN/; accessed 10/10/2021.

UNDP 2014: *Iraq Human Development Report 2014: Iraqi Youth Challenges and Opportunities*. New York.

UNDP: 'Towards National Reconciliation in Libya'. UNDP Project available at https://www.undp.org/libya/projects/towards-national-reconciliation-libya

UNDP (2008): Post-Conflict Economic Recovery. Enabling Local Ingenuity, United Nations Development Programme: Bureau for Crisis Prevention and Recovery (BCPR): UN Publications. New York

UNDP (2018): *Human Development Indices and Indicators, Statistical Update*. New York: United Nations Development Program. New York

UNDP (2019a): *2019 Human Development Report*. Beyond income, beyond averages, beyond today: Inequalities in human development in the 21st century. United Nations Development Programme. New York

UNDP (2019b): Assessing the impact of war on development in Yemen. Sana'a: United Nations Development Program.

UNDP (2019c): Training for All Brochure. Damascus: United Nations Development Programme.

UNDP (2019d): *UNDP Syria Annual Report: Leaving No One Behind*. June 2, 2019. Damascus: United Nations Development Programme.

Bibliography 249

UNFPA (2020): 'UNFPA COVID-19 Response in Libya'. https://reliefweb.int/sites/reliefweb.int/files/resources/unfpa_libya_covid-19_newsletter_1_-_april_2020.pdf.

UNICEF (2019): 'One Woman and Six Newborns Die Every Two Hours from Complications during Pregnancy or Childbirth in Yemen', *UNICEF Press Release*. Retrieved on 21/10/2019, https://www.unicef.org/press-releases/one-woman-and-six-newborns-die-every-two-hours-complications-during-pregnancy

UN ESCWA (2014): *Survey of Economic and Social Developments in the Arab Region 2013–2014*, United Nations Economic and Social Commission for Western Asia, Beirut, Lebanon. ISBN: 978-92-1-128374-7

UN ESCWA (2016): *Syria Five Years at War*. United Nations Economic and Social Commission for West Asia, Beirut, Lebanon.

UN ESCWA (2019): Rethinking Inequality in Arab Countries, Economic and Social Commission for Western Asia, E/ESCWA/EDID/2019/2, Beirut, Lebanon.

UN ESCWA (2020): *Syria at War: Eight Years On*. United Nations Economic and Social Commission for West Asia, Beirut, Lebanon

UN HCR (2019): "Fifth Regional Survey on Syrian Refugees' Perceptions and Intentions on Return to Syria: Egypt, Iraq, Lebanon, Jordan – March", United Nations High Commissioner for Refugees New York.

UN HCR (2019): 'Libya UNHCR Update'. https://data2.unhcr.org/en/documents/download/68641

UN HCR Operational Data Portal Refugee Situations. https://data2.unhcr.org/en/country/lby, accessed 04/12/ 2021.

UN HCR (2020): 'Situation Syria Regional Refugee Response', United Nations High Commissioner for Refugees New York.

UN HCR (2021): 'Situation Syria Regional Refugee Response', United Nations High Commissioner for Refugees New York.

UN OCHA (2020a): Financial Tracking Service, United Nations Office for the Coordination of Humanitarian Affairs. New York. Accessed 20/06/2020.

UN OCHA (2021a): *Humanitarian Needs Overview. Syrian Arab Republic*. United Nations Office for the Coordination of Humanitarian Affairs. Humanitarian Programme Cycle, New York.

UN OCHA (2020b): *Humanitarian Needs Overview Libya*, United Nations Office for the Coordination of Humanitarian Affairs. New York.

UN OCHA (2021b): Global Humanitarian Overview 2022, United Nations Office for the Coordination of Humanitarian Affairs, New York.

UN OCHA (2021c): *Humanitarian Response Plan Libya*, United Nations Office for the Coordination of Humanitarian Affairs, New York.

Urdal, H. (2004): 'The Devil in the Demographics: The Effect of Youth Bulges on Domestic Armed Conflict, 1950–2000', Social Development Papers. Conflict Prevention and Reconstruction Paper No. 14. Washington, DC: World Bank.

Urdal, H. (2006): 'A Clash of Generations? Youth Bulges and Political Violence', *International Studies Quarterly*, 50 (3): 607–629.

USAID (2012): *Assessment of Current and Anticipated Economic Priorities in Iraq*. USAID-Tijara Provincial Economic Growth Program. http://pdf.usaid.gov/pdf_docs/pnadz673.pdf.

Van Parijs, P. and Y. Vanderborght (2017): *Basic Income: A Radical Proposal for a Free Society and Sane Economy*. Cambridge, MA: Harvard University Press.

Van Veen, E. (2019): 'The Geopolitics of Syria's Reconstruction: A Case of Matryoshka', *CRU Policy Brief*. Den Haag, Netherlands: Netherland Institute of International Relations. https://www.clingendael.org/sites/default/files/2019-04/Geopolitics_of_Syrias_reconstruction_April19_final.pdf

Vandewalle, D. (1986): 'Libya's Revolution Revisited'. Middle East Report 143 (November/December), no page numbers.

Varvelli A. et al. (2017): 'State Building in Libya: integrating Diversities, Traditions and Citizenship'. The Monograph of Reset DOC.

Venieris, Y. P., and D. K. Gupta (1986): 'Income Distribution and Sociopolitical Instability as Determinants of Savings: A Cross-sectional Model', *Journal of Political Economy*, 94 (4): 873–883.

Verme, P. (2014): 'Facts and perceptions of inequality', in P. Verme, B. Milanovic, S. Al-Shawarby, S. El Tawila, M. Gadallah, and A. El-Majeed, ed., *Inside Inequality in the Arab Republic of Egypt: Facts and Perceptions across People, Time, and Space*. Washington, DC: A World Bank Study, pp. 55–100.

Vreeland, J. (2008): 'The Effect of Political Regime on Civil War: Unpacking Anocracy', *The Journal of Conflict Resolution*, 52 (3): 401–425.

Walker, J. (2016): *Humanitarian Impact of Syria-Related Unilateral Restrictive Measures*. National Agenda for the Future of Syria. Beirut: ESCWA.

Walter, B.F. (2006): 'Building reputation: Why Governments Fight Some Separatists but Not Others', *American Journal of Political Science*, 50 (2): 313–330.

Wehrey, F. (2012): *The Wrath of Libya's Salafis*. Carnegie Endowment for International Peace. https://carnegieendowment.org/sada/49364

Wehrey, F. (2019): *A Minister, a General, and the Militias: Libya's Shifting Balance of Power*. Carnegie Endowment for International Peace. https://carnegieendowment.org/2019/03/19/minister-general-and-militias-libya-s-shifting-balance-of-power-pub-78632

Weingast, B.R. (1995): 'The Economic Role of Political Institutions: Market-Preserving Federalism and Economic Development', *Journal of Law, Economics, and Organization* 11 (1): 1–31.

Weller, M., B. Metzger, and N. Johnson (2008): *Settling Self-Determination Disputes: Complex Power-Sharing in Theory and Practice*. Leiden and Boston: Martinus Nijhoff.

Weller, M. and K. Nobbs (2010): *Asymmetric Autonomy and the Settlement of Ethnic Conflicts*. Philadelphia: University of Pennsylvania Press.

WHO (2021): 'Libya Health Response to COVID-19 WHO update # 30. Reporting Period: 1–31 August 2021'. https://reliefweb.int/report/libya/who-libya-health-response-covid-19-libya-update-30-reporting-period-1-31-august-2021.

Williams, P., T. Sommadossi, and A. Mujais (2017): 'A Legal Perspective on Yemen's Attempted Transition from a Unitary to a Federal System of Government', *Utrecht Journal of International and European Law*, 33 (84): 4–22.

Wimmer, A., L.-E. Cederman, and B. Min, (2009): 'Ethnic Politics and Armed Conflict: A Configurational Analysis of a New Global Data Set'. *American Sociological Review*, 74(2), 316–337.

WIR (2018): World Inequality Report 2018, written and coordinated by F. Alvaredo, L. Chancel, T. Piketty, E. Saez and G. Zucman, World Inequality Lab.

Witte, C.T., M.J. Burger, and E. Ianchovichina (2020): 'Subjective Well-Being and Peaceful Uprisings', *KYKLOS*, 73 (1): 120–158.
World Bank (1999): *The Transition from War to Peace: An Overview.* Washington DC: The World Bank.
World Bank (2011): *Reducing Conflict Risk: Conflict, Fragility and Development in the Middle East and North Africa.* Washington DC: World Bank Sustainable Development Department, Middle East and North Africa Region.
World Bank (2012): Rapid Assessment of the Libyan Labor Market. World Bank. Washington, DC.
World Bank (2012a): Investment Climate Assessment, Report No. 77096-IQ. Washington, DC.
World Bank (2012b): Private Sector Development in Iraq: An Investment Climate Reform Agenda. MENA Knowledge and Learning, Quick Notes Series, No. 74. Washington, DC.
World Bank (2014a): *Republic of Iraq-Public Expenditure Review: Towards more Efficient Spending for Better Service Delivery.* Washington DC.
World Bank (2014b): Iraq, the Unfulfilled Promise of Oil and Growth Poverty, Inclusion and Welfare in Iraq, 2007–2012, volume 1, Report No. 92681-IQIRAQ. Washington, DC.
World Bank (2017a): *The Economics of Post-Conflict Reconstruction in MENA.* Washington DC: The World Bank.
World Bank (2017b): *The Toll of War. The Economic and Social Consequences of the Conflict in Syria.* Washington DC: The World Bank.
World Bank (2017c): *Iraq - Systematic Country Diagnostic (English).* Washington, D.C.: World Bank Group.
World Bank (2018a): *Iraq Economic Outlook - Spring 2018 (English): MENA Economic Outlook Brief.* Washington, D.C.: World Bank Group.
World Bank (2018b): Iraq Economic Monitor, From War to Reconstruction and Economic Recovery, With a Special Focus on Energy Subsidy Reform. Washington, DC.
World Bank (2018c): *Iraq Economic Monitor: Towards Reconstruction, Economic Recovery and Fostering Social Cohesion.* Washington DC.
World Bank (2018d): Jobs in Iraq: A Primer on Job Creation in the Short-Term. Jobs working paper, 22. Washington, DC.
World Bank (2019a): 'International Bank for Reconstruction and Development and International Finance Corporation and Multilateral Investment Guarantee Agency Country Engagement Note for the State of Libya for the Period 2019–2021'. *Libya - Country Engagement Note for the Period 2019-2021 (English).* Washington, DC: World Bank Group.
World Bank (2019b): *The Mobility of Displaced Syrians An Economic and Social Analysis.* Washington, DC: World Bank. doi:10.1596/978-1-4648-1401-3.
World Bank (2019c): *Doing Business 2019: Training for Reforms.* 16th ed. A world Bank Group Flashing Report. Washington, DC.
World Bank (2019d): *World Economic Indicators.* Washington, DC.
World Bank (2020): Iraq Economic Monitor: Navigating the Perfect Storm (Redux) (English). Washington, D.C.: World Bank Group.
Wright, J., Franz E., and Geddes B. (2014): 'Oil and Autocratic Regime Survival', *British Journal of Political Science*, 45 (2): 1–20.

Wucherpfennig, J., P. Hunziker, and L.E. Cederman (2016): 'Who Inherits the State? Colonial Rule and Postcolonial Conflict', *American Journal of Political Science*, 60 (4): 882–898.

Wyplosz, C. (2005): 'Fiscal Policy: Institutions versus Rules', *National Institute Economic Review*, 191 (1): 64–78.

Yadav, S. and M. Lynch (2018): 'Why It Won't Be Easy to Resolve Yemen's Many Wars', *The Washington Post*. Retrieved June 1, 2019, from The Washington Post website: https://www.washingtonpost.com/news/monkey-cage/wp/2018/01/25/why-it-wont-be-easy-to-resolve-yemens-many-wars/?noredirect=on&utm_term=.12cd09d7533a

Ye, F. and S.M. Han (2019): 'Does Ethnic Inequality Increase State Repression?' *Canadian Journal of Political Science*, 52: 883–901.

Yotam, M.Y. (2019): 'Political Responses to Economic Shocks', *Annual Review of Political Science*, 22 (1): 277–295.

Young, K. (2017): *War at Any Price: Domestic and Regional Economic Consequences of Yemen's Civil War*. Washington, DC: The Arab Gulf States Institute.

Yousif, B. (2007): 'Economic Restructuring in Iraq: Intended and Unintended Consequences', *Journal of Economic Issues*, 41 (1):43–60.

Yousif, B. (2012): *Human Development in Iraq: 1950–1990*. London: Routledge.

Yousif, B. (2016): 'Iraq's Stunted Growth: Human and Economic Development in Perspective', *Contemporary Arab Affairs*, 9 (2): 212–236.

Youssef, J. and C. Zaki (2019): 'A Decade of Competition Policy in Arab Countries: A De jure and De facto Assessment', ERF Working Paper #1301, March.

Zinn, C.M. (2016): 'Consequences of Iraqi De-Baathification', *Cornell International Affairs Review*, 9 (2): 80–100.

Websites:

1 https://www.reuters.com/article/us-libya-security-economy-exclusive/exclusive-libyas-u-n-backed-government-readies-new-war-funding-but-hopes-vital-business-to-continue-idUSKCN1S21M6
2 https://www.hrw.org/fr/world-report/2019/country-chapters/325756
3 http://www.libyabodycount.org/table
4 https://www.humanitarianresponse.info/sites/www.humanitarianresponse.info/files/documents/files/2019_lby_hno_draftv1.1.pdf
5 https://www.unicef.org/appeals/files/UNICEF_Libya_Humanitarian_SitRep_March_2019.pdf
6 https://www.who.int/hac/crises/lby/sitreps/libya-infographic-health-situation-october2017.jpg?ua=1
7 https://www.humanitarianresponse.info/sites/www.humanitarianresponse.info/files/documents/files/2019_lby_hno_draftv1.1.pdf
8 https://cspps.org/Polarised-Nation-covid19-libya
9 http://uis.unesco.org/en/country/iq, accessed 21/10/2019.

Index

Note: **Bold** page numbers refer to tables; *italic* page numbers refer to figures and page numbers followed by "n" denote endnotes.

accountability 9, 10, 21, 27, 31, 33, 39, 109, 115, 145, 149, 160, 161, 165, 168–170, 194, 206, 208, 211
Acemoglu, D. 149n3, 169
Africa 61; economies in 10, 35; finance political and military adventures in 190; GDP/capita in 194
Afrobarometer surveys 77–78
Alaaldin, R. 129
Alawite community 103
Ali, H. 176
al-Islah party 152
Alvaredo, F. 8, 30
anocracies 55–57
anticompetitive behaviour 44, 48–49
Anti-Money Laundering and Combating the Financing of Terrorism (AML/CFT) law 213
Arab authoritarianism 220
Arab Coalition 153, 154, 165, 172, 180, 181, 183n25
Arab countries 5; dominant issue in 13; education system 32; experiences in 15; inequality in 30–31; labour markets in 31, 32; rates of unemployment and youth employment **8, 31**
Arab democracy deficit 16
Arab economies 10, 13, 29, 33, 36
Arab–Israeli war 151
Arab Nationalism 187, 188, 190
Arab region 9, 17; case of 17; conflicts in 4; degree of inequality in 8; democratic order 1; economic growth in pre-2010 period 5; 'exceptionalism' of 219

Arab revolutions 58
Arab Spring 9, 58, 102; Doing Business set of indicators 46, **46**; perceptions of corruption 31; protests 206; 'Revolution of Change,' 2011 152; sustained growth 30
Arab uprisings, in 2011 4, 7, 9–10, 14, 33, 61; double-digit unemployment 12–13, 34; economic factors 29; in Libya 37, 185, 208, 216, 219; political literature on 11; reforms in MENA region 45; social contract 55; social justice associated with 30; in Tunisia 1
Arab World 10, 22n2
Arampatzi, E. 9, 31
Article 116 of the 2005 Iraqi constitution 142
Article 144 of the Iraqi constitution 143
Article 10 of the Syrian constitution 102
Asal, V. 61, 63
al-Assad, B. 99–101, 104
'authoritarian bargain' 8, 17, 31, 32, 102
'authoritarian upgrading' 17, 22n7
Awadallah, B. 27, 32, 58
Azmeh, S. 99, 103
Al Azzawi, S. 30

Ba'ath- era economic policies 123, 126
Ba'athist regime 127
Baghdad 130, 132, 142, 143, 147
balanced growth, macroeconomic policies for 35–43
Barakat, S. 165
Barnes-Dacey, J. 112
Basedau, M. 61
al-Beidh, A.S. 152

Index

Benomar, J. 166
Besley, T. 23, 59
Bodea, C. 4, 13, 23, 56, 61–64, 66n14
Bol, D. 21
Bormann, N.C. 69, 83–85, **89–90**
Brancati, D. 81
Bunce, V. 79

Cammett, M. 68, 91n4, 94n32
Campante, F.R. 27
Castillo, G. del 16, 34
CBI *see* central bank independence (CBI)
CBY *see* Central Bank of Yemen (CBY)
Cederman, L. 59, 61–63, 65n11, 65n12, 66n13, 77, 81, 83, 84
central bank independence (CBI) 36, **37**, 52n2
Central Bank of Yemen (CBY) 179–180
Cheikh, O. 166
Chong, A. 47
Chor, D. 27
civil conflicts 4, 12, 13, 16, 17, 23, 27, 52, 54–58, 60, 61, 64, 138, 154, 181, 185, 216, 222
civil resistance, types of 4
civil society 103, 116, 160–161, 212; initiatives 108; organizations 168–169, 188, 208, 212
civil war 1, 11, 12, 23, 57–62, 64, 67, 83, *90*, 91n2, 109, 154
Coalition Provisional Authority (CPA) 123, 128–129, 132
Cold War 67, 173, 185
Collier, P. 54, 59, 154
colonial histories 71–74
competition law 45, 48
Conroy, C. 34
'consensus' democracy 68
consociationalism 68, 69
'constraining' power-sharing 86
contingent effect of political inequality 61
Cordesman, A. 137, 143
Covid-19 pandemic 20–22, 146–147
CPA *see* Coalition Provisional Authority (CPA)
Crane, D.A. 48

Al-Dabaiba, A.M. 192
Daher, J. 114, 115
Daw, M.A. 203
de-Ba'athification 128, 129
delivery of public services 138–140

de-merit goods 49
democratic change, in post-conflict phase 17
democratic political institutions 55–56
democratic stability 74–75; power-sharing and national identification 76–78
democratization process 17, 75
Derviş, K. 34
determinants of power-sharing 71; colonial histories 72–74; factionalism 71–72; precedent-setting 72
Devarajan, S. 9, 26, 27, 30
disarmament, demobilization, and reintegration (DDR) agenda 115, 117
discontent factors 4; economic factors 4–5, **5**, *6*, 7–10; political and institutional factors 10–11; social factors 11–13
dispersive institutions 82
dispersive power-sharing 71, 75, 76, 79, 81–83, 86
distribution of nominal political power 68
Dixon, J. 60
Dodge, T. 138
Doing Business set of indicators 46, **46**
domestic peace agreements 222
'downgrading' ethnic groups 81
downward mobility 7, 28
Dresch, P. 158

economic agenda for post-conflict reconstruction 23–26; challenges 26–34; foreign direct investment 43; macroeconomic policies for balanced growth and employment 35–43
economic challenges: in Arab countries 220; in Iraq 146; reconstruction 28–33; in Yemen 173–174
economic factors 4–5, **5**, *6*, 7–10
economic growth 18–20; in Arab economies 29; Arab region 5; in Libya 187, 194; and stability 15, 32; in Syria 29, 100–101; in Yemen 29
economic inequality 8, 10, 12, 13, 15, 33, 54, 58–59, 61–64
economic liberalization 99–101
economic reforms 26; benefits of 103; cost of 101; design and implementation of 17, 24; and policies 25, 34, 50, 221; reconstruction challenges 26–27; series of 99
Eggertsson, T. 148

Egypt 100–102, 185–187; downward mobility in 28; wake of Arab–Israeli war 151; youth unemployment in 7, **8**
Elbadawi, I.A. 4, 23, 27, 52n3, 52n4, 179
electoral power-sharing 69, 169, 181
Elkins, Z. 76
employment: in Arab Countries **31**, 31–32; by economic sector and employer *141*; macroeconomic policies for 35–43; youth (re) training and 117
enforcement of property rights 19
Englebert, P. 25, 59
Esteban, J. 12
Estrin, A. 47
ethnic armed conflict 61
ethnic civil war 57, 81
ethnic-group level 13
ethnic groups 62–64, 65n8, 72, 73; with agency and strategy 57; civil war 62; and economic inequities 54; inclusion of 81; income and wealth inequality 61; oil-rich and poor countries 63; political inclusion of 78; political inequality between 76; power of 58
ethnicity 13, 57, 65n4
Ethnic Power Relations (EPR) data 57–58, 65n4, 72, 76, 81, 93n24
ethno-federalism 79–80
Europe 116; lack of engagement 112; worst-affected countries in 21
European Bank for Reconstruction and Development 113
European donor counties 113
exceptionalism 219
exchange rate management 19, 41–42
exchange rate regimes 51
Extractive Industries Transparency Initiative guidelines 161

factionalism 71–72
factors of discontent 4; economic factors 4–5, **5**, *6,* 7–10; political and institutional factors 10–11; social factors 11–13
FDI *see* foreign direct investment (FDI)
FDL *see* Forum for Democratic Libya (FDL)
Fearon, J.D. 54, 55, 59–60, 68, 81, 92n12
federalism 165, 188
financing reconstruction 109–111
fiscal authority 39
fiscal council 40–41
fiscal policy 37–39, 51; commodity price shocks 41; design 19; reforms 39–41

fiscal rules 40, 179
FitzGerald, V. 122
fixed rule 68, 217
forced regime transitions (FIRCs) 75
foreign aid 26, 38, 42, 119
foreign direct investment (FDI) 19, 43, 51, 128, 210, 211
foreign policy of Iran 162
Forum for Democratic Libya (FDL) 212
Fukuyama, F. 124, 144, 149n7
functionality, of federal institutions 70

Gaddafi, M. 187–191, *189,* 200, 212
Germann, M. 80, 94n29
Gingerich, D. 22
Gini coefficient 9, 22n2, 30, 58
Glassmyer, K. 79, 91n4
global financial crisis 101
GNA *see* Government of National Accord (GNA)
Gordon, J. 127
Goulden, R. 101
government budgets 12
government finances 18, 20, 37, 41, 42, 51, 147
government institutions 45, 102, 115, 177
Government of National Accord (GNA) 198–201
Graham, B.A.T. 69, 70, 74–75, 78, 86, **87**
greed-based factors 64
greed-based literature 63
greed *vs.* grievance issue 4
'Green Book' (Gaddafi) 188, 190
grievances-based literature 63
Griffith, M. 166
Gross Domestic Investment, in 2013–2015 131
Gross Fixed Capital Formation 127, 132
Gulf Cooperation Council in 2011 165
Gulf War in 1991 121, 131
Gunter, F. 144, 150n15
Gurr, T. 58

Hadi, A.-R.M. 151, 152, 165, 166, 168, 184n32
Haftar, K. 199
Hartzell, C. 68
Hashemite identity 182–183n17
Hashemite kingdom of Jordan 151
Hashemite rule in Yemen 162
Heydemann, S. 108, 109, 112
Hlasny, V. 30
Hoddie, M. 68
Hodgson, G. 122

Index

Hoeffler, A. 54, 59
horizontal economic inequality 12, 62–64
Houle, C. 13, 23, 58, 61–64, 65n4, 65n6, 65n9, 66n14
housing, land, and property (HLP) rights 44
al-Houthi, A.M. 153
Houthi movement 152–154, 162–166, 168, 169, 171–174, 179, 181
Huber, J.D. 12
Human Development Indices 29, *29*, 219
Humphreys, M. 59
Huntington, S.P. 56
Hunziker, P. 61, 63
Hussein, S. 121, 125, 138

Ianchovichina, E. 9, 27, 30
ID *see* Iraqi Dinars (ID)
Idris, I. 132, 188
IFIs *see* international financial institutions (IFIs)
Imady, O. 113
IMF 121, 123, 138, 139, 143–144; Article IV report of 2013 193
inclusive model for reconstruction 206
inclusive power-sharing agreement 71, 76, 169–170
inclusive power-sharing institutions 221
income and wealth-based horizontal inequality 33, 61
inequality 8–10; in Arab countries 30–31; ethnic or sectarian groups 34; intergenerational inequality 12; inter-group inequality 12; intra-group inequality 12; poverty and, multi-dimensional indicators of 99, *100*; religious intergroup inequality 12; sectarian inequality 34; sectarian inter-group inequality 12; social inequality 11
inflation control 35–36; monetary policy reforms 36, **37**
Institute for Economics & Peace 140
institutionalized power-sharing 71
Internally Displaced Persons (IDP) and Returnee Report 201–202
International Bank for Reconstruction and Development 113
international community 75, 112, 115, 116, 119, 171, 173, 181
international financial institutions (IFIs) 128, 144
International Organization for Migration (IOM) Displacement Tracking Matrix 201
international organizations 103, 108, 110, 115, 116, 118, 168, 172
international sanctions 97, 106, 107, 110, 117
Iran: attack on 125; foreign policy of 162; and KSA, conflict between 162; and Kuwait conflicts 125; labour supply in 145; 1980s conflict with 29; role in Yemen 163; service sector workers in 150n7
Iran–Iraq war in 1980 125, 126
Iraq 121; age structure data 145; armed and security services 129; armed forces 128; budget law of 2019 136; bureaucracy 147; central government 123; developmental structures and institutions 124; economic challenges 146; economic decline 122–123, 128; economy (*see* Iraqi economy, 2003–2020); enterprise registration rules 145; expenditures in 37; foreign debt 128; Governing Council 129; Household survey, 2012 140; human development indicators 121; illiteracy in **140**; inflation rate in 135; labour market and income reforms 145; long-term institutional decline 124; oil exports 126, 143; oil-producing economy 126; oil reserves 142–143; political decisions in 122; political economy 128, 144; Polity IV Country Regime measure 125; power-sharing arrangement 148–149; public services 139, 140; reconstruction 132; sectarianism 130; social contract 124, 148; statist economic policies 123; targeted Social Protection Net 139; TFP growth 7; US invasion of 130; welfare programme of in 138; youths of 132, 144
Iraq Human Development Report 132
Iraqi Constitution of 2005 149n1
Iraqi Dinars (ID) 133, 135
Iraqi economy, 2003–2020 121; basic income **145**; brain drain and slow reconstruction 130–133; centrality of the state and the policy landscape 143–146; Covid-19 pandemic and its effects 146–147; CPA policies 128–129; dangers and opportunities of oil

abundance 142–143; economic sector and employer *141*; fiscal balance, 2004–2020 *134*; governance indicators, 2002–2017 *139*; government revenues and jobs growth *137*; gross capital formation *132*; institutional decline and social contract 124–125; job creation and poverty 140–141; long-term decline in capabilities 122–123; military and health expenditures *136*; oil abundance and role of the state 123–124; oil and key macroeconomic variables *134*; oil dependence 133–135; overstaffed and under-skilled public sector 135–138; political impasse and insecurity 129–130; rise and collapse of development 125–127; social welfare and delivery of public services 138–140; TFP and GDP *129*; Transparency International's Corruption Perceptions Index **138**; unemployment and consumer prices *135*; value added by economic sector *133*; violence and growth *131*; wages and salaries *130*
Iraqi Governing Council 129

Joint Meeting Parties (JMP) 152
Jones, C.I. 29
Jones, Z.M. 56

Keller, J. 45
Khan, A. 35
Khashanah, K. 104
Khazai, S. 143
Kingdom of Saudi Arabia (KSA) 151, 162–164, 180, 183n19
Klenow, P.J. 29
KSA-led Arab Coalition 154
Kurdish communities, in Syria 103–104
Kurdish Regional Government (KRG) 142

labour market 18, 144; in Arab countries 31; female participation in 101; indicators 7; reforms 51
Laitin, D.D. 54, 55, 59, 60, 68, 81
LAL *see* Local Authority Law (LAL)
large-scale civil violence 11
Latin America 9, 10, 22, 33, 39, 47, 190, 215
Law Number 10 of 2018 112
Lawrence, A.K. 11
Lebanese civil war 154

Lebanon 97, 98, 102, 103, 106, 107, 110, 119, 162, 169, 209
Le Billon, P. 137
Leckie, S. 44
legitimacy 25, 50
LIA *see* Libyan Investment Authority (LIA)
Libya: Arab uprisings in 185; armed conflict and civil war 200; brutal civil conflicts in 16; conflict (*see* Libyan conflict); decentralized nature of governance in 207; domestic politics of 185; economic conditions prior to 2011 192–197; economic costs of 202–205; economic growth of 187, 194, 209–216; economic migration 201–202; elections in 208; ethnic fractionalization 191, *191*; expenditures in 37; financial aggregates in **193**; financial reserves 186; GDP growth, 2000–2020 in *203*; health system 204; index of state fragility 196, *198*; international involvement in 209; labour market 196; migration and international involvement 208–209; multi-dimensional military conflicts in 17; national and international initiatives 185; political and socioeconomic map of 186; political system 201; post-conflict reconstruction in 206; Refugee Convention 202; social contract 205–216; in transitional justice 207; transition process in 201; unemployment rates *196, 197*; UNHCR 202
Libyan Arab Republic 189
Libyan Central Bank 199
Libyan conflict 185–186, 197–198; development path prior to 2011 186–197; economic costs of 202–205; government and lack of central authority 198–200; international actors 201; migration 201–202; security 200; social contract (*see* social contract); war profiteering and corruption 200–201
Libyan General National Congress 193
Libyan Investment Authority (LIA) 194
Libyan National Army (LNA) 199
Libyan National Oil Corporation 202
Libyan Political Agreement, 2015 198
Libyan Revolutionary Command Council 189

Lijphart, A. 56, 68, 70
Lipset, M.S. 56
LNA *see* Libyan National Army (LNA)
Local Authority Law (LAL) 158
López de Silanes, F. 47
Lowcock, M. 173
Lupu, Y. 56

macroeconomic conditions 99
macroeconomic indicators **28, 36,** *100*
macroeconomic management 18, 51
macroeconomic policies 14, 18, 51; for balanced growth and employment 35–43; for post-conflict recovery 178–180
macroeconomic structural reforms 19, 26, 51, 215–216
'macro-level' power-sharing 71
al-Mahdi al-Senusi, M.I. 187
Mahler, A. 64
Makdisi, S. 27, 154
Malesky, E. 68, 91n4, 94n32
Malik, A. 27, 32, 58
'marathonic' peace moderation in Yemen 166
market liberalization and regulation 45–48
Marshall Plan 113
Martins, P. 35
Marxist 'People's Democratic Republic of Yemen' (PDRY) 152, 159
Mattes, M. 68, 82
Mayoral, L. 12
McGarry, J. 79, 80, 92n7
merit goods 49
Mesquita, B. de 60
microeconomic issues and policies 43–44; market liberalization and regulation of competition 45–47; property rights reforms 44–45; regulation and interventions 48–50
microeconomic reforms 25–26, 38
Middle East and North Africa (MENA) region 9, 31–32, 101, 136, 140, 146, 185; case for 18; conflict in 12, 34; dominant factor in 13; economic and social indicators 4, 5, 37, 38, **156**; experience of 50; GDP/capita of oil exporters in *195*; geopolitics and foreign intervention in 13; oil exporters in 194; politico-economic equilibria 11; post-conflict countries in 35; post-conflict transition of 85; and upper-middle- income countries (UPC) 192; war-affected countries in 167; wave of reforms in 45
military power-sharing 79, 91n4
missing markets 49
modern fiscal management 40
monetary policy reforms 36, **37**
Montalvo, J.G. 11
Morrison, K. 60
Mottaghi, L. 26
Muller, E.N. 55
multi-national federations 79
multinomial logit regressions **88**

Nabli, M. 28, 45
National Dialogue Conference (NDC) 152–153, 165, 181
National Oil Corporation (NOC) 199, 202, 209
national peace 13–16; challenges 17–20; Covid 19 pandemic impact 20–22
national post-conflict reconstruction work 15
national regulatory agencies (NRAs) 49
national *vs.* ethnic identification, by power status *90*
natural monopolies 48
natural resource wealth 60
NDC *see* National Dialogue Conference (NDC)
Neaime, S. 102
'neighbourhood effect' 104
network utilities 47
new social contract 10, 20, 27, 33, 44, 119, 142, 166, 168, 181, 205–206; Libyan economy 209–216; migration and international involvement 208–209; peace-building and reconstruction 207–208; reconstruction 206–207
Nigeria 70, 77, 83, 93n23
NOC *see* National Oil Corporation (NOC)
Nomikos, W. 69, 71, 72
non-democracies high unemployment 8
non-state actors 166, 207
North, D.C. 148, 222n1
NRAs *see* national regulatory agencies (NRAs)

OCHA *see* Office for Coordination of Humanitarian Affairs (OCHA)
OECD 25
Office for Coordination of Humanitarian Affairs (OCHA) 115;

Humanitarian Needs Overview 204;
Humanitarian Response Plan 204
oil and conflict risk 59–61
Oil for Food Programme 127
oil-poor countries 63
oil price volatility 13, 42, 194
oil-producing ethnic groups 63
oil production 60, 61, 63, 64, 133, 196, 202, 206
oil resources 16, 17, 23, 61, 62, 64, 142, 148, 161, 221
oil revenue 24, 55, 60, 62, 63, 99, 123–125, 132, 133, 135, 136, 141, 142–146, 156, 160, 161, 187–189, 194, 199, 209, 214
oil-rich countries 42, 62–64
O'Leary, B. 79, 80, 92n7
'Operation Decisive Storm,' in March 2015 153, 164
organized crime 49–50, 154
Østby, G. 58–59

Paasonen, K. 12, 34
Paine, J. 60
participants, in war economy 10, 33, 49, 57, 165
PDS *see* public distribution system (PDS)
peace-building process: Libyan conflict and (*see* Libyan conflict); post-conflict economic reconstruction 151; and power-sharing (*see* power-sharing (P-S))
'peace dividend' 19, 37, 40, 51
Pelletier, A. 47
people's property rights 45
Persson, T. 23, 59
phased economic reform process 168
Philips, C. 103, 104
Pierskalla, J.H. 61, 64
Pissarides, C. 32
political elites 25, 148, 154
political exclusion 27, 56–58
political institutions 17, 22–24, 55–57, 61, 63, 69, 76, 108–109, 119, 123–125, 148, 161–162, 168, 169, 222
political opportunity theory 21
political reforms 27, 101–103, 105, 118, 124, 220, 222
political violence 4, 9, 23, 55, 56, 125
post-conflict economic recovery 14, 50, 109
post-conflict engagement, entry points for *113*

post-conflict reconstruction 43, 50, 221
post-conflict recovery 109; European and international involvement 111–112; financing reconstruction 109–111; restoring livelihoods 116–118; rethinking reconstruction 112–116
post-conflict reforms 25, 35
post conflict transition 4, 14, 19, 20, 38, 39, 85, 198
post-war fiscal policy 178–179
post-war macroeconomic policies 181
post-war monetary policy 179, 180
post-war reconstruction plans 178
post-war reunification, of CBY 180
post-war Yemen 167; economic recovery 171–176; political and social reconciliation 167–171; post-war economic agenda 176–180
power-sharing (P-S): consequences of 74–85; determinants of (*see* determinants of power-sharing); formula, in Yemen 169; institutions 23, 67–68, 70, 76, 78, 79, 85, 86, 216; measurement of 68–71
principles: accountability and impartiality of 168; of democracy 50; of good governance 39; National Dialogue Conference principles 181; of proportionality and autonomy 68; of sustained economic growth 38
privatization of SOEs 47, 129
pro-market liberalization reforms 45
property rights reforms 44–45
proposed economic reforms and policies 25, 50
Przeworski, A. 10, 33
public distribution system (PDS) 127, 138, 139, 144
Public-Private Partnership (PPP) Law 114
public services, delivery of 138–140

Al-Qarawee, H.H. 130
quality of life 9, 10, 30, 33

Ray, D. 12
Ray, S. 76
reconstruction 97; agendas 48–49; challenges (*see* reconstruction challenges); feasible peace-building and 207–208; inclusive model for 206; international involvement in 206; policies 24, 25, 50, 122; premises of 13–16; reforms 47

reconstruction challenges 26–28; economic challenges 28–33; political challenges 33–34; social challenges 34
registered civil society organizations 169
registration system 44, 45
religious intergroup inequality 12
rentier-based political economy 99
rent-seeking models 57
repression effect 60
Republic of Yemen (ROY) 152
restoring HLP rights 44
Reynal-Querol, M. 11, 65n4
Riyadh 153, 163, 168
Robinson, J.A. 149n3, 169
robust judiciary system 169
Rodrik, D. 143
Roeder, P. 79
Rokkan, S. 56
Ron, J. 59
Rørbæk, L.L. 34
Ross, M. 60
Rougier, E. 11
ROY *see* Republic of Yemen (ROY)
rule of law 18, 21, 24, 45, 78, 137, 138, 208, 210, 214
ruling group 23, 73
Russell, K. 78
Russian Federation 83

Sachs, J. 214
Sadaka, R. 154
Safadi, R. 102
Salafism 162
Saleh, A.A. 152, 162; General People's Congress (GPC) party 160; patronage system 160–161
Salih, K.E.O. 27
Salisbury, P. 165
Sambanis, N. 75, 79, 80, 83, 84, 86, **89–90,** 91n4, 92n9, 93n29, 94n29, 169, 216–217
Santayana, G. 1
Sassoon, J. 131
Savun, B. 68, 82
Schmidt-Hebbel, K. 40, 41
Schulhofer-Wohl, J. 75, 86
secessionist groups, in South 166
secession of Kosovo/Kosova 83
sectarian inequality 34
sectarian inter-group inequality 12
sector-based approach 116, 119
Security Council resolutions 166
Sedik, T.S. 21
Selby, J. 98, 99

semi-sectarian conflict 104
separatist conflict 83
Shari'a law 214
Shkirat Agreement in December 2015 198
Shura Council (Majlis al-Shura) 159–160
Sides, J. 76
SIPRI 37
Skhirat Agreement 207
Smallholder Support Programme 118
SMEs 214, 215
Smith, B. 60, 65n1
social contract 25, 27, 102, 105; institutional decline and 124–125
social factors 11–13, 54, 220
social inequality 11
social market economy 99
Social Protection Net 139
Social Redevelopment Fund 116
social welfare 138–140
SOEs *see* state-owned enterprises (SOEs)
Soto, R. 23, 40, 52n4, 179
Southern Peaceful Movement (SPM) 158
Southern Transitional Council (STC) 154
sovereign wealth funds (SWF) 52n3
Special Inspector General for Iraq's Reconstruction 132
SPM *see* Southern Peaceful Movement (SPM)
state-owned enterprises (SOEs) 47, 129
state's policy of economic liberalization 99
STC *see* Southern Transitional Council (STC)
Stewart, F. 122
structural reforms post-conflict 25
Sunni Islam 162, 181n1
Sunni Muslim Brotherhood 103
sustainable reconstruction 18, 24, 32, 35, 50
sustained economic growth and stability 15, 32, 38, 148
SWF *see* sovereign wealth funds (SWF)
Syria: agricultural sector 117; banking sector 110; brutal civil conflicts in 16; business community 110; civil war 22n8, 108; communities 112; conflict (*see* Syrian conflict); conundrum in 112; economic growth in 29, 97–98, 107; exclusionary political system 102; expenditures in 37; financing for private sector-led reconstruction in 110; Gini coefficient of income in 30;

global financial crisis 101; healthcare system 97; heavy-handed security 104; humanitarian relief for 111; identity pre-crisis 104; Kurdish communities in 103–104; multi-dimensional military conflicts in 17; nominal GDP 106; political reforms 102, 103; political situation in 102; post-conflict security and economic recovery in 109, 119; primary objective in 116; refugees 110, 114; regime and international community 98; stability and security 111; state institutions 105; upward mobility in 28; youth unemployment in 7, **8**
Syrian Centre for Policy Research 108
Syrian Commission for Family Affairs 105
Syrian conflict 97, 109, 118, 119; climate change 98–99; economic conditions and economic liberalization 99–101; political/institutional impact of 108–109; social dimension 103–104; stalled political reforms and rising corruption 101–103; timeline *99*; weak and inflexible institutions 104–105
Syrian government 102, 103, 110, 115, 117
Syrian-led political process 111
Syrian regime 113–114, 116

Tanzania 77, 92n17
Tehran's policy 163
territorial autonomy 79, 83, 84; on post-conflict risk of war recurrence **89–90**
territorial power-sharing 76
TFP *see* total factor productivity (TFP)
theory of democratic survival 74
Tilly, C. 11
total factor productivity (TFP) 7, 22n1, 128, *129*
Toukan, M. 83, 84, **89–90**
traditional money-metric macroeconomic measures 133
Transparency International's Corruption Perception index **37**, 137, **138,** 161
tribalism 188, 190, 216
Tripp, C. 127
Tull, D.M. 25
Tunisia 1; case of 16; upward mobility in 28; youth unemployment in 1, 7, **8**
Turkish Cypriots 70
Turkish invasion 70

Turkish military intervention 201
Turkish Republic of Northern Cyprus 70, 83

UCDP/ACD data on conflict 75
UCDP/PRIO Armed Conflict Dataset 62, 86
Ulfelder, J. 60
UNDP *see* United Nations Development Programme (UNDP)
unemployment 7–8, **8,** 31–33; in Arab countries **31,** 31–32; and food insecurity 98; high levels of 196–197; and informal activity 20; in MENA region 50
UNESCWA *see* United Nations' Economic and Social Commission for Western Asia (UNESCWA)
UN High Commissioner for Refugees (UNHCR) 115
United Nations (UN): Integrated Food Security Phase Classification 172; intervention 69; peacekeeping/peace missions 67; supported peace negotiations 198; Training for All initiative 110
United Nations Development Programme (UNDP) 103
United Nations' Economic and Social Commission for Western Asia (UNESCWA) 97
Univariate Box-Jenkins (UBJ) three-stage model-building process 176
unorganized crime 49
UN Resolution 2216 165, 166, 170
UN Resolution 2254 111
UNSCR 1325 208
UN Security Council 153, 165, 170
UN-supported agreement 207
UNU-WIDER database 30
upward mobility 28
Urdal, H. 12, 34

Vanderborght, Y. 144
Van Parijs, P. 144
Van Veen, E. 111
Véganzonès-Varoudakis, M.A. 32
Verme, P. 9, 31
Vogler, J.P. 22
Vreeland, J. 56

Walter, B.F. 72
Warner, A. 214

Index

war recurrence 78–81; conditional effects of dispersive power-sharing 81–82; data 94n35; power-sharing in shadow of external intervention 83–85; territorial autonomy on post-conflict risk of **89–90**
Weede, E. 55
well-defined property rights 44
WFP *see* World Food Programme (WFP)
WHO *see* World Health Organization (WHO)
Wimmer, A. 57
Witte, C.T. 4
World Bank 9, 131, 135, 137, 138, 140, 142–145, 147, 155, 168, 192, 202; World Development Indicators 176
World Food Programme (WFP) 183n28
World Health Organization (WHO) 204
World Inequality Database 22n2
World Values Survey (2010–2012) 76
World War II Europe 113
Worldwide Governance Indicators 137
Wright, J. 60
Wucherpfennig, J. 58, 72, 73, 92n14

Xu, R. 21

YAR *see* Yemen Arab Republic (YAR)
Yemen: affairs 171, 180; agriculture sector 156; Arab–Israeli war 151; brutal civil conflicts in 16; case of 154; civil society 161; and civil war 155; combatants 151–152; conflict in 161, 172, 176; Covid-21 crisis in 173; crisis 166; downward mobility in 28; economic growth in 29; electoral system in 159; elites 158; expenditures in 37; failed political transition, legacy of 164–167; foreign intervention in 162–164; fragile state institutions 180; Hashemite rule in 162; human development in 172; humanitarian crisis in 173; al-Islah party 152; Joint Meeting Parties 152; leadership 169; local communities in 170; 'marathonic' peace moderation in 166; Marxist 'People's Democratic Republic of Yemen'152; and MENA selected economic and social indicators **156**; multi-dimensional military conflicts in 17; National Dialogue Conference 152–153, 155; National Population Council 182n13; oil resources in 160, 161; 'Operation Decisive Storm,' in March 2015 153; peace and stability in 181; political and social reconciliation in 168; political economy 155; post-conflict economic performance in 178; post-war Yemen (*see* post-war Yemen); poverty 155; power-sharing formula in 169, 181; pre-conflict contributions of economic sectors *157*; pre-conflict development profile of *157*; pre-war monetary institutions and policy in 179; real GDP in 176; reconstruction of 181; religious culture 162; Republic of Yemen 152; roots of conflict in 154–164; sects in 162; social fabric 171; Southern Transitional Council 154; TFP growth 7; traditional elite 182n10; Transparency International's Corruption Index 161; UN envoys in 166; urban areas 159; violent conflict in 180; war-devastated health infrastructure 173; water resources 155; western engagement in 169
Yemen Arab Republic (YAR) 151, 152
Yemen Data Project 172
Yemeni Defence Ministry 163–164
Yemeni National Movement 183n18
Yousif, B. 125, 127
Youssef, J. 45
youth bulges in Middle Eastern economies 12
youth employment **31,** 32, 117, 118
youth (re) training and employment programmes 117

Zaki, C. 45
Zaydi Houthis 162
Zaydi Shi'ism 151
Zaydism 162, 181n1